THE ARAB NATIONAL PROJECT IN YOUSSEF CHAHINE'S CINEMA

THE ARAB NATIONAL PROJECT IN YOUSSEF CHAHINE'S CINEMA

MALEK KHOURI

The American University in Cairo Press
Cairo New York

First published in 2010 by
The American University in Cairo Press
113 Sharia Kasr el Aini, Cairo, Egypt
420 Fifth Avenue, New York, NY 10018
www.aucpress.com

Copyright © 2010 by Malek Khouri

All rights reserved. No part of this publication may be reproduced, stored in a retrieval system, or transmitted in any form or by any means, electronic, mechanical, photocopying, recording, or otherwise, without the prior written permission of the publisher.

All stills in this book are courtesy of Misr International Films
(Youssef Chahine & Company).

Dar el Kutub No. 14134/09
ISBN 978 977 416 354 8

Dar el Kutub Cataloging-in-Publication Data

Khouri, Malek
    The Arab National Project in Youssef Chahine's Cinema / Malek Khouri.—Cairo:
The American University in Cairo Press, 2009
    p.   cm.
    ISBN 978 977 416 354 8
    1. Motion pictures
    2. Shahin, Yousef 1926 – 2008
    791.43

1 2 3 4 5 6   14 13 12 11 10

Designed by Fatiha Bouzidi
Printed in Egypt

CONTENTS

Preface and Acknowledgments   vii
Introduction   xi

1. An Unfinished Project: Chahine and the Arab National Project   1
2. Popular Cinema and Conceptualizing Class and Social Change   17
3. Political Intervention and the Struggle for National Unity and Liberation   33
4. Institutional Shifts and Political Divergences   53
5. The Prodigal Director   89
6. Identity and Difference   115
7. Resistance, Heterogeneity, and Historical Memory   135
8. Queer Transgression and Postcolonial Ambivalence   147
9. Religious Fundamentalism and the Power of History   167
10. National Liberation in the Age of Globalization   185
11. Chahine as an Author and as an Arab Organic Intellectual   215

Notes   237
Bibliography   251
Index   269

PREFACE AND ACKNOWLEDGMENTS

My interest in Youssef Chahine's cinema goes back to my high school years in Sidon, Lebanon in the mid-1970s when his film *al-'Asfur* (The Sparrow) became an icon for all leftists in the city and across the country. Sheikh Imam and Ahmad Fu'ad Nagm's soundtrack song *Masr yamma ya Bahiya* (Mother Egypt, You 'Beautiful' Bahiya) assumed legendary status around the Arab world particularly among young people along with multiple other Imam/Nagm songs of dissent and resistance. For this generation, just coming out of the difficult period of the 1967 Arab defeat in the war with Israel, the film along with other songs by the Imam/Nagm duo represented hope and new possibilities for change and resistance.

When I was doing my film studies degree at Carleton University in Canada, one of my professors, Zuzana Pick, saw my interest in Chahine's work and encouraged me to do an independent study course on Chahine, who she saw as one of the most important 'third world' filmmakers. The outcome of this course was my first attempt at compiling a bibliography of material on the filmmaker. I kept this bibliography for many years but never pursued any further work on it—that is until I finished my PhD over two decades later and began my career as a film studies university professor. Once again, Zuzana Pick's unrelenting encouragement was instrumental in persuading me to start where I have long left off with my scholarly project on Chahine. For her, not having a comprehensive study on Chahine in English represented an important gap in film studies. She also saw that, with my background and interest in the filmmaker's work, I was in a privileged position to pursue such a job. Therefore, it is not an exaggeration to say that if it were not for Zuzana's diligent encouragement and friendship over the years, this book would have never materialized. I therefore dedicate this book to her: a dear mentor and friend, and a meticulous and first-rate scholar of 'third world' cinemas.

My appreciation goes to my colleagues in the film studies program and the Faculty of Communication and Culture at the University of Calgary for their support of the project and my work on Arab cinema.

My thanks go to my colleagues at the Department of Performing and Visual Arts at the American University in Cairo for their friendship and support during my assignment as the director of the Film Program. Your collegiality gave me a great leverage to finalize this book and put it into print. Randi Danforth, senior development editor at the American University in Cairo Press, has been great in her support for this project, and in keeping me in check whenever I needed a push to wrap up my work on time. From the Press I would also like to thank Abdalla Hassan, project editor, who made a great contribution to the book by meticulously copyediting the final draft. My research assistant in Cairo during the preparation of the final draft, Mariam Mekiwi, was a great support, and I would like to thank her and wish her the best in developing her future career in film.

The archival material available at the Egyptian Catholic Center for Cinema remains instrumental for any serious research on Egyptian cinema, and such was its contribution to this book. My thanks go to this leading Arab film study institution, which, in spite of its limited resources, has maintained one of the most comprehensive and professional archival collections of documents on Egyptian and Arab cinemas. My thanks also go to Marianne Khoury in Misr International Films (Youssef Chahine & Co.) for her encouragement and for providing all the photo stills for the book. I am confident that Chahine's legacy is alive and reverberating, and will continue to expand its impact on and maintain its spirit through the work of Marianne and Gaby Khoury as they lead the filmmaker's unique institutional creation.

My dear and great friend Barbara Rockburn was instrumental in helping me write better by patiently and attentively reading and editing my manuscript. My thanks to my dear friend Amro Sayed and his family in Cairo who never yielded in helping me adjust to living and working in Egypt during the long periods of research over the last six years.

This book also owes a great deal to the University of Calgary, which offered me a Starter Grant to initiate this project. This book has been made possible by a Standard Research Grant by the Social Sciences and Humanities Research Council in Canada.

Of course, this book is driven by the goal of encouraging other scholars to pursue the study of Egyptian and Arab cinemas. This is probably among the most influential yet most understudied cinemas in the world today, and any effort in this regard by young scholars would be of major significance to film studies around the world.

Last but not least, I am, as always, immensely grateful to my mother Huneineh and my father Mounir for their unrelenting love and support to me throughout my life. You have been my inspiration, my comrades, my best friends, and my greatest love.

INTRODUCTION

No other filmmaker in the history of Arab cinema has witnessed, contemplated, and consequently captured in his work so many facets of the changes and upheavals in the modern Arab world as Egyptian filmmaker Youssef Chahine. Nor has any other Arab filmmaker's career as Chahine's, which stretched close to sixty years, attracted as much attention among western film critics and international film festival circuits. This book is particularly concerned with countering the tendency among western critics and scholars to universalize Chahine's work within a preconceived third worldist status. In this regard, this book repositions his cinema's relationship to its Arab environment, sources, and esthetics in the context of its propinquity with what is commonly referred to as the Arab National Project. More precisely, the book focuses on how Chahine's work has consistently contributed to the deconstruction of the myth of a homogenous Arab national identity, while simultaneously reconstructing the concept of the Arab nation and Arab national identity as heterogeneous and integral to a long-term modernist project for national self-determination as well as economic, social, and cultural renovation and progress.

Over Chahine's long film career his proactive involvement in his society's struggles during some of the most turbulent periods of contemporary Arab history has resulted in a body of work that illuminated the dynamics of the contemporary re-emergence of the Arab national project in the aftermath of Gamal Abd al-Nasser's 1952 revolution in Egypt. Chahine's work includes forty-four films and embodies a rich and critical survey of the social, political, and cultural history of Egypt and the Arab world in the twentieth century.

Born in Alexandria, Egypt in 1926 of Christian-Lebanese descent, Chahine earned the respect of the Arab world while garnering international attention and awards at film festivals in Moscow, Venice, Berlin, and beyond. His 1997 film *al-Masir* (Destiny) was awarded the fiftieth anniversary Palme d'Or at the Cannes Film Festival. This book examines films made from the 1950s through to his last film, *Heya Fawda* (Chaos, 2007). It analyzes the content and formal components of his films as they interact with cultural, social, and political specificities of various periods in contemporary Egyptian and Arab history. It also accounts for the dynamics of the production and reception of his films—particularly in interaction with local systems of cultural and film practice—as received by Egyptian and Arab film critics and audiences.

Chahine's work is sited within a corpus of social and cultural concerns vis-à-vis the protracted struggle for Arab national self-determination and modernization. His films foreshadowed the upheavals that rocked the Middle East since the early 1900s—times of war and civil strife whose fodder would be the hungry, the orphans, the workers, the peasants, and the unemployed. Since the 1990s his films tended to chronicle the rise of Islamic fundamentalism among unemployed urban youth channeling their anger into reactionary religious and political obscurantism. But his films also attest to the intrinsic dilemmas generated by Arab national liberation—social change, a love/hate relationship with the west, gendered and sexual relationships—all in conjunction with Arab society's struggle to grapple with the prospects of modernity and modernization. This book demonstrates how his films function as agencies of modernist cultural practice through an exploration of their postcolonial narrative delineations of social inequalities, colonialism, capitalist globalization, ethnic and religious heterogeneity, non-normative sexuality, the Palestine question, the current anxieties associated with the rise of religious fundamentalism, and their effects on contemporary Arab societies.

While critical interest in Arab cinema in general, and in Chahine in particular, has been relatively strong in Europe—especially France—and among film critics in Africa, Asia, and Latin America, familiarity with his work has been very limited among North American film enthusiasts and critics. Over the last decade, however, there has been increasing interest in North America in films from countries with primarily Muslim and Arab populations. Arab films have been enjoying a greater presence in film festivals and repertory theaters in Canada and the United States, and a vibrant corpus of English-language scholarship on Arab cinemas and cultures is slowly emerging. This interest is also manifest in the activities of film and media studies groups, as seen in the Society for Cinema and Media Studies' recent creation of a

Middle East Caucus. Egyptian cinema is among the most successful studio-based national film industries, and its vast production sustains a major weight throughout the Arab and Muslim worlds, as well as in south and west Asia and Africa. Nevertheless, Arab cinema continues to be relegated to the margins of English-language film studies; the scant body of North American scholarship on Egyptian cinema is clearly disproportionate to this cinema's status as one of the world's most influential, entrenched, and enduring national cinemas.

Though Egyptian cinema occupies a paramount position within contemporary Arab political and cultural discourse, the bulk of critical attention has traditionally been limited to very few filmmakers, such as Salah Abu Seif, but more attentively to Youssef Chahine. His films have consistently attracted the attention of film festivals and critics, and in 2001 the British Film Institute published Ibrahim Fawal's *Youssef Chahine*—the first English-language book devoted to Chahine and his oeuvre—as part of their series on world directors. Fawal's undertaking was an important breakthrough, representing the first attempt to present an Arab perspective on Chahine to a western readership. And while Fawal's book positioned Chahine's cinema as a cultural practice within a specific sociohistorical praxis, his was largely an auteurist approach that did not reflect on the ideological affectivities of the filmmaker's work or contemplate the linkages between his thematic and formal strategies. As a result, Chahine's films were approached in ways that minimized their ideological workings within specific moments in Arab history.

More recently (2009) and in Arabic, veteran Lebanese film critic Ibrahim al-Aris finally released his long anticipated book on Chahine *(Youssef Chahine: The Child's Vision and the Rebel's Fist)*. Albeit impressionistic in much of its assessment of the filmmaker's work, the book provides a most comprehensive reading of Chahine's film repertoire. Written by a leading Arab film and cultural critic with a long personal friendship with Chahine and his rich insight on Arab cinema, al-Aris's book is a must-read for any serious researcher on the filmmaker and on the history of Arab cinema as a whole.

Generally speaking, analyzing any film that originates within an Other's cultural space and perspective is fraught with potential pitfalls. Among the most acute of these is the readers' inclination to project their own cultural matrices on the text. This is much in evidence in western scholarship where critical categories attempt to tame foreignness to adapt to its own cultural traditions. Such processes not only misrepresent, but ultimately subvert and render inferior other cultures and societies. When it comes to reading cultural practices originating in the Arab world (and by extension Muslim societies in general), this usually translates into political encoding—thereby reverting to the historical dichotomy that pits western civilization as a beacon of secularism and rationalism against an Arab/Muslim culture that is inherently irrational, fanatical, violent, and anti-progress. My inclination in this study is to offer an alternative to this theoretical assumption once described by Edward Said as the "corporate institution" of the Orient.[1]

This study looks at how postcolonial subjectivities in Chahine's films, as embodied in their characters and themes, are shaped through his modernist narrative and formal strategies. It explores how these films incorporate heterogeneous and multitemporal cinematic models to present their subject matter; correlating popular and high art, contemporary and earlier history, and local and foreign perspectives. Special attention will be given to exposing the ways in which his films reposition culture in the politics of history, social agency, and change. Chahine's films' unique twofold relationship with the traditions of both popular and art cinemas will be addressed in conjunction with an examination of their function as organic agencies within the historical junctures in which they were created and received. As such, the study will account for how these films informed—and were informed by—the paradoxical dispositions of an activist and an effectively counter-hegemonic discourse. To paraphrase Gramsci, such a discourse offers an ideologically common-sense alternative fundamentally opposed to the hegemonic ideology of dominant power structures and alliances. However, my theoretical premise also problematizes and ultimately challenges the universal (read 'colonial') utilization of notions such as hegemony, postcolonialism, and modernity and what they entail when applied to the study of Arab cinema. Therefore this study resituates these terminologies in proximity to Egyptian and Arab cultural and historical contexts. The notion of hegemony, and by extension, counter-hegemony, and its relationship to postcolonial cultural practice will be considered in depth.

Hegemony, under less advanced capitalist colonial and postcolonial conditions, informs and is informed by rudiments that are largely different from those that exist under advanced capitalist or imperialist conditions. Therefore, the nature and social composition of hegemonic and counter-hegemonic relationships in the Arab world will be addressed here in a different context than that of western cultural critics looking at hegemonic structures within advanced capitalist societies. Hegemony, as applied to postcolonial subjectivity in Chahine's cinema, accounts for the *internal* dynamics of class, gender, sexuality, ethnicity, and so on, within Arab and Egyptian societies; but it also poses these dynamics in interaction with *externally* grounded colonial and neocolonial power structures. Within these pages Chahine's films are positioned vis-à-vis internal *and* external ideological hegemonies and power structures and, by extension, in relation to political and social historical blocs and alliances that are specific to postcolonial conditions. It is within this paradigmatic breadth that my study attests to Chahine's counter-hegemonic cinema in conjunction with its incorporation of specifically postcolonial Arab notions of modernity and modernization, as well as modernist cultural practices.

The use of the term 'modernity' in this book accounts for characteristics that are historically and culturally specific. As mediated social, economic, political, and cultural entities, Chahine's films are largely associated with modernist themes and strategies that find their roots in a mid-nineteenth-century Arab Renaissance movement (or *al-Nahda* in Arabic). Vigorous discussions around the exegesis of religious texts during this period soon expanded to include wide and spirited debates around the need to break away from the sanctification of language and texts. What ensued was the development of a sense of modernity and modernism that impacted on broader intellectual circles; promoting the renewal *(tajdid)* of Arab critical, artistic, and literary discourse to counter centuries of intellectual stagnation *(jumud)* under Turkish-Ottoman rule. Consequently, the Arab intellectual adaptation of modernity *(hadatha)* in the late nineteenth and early twentieth centuries became increasingly associated with first, recovering progressive Arab and Islamic heritage in philosophy, literature, arts, and language; second, the dynamic development of classical Arabic language toward making it more reflective of and accessible to all social strata and contemporary art, literature, and sciences; and third, a renewal of Arab literature and arts, making them more accountable and relevant to the concerns of Arab society. On the political level this simultaneously challenged colonial hegemony (initially, of the Ottoman Empire, and later of western colonialism) and hegemonic internal power structures, including proponents of social reaction and conservatism within Arab societies themselves. This take on modernity and modernism enhanced and informed Chahine's narrative structures and themes, as well as the signature formal textures and patterns that mark them.

Throughout this book I occasionally use the term 'third world' while alluding to non-western cinemas. This expression has been reinscribed by many scholars of Latin American, West Asian, South East Asian, African, and Arab cinemas by way of reclaiming a counter-hegemonic utility of an originally Eurocentric and inferiorizing term, which partly referenced non-Hollywood and non-Eastern European (specifically socialist bloc countries) cinemas. For a long time, third world cinemas formed the silent majority of world film production which, when not ignored, was treated with aloofness, as if it was merely the subaltern specter of the 'real' cinema of North America and Europe. Through their resilient, proficient, innovative, and inspiring work many of the filmmakers (and Youssef Chahine is one excellent example) and film industries working throughout the non-western world were able to sustain and develop cinemas that worked under very difficult political and economic conditions as they emerged (and continue to emerge) from colonial and post-colonial hegemony. For its part, this book hopes to reaffirm a useful reapproximation of a terminology that refers to collectively, and indeed heterogeneously distinguished cinemas that are produced outside the realm and control of 'western' film industries both east and west.

Youssef Chahine embarked on his filmmaking career in the late 1940s, just as the turbulent reality of the Egyptian and Arab anticolonial struggle began to take new forms and acquire increased momentum. With several Arab countries gaining their independence from France and Britain, the Arab world was confronted with what would become its most volatile national political issues: the uprooting of Palestinians from their homeland and the creation of the state of Israel. In the first film of his autobiographical trilogy, *Iskindiriya... lih?* (Alexandria... Why?, 1978), Chahine contemplated the period and chronicled how this informed and shaped his personal, political, and artistic development. As he began to respond to the climate of social and political crisis that had beleaguered the region since the late 1940s, Chahine sought ways to enhance social awareness through films informed by a range of national and international political and artistic confluences.

Chahine amassed an impressive body of work that bridged gaps between theory and practice; gaps that characterize the artistic convergences of *organic intellectuals*. His oeuvre consists mainly of films, but also includes critical writings and the many interviews he granted over the years concerning his films and his politics. The circulation of this body of work disseminated the objectives and goals of the predominantly entertainment-oriented cinema of Egypt and the Arab world, but also contributed to the formation of a socially and politically conscious—and distinctly Arab—film practice.

One of the goals of this book is to explore the institutional and esthetic foundations of Chahine's cinema while recognizing that its history and its practices owe as much to the self-defining consciousness of the filmmaker as to the social, political, and cultural formations that contributed to its development. Another goal is to profile the possible points of intersection between politically oriented cinematic practices developed in diverse national contexts and the conceptual framework of Chahine's cinema as part of a national Arab cinema.

It is my view that to consider the virtually simultaneous development and growth of Chahine's cinema and the protracted evolution of the national Arab project represents a potentially productive critical approach to an otherwise complex body of cinematographic work. This approach enables us to concurrently consider the contextual and ideological factors that informed Chahine's cinematic practice and its history, and allows for a diachronic layering of the instances that have mediated the growth of Chahine's influence within Egyptian and Arab cinemas and, equally as important, among Arab intellectuals and artists. Furthermore, this approach permits us to trace the marked cinematic tendencies within specific films as foundational elements identifiable within Egyptian and Arab political and cultural formations as well as within supranational formations and projects.

Through nearly sixty years of experimentation and consolidation, reevaluation and redevelopment, Chahine's cinema can be seen as a site that consistently empowered and enhanced a variety of cinematographic practices, within Egypt itself and across official Arab state boundaries. Whether as a unified project, or merely as a rich alliance of practices that consolidated what otherwise could not be connected, this cinema gained a wide reputation within Egypt and the Arab world as one that many Arab filmmakers, producers, actors, and technicians aspired to learn from, or, at the least, to be associated with. Therefore, as a body of work, Chahine's cinema accommodates disparate practices into a whole, in the same way that the term *Arab* organizes and encompasses the heterogeneous formation that brings together peoples of the immense land stretching from the Arabian Gulf and Iraq in the east, to Morocco and Mauritania in the west: a multiethnic, multiracial, multifaith, and multilingual hybrid with a six-thousand-year history. It is within this hybrid that Chahine's cinema has been able to nurture the idea of an Arab identity that (even as it continues to be challenged and contested) is informed by shared histories of growth and unity which were particularly associated with the zenith of the Islamic classical epoch between the seventh and fourteenth centuries, through later divisions, conciliations, and anticolonial struggles, to the current regional and collective attempts at social, economic, and political modernization and development.

Appealing to the ideals of Arab unity, social justice, solidarity, and a heterogeneous national identity, Chahine's cinema informed and was informed by the values through which Arab histories and cultures have been mediated. As such, these principles shaped the discursive foundation of Chahine's cinema, and ultimately became the basis in the quest for a pan-Arab identity that has characterized his cinema. These ideals, to which Chahine often alluded in his films, interviews and commentaries, enabled him to constantly refashion and reconstitute his cinematic practices. Inasmuch as Chahine's cinema accentuated the distinctive inflections of Egyptian struggles and culture in its manifestations of modern pan-Arab national histories and dilemmas, it spoke to the aspirations and dreams of a wider Arab audience. In this way, Chahine was always able to constitute his cinema within the Egypt he knew and loved, and within an Arab world he saw as his natural element.

Chahine's ideological preoccupation with a multifaceted national project based on unity within diversity helped his cinema to expand and consolidate itself by incorporating that diversity into his own well-defined sense of artistic preoccupations. The unique status of Chahine's cinema both as an intellectual and a cinematic project is largely related to his capacity to exploit the social and political impact of cinema as cultural practice. Despite the many political obstacles he encountered along the way, his cinema's modernist impulses provided the organic structure he required to rearticulate the Arab national project.

Chahine's cinema both challenged and preserved traditional practices in Egyptian and Arab cinema. Much of this cinema's history tends to confirm coalitionist, rather than independent, strategies and industrial cinematic practices. Historically, the term "Hollywood on the Nile" in reference to Egyptian cinema reflected at its extreme the appeal of a homogeneity within the Egyptian filmmaking industry as a normative form of cinematic expression; it also reflected the western tendency to marginalize national cinematic practices whose local appeal did not extend to Hollywood's traditional audiences. In the case of Chahine's cinema, the advocacy of alternative, oppositional modes and industrial strategies was also synonymous with a desire to appeal to a wider audience that is more familiar with traditional cinematic techniques and approaches. While Chahine's film practices have historically challenged the homogenizing accounts of local cinema, they simultaneously provided a space where diverse cinematic practices converged and interacted. In this way, Chahine's cinema has been the site where consensual models of industrial growth and creative merit can be de-centered and where new affiliations can be forged. Even Chahine's creation of his own film production company reflected a strategy that sought to articulate new dynamics of alternative filmmaking practices and connections. This allowed Chahine to maintain the financial basis necessary to attract and produce not only his own films, but also the work of new and non-traditional filmmakers and apprentices. When his critics accused him of producing unpopular, elitist films, Chahine shot back, "How do you think I keep directing and producing if my films were not popular and were not making money?" In the end, Chahine's work conveyed the tensions of the filmmaker's struggle to coalesce political and stylistic avant-gardism with those of accessibility and mass appeal.

The longevity of Chahine's filmmaking career, its presence and influence over nearly six decades, sets his cinema apart within the Arab world. His cinema sustained its political and national relevance by insinuating itself into sociopolitical concerns via an ideology and estheticthat remained conscious of the changing conceptual dynamics of cultural discourse in the Arab world. By accessing alternative modes of production and consumption and through an eclectic stylistic approach, Chahine's cinema refurbished classical definitions of political cinema. But while his production methods and esthetic approaches may have been customized occasionally to account for changing personal, social, political, and cultural contexts, what remained consistent was Chahine's resolve to use film as a tool for social and political change. He challenged traditional forms of national political expression, and was a strong advocate of national cultural autonomy and anticolonial struggle. As such, Chahine's body of work represents a partnership between cultural politics and social history; his work has as much to do with an ideological agenda as with an institutional negotiation of esthetic options for Arab filmmaking.

All films ultimately make choices in settling narrative dilemmas, and one way or the other assume some position in relation to specific historical, social, ethical, and political questions. As such, film mediates views and perspectives by informing the audience of social and political realities. My methodological approach in this book utilizes the study of form as an extension of wider systems of cultural interactivity. It accounts for three critical elements, each with its own dynamics overlapping the others, evolving to create a common field of intersection. These elements include the filmic text (the organization of the film and its codes and sub-codes), its production (where a wide range of determinants shape the actual creation of films and ultimately mould the cinematic text itself), and its reception (subjectivity—as evidenced in audience expectations, reactions, and engagement with films—rooted in historical and cultural familiarity with various cinematic practices).

Although I have examined a variety of discursive sites, including academic critiques, editorial commentaries, and trade journal accounts, as well as popular press reviews and interviews with the filmmaker, I am not offering a detailed reception study per se. Instead, this book engages in a contextual analysis of a filmmaker's cinematic circulation within the larger national and cultural world outside the texts themselves. Thus my references to critics and press commentaries are not meant to stand in for the audience at large, but rather to point out how Chahine's body of work was galvanized within a broader cultural discourse. As such, contemporaneous Arabic- and English-language academic and non-academic books and journals, as well as local mainstream magazines, newspapers, and journals, provided an important resource. These sources were accessed mainly in Cairo, Beirut, Damascus, and Paris through local archives and private collections.

I have mapped out various areas of inquiry—history, national liberation, class and social change, queer sexuality, cultural heterogeneity, and stylistic authorship—to explore interactive connections between Chahine's cinema and the national tendencies that contributed to its shaping. To the extent that Chahine's consistent presence in and influence on Arab cinema is contiguous to a commonality of purpose, I examined a range of critical motifs in light of their relevance to his cinema. This approach allows for a detailed study of specific films that were made under various historical and institutional contexts. The study of these films surveys the significance of their political preoccupations and esthetic thrusts, and their possible impact on Arab national discourse. In selecting these films I tried to account for the critical impression they left within the history of Arab cinema as well as their analytical utility in pointing out connections with their Arab contextual sphere.

Despite the current tendency to ignore or to de-emphasize historical context in film studies ventures, this book remains cognizant of the expediency of such a survey, and situates Chahine's cinema historically within the national Arab project. The study is also conscious of the evolution of Chahine's cinema and how it adaptively reflected upon social, political, and ideological struggles over several key moments in Egyptian and Arab histories. Specifically, the four consecutive historical junctures critical to understanding the ideological hegemonies active in the films discussed are: a) the 1950s to the early 1960s. Key events of this period include the Nasser revolution against the monarchy, the Suez crisis, the Algerian crisis, Syrian-Egyptian unity, and the Yemen war; b) the mid-1960s to the early 1970s. Of special significance are the Arab defeat in the 1967 war with Israel, apprehensions over revolutionary change, the Jordanian/Palestinian war, and the death of Nasser; c) the 1970s and 1980s. This was the era of the October War, civil war in Lebanon, détente with the United States, Anwar Sadat's alliance with Islamic fundamentalism and the crackdown on the secular left, the peace treaty with Israel, and the assassination of Sadat; and d) the 1990s to the present: a time of shifting political paradigms, the rise of Islamic fundamentalism, the Oslo Accords, capitalist globalization, and the events of September 11, 2001.

While this ordering provides a backdrop for my analysis of the films, the chapters of the study are organized in conjunction with specific themes that reflect key aspects of a modernist social/political/cultural formation. Each of these themes explores one aspect of Chahine's modernist discourse within the national polemics of the four historical periods of interest. In turn, each theme becomes the focal point of a chapter. The first chapter defines the contextual parameters of the notion of an Arab national project *(al-mashru' al-'arabi al-qawmi)*. The emphasis here is on discussing the historical changes that have impacted the social, political, cultural, and esthetic definition and redefinition of this project. The chapter sheds light on the nature of this project as an unfinished endeavor, one that continues to be contested, reshaped, and reframed, yet remains the goal and rallying cry for Arab independence, social change, and modernization. This chapter also introduces an overview of the notion of modernity within its Arab and cinematic context; examining Arab cinema on the eve of Nasser's 1952 revolution and shortly thereafter. This period is extremely important for our assessment of Chahine's body of work as it coincides with the inception of his film career.

Chapter two describes how, through an alternative approach to popular cinema, Chahine explored social experiences that were marginalized or excluded from homogeneous representations of nationhood. This is assessed through Chahine's films of the early 1950s, which exemplify his early and nascent interest in issues of class and social change. The chapter discusses how this initial preoccupation informed his later work and complemented Egyptian political developments at the dawn of the Nasser revolution. The third chapter addresses Chahine's popular cinematic rendezvous with ideas of anticolonial struggle and Arab unity through his films of the late 1950s and early 1960s; the films that shaped his reputation as a champion of pan-Arab solidarity and the Nasser revolution.

Chapter four connects Chahine's frustrated personal and political encounter with public sector bureaucracy to production conditions following the 1967 Arab defeat. While his films during this period did not engage in an explicit critique of the Nasser revolution, they were nevertheless informed by a more nuanced sensitivity toward the political and social dynamics of that revolution, as well as to the dynamics and possibilities of reversing its social and political agenda. Chahine's films on the building of the Aswan High Dam, the role of intellectuals and the bourgeoisie in social revolution, and the fate of peasants under feudalism, offered a new and darker view of the future and foreshadowed Chahine's later—even darker—cinematic position on the fate of the Nasser revolution and the Arab national project.

Chapter five chronicles the filmmaker's progression to more damning critiques of the situation which led to the 1967 defeat and Egypt's divergence from the ideals of the revolution. The burden of Nasser's 1970 death is felt in the nostalgic tone of Chahine's depictions of lost possibilities and through his palpable anticipation of catastrophe.

While his earlier films tended to overlook the underpinnings of difference and heterogeneity on the construction of national identity, in the late 1970s and into the 1980s Chahine began addressing religious, cultural, and sexual differences. In chapter six I assess *Alexandria... Why?* (1978), the first installment of Chahine's Alexandria trilogy, and its incorporation of difference itself as integral to Chahine's evolving conception of Arab national identity. Chapter seven builds on this by addressing *Wadaʿan Bonaparte!* (Adieu Bonaparte!, 1985), Chahine's historical drama promoting a heterogenic national consciousness and endorsing unity in the struggle against colonialism, both past and present.

Sexuality and its representation—historically a taboo in Arab social and cultural discourse—is discussed in chapter eight. The chapter looks at the ways Chahine seeks to identify new expressive territories that not only subvert accepted esthetic standards, but also claim a public space for topics suppressed in the private sphere. The chapter offers an analysis of Chahine's appropriation of non-normative sexuality, and argues that his subtle inclusion of queerness in his films augments the theme of heterogeneity as an elemental component of a renovated Arab national identity. While this chapter alludes to how Chahine's cinema furthered critical and reflective approaches to identity and social change, at stake here is the manner in which his films problematized the social, religious, and cultural erasure of non-normative sexualities while privileging collective identities as embattled sites of representation and discourse.

Chapter nine offers a detailed analysis of *Destiny* (1997), a key Chahine film that focuses on one of the major preoccupations of Arab intellectuals in the 1990s—religious fundamentalism. The chapter describes and contextualizes the filmmaker's battle against dogmatism, mining the past to render the current national impasse ripe for a modernist intervention. Chapter ten offers an analysis of Chahine's response to the heightened Arab awareness of the politics of globalization in the aftermath of the September 11, 2001 attacks. Chahine's work during this period tends to indulge in a discussion of the concept of the Other and how it affects both the colonizer and the colonized. Here I analyze the director's last films and how they re-established Chahine's appeal with mainstream Egyptian and Arab audiences.

The final chapter focuses on Chahine the author and organic intellectual; offering a critical assessment of his eclectic stylistic approach, his idiosyncratic cinematic perspective, his avant-garde formal strategies, and how they were all informed by his stance on the various social and national conditions that characterized each period of his career. Traditionally, the definition of an activist cinema—conceived as always open, never complete—was linked to oppositional strategies capable of challenging mainstream modes of cinematographic production and consumption. In Chahine's case there seems to have been an amalgamation of various popular and experimental practices, which were enhanced by his conscious pursuit of the roles of architect of change and political activist. This observation gives way to a discussion of authorship in Chahine's cinema; a cinema cultivated within a political framework that shifts agency away from narrowly defined notions of creativity.

In addition to the comprehensive bibliography on Chahine, I have chosen to include an additional list of resources that are of interest to all current and future researchers on Arab cinema. Academic work on Arab film in general remains severely underdeveloped, and any work on Chahine himself is impossible without a good background in and an understanding of Arab film history and cultural politics. This additional list fills an important reference gap in the study of Arab cinema and a contextual breadth for reading and positioning Chahine's unique contribution to national Arab cinema and culture. It provides current and future researchers a broad and updated engagement with scholarly work on this still relatively unexplored cinema and its masters.

Through its conceptual framework, Chahine's cinema has placed modernity at the service of experimentation and heterogeneity. Moreover, the critical modernism of Chahine's films operates within a consciousness of multiple and yet-to-be-told narratives of cultural identity. This principle upon which fixed ideas of Arab identity have been challenged and new utopias imagined, is exemplified in Chahine's belief that the ideological pretext of the Arab national project remains incomplete, persisting as the elusive essence of the Arab social and cultural consciousness.

1

AN UNFINISHED PROJECT: CHAHINE AND THE ARAB NATIONAL PROJECT

This chapter provides a contextual survey of the nature and development of the Arab national project, and how it impacted the revitalization of Arab cinema as constituent of a modernist national project. While Chahine's cinema was informed by contemporaneous social, political, and cultural developments in the Arab world, it was also augmented by the persistent ideological and intellectual anxieties that have troubled the region since the early 1800s.

The protracted struggle for modernization, democratic reform, and social justice in the Arab world has variously informed and been informed by struggle for Arab national independence and unity, itself an enduring endeavor. The dynamics of anticolonial resistance and the struggles for national self-determination within the region continue to interact with the lingering battle for socioeconomic development and democratic change. Hence, this book's allusions to the *Arab national project* and its impact on Chahine's work inevitably refer to a project far from achieving its main goals and objectives. It must be stressed that this project has been evolving over two centuries that have seen major sociopolitical upheavals and actions that have impinged on the Arab national agenda, often redefining its priorities. As such, the Arab national project should be looked at as one in formation; part of an organic process that has witnessed its share of successes and failures, but nevertheless has steadily and increasingly assumed heterogeneous and inclusive bearing and disposition.

THE ARAB NATIONAL PROJECT AS AN UNFINISHED PROJECT

The ideological and conceptual roots of Arab nationalist political and cultural discourse over the last two centuries are located in the nineteenth-century movement known as al-Nahda (the Renaissance), and epitomized by the anticolonial struggle for national self-determination under the Ottoman Empire. Between 1831 and 1840 Egyptian ruler Muhammad Ali and his son Ibrahim made the first attempt in modern history to create a larger united Arab state encompassing Egypt and Greater Syria (which then included present day Lebanon, Palestine, and Jordan). The campaign was eventually crushed by a joint political and military operation initiated by the Ottoman Empire in an alliance with imperial Britain tacitly sanctioned by other European colonial powers. But despite its failure, Muhammad Ali's attempt advanced the intellectual and political maturation of the struggle for Arab unity, independence, and modernization.

The first attempt to create a united Arab state reflected the mounting influence of an emerging national bourgeoisie on the old feudalist structure. The foundational ideologies of this emerging class echoed those of the European bourgeoisie during the Renaissance and affirmed by the French Revolution. The emergence of al-Nahda movement specifically reflected an appreciation of the linkages between anticolonial resistance and the struggles against social and political injustice, and religious sectarianism and dogma. Initially advocating the negotiation of Arab emancipation within the framework of the Ottoman Empire, this movement aspired to integrate Islamic and Arab heritages within the humanist traditions of contemporary Europe. The movement sought to create a more inclusive social contract; encouraging women and religious and ethnic minorities to embrace and engage in Arab public life.

Historically, advocates of pan-Arab unity have sought the democratic unification and national self-determination of Arabic-speaking peoples.[1] And contrary to what Orientalist discourse customarily suggests, Arab nationalism has advocated national identity as a preferable alternative to religious, ethnic, and tribal sectarianisms, promoting secular forms of government and engaging a wide cross-section of the region's ethnic and religious mosaic.[2]

To be sure, on the cultural level it is impossible to separate Arabism and Islam. Notwithstanding the need to be cognizant of the nuance between the Arab national project as a relatively modern enterprise and today's politicized Islam as a separate project with critical significance within the Arab and Muslim worlds, the Arab national project was not preoccupied by the separation between Arabism and Islam. If anything, it has always been clear that the audience that project addressed was and is overwhelmingly Muslim. Furthermore, the Arab national project was consistently and largely based on the appreciation of the modernist civilizational aspects of Arab culture after the emergence of Islam. This is why most Arab nationalist movements of the twentieth century recognized unequivocally the centrality of Islam and Islamic culture in their versions of the Arab national project. This occured despite the fact that many of the intellectuals behind these movements came from Christian backgrounds.

By the late 1940s and early 1950s political leaderships in the region, which led the struggle for independence from colonialism in Syria, Lebanon, and Iraq, were losing support within their constituencies. On the other hand local leadership in other Arab regions such as the Trans-Jordan, the Arabian Peninsula heartland, Yemen, Aden, as well as various Gulf emirates had close relationships with British colonialists. Jordan and Saudi Arabia in particular enjoyed relative autonomy. The North African region, including Morocco, Algeria, Tunisia, and Libya, was still under direct colonial rule, albeit under different and various pretexts. Egypt in the late 1940s and early 1950s maintained a special status whereby the British mustered almost total control over the government, and British troops maintained a strong presence in the country. Regimes of the countries that participated in the 1948 War in response to the creation of the state of Israel, including Iraq, faced the brunt of criticism for their armies' humiliating defeat in Palestine.

Arab nationalist groups, particularly in the Levant, differed politically from each other, and competed fiercely over the leadership of the growing anti-government opposition movement in post-independent Arab states. However, for most of these groups an anti-imperialist and socialist political perspective was the norm, and in this regard at least, they could agree on the goal of ridding the Arab world of pro-colonial governments, and on the need to replace them with new regimes that were capable of restoring Arab dignity and unity. They also saw in unity a critical ingredient for social and economic progress and reform within the region. Of course, differences between these groups were at times fierce, but there were also political moments when they created effective alliances. Within this general nationalist framework, two major camps competed for the leadership of oppositional forces in the area: the leftist nationalists associated mainly with the Baath Arab Socialist Party, and the Marxist-oriented Communist parties. Both of these groups had important grass roots followings, particularly in the Levantine countries of Syria, Lebanon, and Iraq. Another nationalist group that also sought unity—but with the perspective of the pan-Levant area of Greater

Syria—was the Syrian National Social Party. Egypt had a different situation; while Communists enjoyed some level of support among intellectuals and some working class circles, pan-Arab nationalists did not enjoy as much influence as they did in the Arab east. The major opposition to King Farouk and to the British colonial presence in the country circulated within secret networks in the military where the seeds for overthrowing the king's regime would be planted and cultivated.

Thus it must be stressed that despite their differences, the pan-Arab impetus was as dear to the popular masses of the Arab world—particularly in the Levant and Egypt—as was the drive toward social and economic reform discourse. As a result, a two-fold socialist/nationalist discourse would shape the philosophies of pan-Arab nationalist forces for at least two decades to come. This confluence came to constitute a major element of the political discourse of the nationalist regimes that would begin to emerge in the 1950s in Syria, Iraq, and Egypt.

To summarize, early manifestations of a contemporary Arab national movement coincided with the European colonization of the region in the aftermath of the collapse of the Ottoman Empire. This resulted in the segmentation of the Arab world into various nation states. The second phase occurred in conjunction with the emergence of the Arab national liberation movement against western colonialism, the colonization of Palestine, and the movement advocating Arab unification. This phase was characterized by largely romantic political experimentations, which in the end were unsuccessful in achieving any substantive or enduring progress toward the movement's goals. In the end, the failure of contemporary Arab nationalist movements and groups in the postcolonial era resulted in a deep disillusionment with the entire pan-Arab modernizing project and a general despair among the masses of any possibility of reform. Arab states which first embraced the rule of nationalist-oriented governments in the 1950s, 1960s, and 1970s eventually witnessed the gradual failure of these governments in pursuing their nationalist goals. Adding to the Arabs' disillusionment with the national project was the failure of Arab states to coordinate their efforts to deal with the Palestinian dilemma, which people in the region consider to be a major historical, political, national, and humanitarian calamity.

Today, there is a deeply rooted feeling among Arabs that their struggle for national liberation remains part of an unfinished project. A political malaise—characterized by the general presumption that national economic resources remain essentially under the control of neocolonial powers—continues to be fueled by the persistent denial of the right to self-determination for the Palestinian people, the launching of two major American military interventions in less than fifteen years, the placement of hundreds of thousands of foreign troops within several Arab countries, and American threats against Syria. Within this atmosphere, Arab nationalism today is not simply an ideological or political agenda. Rather, it has assumed the shape of a community which is personally held and culturally expressed. As such, Arab nationalism in the first decade of the new millennium is a dynamic form of an "imagined community," to use Benedict Anderson's term, constituted by social practice and formations, which informs and is informed by Arab cultural practices, including cinema.

An important backdrop to the development of this form of nationalism over the last two decades has been the rising influence of fundamentalist groups and various forms of religious dogmatism. Many Arab intellectuals feel that this wave has hindered the process of democratization and social modernization in the area, and contributed to the state of stagnation that has been afflicting the pursuit of national self-determination and unity. A recent conference held in Damascus brought together intellectuals and representatives from across the Arab world to discuss issues relating to what was considered a "state of existential crisis" faced by the Arab peoples. Participants identified the essence of this crisis in the following manner:

> In discussing the relationship between globalization and the national question, and in analyzing its backgrounds and effects, the attendants concluded that there is an urgent need to re-evaluate some of what used to be considered a given. Among the key issues that were discussed was religious sectarianism and the means to confront it. [We agreed] that such sectarianism only flourishes and grows as the progressive national outlook gives ground and approaches a state of crisis . . . the conference also agreed that the entire future of the Arab world becomes in the balance when national and civilizational consciousness retreats, and is replaced by reactionary stances and ideas that are rooted in religious discord, confessionalism, and ethnic and tribal divisions.[3]

Other Arab nationalists are even more explicit in identifying the nature of the current crisis; they refer to the class-based character of postcolonial Arab regimes that they consider to be in alliance with old and contemporary colonial interests in the region:

> European revolutions were led by a rising bourgeoisie, and were interlinked with the rise and development of capitalism. The bourgeoisie in the Arab

world has never been a productive class and therefore was never a vanguard class. As a result this class was easily and directly manipulated by imperialist strategies and the world capitalist system . . . . Eventually, each Arab state was built around structures that encouraged [internal] divisions, and tailism [to colonial politics]. These structures enhanced and accommodated earlier colonial division of the region initiated in the Sykes-Picot Agreement in the aftermath of the First World War. A state of crisis was further exacerbated by the creation of the state of Israel in the heart of the Arab world . . . perhaps the most dangerous aspect of today's [Arab] national crisis is the strategies of marginalization and of division, as they both enhance unilateral American hegemony. Unfortunately, the Arab national project, which remains the only viable strategic and historic alternative, is yet to be translated into and built upon the notion of democracy with all its epistemological, intellectual, political, social, and economic parameters . . . this has been the essence of our national collapse.[4]

Over the last fifteen years, similar concerns have been raised in the context of attempts to refashion national Arab cultural discourse in literature, poetry, visual arts, music, theater, and film. The general state of stagnation afflicting the Arab national liberation movement seems to have enhanced the emergence of vigorously self-critical attitudes in approaching social, political, and cultural realities in the region. In hindsight, this interest in the critical and uncompromising evaluation of mistakes, roles, and ideological preconceptions has reinvigorated Arab cultural discourse with a new vivacity that, in many ways, echoes what was taking place in the early stages of the development of al-Nahda movement in the nineteenth century.

MODERNITY AS AN ARAB CULTURAL CONTINUUM

The notion of modernity and the modernist revamping of the Arab world have consistently impacted on the discourse of the modern Arab national liberation movement as well as on the general parameters of its counter-hegemonic vigor. The term *modernity* integrates an outlook toward lived experience that encompasses various political, ideological, and cultural paradigms. The term *modernization*, on the other hand, refers more specifically to the processes of change that result from the introduction of certain technologies, such as the technology of cinema, into various spheres of private and social life. However, it is crucial to stress that my employment of both terms in this book also considers the contextual specificity of Arab history, philosophy, and culture.

My emphasis on contextualizing the use of modernism-related terminology naturally poses a challenge to the universal (read 'colonial') use of the notion of modernity and proposes a utility which accounts for the specificity of the postcolonial cultural text. As such it provides an Other's postcolonial — and in this case a specifically Arab postcolonial — approach to modernity. Furthermore, my use of the terminology offers an alternative to what Edward Said characterized as the "corporate institution of dealing with the Orient,"[5] in this case as it pertains to western scholarship on Arab culture in general and Arab cinema in particular. The goal here is to propose some crucial and often disregarded theoretical and methodological considerations for those interested in pursuing further research on Arab and Egyptian cinemas as well as postcolonial film texts in general.

Since its emergence in the mid-1800s al-Nahda movement simultaneously informed and was informed by a strong emphasis on social and cultural heterogeneity as integral to achieving self-determination and national independence.[6] Within its own historical and cultural parameters al-Nahda articulated paradoxical dispositions of a project which was not dissimilar in its outlook to how modernist renewal was historically expressed, for example, within a Latin American context, that is as "neither a break from the past nor a new way of describing and categorizing the present; [but] instead [as a rearticulation of] the process whereby historical and cultural formation mediate and condition contemporaneity."[7] Arab modernity and renewal, however, more specifically emphasized, first, the dynamic recovery and preservation of Arab and Islamic history, literature, and language; second, the development of classical Arabic language and utility while making it more accessible to and informed by the realities of contemporary life, arts, literature, and sciences; and third, seeking renewal and continuity in the process of developing literature and the arts by deepening their social relevance and stressing their connection with the wider heritage of humanity. Modernity as a specifically Arab frame of reference equally finds its origins within a paradigm whereby Arab intellectuals (particularly from the mid-nineteeth to early twentieth centuries) began to pursue an anticolonial project for progressive political, social, economic, and cultural renewal.

As we saw earlier, al-Nahda movement began to develop in the mid-nineteenth century when much of the Middle East was under the control of the Ottoman Empire. This movement epitomized the struggle to reaffirm Arab identity and sought ways to assert the Arab right to self-determination. Equally as important, Arab intellectuals of the time aspired to a transformation that involved the cross-fertilization and integration of Islamic and Arab heritages with the humanist traditions of the European Renaissance, the ideals of the French Revolution, and the nineteenth-century scientific and industrial Enlightenment. As such al-Nahda saw itself primarily as a modernist and modernizing movement combining various political, social, and intellectual/religious features.[8]

Religious Muslim Arab intellectuals of the mid-nineteenth century such as al-Afghani, Muhammad Abdu, and Abd al-Rahman al-Kawakibi consistently stressed the need to overcome the barriers between Islam and philosophy that arose after the burning of the books of Cordoba's philosopher Ibn Rushd—an event that later became the topic of a major Chahine film. These intellectuals emphasized the need to break away from traditional dogmatic readings of the Qur'an and embraced openness in interpreting the religious text. Essentially, this group of theologians sought to rejuvenate and modernize the process of understanding the religious text in a way which—as Ibn Rushd himself described seven centuries earlier—respected the primacy of reason, fought intellectual and religious mysticism, and by extension promoted philosophical rationalism as well as scientific modernization and social progress.

Discussions around the interpretation of the religious text soon expanded to include wider and even more vigorous debate regarding the need to break away from the sanctification of language and written texts in general. What ensued was a movement which put a specifically Arab spin on the notion of modernity. This movement was later implicated in a wide literary and artistic body of work that promoted a renewal *(tajdid)* of critical and literary practice; giving it a progressive role in Arab politics after centuries of what was considered to be intellectual stagnation *(jumud)* under the Ottoman rule.[9]

By the 1920s (and again during the period of struggle for national liberation in the 1940s and 1950s) a heterogeneous movement involving a broad spectrum of anticolonialist, socialist, and left–liberal groupings began to introduce and incorporate various aspects of early twentieth-century western-based modernism in the arts and in literature. Within this paradigm many Arab artists saw themselves and their role as part of a new cultural thrust, one which involved the recuperation of cross-historical, cross-cultural, cross-textual, and inherently political traditions. In other words, the openness toward and the recognition of the polity of the text constituted the essence of Arab modernity.

AN OVERVIEW OF ARAB CINEMA AS A MODERNIST PROJECT

Arab cinema emerged around the same time as the Arab world itself was embroiled in the challenges of modernization and concerns over the growing struggles for independence, Arab unity and national self-determination. As such, Arab cinema grew and was largely fashioned via a modernist symbiosis that informed and was informed by a budding national identity struggling to affirm its heterogeneity and find a new role for itself in the continuing fight for national liberation.

Dating from the 1895 screenings of the Lumière brothers' films in Alexandria, cinema as a cultural practice has had a major impact on the Arab world, not simply in terms of its content and as a modern invention, but also because of its articulation of a new textual mode of communication. Social discourse on the function of the image, the strategies of the narrative, the place of the audience, and the advent of new cultural codings had a major impact on Arab intellectual circles at the turn of the twentieth century. As such, cinema quickly became associated with the notion of a modernist text and as a new site for the Arab struggle for modernization.

Earlier al-Nahda discussions on the interpretation of religious texts later expanded to include a call to break away from traditional sanctification of language and its use in literary and artistic work. By the early 1900s even traditional critical interpretations of classical literary Arabic texts, including those of the pre-Islamic period *(al-jahiliya)* came under fierce scrutiny. This opened the way for vigorous discussions on the historicity and interpretive value of language and the text. A major development in this regard was the publication of Egyptian writer Taha Hussein's groundbreaking book *On the Jahili Literature*. Other major literary figures and social and cultural reformists who contributed to this re-evaluation process during the period included Gibran Khalil Gibran, Jirgi Zaydan, Amine al-Rihani, Qasim Amin, among others.

With the collapse of the Ottoman rule after the First World War and its replacement with western colonial hegemony, new alignments of anticolonial forces were beginning to take shape. From the 1920s through to the 1950s the anticolonial movement in the Arab world was comprised of forces whose outlook was more open than ever to western ideals in political and cultural discourse. Liberal, socialist, and Marxist ideas increasingly asserted their presence among Arab intellectuals, heralding a closer examination of the new artistic and cultural trends that were emerging at the time in Europe and the former Soviet Union.[10]

These realignments constituted the nucleus of a modernist, Arab-nuanced cultural discourse. Located within al-Nahda's philosophical emphasis on opening the use of language and the interpretation of the text (rather than the closing of its use to specific forms and conventions), and as means of challenging colonial hegemony and conservatism, the Arab appropriation of the modernist text increasingly became characterized by both a stylistic emphasis on heterogeneity and interactivity, and a conscious awareness of the polity of the artistic text.

From its early beginnings in the 1920s and through its uneven development over the last century Arab cinema in general, and Egyptian cinema in particular, evolved and reinvented itself by incorporating heterogeneous stylistic and generic approaches. Egyptian film, buoyed by its nationally based and operated studio system, has maintained a broad popular appeal among its national audience,[11] even while sustaining a concomitant interest in various popular and high art cinematic traditions on the levels of production, circulation, and consumption. Thus the social realist movement which arose in Egypt after the 1952 revolution against the monarchy coexisted with and fed upon the success of the generic and stylistic conventions of classical Hollywood cinema. By the late 1960s and early 1970s classical Hollywood stylistic strategies as adapted in the Egyptian popular cinema were being informed by an interest in neorealism and, to a lesser extent, avant-garde filmmaking techniques.

Western modernist impulses—arising from western art and literature of the early and mid-twentieth century—were also assimilated by Egyptian filmmakers as equally valuable and complementary rather than antithetical to Arab national and cultural modernist traditions. The incorporation of western versions of modernism by these filmmakers was partly based on a refashioning, liberating, and revitalizing of the modalities that complemented their indigenous modernist traditions and history.

Following Gamal Abd al-Nasser's leftist national revolution, the public sector in Egypt began to play a major role in supporting socially and politically dedicated, modernist, 'third worldist' cinema. By the early 1950s Egyptian cinema was integrating a loose adaptation of various realist cinematic trends including French poetic realism, Italian neorealism, and socialist realism.[12] It was also incorporating a mixture of approaches associated with Soviet dialectical formalism, particularly those articulated by Sergei Eisenstein and Dziga Vertov, as well as the expressionistic techniques and innovations introduced by classical German filmmakers of the 1920s.[13]

The interest in a wide range of modernist trends was fashioned via a symbiosis of themes and the incorporation of local settings and experiences. By 1958, Chahine's *Bab al-Hadid* (Cairo Station) would clearly reflect this symbiosis through its utilization of techniques from neorealism, German Expressionism, Soviet montage, and the French New Wave, even while maintaining a fundamentally classical Hollywood plot structure. By building upon their own national modernist paradigm which emphasized opening the parameters of the text and its utility beyond traditional restrictive rules of engagement, many Arab filmmakers considered themselves to be salvaging a cross-historical, cross-cultural, cross-textual, and inherently political cinematic project.

EGYPTIAN CINEMA JUST BEFORE THE REVOLUTION

In the pre-revolution period between 1945 and 1951, Egyptian cinema experienced such huge growth that there was often difficulty in finding enough actors and technicians to service the huge output of films. According to film director Mohammad Khan, "directors made do with singers and dancers and no longer bothered to train or discover new talents."[14] Khan provides a broader historical context to this staggering growth within the Egyptian filmmaking industry.

Egypt took part in the Second World War on the side of the Allies, under the Anglo-Egyptian agreements, and provided Britain with certain strategic bases. This led to the emergence of a new social class with larger material resources. A large number of companies that never had any connection whatsoever with the film industry, set up in production. Apart from the large number of new film companies, other film firms were set up whose real purpose had no relation to the cinema. These firms, some of which were even unlicensed, were trading in unexposed film on the black market. They obtained such stock from the Ministry of Social Affairs, which was responsible for its distribution, at the ordinary price. Unexposed film was imported from abroad. They then resold it to licensed companies at exorbitant prices.[15]

The Egyptian film industry became firmly established along the Hollywood model, with a huge star system where some of the actors' fees frequently reached nearly half the budget of an entire film.[16] The number of movie theaters during this period jumped from a hundred in the mid-1930s to 244 in 1949, while four new modern film studios were created in addition to the major state-of-the-art Misr Studio. Film production itself rose to over fifty films a year between 1945 and 1950, creating a huge market for Egyptian film in other Arab countries and allowing the Egyptian film industry to firmly establish a pan-Arab influence, which it continues to enjoy today. Furthermore, Arab capitalists began to see the great potential for profit in the successful industry. An early manifestation of this interest was seen in the major role played by Lebanese distributors who became involved in promoting Egyptian films throughout the Arab region and even within Egypt itself. In conjunction with this explosion in filmmaking and distribution, the number of Egyptian directors doubled.

This mostly profit-oriented approach to filmmaking, however, resulted in a hodgepodge cinema, which was designed to satisfy all tastes to the extent that it became difficult to classify even in terms of commonly known generic terms. Khan gives an example of a typical movie poster of the period announcing "A dramatic comedy, love story with songs and dances."[17] Films of this period were mostly divided into two groups—melodramas, and farces and comedy revues, which were usually punctuated by song and dance. One factor which may have helped institutionalize the Egyptian film industry's reliance on melodramas and formula musicals was the government's introduction of new rules in response to the increasing political tensions within the country.

Along with the impressive successes of the Egyptian film industry came the increased tightening of government censorship. New laws introduced by the Ministry of Social Affairs in February 1947 went well beyond traditional concerns over public morality and decency. Explicit rules banned all depictions of "scenes that might offend Egyptians... and issues that appear to support communistic tendencies or offend the system and the monarchy." The law also banned "showing scenes that could encourage disruption of the social order, such as revolutions, demonstrations or strikes," and the depiction of "poverty, peasant life, calls to revolt, and the questioning of traditional customs."[18] Clearly, King Farouk's government was cognizant and fearful of brewing political tensions in the country. The hardships suffered by peasant and working class Egyptians inspired the growth of more vocal grass-roots opposition, which materialized in mass protests against the government in 1946, as well as major strikes and demonstrations by workers in industrial centers such as Shubra al-Khayma, Tanta, and Port Said.

REVOLUTION AND THE EMERGENCE OF A NEW FILM DISCOURSE

By the late 1940s Egypt and the Arab world were entering a period of major political upheaval. The defeat of the Arab armies in the battle to prevent the creation of the state of Israel had resulted in what would become known as *al-Nakba* (the Disaster). The term refers to the political and demographic tragedy that befell hundreds of thousands of Palestinians after the loss of their homeland, transforming them into refugees scattered in neighboring Arab countries. These events contributed to the revolts that occurred in several Arab countries, resulting in the overthrowing of their governments. The revolts not only reflected popular anger over the failures of these regimes to effectively defend Palestinian rights, but also echoed widespread dismay over what was conceived as the direct control over these regimes by colonial powers such as Britain and France, both of which were seen as culpable in the Palestine disaster.

Arabs in most newly independent countries were also fed up with repressive post-feudal social, political, and economic systems of governance. Anticolonial groups and organizations along with socialist, communist, and Arab nationalist parties were gaining wide influence in many Arab states such as Syria, Iraq, Lebanon, and Egypt. In Egypt, Colonel Gamal Abd al-Nasser led a bloodless revolution in July 1952 that overthrew the Egyptian monarchy, which was considered to be directly supported and controlled by the British. That revolution's impact on the development of the national and social liberation movement in the Arab world also played a major role in the emergence of new kinds of Egyptian and Arab cinemas.

Under the new political conditions in Egypt, cinematic depictions of social justice, national liberation, Arab unity, and anticolonial struggles not only became possible but specifically encouraged. In 1955, less than three years after the revolution, the Ministry of Public Information (*al-Irshad*) eliminated the censorship measures imposed in February 1947, and legislated new regulations that remain in place today.[19] According to Egyptian film scholar Ali Abu Shadi, despite its many loopholes and remaining restrictive elements, the new law represented a major advancement on the 1947 regulations.[20] Another leading scholar, Samir Farid qualifies Abu Shadi's view in this regard, and proposes that after the July Revolution, "censorship became limited to issues concerning disturbing public peace and offending moral norms, leaving the interpretation of these two general guidelines to the discretion of the censor." Farid stresses, however, that the legislation under the king was practically a verbatim copy of the U.S. Hays Code, and that it explicitly detailed what was to be banned. This contrasted with the more flexible and widely interpretive nature of the subsequent censorship regulations after the revolution.[21]

Equally as important, the new government policy moved in the direction of social reform and increased state intervention in the economy. This was exemplified in its nationalization of the main sectors of the economy. The government, however, became even more committed to state involvement in the economy between 1956 and 1957, and began to move aggressively from its initial encouragement of private capital investment in the infrastructure, to taking near total control over production. By 1960, around the same time the government effectively took control of most major Egyptian industries,[22] Bank Misr, Egypt's largest bank controlling up to a fifth of Egypt's industrial output, was nationalized.

When it came to the film industry, however, the government initially had no plans to nationalize studios, laboratories, or movie theaters. According to Samir Farid, government intervention came as a direct result of the film companies' push for government compensation for what they claimed to be a loss of revenues from foreign market sales.[23] Nevertheless, the new regime's intervention within the film industry took a different shape from those in other socialist-oriented governments:

> The studios, laboratories, and movie theaters were not totally nationalized, as happened in the socialist countries of Asia and Eastern Europe, and the degree of state ownership ranged from outright purchase to the confiscation of private property and placing it under state guardianship. Nor did the government move against the Egyptian subsidiaries of the large 'imperialist' U.S. companies.[24]

Mohammad Khan also points out that in the post-revolution period the government was even lending money to private film production companies, and that Youssef Chahine himself was among the beneficiaries of this support with *al-Nasir Salah al-Din* (Saladin, 1963), which was produced by Lotus Film (Asia).[25] But irrespective of how the film production, distribution, and exhibition industries came under the control of the public sector, the fact remains that these developments impacted on Egyptian cinema in a major way.

The new situation after the revolution saw a renaissance in almost all areas of cultural production and reception in Egypt. The major changes on the economic, social, and political levels during the first decade of the revolution helped create and vitalize new forms and cultural practices. Art had an important place in this revolution, with, for example, the establishment of the Ministry of National Culture and Guidance, which included the Higher Council for the Protection of the Arts and Literature. In July 1957, the National Organization for the Consolidation of the Cinema was set up by the Ministry of National Culture and Guidance, which gave it the right to initiate legislation and to adopt schemes calculated to develop the art of the cinema, and endowed it with an annual budget of 150,000 Egyptian pounds.[26]

These changes affected Egyptian cinema in ways that had never existed before: new policies and structures were created to encourage and reward film talents, and to support participation in Egyptian-foreign coproductions. As Joel Gordon demonstrates in his unique scholarly survey of Egyptian cinema during the Nasser period, this cinema witnessed a "Golden Age" which helped constitute a pantheon that many Egyptians remain attracted to today, that is inspite of the enormous changes that have affected the country's politics and ideological outlook over the last three decades. Gordon presents the era as the greatest in Egyptian filmmaking and as such he considers it to be a formative one for those involved in today's filmmaking in Egypt.[27] Whether we agree or not with Gordon's evaluation, it remains important to point out specific facts.

The changes to censorship laws themselves included new clauses that sought to discourage the production of films with poor artistic, dramatic, or technical values. The government also sent several film commissions to Latin American and Asian countries to promote the screening and distribution of Egyptian films. In Cairo in 1959 the High Cinema Institute was created, which became the first film school in the Arab and Islamic worlds and in Africa. The institute played a critical role in training a huge number of young filmmakers and professionals and enriched the Egyptian and Arab film industry with a major influx of artistic and technical talent. Within this new atmosphere new film study and discussion groups and organizations were created including the Cairo Film Society in 1960. Mohammad Khan describes the impact of this group:

> [The Society] also served as a second classroom for students of the Higher Cinema Institute. Originally the society was founded to screen artistic films, hold lectures and publish its quarterly bulletin. The Society started with 15 members and now [1969] holds over 500. Having aroused an artistic awareness within its members which included prominent directors and technicians as well, the Society decided to undertake short film production.[28]

An important development took place in Egypt in the aftermath of the revolution. The government began to proactively encourage studying and discussing international trends and developments in filmmaking and theory. In 1960 the government helped organize and support a major festival for Asian and African films in which more than thirty-two countries participated. It also supported financing the translation of twenty-five important academic books on film esthetics and techniques.[29]

Samir Farid shares Khan's evaluation of this period in Egyptian film history and more specifically describes the years between 1956 and 1962 as the "second golden age for Egyptian cinema" after the financial golden period which followed the creation of Studio Misr in the mid-1930s until toward the end of the Second World War.[30] Farid points out that within this six-year period it became common for Egyptian films to be screened at international film festivals such as Cannes and Moscow. In contrast, after the late 1960s it became rare to see Egyptian films at international festivals.[31]

As a result of these changes, the themes and the quality of Egyptian films underwent a transformation. A strong group of Egyptian filmmakers who eventually came to define Egyptian cinema emerged during this period. These filmmakers were among the most successful locally and most recognized throughout the Arab world, and were also able to muster respect within international film circuits; their list includes Salah Abu Seif, Hussein Kamal, Hussam-Eddine Mustafa, Tawfiq Saleh, Farouk Agrama, Shadi Abd al-Salam, among others.

Clearly, the Egyptian film industry was experiencing a golden period of popularity and success and solidifying its position as the center of Arab cinema. On the other hand this cinema was also experiencing its first major rendezvous with political involvement, which created a conscious appreciation of its potential as an agent for social and political change. Revolutionary events in the country would greatly impact on the development of this cinema, and map out new thematic interests and esthetic practices and directions from which Youssef Chahine's work would emerge and evolve.

2

POPULAR CINEMA AND CONCEPTUALIZING CLASS AND SOCIAL CHANGE

This chapter covers the early work of Chahine, which for the most part coincides with the first decade of the Nasser revolution. In the 1950s Chahine made twelve films. During this stage his burgeoning interest in social and national issues and lives becomes apparent in his depictions of peasant and working class life. And despite his dismay regarding many aspects of middle- and upper-class lifestyles, some of his films reflect on the possibility of building bridges between those who come from different class backgrounds yet share a common interest in issues of social and political justice and change. Notwithstanding his interest in the subject, Chahine's cinema never adopted a dogmatic stand on the issues of class and class divisions; rather, it acknowledged the common areas of interest among people from different classes. This was the manifestation of Chahine's early conception of change in the Arab world as one that works toward achieving political, economic, and national independence. This conceptin also suggests that marginalized classes can be empowered even while maintaining a level of cross-class solidarity with an enlightened middle class, the kind of unity which remains needed during the period of national liberation.

EARLY CINEMA AND SOCIAL CLASS

The young Chahine began his filmmaking career in the interval between the old British-supported regime of King Farouk and the new revolutionary government of President Nasser. From the outset, this transitory period reflected tensions between politically conscious cinema and popular film practices. During the early period after the revolution a new realist trend was taking hold within Egyptian cinema. Filmmakers such as Salah Abu Seif showed interest in making films that presented a vivid and less artificial depiction of life among peasant and working class Egyptians. Abu Seif's 1953 film *Rayya wa Skina* (Rayya and Skina) and the 1954 *al-Wahsh* (The Monster) became landmarks in the history of what came to be known as Egyptian social realism.

Chahine began his film career immediately following his return from the United States with an acting diploma from the Pasadena Playhouse in 1948. But instead of seeking work in the theater, his first job was in the publicity department of Twentieth Century Fox in Cairo, where his brother-in-law, John Khoury, worked as a manager. Just before the Nasser revolution, Chahine directed his first feature film *Baba Amin* (Father Amin, 1950), followed by *Ibn al-Nil* (The Son of the Nile, 1951). The latter film was the first Egyptian film to be shot on location outside the studio. It was also a popular success; costing only 13,000 Egyptian pounds to make while grossing over 70,000.[1] Later in the 1950s, while filming a number of thematically and stylistically traditional popular melodramas and musicals such as *al-Muharrij al-kabir* (The Great Clown, 1952), *Sayyidat al-qitar* (Lady on the Train, 1953), and *Nisa' bila rijal* (Women without Men, 1953), Chahine also made *Shaytan al-sahara'* (Devil in the Desert, 1955). The film was set among a group of Bedouins and presented a story of a corrupt king and the attempts to revolt against him, which reflected a post-revolutionary outlook on the role of the last Egyptian king. *Devil* was later followed by *Wadda'tu hubbak* (Farewell My Love, 1957), *Inta habibi* (You Are My Love, 1957), and *Hubb li-l-abad* (Forever Yours, 1959), *Bayn idayk* (In Your Hands, 1960), *Rajul fi hayati* (Man in My Life, 1961), and *Nida' al-'ashiq* (A Lover's Call, 1961). Many of these melodramas and musicals were popular favorites among Egyptian and Arab movie audiences, and reflected Chahine's genuine love for popular American generic traditions. Chahine continued to play with and incorporate this love for American popular cinema into his films throughout his career including some of his most politically astute films of the 1980s, 1990s, and beyond. Some of Chahine's early popular melodramas and musicals of the 1950s certainly alluded to and occasionally criticized the gap between social strata in Egyptian pre-revolution society, or mocked the bourgeois lifestyle, or described the workers' environment in a more or less 'realistic' fashion.

The link between class and popular culture is similar to the one by which class interconnects with the concept of the nation. By the 1950s, Chahine's cinema advocated new approaches to popular culture through a renewed

Struggle in the Valley: Violence as upper class repression.

perspective on rural and working class issues. As early as his second film, *The Son of the Nile*, Chahine's work introduced elements of what would later grow into a celebrated feature of his cinema. The film presents the story of a young man from a peasant background who seeks change in his life and decides to leave his village and go to Cairo. The man succumbs to the temptations of the big city and becomes involved in illegal activities. He eventually finds his way back to his village and finally begins to appreciate the things he had earlier taken for granted. As simple as the film's plot line appears on the surface, it nevertheless foreshadows Chahine's interest in exploring the social fabric and the challenges facing the peasant class in rural Egypt, something that he would explore again in *Sira' fi-l-wadi* (Struggle in the Valley, 1951) and take into masterful height in *al-Ard* (The Land, 1968).

Struggle in the Valley was among Chahine's most successful films of the 1950s, and was among the earlier Egyptian films to unambiguously express an intellectual position favoring the peasants over the feudal lord. In some ways, the film represented rather a continuation of a much established trend or orientation in Egyptian cinema which showed empathy with the fate of marginalized social elements within Egyptian society. Among the important examples of such cinema include Kamal Selim's seminal work *al-'Azima* (The Will, 1939) and *al-Suq al-sawda'* (The Black Market, 1946), which have overtly favored workers and effendis over capitalists. Other examples include 'populist' themes in Youssef Wahbi productions of *Awlad al-fuqara'* (Children of the Poor, 1942) *Ibn al-haddad* (The Son of the Blacksmith, 1944), and *al-Avocato Madiha* (Master Madiha, 1950).

The story of Chahine's film involves the struggle between a young agricultural engineer and his peasant supporters and the feudal pasha who considers the young man's efforts to improve the peasants' cultivation methods as an affront to his control and a depletion of his resources and profit. Audiences conditioned to expect the conventional last-minute reprieve were shocked by Chahine's depiction of the execution of an innocent man. In *Sira' fi-l-mina* (Struggle on the Pier, 1956) Chahine explores the working conditions on the docks of the port of Alexandria through a story about a clash between a young worker and his boss. In turn, the celebrated *Bab al-Hadid* (Cairo Station, 1958) offers a critical look at the microcosm of the Cairo train station through its workers, street vendors, and a union organizer.

STRUGGLE IN THE VALLEY AND THE REVOLUTION IN RURAL EGYPT

A little less than two years after the 1952 Nasser revolution, and on the heels of major agricultural reforms that virtually dismantled the feudal control of Egyptian agricultural lands, Chahine released *Struggle in the Valley*. The film featured Faten Hamama, a well-known and respected actress who had worked with Chahine in his 1950 musical *Father Amin*, and introduced a young Omar Sharif in his first feature film role; many would later credit Chahine with launching the career of this young actor who would go on to become one of the few recognizable Arab actors in the west. The film received enthusiastic reviews and great box office success in Egypt and the Arab world, and gave Chahine his first taste of international recognition when it was nominated for the Grand Prize at the 1954 Cannes Film Festival.

The film offered an unprecedented and vivid portrayal of the exploitation of peasants under the old feudal pasha system. As such the film echoed an earlier commitment by the revolution to side with the Egyptian peasant class in their struggle against repression and exploitation by fewer than three hundred feudal landlords who owned virtually all Egypt's agricultural land. Before the revolution, the pasha class also shared control over other segments of the country's economy including the emerging industrial, trade, and finance sectors in the large urban centers of Cairo and Alexandria. This class also ensured its economic control through its close political collaboration with colonialist Britain, who at the time exercised near-total control over Egypt.[2]

In the film, Ahmad (played by Omar Sharif) returns home after graduating as an agricultural engineer, full of hopes and plans to increase the sugarcane output and bring prosperity to his village, which is located close to Luxor in the south of Egypt. The young engineer begins to experiment and utilize modern ways of plantation and eventually succeeds in offering a major sugar company a product that could compete with the one cultivated in the pasha's land. In coordination with his nephew Riyad, the pasha conspires to flood the village fields and spoil the crops of its peasants. Soon after the villagers recognize his hand in the flooding conspiracy, the pasha plots to kill the village's local leader and then frames Ahmad's father, who is consequently jailed, tried, convicted, and then hanged.

The second part of the film focuses on Ahmad's attempt to prove his father's innocence, and his flight from Salim, the victim's son, who wants to take revenge for his father's murder. As the pasha's daughter Amal (Faten Hamama), who is in love with Ahmad, tries to defend him against the accusations, she discovers the involvement of her father and her cousin. The film ends with a shooting in the Karnak ruins resulting in the tragic death of the father as he tries to defend his daughter against Riyad's wrath. The cousin is arrested by the police.

Struggle in the Valley captures several aspects of the harsh class differences in pre-revolutionary Egypt through a juxtaposition of the luxury setting of the pasha's palace with the starkly poor and basic homes of the village's peasant class. The film also presents a vivid depiction of the incongruous lifestyles of the two classes, particularly through rendering in detail the peasants' hard work compared to the managerial role of the feudal upper classes. In one shot that captures the essence of class difference, we watch Amal as she arrives from Cairo in a car driven by her cousin Riyad. The car dominates the foreground of the frame as it drives over the private asphalt road. In the background, the camera captures a group of peasants working the land. The deep focus shot and its composition visually summarize the nature of the relationship between the two classes and alludes to the power structure that dominated the agricultural system under Egyptian feudalism.

On another level, the film's plot, which concentrates on young Ahmad's struggle to implement new tools and methods to work the land, echoes yet another key post-revolution theme. Modernization, as we saw earlier, has been integral to forging progressive economic changes and social reform. The film engages the idea of modernization interactively with that of social agricultural reform and contemplates the need to overthrow the feudal landlord system. The fact that it is Ahmad, the young and educated engineer who comes from a peasant class background, who has the ideas for reforming the production system and introducing modern technology, complements the film's linkages between modernization and social change. Furthermore, given its setting within a historical period largely associated with British colonial military and political control, the film positions modernization and socioeconomic reform as part and parcel of the struggle for national independence and self-determination in Egypt—a linkage to which Chahine would later return in his 1969 film *The Land*.

An important feature of *Struggle in the Valley* was its originality in its depiction of Egyptian peasants. This fundamentally challenged traditional mainstream Egyptian cinema's disregard for the harsh realities of the peasant class's work and life. Chahine's choice of setting vibrantly exposed class differences in pre-revolutionary Egypt, but more importantly presented a dignified portrayal of the daily lives of peasants; their clothing, traditions, mannerisms, communal connections, and social fabric. In a memorable shot of a group of peasants walking away after they realize the devastation that befell their crops in the aftermath of the river flooding event, we see them stretched over the horizontal center of the frame as if walking in a strong chain-like march. The shot foreshadows the march that they will walk later during the funeral of the slain village leader. The deep sorrow and devastation of the peasants in both walks is matched only by their communal and class solidarity.

While the *mise en scène* of the film favors a detailed interior study of the villagers' homes, their mud walls and structure, their bamboo huts, their sleeping mattresses, and their food utensils, it is contrasted by elaborate long and

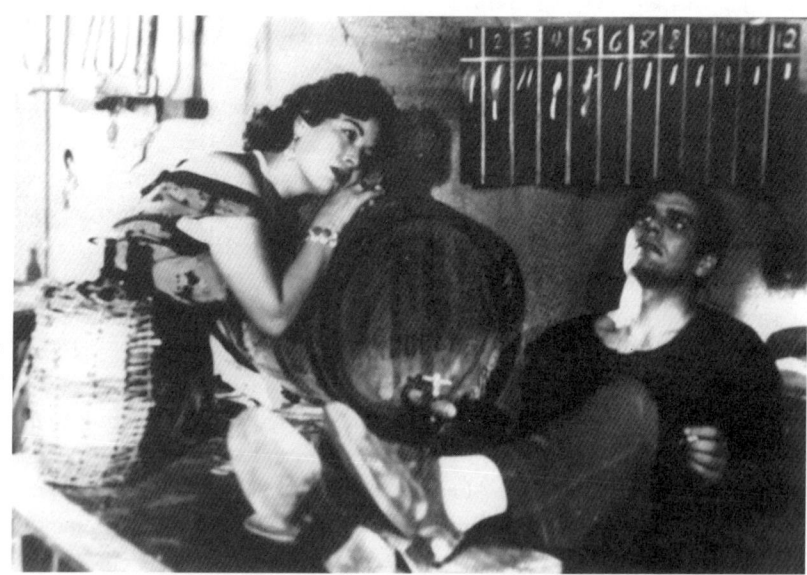

Struggle on the Pier: Social antagonisms in an urban environment.

22   Popular Cinema and Conceptualizing Class and Social Change

extreme long shots of the Egyptian countryside and of the peasants working the fields. As such the film paints a picture that establishes a dialectical connection between the communal and the private lives of the peasants. Chahine's stylistic approach here prefigures what will become integral to his later work. In the words of a prominent Arab film critic, the film "augured some elements in Chahine's style that would eventually become standard in most of his work: an unpredictable rhythm, a poetic engagement, and a detailed attention to composition which makes it fundamental to Chahine's storytelling."[3]

The film was very well received both on the critical and the box office levels. One critic points out that the film was a watershed in Egyptian cinema, in that less than a year after the revolution it was the first to explicitly condemn the feudal system. The reviewer reminds us that the film, though made in 1953, was only released in 1954, less than one year from the time when the pashas in Egypt were considered untouchables and near gods.[4] Another Egyptian critic, while acknowledging the film's melodramatic treatment of class conflict, recognized the contribution of *Struggle in the Valley* as the first Egyptian attempt to cinematically depict to a mass audience the complex dialectic of class based social differences. Ali Abu Shadi begins his article by asking, "irrespective of its power and resilience, can love bestow some level of reconciliation and harmony in a society where lives are so coerced by sharp class differences?" He summarizes the film's attempt to provide an answer:

> The simple answer based on the film's dramatic development is 'no'! Characters are clearly swimming against the tide in a certainty, which does not allow any intrusion into ingrained opposing traditions and values. The film's portrayal of the pasha's character affirms that his motivation inadvertently stems from his own class interests and not simply from bad intentions, whether these intentions were his or those of his nephew Riyad.... In fact the film remains today [1992] among a very few number of films that have dealt with the notion of conflict between feudalism and peasantry in a way that is both serious and humorous. As such, the film at the time took the right step in the right direction.[5]

But Abu Shadi goes on to critique the weak melodramatic ending and how it impacted on the rest of the film's complex depiction of class differences, and suggests that, in the end Chahine could not avoid "falling into the trap of classical happy endings as the pasha's daughter reunites with the farm supervisor's son." Furthermore, Abu Shadi continues, considering their diametrically opposed roots, Chahine did not offer "a realistic prefiguring of the kind of road that these two people would later follow."[6] Commenting on the film many decades later, Chahine himself acknowledged his conscious attempt to deal with the dismantling of the old feudal system as an issue he felt critical to post-revolutionary Egyptian society. But he also noted that his political approach toward the issue was fundamentally "spontaneous," and carried a largely naïve and "emotional condemnation of the tyrant and sympathy for the oppressed."[7]

There is no doubt that the film's melodramatic rendition of the love theme contributed to its success with mainstream Egyptian and Arab audiences at the time. Nevertheless, the film's ideological impact in Egypt of the early 1950s was considerable. With its sensitive depiction of Ahmad and his peasant family, and through its plot and stylistic construction that privileged the peasants' point of view, the film broke a major taboo as far as Egyptian popular culture was concerned. Representations of class as Other were unfamiliar in Egyptian cinema as a whole, let alone in its melodramas. And despite the satisfying resolution of the narrative's immediate crisis, the film's ending remains resolutely open. The textual affirmation of Ahmad's class pride is effectively countered by Amal's fate bereft of her father's palace—an allegorical suggestion of the impending separation between her and her class roots.

Today the film remains an enduring feature on Arab television stations, and its attraction for younger audiences does not appear to have faded. Many Egyptians and Arabs who watch *Struggle in the Valley* are surprised to learn it is part of Chahine's repertoire. Over the years, Chahine has garnered a reputation as a filmmaker whose films are hard to understand, and his films tend to resonate among wider audiences only years after their release. While this may be true in connection with many of his later films, *Struggle in the Valley* seems to have maintained and even transcended the popularity it enjoyed from the date of its release. To the extent that this film's resonance has been able to spill over various historical periods in contemporary Egyptian history, it denotes Chahine's cinematic capacity to converge the popular with the ideologically counter-hegemonic or subversive. This early success in depicting an empowering of Egypt's marginalized classes—and in spite of its prevailing melodramatic tone—eventually helped forge a new kind of Egyptian cinema: a popular cinema with an oppositional agenda (and I am referring here to the lasting resonance of the film's association with the marginalized, which transcends the Nasser government's encouragement of such social commentaries at the time). While Chahine would not consistently adhere to this blending of the popular with the ideologically subversive (at least not in this pure melodramatic model), this early contribution sanctioned new possibilities for early post-revolution Egyptian cinema: the prospect of producing oppositional meaning and calling attention to the power of popular culture.

THE REVOLUTION'S URBAN DIMENSION: *STRUGGLE ON THE PIER*

Struggle on the Pier represented an early attempt by Chahine to focus on the story of an urban working class character. Released three years after the unprecedented success of *Struggle in the Valley*'s exploration of the lives of Egyptian peasants under the feudal pasha rule, *Struggle on the Pier* depicted the problems facing workers and fishermen that pit them against big business operatives in the port city of Alexandria. As in *Struggle in the Valley*, Chahine cast Faten Hamama to play the love interest of Omar Sharif, by then a rising star in Egyptian cinema. The two actors would eventually marry.

The film came out on the heels of the release of a major American film with a comparable setting and storyline. In Elia Kazan's *On the Waterfront* (1954), Terry Malloy (Marlon Brando) is a working class dreamer who runs errands at the docks for a mafia-type boss named Johnny Friendly who controls the dockers' union. Malloy's rebellion against Friendly leads to a battle between the two, which occurs in juxtaposition to a love story between Friendly's sister and Malloy. In *Struggle on the Pier* the story is different, but strikes interesting similarities in the setting (the pier), the corrupt and violent boss, the love triangle as catalyst, and even in the blood connection between the corrupt

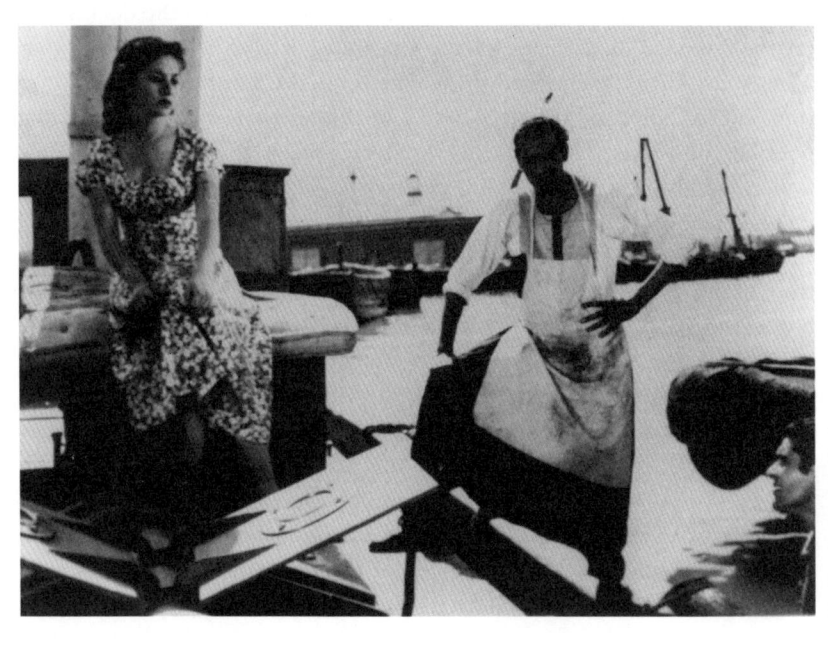

Struggle on the Pier: On location cinematography as political esthetic.

son and the protagonist's love interest. The story in Chahine's film pits Ragab (Omar Sharif), a destitute fisherman who returns home from travel, against Mamdouh (Ahmad Ramzi) the son of a wealthy Alexandrian shipping company boss. Both are in love with the same woman, Hamida (Faten Hamama) who also happens to be Ragab's cousin.[8] As Ragab's jealousy rages he discovers that Mamdouh is actually his brother.

The events of the film all occur in one day; beginning with Ragab's morning arrival in Alexandria and closing with his evening decision to leave the city. The story begins with a shot of a ship entering the Alexandria harbor carrying Ragab, a former fisherman now returning to settle and work in his hometown. Ragab is warmly welcomed back by a large party of friends and relatives. On greeting his mother Ragab asks about his cousin Hamida, to whom he has never expressed his secret love. We also learn that Hamida has never told Ragab of her love for him. Further, it is revealed that Ragab has been always aware of his image as a leader among workers in the harbor and that this was behind his hesitancy to express his love to Hamida.

As Ragab returns, problems erupt on the harbor. Izzat Effendi, the former manager of the company who is now in control of operations in the area, is intent on avenging his dismissal and the owner's decision to replace him with his son Mamdouh. Izzat plots to pit Ragab, with his influence among the workers, against Mamdouh who also happens to be in love with Hamida. Izzat Effendi also initiates plots to create divisions between the dock workers themselves. The dramatic events that follow lead to the revelation that Mamdouh's father, the owner of the company, is also in fact Ragab's father who had had a second marriage with a wealthy woman when he was still a poor harbor worker. The film ends with a reconciliation between Ragab, his father, and his brother Mamdouh, and with Ragab and Hamida acknowledging their love for each other.

An Alexandrian himself, Chahine paints a detailed and loving picture of the city and its people, particularly of those who make their living on the harbor and the sea. The film describes a place full of life, hopes, and struggles. It is also a place where large export and import operations make it a hub of social activities and conflicts. As such the vibrant waterfront setting itself becomes an intriguing motif that resurfaces several times in Chahine's films as an expression of his infatuation with locations that inspire ideas about travel, dreams, and possibilities. This passion would resurface in all his Alexandria trilogy films as well as in his 1970 film *al-Ikhtiyar* (The Choice). It will also recur in the context of another mode of travel in Chahine's depiction of Cairo's train station in *Cairo Station* (1958).

Struggle on the Pier's narrow one-day narrative offered an effective and original utilization of classical linear storytelling and editing techniques. Chahine used a similar approach in *Cairo Station,* and in his first film *Father Amin* (1950), where events begin early in the morning and end with the sunset break of the Ramadan fast. Some suggest that Chahine's early interest in the one-day plot structure stemmed from his theatrical training. Su'ad Shawqi cites an example from *Saladin* (1963) where Chahine uses theatrical techniques to distinguish between events taking place simultaneously in two locations. Instead of editing back and forth between the two events, Chahine manipulates lighting to switch between two separate spaces while maintaining the same frame.[9]

Effective use of time and space and attention to *mise en scène* details would come to be hallmarks of Chahine's cinematic storytelling. Here Chahine provides his audience with a glimpse of a space they had not seen on the big screen. As with *Struggle in the Valley* and *Son of the Nile* (1951)—in which he framed Egypt's peasant and rural landscapes and the position of the human element within it—*Struggle on the Pier* captures yet another facet of Egypt's marginalized social fabric. Offering an efficient and nuanced portrait of a moment in time and space, *Struggle on the Pier* examines the urban setting of the Alexandria waterfront. The film is built around extreme long shots of the sea, the harbor, the big ships and the small fishermen' boats juxtaposed against meticulously designed long and medium shots of the streets and living quarters of waterfront Alexandrians. Ragab's home is built of wood and stands in the water; its interior reverberating with an openness of space which forces fascination with its two-leveled boat design with the lower level largely under water. This visual representation of the relationship between people and their urban environment is utilized to illustrate the film's themes of social struggle and conflict. In one key scene, the workers of the harbor and their families chase Mamdouh, the spoiled son of the shipping company's owner. Mamdouh is framed in oblique shots, while the people chasing him are presented in horizontal and vertical shot lines, emphasizing the social and ethical contrast between the two.

By the mid-1950s Egyptian filmmaker Salah Abu Seif had established a reputation for his sensitive and vivid portrayals of working class Egyptians. His films *Forman Hasan* (1952), *Rayya and Skina* (1953), *The Monster* (1954), and later *The Tough* (1957) all reflected a new post-revolutionary interest in stories about urban working class Egyptians and their problems. Abu Seif's films also established him as Egypt's foremost social realist filmmaker, whose work would not only brilliantly depict details about impoverished urban Egypt, but also contemplate the dynamics of social and political exploitation and repression that affected the working class both before and after the revolution. Even before the revolution, despite attempts by the Farouk government to repress the production of such films, some filmmakers did succeed in venturing into this territory. These early attempts, however, did not come without a price. A prime example is Ahmad Kamel Mursi's *al-'Amil* (The Worker, 1942). Years later, Hussein Sidki, one of the film's actors, said "We were indeed interested and invigorated by problems in our society. The film described the hard work of labor and their efforts to survive despite hardships and low pay. The film was confiscated by the government after few screenings, but played a role in the consequent legislation of labor laws including those relating to the right to form unions."[10]

Chahine's *Struggle on the Pier*, therefore, was not unique in its setting nor in its subject matter. Furthermore, the film did not directly engage the issue of unionization and its impact on the lives of workers. While Ragab is subtly framed as a leading figure among his peers, the narrative does not in any way indicate an involvement in any labor organizing activities. On the contrary, the focus is on the personal dimension of his struggle, and mere sympathy is the motive behind the support of the other workers. In this regard, the film personalizes the labor–management relationship to the extent of reducing it to an issue of individual ethics where the boss's resolve or change of heart essentially determines the rectification of an unjust situation. In fact Chahine's first serious rendezvous with the issues associated with the organizing of labor would occur two years later.

In *Cairo Station*, Qinawi (played by Chahine), a physically challenged peddler who makes his living selling newspapers in the central Cairo train station, is obsessed by Hannouma, an attractive young woman who sells soft drinks from an ice-filled bucket. While she treats Qinawi in a sympathetic way and jokes around with him about a possible relationship, Hannouma is in love with Abu Sri, a strong and well-respected porter at the station who is struggling to unionize his fellow workers to combat their boss's exploitive and abusive treatment. Qinawi decides to murder Hannouma after seeing her having sex with Abu Sri, and the dark ending sees Qinawi being taken away to the mental hospital. The film blends a neorealist approach that centers its focus on marginalized members of society with elements of the horror/slasher generic traditions as well as incorporating moments of melodrama and comedy. As Ahmad Higazi suggests, Youssef Chahine's camera in *Cairo Station* was focused on a world that was long forgotten and ignored by Egyptian cinema, and offered a major contribution to the emergence of new cultural practice, which transcended Hollywood's generic limitations and succeeded in capturing authentic elements of national specificity.[11] The film represents another stage in the evolution of Chahine's interest in the socially aware themes featured in both *Struggle in the Valley* and *Struggle on the Pier*. On another level, though, *Cairo Station*'s travel motif alludes to the enduring human quest to negotiate ancient boundaries drawn by the dogmatic walls of class, ethnicity, and religious faith, and bolstered by the modern social and political Othering of the adversary. It is also in *Cairo Station* that we see Abu Sri (Farid Shawqi), a porter at the train station who is intent on organizing his fellow workers in a union to fight for better wages and welfare. Abu Sri's explicit dissertation on why he believed that the union should play a key part in galvanizing workers in the fight for a better life was a first in Egyptian cinema. Furthermore, the film does not idealize the character of Abu Sri; instead it questions whether his personal machismo is enough to help deal with complex issues such as workers' rights and the fight against exploitation. But most importantly the film does not simply occupy a neutral position vis-à-vis the fate of its characters. It is after all a film about people with lost rights who seek to create a structure to protect themselves from exploitation. It is also about people struggling to survive marginalization and to find a place for themselves in the world.

What is important to note, however, is that *Struggle on the Pier*—along with the films made around the same time by Salah Abu Seif—did indeed venture into uncharted territory as far as Egyptian cinema was concerned. Just as *Struggle in the Valley* did in its depiction of Egyptian peasantry, so did *Struggle on the Pier*'s portrayal of the lives of poor labor families in the port of Alexandria add a new dimension to what melodrama looked like in Egypt. In this regard, it is important to reiterate here that these films helped alter fixed notions about popular culture. The class-based stories in these films served to contest the homogenous and uniform representations of Egypt of earlier melodramas. The stories belie populist bourgeois conceptions of popular culture as embodied in a search for genuineness or a restoration of an ideal past. In this regard, these films created a central space for characters from the marginalized classes and segments of Egyptian society in one of the most popular forms of popular culture.

While Chahine's early cinema would only reflect a budding and mostly naive interest in issues of social justice, there were also important indications of a genuine desire to survey peasant and working class lives in Egypt. Thus, both *Struggle in the Valley* and *Struggle on the Pier* contributed to the emergence of a socially conscious Arab cinema. Even while incorporating the forms and conventions of popular cinema, Chahine offered images of the peasant and working classes—images that had been previously ignored, demonized, romanticized, or marginalized in Egyptian cinema. In the process, Chahine helped forge a new trend in Arab cinema, one which explored aspects of social experience that transcended Egyptian cinema's traditional focus on the lives of the middle and upper classes.

Popular audiences in Egypt were introduced to a new narrative; one which challenged their cinematic and ideological expectations. By simultaneously exploring traditional expressions of popular film culture, its social memory, and its power as an agent for social change, Chahine's cinema was making an early contribution to the development of a cinema that subverted populist and folkloric approaches to the popular.

As is the case in many other third world societies, in the Arab world discourse pertaining to national identity has been largely influenced by social, economic, and cultural factors that advocate modernization and progressive change. But while the bourgeoisie and the rising middle classes have been conceptualized as agents of modernization, popular classes have often been seen as complications to progress and change. In this regard, attracting peasants, workers, and other marginalized classes into the process of modernization has been considered crucial to—and even inevitable for—economic and social progress and the consolidation of the Arab national project. This was more explicitly pointed out by writers of al-Nahda period, when many wrote whole theses appealing to the 'common' (read 'lower') classes to change their traditional 'old fashioned' habits by way of embracing progress.[12]

On the other hand, folklore was selectively emphasized as integral to the new national identity because the tales were thought to embody a national heritage. Nevertheless, with the emergence of organized efforts toward Arab national unity, which began with the consolidation of power of new left–nationalist regimes, popular culture became integrated into the fabric of Arab national culture. Mainstream art discourse in the 1950s, for example, encouraged and even celebrated local song and dance traditions.[13] Furthermore, traditional and modern forms of cultural representation in the Arab world were encouraged to amalgamate and coexist. In this regard, the long and rich cultural history of the region offered an immense range of expressions and representations that reflected this encounter between precapitalist and capitalist forms of cultural exchange.

In addition, the Arab world has produced distinctive forms of popular culture that, while originating in the past, have been transformed by mechanical reproduction.[14] As such, the contrasting outlooks and dissimilar experiences of popular culture after the 1952 revolution were encouraged to merge into a new Arab national and cultural practice. In this context, the notion of popular culture in the Arab world at the time appeared to simultaneously serve to challenge homogeneous conceptualizations of Arab identity and to discard the position that situates popular culture in a search for authenticity or a return to original sources (such as in the case of seeking religious purity and tradition).

Many Arab intellectuals in the aftermath of the Nasser revolution, however, began to engage with the issue of popular culture as a critical and self-questioning process. Rather than endorsing popular traditions as normative practice, they sought to deconstruct and reconstruct their subversive power of these tradtions. In this regard, Egyptian novelists, playwrights, and poets such as Naguib Mahfouz, Abd al-Rahman al-Sharqawi, Yusuf al-Siba'i, Yusuf Idris, Lafred Farag, Lotfi al-Khouli, and Salah Jahin—all of whom became hallmarks of Egyptian cultural life during the Nasser period—explored the processes by which class-based ideologies regulate nationality and erase social conflict. Similarly, other intellectuals contributed to the reimaging of popular culture via the engagement of new approaches to social inequality and oppression. And Youssef Chahine and Salah Abu Seif would emerge in the 1950s as leading figures of a new stylistically and thematically conscious Egyptian and Arab tradition; one which would introduce the socially marginalized into the evolving hub of popular culture, the cinema.

Popular cinema as it was being refashioned by Chahine and others in the early 1950s certainly mirrored tensions between tradition and modernity. His popular melodramas of the decade not only refigured the subversive power of popular cinema, but also deconstructed the representations and discourses that have limited the self-representation of Egyptian and Arab peoples. In his early films, Chahine seemed to celebrate the mere capacity to point out the reality of class differences and class struggle. As such, his films evoked the social contradictions and possibilities of both the pre- and post-revolutionary periods. Thus, this chapter has shown that through his love for cinema—largely growing out of his genuine passion for classical popular Hollywood cinema—Chahine sought to create new spaces to challenge dominant narratives. Revolutionary events in Egypt in the early 1950s clearly opened the door for a new kind of political engagement by film and cultural intellectuals in the country. These events provided the base on which new generations of filmmakers working within the newly prosperous Egyptian film industry could build on the earlier successes of popular cinema. In this regard, the revolution's early emphasis on the social component of economic and political change in the country helped forge a new cultural discourse which began to impact on Egyptian and Arab popular cultures. Chahine's early cinematic undertakings embody the infant formations of this discourse.

3

POLITICAL INTERVENTION AND THE STRUGGLE FOR NATIONAL UNITY AND LIBERATION

The first serious Arab cinematic attempt to tackle the issue of anticolonial struggle came in 1958 by way of a film that told the story of a real-life Algerian resistance fighter who had been caught by the French army. *Jamila* (Jamila, the Algerian) became an instant hit in Egypt and across the Arab world and contributed to galvanizing wide solidarity with the Algerian resistance to French colonialism. The film exemplified the emergence of a new kind of Arab cinema, and in many ways it reflected issues that were raised by the new political establishment in Egypt. As such, *Jamila, the Algerian* complemented the emerging left–nationalist Nasser regime's policies in Egypt and in analogous rising governments in Syria, Iraq, and Yemen—all of which took power between the late 1950s and 1960s. Furthermore, the film informed and was informed by postcolonial popular discourse that was emerging across the Arab World in response to chronic underdevelopment, social and class exploitation, political repression, and colonial subjugation.

Jamila came on the heels of the Egyptian victory which saw the retreat of the trilateral forces of Britain, France, and Israel that had attacked Egypt in the aftermath of the Nasser government's decision to nationalize the Suez Canal in 1956. After a fierce resistance by the Egyptian army and popular resistance in several Egyptian cities around the Suez area, and after a strong pan-Arab and international solidarity campaign against the attack, an agreement was reached in the United Nations in which the British and French armies were asked to retreat from the areas they occupied during the attack. The Israeli forces that occupied the Sinai Peninsula withdrew to the prewar borders. The conclusion of the crisis affirmed Egypt's national control over a long-standing symbol of colonialism in the country. As a result the Egyptian victory heightened the popularity of Nasser and his status not only as a national Arab hero but also as an international anticolonial fighter. In this context, *Jamila* reflected the grass roots sentiments in the region and informed its preoccupation with issues of national liberation.

Algerian resistance against French colonialism was widely supported by the Nasser government and enjoyed popular support across the Arab world. Eventually, with the success of the Algerian resistance and the declaration of Algeria's independence in July 1962, a wave of pan-Arab sentiment was fueling Arab masses. The role that Nasser played gained momentum both inside and outside Egypt. In the same year *Jamila* was released, Egypt and Syria declared their merger in the United Arab Republic as a first step toward a pan-Arab state. The merger reflected strong grass roots support in Syria, and Nasser—by then a popular hero-figure throughout the Arab world—became the first president of the new republic. While the union only lasted until 1961, the sentiments it generated as the first contemporary attempt at forging a united Arab state left a long-lasting, though controversial, legacy regarding the Arab unification project. In 1963, Chahine's film *Saladin* addressed this critical moment in contemporary Arab history.

CHAHINE AS A BUDDING ACTIVIST FILMMAKER

If the revolution took ten years before it began to pay attention to cinema, Chahine himself took several years to fully absorb the political and social changes resulting from the revolution. Chahine himself regularly attested that his interest in politics in the early 1950s was largely naive and was reflected in a raw "rejection of the king and his entourage, and the values and practices of the bourgeois class."[1] This position stemmed mainly from his personal experience and a humanist impulse. As such, Chahine's early films did not indulge in critical observations of social contradictions as they affected political change on the national level. Nevertheless, Chahine did respond to the changes in Egyptian society as a result of the Nasser revolution and its socialist discourse, which was inspiring urban and rural populations in Egypt and around the Arab world.[2] By the late 1950s, however, Chahine's commitment to social and political change in Egypt and in the Arab world appeared clearer and more focused, and seemed to reshape his role as an activist. The popularity of the Nasser government was unprecedented in the Arab world, and the 1956 Suez War, the Algerian war of independence, and the struggle for Arab unity became hallmarks of Arab political discourse in 1950s and early 1960s. In this context, Chahine's increasing support for the left–nationalist government's policies should be understood as a response to its social reforms, which were positively affecting the lives of millions of peasant and working class Egyptians, and to its engagement with the grass roots anti-imperialist movement that was sweeping the entire Arab region. Therefore it was no coincidence that Chahine's most popular films of the post-revolution decade were also the most explicit and unswerving in their depictions of anticolonial resistance (*Jamila, the Algerian*), and Arab unity and the struggle for Palestine (*Saladin*). Walid Shmeit describes Chahine's political evolution during this period as a turning point in his long filmmaking career:

> This stage comprised new and more important films that uncovered Chahine's anxieties, his constant search for an identity, and the crystallization of his understanding of the role of cinema as an instrument of participation and guidance. This was reflected in his response to and assimilation of major events not least of which were the socialist decrees, the building of the High Dam, the struggle for Arab unity as upheld by the Nasser revolution, and solidarity with the Algerian revolution. More than anything else, what characterized this period was its integration of the notions of political commitment and the celebration of the role of the artist and his/her solidarity with anti-imperialist struggles and against foreign hegemony. For Chahine at this point, the issue was not simply about expressing indignation against the bourgeoisie and the upper classes, or a utopian or emotional empathy with the poor classes of peasants, workers, and the city's marginalized; Chahine's preoccupations had already developed, branched out, and were now reflected in his deep trepidatious reaction to what was galvanizing Egypt and the entire Arab world. The Algerian revolution was a central chapter in the Arab struggle against imperialist hegemony, and Saladin's confrontation with the Crusaders represented a prime historical lesson on the possibility of achieving Arab unity and the ability to confront external challenges. This is exactly what Chahine wanted to say in Jamila, the Algerian (1958), and Saladin (1963).[3]

During this period Chahine developed his mastery of large-scale cinematic productions; working with large numbers of actors and personnel and using technologically sophisticated equipment—often in regions without the

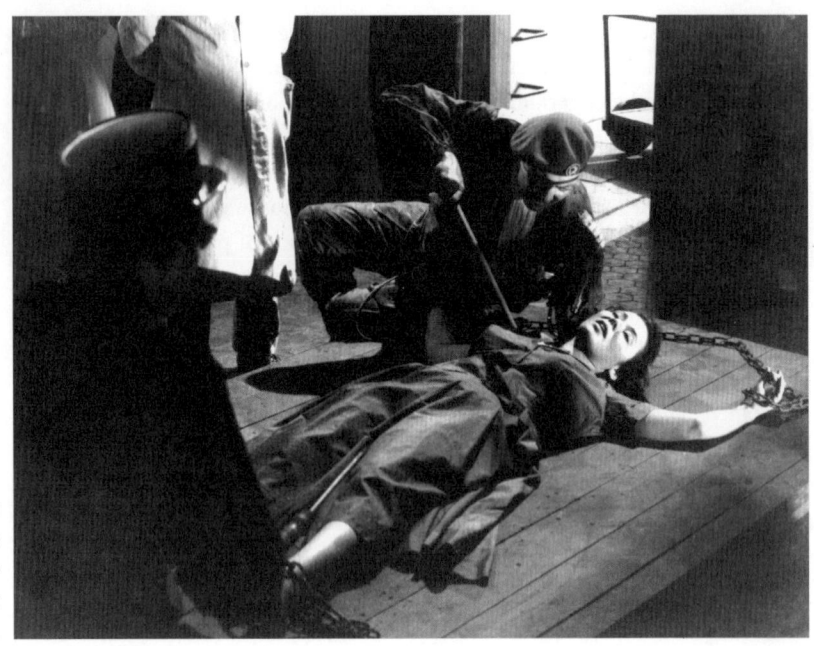

Jamila: Chahine as an expressionist filmmaker.

most elemental amenities of progress, like electricity—he sought to reconcile inconsistent development with the resourcefulness of social traditions.

Substantial government support of Chahine's filmmaking apprenticeship on projects such as *Jamila* and *Saladin* was reflected in his growing comfort level in taking on different kinds of film ventures. In *Saladin*, for example, large-scale production techniques and modern technology, along with his cinematic artistry and maturing editing techniques allowed Chahine to produce an impressive epic film with only a small fraction of the budget and resources of a comparable Hollywood production. In this context, Chahine was effectively cultivating indigenous third worldist methodologies to overcome the limiting effects of underdevelopment.

On another level, this period also signaled the beginning of what would become a major component of Chahine's film career: participation in international film festivals. The escalation of his involvement in such events played an important role in shaping the thematic, stylistic, and institutional aspects of Chahine's filmmaking interests, even while enhancing his international status. *The Son of the Nile* first introduced Chahine's oeuvre to film critics at the 1951 Cannes Film Festival, who characterized it as an important "attempt to move Egyptian cinema from the realm of the song and dance melodrama."[4] In the 1950s Chahine was second only to Salah Abu Seif in attracting international attention, but, according to one contemporary film critic, Chahine's ubiquitous festival presence soon led to his becoming known as the "festivals' director."[5]

In the Alexandria trilogy Chahine refers to his preoccupation with international recognition. In a 1959 interview after the successful screening of *Jamila* at the Moscow International Film Festival, Chahine reflected on the importance of being acclaimed in international film circles:

> I'm not defending Arab cinema if I say that it is working in the worst and poorest conditions . . . the fact is that making a good film is virtually a miracle under such conditions. If better conditions were to materialize to support this cinema over the next five years, I guarantee you that we can become serious competitors and contenders for first prizes in all international festivals.[6]

Irrespective of his motivations, Chahine would eventually capitalize on his international reputation in an effective manner, garnering technical and financial support for the production of most of his later films, particularly those produced after the end of the Nasser period. This reputation would also provide a convenient shield against implicit and explicit local attempts to censure his films at various periods of his career.

JAMILA, THE ALGERIAN

Two years after the Suez War of 1956, and four years after the beginning of the Algerian war of independence, Chahine began to make his first explicitly political film. *Jamila, the Algerian* was the fact-based story of a woman who casts off her complacency and joins the Algerian National Liberation Front (FLN) in its fight for Algeria's independence. Jamila Bouhired is eventually caught by Bigeard, a French officer who heads operations against the FLN network. She is tortured but refuses to talk. When French and worldwide public opinion awakens, the French lawyer Vergès comes to her defense in what degenerates into a show trial. From today's perspective, some contextual clarifications are important to untangle the composite relationship between the film and its history.

French colonialism in Algeria began in 1830, and by the early twentieth century was accompanied by a campaign to transform the entire country into a French territory on all levels of culture, law, and language. The French occupation of Algeria ended in July 1962 following a bloody struggle that some estimate cost almost one million Algerian lives. The rebellion against French occupation began in 1920 and developed into a full-scale war of independence by the end of the Second World War. Many Algerians supported France, but in the end France launched a fierce battle to suppress any hopes for independence. Jamila was among hundreds of thousands of Algerians who supported the FLN. Algerian grass roots support for the group expanded and independence became an Arab and international rallying cry for anticolonial solidarity.

The Egyptian government played a major part in supporting the FLN politically, financially, and militarily. Among the writers who contributed to the film's script was Egyptian novelist Naguib Mahfouz, whose social realist work at the time complemented the Nasser revolution's emphasis on social justice and national liberation. As one of the leading fighters in the Algerian war of resistance, Jamila's name became a household word in the Arab world.

Ibrahim Fawal describes the atmosphere within which Chahine made his filmic account of the legendary Algerian hero:

> Voice of the Arabs [an Egyptian radio station with a large Arab following at the time], broadcast the triumphs and defeats in every battle and skirmish. It turned Jamila's heroism into the stuff of legends. A simple young girl who had been tortured at the hands of the colonialists, Jamila transcended her oppressors and wrenched the hearts of an entire nation. She became the Arabs' Joan of Arc.[7]

Magda, a popular actress in 1950s and 1960s Egyptian cinema, campaigned to produce the film and play the leading role. During the preparation of the film, the emphasis was clearly on Magda, rather than Chahine, who was not yet as well-known among the Egyptian and Arab public. But while the contemporary press gave more attention to the producer/actor, a few articles reflected on Chahine's state of mind as he embarked on the project. In one interview the filmmaker stresses how political enthusiasm was the main reason behind his interest in the film:

> [D]espite many technical problems and lack of professionalism that were hindering the progress of the work, I remained confident that I would be able to achieve the goal of making a film which does not simply idealize the story and the struggle of Jamila, but rather utilizes it to alert audiences to the difficult and on-going struggle of the Algerians and of all Arabs against colonialism.[8]

With its ripped-from-the-headlines anticolonial tale, *Jamila* became an instant hit on Arab screens. The film was screened around the world, including,

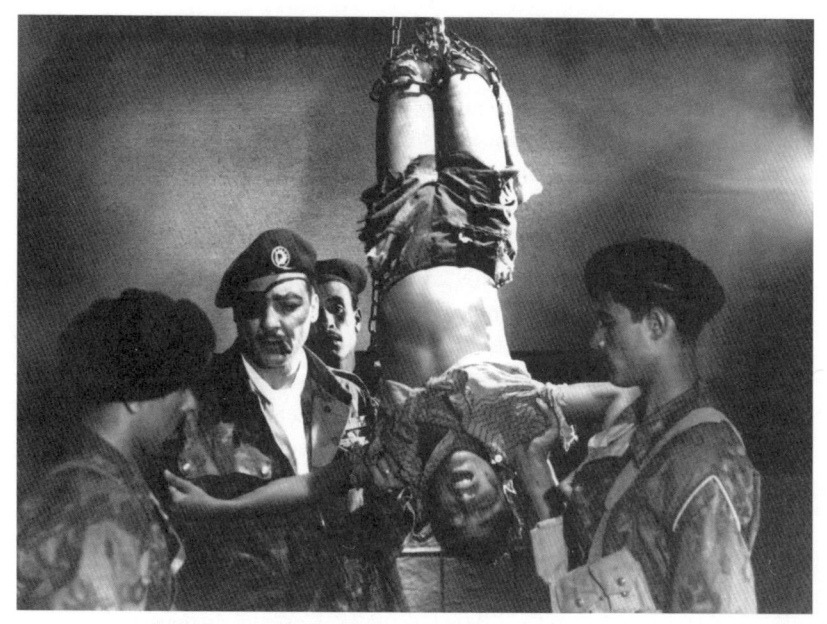

Jamila: Torture as colonial terror.

most notably, Czechoslovakia, Hungary, Germany, Pakistan, Afghanistan, India, and China—where people had never before seen an Egyptian or Arab film.[9] In the Soviet Union the film "drew attention and praise at the 1959 Moscow International Film Festival and won the Festival's top award."[10]

The film begins with an early Second World War sequence in which France was still promising independence and freedom to Algerians—as soon as the war ended. The sequence offers a collage of documentary shots of events punctuated by a voice-over by Egyptian radio announcer Ahmad Said: a well-known figure in the Arab world, particularly for his fiery commentaries during the 1956 Suez Canal War. The footage juxtaposes images from the Second World War with a background commentary relating the Algerian sacrifices suffered in support of France's fight against the Nazis in exchange for their promised independence after the war. Said's voice laments France's deception: "The pledge was a sham and France duped us." As a result, Said continues, Algerians paid the price for France's victory, "and they lost 45,000 people." The sequence ends with reconstructed images of a young Jamila and her uncle as he comes to take her to live with him in his village. The film then depicts her school days and her later discovery that the village had been infiltrated by French soldiers who imposed a reign of terror on its inhabitants in the aftermath of the war.

From the outset, the film focuses on how its protagonist always felt that her country's resources never truly belonged to its people. The film's introductory

Jamila, the Algerian 39

commentary, now including reconstructed shots of Jamila, describes how she used to ask her uncle about "who owns the beautiful villas and palaces that surround the village, and how she was told that they belonged to the French." Jamila, the commentary continues, always hoped that one day these places, as well as other Algerian *khayrat* (blessed resources), would someday belong to the Algerians instead of the colonialists. After this semidocumentary segment, the film goes on to relate the story of her evolution as an independence fighter.

Jamila joins university to study law, only to recognize that she is studying the Napoleonic legal system, most of which has nothing to do with Algerian culture or concerns. On her way to school one day a bomb is detonated near a French police station, and Jamila realizes her best friend Amina might have been behind the attack. French police come to school to arrest Amina, but before they can she commits suicide by swallowing poison. Jamila returns home thinking about the incident and questions her uncle about the situation with France and the burgeoning resistance against its occupation of Algeria. As he urges her to concentrate on her studies, her questions become more pointed. After Yusuf, a famous leader of the rebellion, takes refuge in her uncle's house, she realizes that her uncle is part of the anticolonial network. After that Jamila insists on being allowed to join the rebel army. After a series of events illustrating Jamila's participation in operations against the French, her uncle is killed in a massacre in the al-Kasbah district by French soldiers. Later, after being wounded in a botched maneuver, Jamila is captured and taken prisoner.

Much of the remainder of the film concentrates on the physical and psychological torture and abuse she endures during her interrogation, which culminates in her presentation before the tribunal that eventually sentences her to death despite the passionate pleas by her French lawyer. *Jamila* makes a point of emphasizing the role of women in the Algerian revolution; featuring the depiction of several female resistance fighters including Bou-Azza, Simonne, and Hasiba—all of whom we see coordinating military operations against the French with Jamila. The film, however, does not depict the aftermath of the trial nor Jamila's eventual release after a worldwide campaign supporting her and the Algerian struggle for independence.

Chahine's largely formalist *mise en scène* effectively conveys both the tense and charged atmosphere of the times. The shots of the trial, for example, are particularly stylized to emphasize Jamila's moral superiority over her accusers. The film's minimalist courtroom setting focuses attention on the differences between what Jamila and her accusers represent. In one shot Jamila is placed in the foreground at the center of the frame, while her lawyer and the prosecutor are placed in the background to the right and left of the screen, respectively. Here, the lighting enhances Jamila's heroic status by haloing her head angelically with an overhead key while the bodies and faces of the two men are marked by dark shadowy streaks. Similarly, the torture scenes are shot with an eye to the symbolic rather than mere gore and blood. As Mohammad Khan suggests, the "long torture sequences were not merely sadistic but reflected the whole Algerian struggle for freedom."[11] Chahine also substitutes decorated interior sets for most of his exterior shots, particularly those depicting Jamila's urban neighborhood. The highly stylized set highlights the connections and links that unite Algerians and allow them to lend support to each other in their resistance efforts. In particular, the interconnected Kasbah rooftop and balconies initially used by Jamila and her friends to visit each other, eventually become the venues and routes through which resistance fighters emerge as integral elements to the cultural, political, and locational foundation of their society.

The film was enthusiastically received across the Arab world and internationally. In a very short time, *Jamila* created a new paradigm for Egyptian and Arab filmmaking; it was clearly bound to processes that extended across a variety of registers, and as such its political agenda was affected by historical factors, which in turn informed its reception and circulation. The film operated within the ideological premises of a left–nationalist Arab national liberation perspective and complemented the views of the anticolonialist movements of the 1950s; it also derived power from the rising interest in engaging a renewed sense of Arab national identity. Contemporary critic Anwar Abd al-Malik describes how he was initially hesitant to see the film because he was apprehensive about watching "yet another propagandistic flick."[12] "What I, along with a big group of foreign correspondents saw," he continues, "was a powerfully charged, politically effective, and artistically serious and solid piece of work.... Indeed it was a respectable contribution to the struggle for liberation and humanism which Algeria and its revolution symbolized during this time."[13] Another critic, Saad Nadim, thought that the film was a victory for a new kind of Arab cinema. He compares the massive effect of the film with that of Mehboob Khan's 1957 film *Our Mother India*:

> In less than a week, Cairo saw two major films, Our Mother India and Jamila, the Algerian. If anyone has doubts about the need for solidarity between the peoples of Asia and Africa, seeing these two films assures us of the unity of our struggle in the face of colonialism, that is irrespective of its form and methods. If India has chosen the weapon of passive resistance at a specific

stage in its struggle against British colonialism, the increased viciousness and aggressiveness of French colonialism today has reached the extent that only armed resistance can rise to the challenge.[14]

The success of the film pointed out how popular cinema can function as a tool for furthering the cause of national liberation in the Arab world. As such, *Jamila* offered a blueprint for a critique of colonial and neocolonial policies in the Arab region; it represented an intervention in favor of a more socially and politically engaged cinematic practice, and in this regard hinted at the role of the organic intellectual in national politics.

Given that the film was closely tied to the ongoing manifestations of the anticolonial struggle in the Arab world and to a new approach to popular filmmaking, its position within Egyptian and Arab cinemas was certainly groundbreaking. While its political agenda mainly relied on the linear paradigms associated with classical Hollywood and mainstream Egyptian film practices (in turn traditionally linked with manifestations of hegemonic ideological cultural practices), *Jamila* functioned within parameters that were new to Arab cinema. The film operated transversely across the artificial boundaries, which tend to distinguish between popular film and the interventionist approaches of socially and politically committed cinema, and as such successfully challenged the illusion of incongruity and put it to the test.

THE IMAGE OF NASSER IN ARAB CINEMA, THE STRUGGLE FOR NATIONAL UNITY AND CHAHINE'S *SALADIN*

When Chahine embarked on the making of *Saladin* (1963), the atmosphere in Egypt and the Arab world was still experienced the negative effects of the failure of the attempt to create a United Arab Republic (UAR). The disbanding of the union in the aftermath of a secessionist military coup d'état in Syria in 1961 was a major blow to the Nasser revolution and its pan-Arab project. While the move in Damascus exposed frustrations with repressive Egyptian administrative and political practices in Syria within the military and economic elite, the secession, nevertheless, did not reflect the deep-rooted pro-Arab unity sentiments in Syria. Just two years later a counter coup took place in Damascus, restoring pro-union supporters to power. The United Arab Republic, however, did not re-emerge after the change of leadership in Damascus, and Egypt alone remained in the union until its name was changed in 1971 after the death of Nasser.

These political changes, however, did not diminish the pro-unity sentiment in the Arab world, neither did it substantially change the level of support that Nasser's own Arab unity project enjoyed among Arab masses. Chahine elaborates on how he saw Arab unity, Nasser's role in it, and how changes after his death affected the Arab national project and its unity aspirations:

> We need to be cognizant of our Arab national identity. Nasser realized that, and reminded us that being Arab is what unites us.... Single Arab states will always face major problems, but a united Arab nation represents a major power. The west continues to ferment divisions among us by exerting more control. Unfortunately, we as Arabs continue to fall into the trap of narrow single state chauvinism. Sadat tried to drum up Egyptian chauvinism.... I never felt as humiliated as much as I did under the Sadat regime. Nasser used to say to us, "Lift up your head, my brother." This is why I consider myself to be an Egyptian, an Arabist, and a humanist all at once.[15]

Nearly three decades after his death, and thirty-six years after *Saladin*, filmic depictions of Nasser continue to attract audiences and engage Arab political discourse.[16] Nasser-related motifs and nationalist anticolonial songs from the 1950s and 1960s are often featured in new Arab films. While some of these cinematic references indulge in a nostalgic view of Nasser and his role during a critical period in Arab history, one cannot underestimate the anticolonial and pro-modernization resonance such references hold for Arab

Saladin: An early commentary on the manipulation of religion (photo: Fawzi Atallah).

The Image of Nasser in Arab Cinema 43

audiences even today. A key example of how Nasser-related themes reflect the Arab impetus to modernization and national self-determination is found in Mohamed Fadel's 1996 film, *Nasser 56*. The film became one of the most successful box office hits of the 1990s in the Arab world.

Nasser 56 tackles the dispositions of economic and social change in the context of internal and external politics. By focusing on Nasser's nationalization of the Suez Canal in 1956 and the reaction by western colonial powers—aided by Israel—the film offers a polemic against the contemporary anti-western rhetoric from religious fundamentalists. In contrast to such rhetoric, the film presents an image of a leader who offered concrete steps toward national self-determination during the Suez crisis. In this regard *Nasser 56* linked the struggle for economic and social development as embodied in the nationalization of the Suez Canal and the building of the Aswan Dam with the anticolonial struggle.

Mounir Radi's film, *Ziyarat al-sayyid al-ra'is* (The Visit of Mr. President, 2002) even more explicitly laments the passing of the Nasser era by contrasting it with the era that followed. Radi draws unequivocal links between Sadat's attempt to Americanize Egypt and the rise of religious sectarianism, and their negative effects on Arab national identity. More recently, in Sharif Arafa's *Halim* (2006), a film about Abd al-Halim Hafiz, one of Egypt's most beloved modern-day singers, the Nasser shadow forms the backdrop to a period of missed opportunities in Arab history. A contemporary of Nasser who died only a few years after him, Hafiz is presented as an ally of Nasser who contributed to the rejuvenation of a proud sense of national identity and empowerment.

The creation of the United Arab Republic itself was informed by a political moment in which the notion of unity itself was high on the agenda of political discourse; the eventual failure of that union exacerbated internal tensions—even among those who agreed on the general parameters of the pan-Arab project. Thus Chahine's film on the twelfth-century Muslim leader Saladin clearly informed and was informed by this critical moment in contemporary Arab history, with all its preoccupations, hopes, and anxieties over the prospect of national unity.

This "most pivotal film of the 1960,"[17] in respect of its depiction of the relationship between Christians and Muslims, presented a fictional account of a battle that pit Saladin, ruler of the areas surrounding the Latin kingdom of Jerusalem, against the Faranga[18] who controlled the city. The film first depicts the Faranga's attack on a convoy of Muslim pilgrims on their way to Mecca—a group that includes Saladin's sister. Despite many logistical obstacles, Saladin launches a campaign in which he retakes Jerusalem and the surrounding areas that had been controlled by the Crusaders.

In response, the French, Germans, and English joined forces to launch the Third Crusade, led by Richard the Lionheart of England. While the city of Acre is retaken by the Crusaders, Saladin succeeds in thwarting the recapture of Jerusalem. In the end negotiations between Saladin and Richard (admired by Saladin as the only honorable infidel leader) result in the return of the city to Arab rule.

The film does not depict the conflict as one motivated by religious ideals, but rather as one precipitated by the European attempt to control Muslim and Arab lands. In this regard the film offered an unequivocal perspective which placed "Arab identity above religious affiliation or, to be more precise, it reassert[ed] the conviction that 'religion is for God and the homeland is for all.'"[19] Chahine's Saladin does not fight the crusaders because they are Christians, but because they are invaders.

> In Saladin, I was not hesitant in telling Christians that they were wrong in coming over to occupy our land. I, myself a Christian, have lived in the heart of Muslim culture where 90 percent of the people whom I loved were Muslims.... From the times of Andalusia to [today's] Alexandria, the idea of diversity within a predominantly Muslim culture has been much more integrated than it has ever been within mostly Christian societies. These are not just words.... This is how I exactly feel.[20]

The film emphasizes the fact that Arab Christians suffered from the Crusades as much as the Muslims, and that many of them even fought side-by-side with the Muslims to defeat the Faranga. In the film, one of Saladin's closest advisors and military lieutenants is 'Isa al-'Awam, an Arab Christian who fights the Crusaders because he believes that "religion is for God and homeland is for all." Al-'Awam makes a significant contribution to Saladin's campaign that ultimately results in King Richard's defeat. On another level, Chahine stresses Saladin's compassion, which in the end enables him to achieve a two-fold victory, one through battle and the second through his benevolence. The film positions Saladin as a man of moral integrity, in radical contrast to the way he has traditionally been imagined in western cinema. Chahine's Saladin is a symbol of fairness and chivalry; he loves sciences, promotes tolerance, and abhors war—fighting only to defend his people, their land, and their values.

Chahine envisaged Saladin's victory as one instructive to modern Arabs, illustrating the need to confront one's own dilemmas with dignity and determination:

Saladin: Visual proficiency to create an epic of Hollywood proportion (photo: Fawzi Atallah).

Before achieving victory against others one needs to first conquer one's own demons, prepare the adequate power to confront the invader or those who are planning to oppress him.... You need to provide the means for the success of such confrontation, and this is why the film emphasizes issues such as education, organization and unifying resources. Saladin was able to defeat the Crusaders because he succeeded in uniting people and adequately prepared for his battles.[21]

For Chahine, national unity is integral to Arab efforts to rid themselves of colonial domination, but a determined and well-organized effort to modernize their social, economic, and political structures is equally important. Only through unity and modernization can Arabs muster a well-defined and coordinated struggle for liberation from colonial hegemony.

Chahine's masterful visual and technical cinematic abilities are manifested in his dazzling use of color, which assumes a story-telling significance in *Saladin*. In one incident, instead of showing the actual killing of Muslim pilgrims during an attack by the Faranga, Chahine depicts the horrific episode through a montage of close-ups of the victims' white robes—the religious dress of Muslim pilgrims—as they are splattered by red blood. The frame is then punctuated with disorienting rotating shots of a sword on a white background; the camera movement first obscures, then reveals a white robe as it gradually turns red. These images are juxtaposed with rapidly cut long shots of the actual attack as it took place in the desert. The focus is clearly on the symbolic rather than on literal interpretation and presentation.

Recognizing that his audience would include both Muslim and Christian Arabs, Chahine sought to underplay Christian–Muslim enmity, admitting that the chaotic fragmentation of the images of the charging Faranga was used to "create the impression of violence without showing actual violence."[22] Freeze-frames are also utilized to this effect, as in the battle scene when the Arab and Faranga armies approach each other. Just before the two armies actually collide, a shot of each is frozen in time allowing the audience to better discern the visual details of the moment and to contemplate its ferociousness.

Chahine also utilizes his theatrical background and training to cinematically highlight the clash between Saladin's moral perspective and that of the Crusaders. In a spectacular scene that contrasts Louisa's trial with that of Acre's governor, Chahine uses an original technique to allude to the similarities between Saladin and King Richard as two honorable men caught in a moment bigger than themselves. Rather than cutting between the two or using a split-screen technique, Chahine effectively utilized the wide-screen Cinemascope image by building the courtroom sets side-by-side to exhibit each simultaneously on opposite sides of the frame. The alternating application of lighting alone indicates which set and scene should command our attention.

Chahine's sentiments on the issue of Arab unity were clear from the beginning, and in a later interview about *Saladin* he reiterated his on-going commitment to the pan-Arab project.[23] But considering his experience with *Jamila* and other socially conscious films of the mid-1950s, Chahine was quick to argue that he was not merely making pro-Nasser propaganda, noting that his main motivation was to create an epic film countering the Hollywood tradition:

> Let me be clear: perhaps the government back then, among other things, did have this goal in mind [showing support for Nasser's effort to unite the Arab world]. Of course, my feelings about the issue of Arab unity back then were very strong . . . and today they have become even stronger, albeit more studious and substantive. But when I made the film I was simply trying to prove that I could make historical epics and battle scenes without even needing the huge budgets that Hollywood uses for the production of such films.[24]

Chahine reiterated his desire to make an historical epic in a more recent interview, in which he emphasized that making a Hollywood-esque historical epic with only 120,000 Egyptian pounds—a small fraction of a Hollywood budget—represented an important challenge both personally and politically:

> The challenge was to do it smart, and the idea that you were braving yourself to do what the Americans at the time were expertly doing was the most intriguing part of the project. We were given all kinds of resources: horses, costumes and everything! The script, on the other hand, also specified eight battle sequences and at the time I thought it would be a miracle if I was able to do even half a battle. But then I told myself I was going to do the eight battles . . . just to show the Americans that we could do it![25]

Even considering Egypt's modest financial and technical resources, Chahine managed to successfully create a spectacular historical epic in the Hollywood tradition; indeed "his visual competence made miracles with the battle scenes and added depth to others."[26]

Originally, the film was supposed to be directed by Ezzaddine Dhulfuqar, a well-respected Egyptian filmmaker. Dhulfuqar, however, had problems with the producer, who later offered the project to an enthusiastic Chahine. The film script was based on ideas originally developed by leading Egyptian female film producer Asia Dagher, along with two major Egyptian novelists of the time, Yusuf al-Siba'i and Abd al-Rahman al-Sharqawi. While there had been many Egyptian pre- and post-revolution attempts to produce historically inspired films, *Saladin* was the first to consciously draw attention to its modes of production as compared to those of western studios. Theatrical and print advertisements touted its Cinemascope technology (a first in Arab cinema), its star power (an ensemble featuring many popular Egyptian actors), and its massive number of extras.

The context within which the film was produced and released enhanced its fashioning as an unabashedly political film; enthusiastic Arab audiences would loudly chant "Nasser!", acknowledging the correlation between the twelfth-century battles and Nasser's fight to unite Arab people and liberate Palestine. Indeed, it was nearly impossible for a 1963 audience to *not* see the link between the film's story and the Arab–Israeli conflict.

Ibrahim Fawal describes how the film constructed a connection between the Crusader's occupation of Jerusalem and the Palestinian exile, and how the issue of Arab unity directly impacted the film's appropriation of the struggle for Palestine. He also alludes to how the title's implicit Nasser reference (the Arabic name of the film, *al-Nasir Salah al-Din*—"the victorious Saladin"— binds a two-pronged reference to the two men and their victories) was meant to send a message of hope to Palestinians and other Arabs:

> In both cases, the perception was that under the guise of religion, a sacred Arab city was descended upon by waves of outsiders who, unprovoked,

proceeded to dispossess the rightful owners and inhabitants and to wreck havoc in their life. The fragmentation of the Arabs in their city-states during the time of the Crusades, however, was far worse than the fragmentation of the Arabs in modern times. At that time there were dozens of Arab city-states, each ruled by an independent and often paranoid prince or a sultan, always envious or fearful of the others. Thus it was easy for the Crusaders to decimate most of them and to establish a foothold, some of which lasted nearly two hundred years. It took a brave and wise Saladin to unite the Arab and liberate Jerusalem. This is how the Arabs in the 1960s saw Nasser—in reality or in hope. To listen to some of the dialogue from the film itself is to imagine how it must have replayed itself between Arabs and Israelis. Saladin's message of strength in unity, tolerance, and the necessity of defending one's country interacts with Chahine's political philosophy.[27]

While Chahine's *Saladin* project was borne of his drive to produce a Hollywood-like historical epic, the key significance of the film remains entrenched in the way it engaged the political discourse of the day, and how it refashioned the ideological and political use of a popular Hollywood genre as a new kind of Egyptian and Arab film. The film's resonance across the Arab world and its continued audience appeal today, as evidenced by its repeated television screenings, indicate its lingering political relevance. Over twenty-six years after the film was released, one local critic wrote, "I asked a friend of mine, a woodworker, did you see the film *Saladin* last night and he said, If this film was shown a hundred times in a hundred days I would still sit and watch it."[28]

The popularity of the film today denotes an enduring nostalgia for Nasser's leadership and a longing for strong, unswerving guidance in the struggle for Arab economic and political independence. It also indicates a renewed sense of national identity, and a continued grass-roots preoccupation with the fate of the Palestinians and their struggle for self-determination. In a contemporary assessment of the overwhelming popular success of the film, a local newspaper described how *Saladin* played to full houses in almost every large theater in Cairo and Alexandria for weeks in order to allow people to watch it along with their entire families:

> This is a film which makes us all feel proud . . . and it is a miracle indeed that it was made in the first place! What is also significant is the film's avoidance of using an an overbearing propagandistic approach to glorify its Arab characters, and its dodging of any sloganeering on how ideal Arab history and traditions were before. The film also rejects any sectarian

or chauvinistic characterizations of Islam; more interestingly, the film effectively focuses on the unity between Arab Muslims and Christians within the Saladin army, and their unity in the defense of Arab lands against invading European troops. On another level, the love story that develops between an Arab and a Faranga woman assumes its own significance: after all, Arab struggle has never been about hating foreigners, but rather about defending our lands and our freedom.[29]

For Arab cinema, the film was by all accounts a first: its production illustrating what the cinema of a poor third world country can achieve when supported by political and professional will.

As such, the film represented a strong and optimistic beginning for the technical and artistic development of a new Arab film project. It also represented "a first attempt to counter colonial stereotypical representation of Arabs, their history and culture as backward and evil."[30] More specifically, the film demonstrated how a successful and popular Hollywood genre could be refashioned to tell a historical story from the perspective of a newly de-colonized country. This was a major statement for Egyptian and Arab cinema at a time when the discourse on national liberation was as much about self-determination as it was about empowering de-colonized nations to re-envision themselves and re-read their history without the filters imposed by the colonizers.

While the film presents a broadly authentic overview of the historical events associated with the twelfth-century conflict, it certainly takes liberties in its interpretation and depiction of specifics. Some contemporary reviewers of the film pointedly criticized Chahine's loose historical interpretation as one employed at the expense of emphasizing the dialectical depth of historical discourse. An Egyptian critic pointed out that while it effectively used Eisenstein's dialectically punctuated cinematic storytelling montage technique it still tended to manipulate historical events and history. As a result, the film failed in articulating events within their historical dialectic and in turn failed to point out the dynamics of social and political conflict.[31] Conversely, another critic sees a more important significance to the film's play with history by way of projecting a message about present-day politics. Describing the political resonance within which the public interpreted the film Rushdi Saleh, writes that,

> within total collapse and destruction, fear and defeat, the real Saladin emerged and looked at history, and found that there was no hope for him except through uniting Arab mini-states under one banner to confront their

enemies and to liberate Jerusalem and recover their stolen land . . . this is a historical moment that we need to once again look at and absorb. Saladin did an excellent job of reminding us of that moment!"[32]

Clearly, the interpretive and thematic cinematic punch takes precedence over the film's authentic historical references. The film freely redraws and refashions its citations even regarding commonly known religious practices. In one memorable scene, we hear in the background the hymns of Christmas as we gaze at a snowy celebration of the midnight mass. In the background we hear the muezzin's call to prayer. Of course the muezzin does not call for prayer at midnight, but Chahine uses the familiarity with the two religious references to reiterate a powerful message that rejects religion-based sectarianism.

Chahine certainly does not claim authenticity in his historical reach. As Joseph Massad argues, "historical epics are not simply used by Chahine to illustrate historical events, but as lens[es] on the present. In this sense, his epics emerge as national allegories."[33] In *Saladin*, Chahine does not present a history, but rather a historical account, a practice that he will recreate later in several films that deal with specific Arab historical settings, including *Adieu Bonaparte!* (1985) and *Destiny* (1997).

Saladin rewrote and reinterpreted history with an eye to the present. As such, the film offered a new way of dealing with history, and despite the criticisms of how it took liberties with historical accuracy, Chahine was still able to present a view of Saladin that did not intentionally attempt to mislead in its portrayal of the man himself. As Mohammed Khan points out, "The film at least was not as naive as the Hollywood production of David Butler's *King Richard and the Crusaders* (1954), which presented the great Saladin as if he was Chief Yellow Horn out its stock of Red Indians."[34]

With Chahine's recounting of the Arab people's medieval history, he was intent on relating how this history impacted their recognition of their own place within it, as well as how this history shaped their conception of their national identity. To this end, Chahine basically chose to reconstruct popular history, seeking to give expression to a past and a present that were both scarred by violence but filled with possibilities. By recognizing that the systemic destruction of popular memory has been instrumental to the colonial domination of the Arab world as well as other underdeveloped parts of the de-colonized world, Chahine saw in history, both medieval and current, a living expression of resistance and political change. As such, collective memory became a resource to contest the presentation of history as a secluded scholarly exercise with no impact on understanding the present or contemplating the future.

In retrospect, given the predominance of national history and historical experiences within his cinema, Chahine's early popular cinema further linked him to distinctive political, social, and cultural engagements. The popularity of both *Jamila* and *Saladin* challenged the uniform appropriation of popular cinema as empty and as ideologically loyal. Furthermore, the popularity of the two films also pointed in the direction of Chahine's cinema's potential as an agent for a national renaissance. Despite the change from his 1950s class-oriented work to his later engagement with explicit national politics by the early 1960s, Chahine's cinematic practice was clearly and increasingly being informed by a new sense of its place within history and within the process of social and political change within the Arab world. To the extent that their impact spilled over the national borders of Egypt, Chahine's *Jamila* and *Saladin* informed and were informed by the agenda of a new Arab cinema; one largely encouraged by the left–nationalist revolution and Nasser's leadership in Egypt. Because these films sought to empower collective experiences that were being generated within a clearly crucial political moment in contemporary Arab history, they also accommodated rather than restricted the enrichment of Arab national discourse. As such, they presented an essentially new mode of filmmaking—as opposed to the historically sanctioned practice—that sought to produce revamped meanings and underscored the power of collective anticolonial national resistance in Arab popular culture.

4

INSTITUTIONAL SHIFTS AND POLITICAL DIVERGENCES

Just after the production of his 1963 film *Saladin* Chahine entered a new stage of his career. The new phase saw important political, institutional, and stylistic shifts begin to take hold in the filmmaker's cinema. Even before the devastating defeat of the Arab armies, including Egypt's, following Israel's trilateral attack on Egypt, Jordan, and Syria, and its June 1967 occupation of the Gaza Strip, the West Bank, and the Golan Heights, Chahine's cinema was beginning to reflect an increasingly critical position vis-à-vis government policies and practices. While Nasser's charisma and his genuine popularity among the Egyptian and Arab masses remained as strong as ever, there were also clear signs of bureaucratic fissure, corruption, and an intolerance of dissent in Egypt and other left–nationalist Arab regimes.

Simultaneously, new developments within the Egyptian film industry foreshadowed the decline of private sector production and distribution enterprises. With the gradual nationalization of studios and theaters as a result of increased economic and political pressure and the increased role of the government in the film distribution process, the entire dynamic of the Egyptian film industry was shifting. And while these changes helped forge new world-class government-supported film training institutions, creating new opportunities for young filmmakers, and contributing to the development of a vibrant Arab film culture, the public sector struggled. The new film bureaucracy came mainly from outside the film community and hence was not capable of understanding the issues involved in this complex area of cultural activity. While most filmmakers supported in principle the emergence of the public sector and its involvement in encouraging the development of a more socially and politically engaged cinema, as well as its effort to improve the quality of filmmaking in the country, they were also beginning to suffer from the heavy-handed shadow of government bureaucracy and its practices. And while government intervention did not regulate against or censor the production or screening of films with controversial topics, it nevertheless did not allow for the flexibility some filmmakers associated with the private Egyptian film industry. As a result, relationships between filmmakers and the government became increasingly strained, and some filmakers began to seek alternative ways to make their films.

STATE INTERVENTION, GROWTH, AND INSTITUTIONAL SHIFTS

By the early 1960s the Egyptian government's involvement in film production and distribution had become larger and more widespread. With the creation of the public sector, more and more private producers and companies were being pushed out. While private film producers continued to make films, albeit in increasingly limited numbers, and the government ostensibly allowed them to establish studios, laboratories, and production and distribution companies, the fact remained that no new companies were created during this period.[1] And in 1963, as the first cohort of students from the High Cinema Institute graduated, the government's public film structure and institutions were, in fact, "not able to provide them with an opportunity to direct a film, even a short film."[2]

Just prior to the 1967 defeat, Egyptian critical film discourse had been bogged down in endless debates around what were essentially semantic differences in proper terminology to define the kind of cinema for which they strived. According to Samir Farid:

> During this period, an oft-used expression in Egyptian cinema was 'al-film al-hadif' [the film with a purpose] — purpose in the sense of political propaganda for socialism. The expression 'al-film al-jad' [the serious film] was also used; in this case, 'serious' meant political propaganda. Egyptian films moved away from dealing with contemporary reality, for everything was 'fine' in the present. Most of the films of the public sector took place in the 'hated' past.[3]

But with the 1967 defeat, Egypt, along with other left-nationalist Arab regimes entered into an unprecedentedly precarious period. The following years leading up to the October 1973 War were ones of uncertainty and cynicism. As Farid points out, Egyptian cinema itself was "drowning in 'purposeful' and 'serious' films" with hardly any popular appeal, "this at a time when cinema in Europe and the United States" was undergoing a revival ('nouvelle vague' in France; 'free cinema' in Britain; 'new cinema' in Germany, Poland, Hungary, Czechoslovakia, India, Japan, and Brazil; underground cinema in New York).[4] Ziyad Fayed attributes this new situation to the creation and solidification of the public sector in 1961. Fayed considers the expansion of Egyptian public sector film production as a "disaster" which afflicted Egyptian cinema, writing,

> the implementation of the July 1961 socialist laws and the nationalization of studios and theater, the Arab boycott of Egypt, and the new involvement of Egyptian (along with Arab and particularly Lebanese) distributors in producing films, and the beginning of television broadcasting all contributed to the beginning of collapse of the Egyptian film industry.[5]

Another Egyptian film critic shares a similar view on how the rise of public sector production, along with the rise of television, played a negative role in the development of the Egyptian film industry. Mustafa Darwish argues that the industry continued to grow *in spite* of the "tremendous obstacles" including "the nationalization of studios and theaters in the 1960s, and the decline of theater when confronted with television, which the state supported." Nationalization and television together forced the submission of the moving image to the public sector, "an ineffective, inefficient dinosaur marked by excess labor, accumulating debt, and the squandering of public funds," Darwish suggests.[6]

Clearly, the blame here is put solely on the public sector in a way that underestimates, if not totally ignores, the positive aspects that this sector played in the history of Egyptian cinema. Both Darwish and Fayed's critiques take virtually no notice of the major contributions this sector made prior to—and even after—the implementation of more stringent regulations on the private film industry. Furthermore, Fayed's critique does not account for the political fatigue and corruption that functioned beyond the sphere of the cinematic public sector itself.

According to Samir Farid, a huge number of films were made during this period with the support of the public sector, resulting in the emergence of many new talented filmmakers—most of whom were graduates of the High Cinema Institute. Among the more renowned alumni were Mamduh Shukry, Ali Abd al-Khaliq, Ashraf Fahmi, Nader Galal, Shadi Abd al-Salam, and Said

Marzuk.[7] For his part leading Egyptian scholar/critic Ali Abu Shadi presents a strongly sympathetic assessment of the public sector issue as it relates to Egyptian cinema and counters the attacks on it after 1972 and beyond. Abu Shadi goes further and suggests that despite many logistical and financial obstacles and limitations, the public film sector was instrumental in maintaining cinema in Egypt both as an industry and as a trade; this in addition to its major share of films that were distinguished for their high level of artistic and intellectual skill. Presenting the first detailed quantitative and qualitative analytical survey of the film output of the period between 1963 and 1972 (the period of the film public sector), Abu Shadi concludes that despite all "unfounded claims," not one single filmmaker stopped working during this period.[8] He suggests that the public sector "in fact allowed a working chance to sixty filmmakers out of eighty five who directed a total of 430 films during the same period." These sixty directors presented 149 films from the list that included 153 films produced by the public sector. The remaining six were international coproductions made by non-Egyptian filmmakers."[9] The end result demonstrates that the contribution of the public sector exceeded by far that of the private sector when it came to giving a chance to new film talents to emerge: "The public sector produced 30 percent of general output of the Egyptian film industry during its ten year tenure, yet it was able to give a first directing chance to twenty-six filmmakers . . . while seventeen first time directors were given a chance by the private sector at the time when its share of productions during the same period was 70 percent."[10]

According to Sami al-Salamuni, a leading Egyptian film critic and scholar, the prevailing trend in the post-Nasser period was to just throw out the baby with the bathwater. Salamuni argues that intentionally or not, some post-Nasser critics began to contribute to the gradual erasure of collective memory in relation to a significant if not key period in Egyptian film history:

> When we remember The Land [Chahine, 1968] we cannot but recall that it was produced by the public sector, along with al-Mumya [The Mummy], al-Bustagi [The Postman], and al-Haram [The Shame]. Tens of other films and new names emerged as a result of the support of the public sector in what is referred to as the 'sixties cinema' which would not have been possible without the support of this sector, which we still lament the loss of. We can imagine Youssef Chahine asking for an external distribution loan from a Lebanese distributor for his film The Land who would have probably told him that there is no market for films about peasants and their jalalib [Egyptian peasant traditional dress].[11]

While Roy Armes would later disparagingly characterize the political output of Egyptian filmmaking during this period as somewhat "like the 1952 revolution in its early years, [and that it] remained an expression of petty-bourgeois nationalism,"[12] he nevertheless reiterated the importance of the public sector in helping forge the careers of new filmmakers along with some of the milestones in the history of Egyptian and Arab films:

> [I]n effect the public sector produced all the films of any importance during the period 1963–71. [Samir Farid] lists some of the major achievements as including The Sin (1965), by the prolific Henry Barakat (b. 1914); The Postman (1968), by a newcomer, Hussein Kamal (b. 1932); Tawfiq Saleh's The Rebels (1968), Abou Seif's The 68 Trial (1968), and Chahine's The Land (1970[sic]).[13]

On another level, Fayed's and several other post-Nasser critics do not account for the major changes impacting intellectual public discourse on film in Egypt, and, by extension, in other Arab countries. Considering that most new critics became the main contributors to Egyptian mass newspapers, magazines, and film journals, an emerging and increasingly influential group was bringing new and more complex perspectives into Egyptian and Arab popular film culture. The work of this group enhanced further development of Arab film culture:

> The second half of the sixties also saw the emergence of many film critics who came to cinema from literature, theater, or philosophy. After the 1968 demonstrations, a group of young filmmakers and critics founded Jamaat al-Cinema al-Jadida [the New Cinema Group], which helped chart a new path for cinema in Egypt and the rest of the Arab world.[14]

The Group began to publish *al-Sinima*, the first serious specialized Arab film journal dedicated to discussions on Egyptian, Arab, and international cinemas. Soon after, Nadi al-Sinima fi-l-Qahira cinematheque was created in Cairo. The club organized screenings of masterpieces of international cinema and followed these screenings with public discussions with film enthusiasts, filmmakers, artists, and critics. During the same period, prominent Egyptian writers such as Abd al-Rahman al-Sharqawi, Lotfi al-Khouli, Ihsan Abd al-Kouddous, Salah Jahin, and even Naguib Mahfouz began to get involved in film ventures for the first time, and filmmakers including Chahine would utilize their talents by adapting their novels or having them cowrite his film scripts.

CHAHINE AND THE EARLY PUBLIC SECTOR EXPERIENCE

In spite of his general backing for government involvement in supporting the arts including film, Chahine's own experience with the public sector remained limited and at times even icy. In the end, Chahine only made three films with the support of the public sector: *al-Nas wa-l-Nil* (The People and the Nile, 1968), *The Land* (1969), *The Choice* (1970). Within the Egyptian film industry there were signs of increased fatigue and unease that were only exacerbated by bureaucratic government practices. This led some filmmakers, including Chahine, to seek alternative ways to make films without involving the officious hand of the government. In 1965, during a period of rage against local government bureaucracy, Chahine simply decided to go to Beirut to produce and direct a Lebanese musical, *Bayya' al-khawatim* (The Ring Seller, 1965), with the legendary Lebanese singer Fayruz. The film was an adaptation of an operetta by the Rahbani Brothers, a celebrated Arab musician/poet duo. Chahine compared the reason for his temporary departure from Egypt to that of the protagonist in his 1964 film *Fajr yawm jadid* (Dawn of a New Day, 1964). He explained, "I felt that the socialism we were dreaming about consciously and instinctively had become a bureaucracy, and authoritarian, and the bureaucrat had become king, and this was very clear within the film sector. I was fed up and I needed a break."[15] However, the attempt to move his work to Lebanon failed, and Chahine returned to Egypt, to work again in the government-controlled public sector.

Youssef Chahine's films in the period following the release of *Saladin* reflected emerging anxieties within Egyptian society itself and across the Arab world concerning the direction of the Nasser revolution. The war in Yemen that pit the Egyptian army in support of nationalist forces against the Saudi and western backing of the old autocratic Imam regime was draining the Egyptian economy and raising concerns about the mounting death rate in the Egyptian military. The failure to forge a union with Syria represented a major blow to the political aspirations of pan-Arab nationalists and resulted in creating new divisions among them. Within Egypt, disillusionment with bureaucratic controls and the systemic repression of dissent was growing, even among left–nationalist intellectuals.

Chahine's *Dawn of a New Day* (1964), did not directly address these issues. Instead it chose to focus on the inability of the bourgeois class to deal with and absorb the new changes in society, and how this played a major role in jeopardizing the work of the revolution. Through the story of an older upper-class Egyptian woman who falls in love with a young working-class student, Chahine sought to depict obstacles as well as possibilities in the post-

Dawn of a New Day: Cairo from the tower: Different outlooks on the same city.

revolution movement to modernize social and economic relations. But with the crushing Arab defeat of 1967, Chahine's work became even more focused on the issue of class and its role in revolutionary change. While his Egyptian-Soviet coproduction *The People and the Nile* (1968) and his widely celebrated 1969 film *The Land* implicitly criticized the bourgeois and petit-bourgeois elements controlling the Egyptian revolution, *The Choice* (1970) was quite explicit in its depiction of the emergence of a parasitic nouveau riche within Egyptian society—a class he felt was killing the aspirations of the revolution and isolating it from its constituency among the working classes. The film was later screened at a Carthage Film Festival celebration of Chahine's body of work in 1971. It was during this event that Chahine began to lay the foundations for his collaboration with the Algerian government agency that would soon produce his film *The Sparrow* (1972).

Although none of his films of the period realized the successes enjoyed by popular melodramas and musicals such as *Abi fawq al-shajara* (My Father on the Tree, Hussein Kamal, 1969) and *Khalli balak min Zuzu* (Keep Your Eye on Zuzu, Hasan al-Imam, 1972), Chahine's films were opening new horizons and garnering new respect in the Arab world and on the international level, especially among film critics. On another level, the joint Egyptian-Soviet production of *The People and the Nile* and the Algerian-produced *The Choice* awakened Chahine to the possibilities associated with seeking outside support for his work. This production practice would characterize the future development of Chahine's work, and would impact its thematic as well as its stylistic perspective.

THE POST-REVOLUTION UPPER CLASS IN DAWN OF A NEW DAY

Dawn of a New Day (1964) is a complex film about alienation, and while certainly a sad tale, in the end it remains resolutely optimistic. On the surface, the film is a post-revolutionary drama about a forbidden relationship between a married woman and a younger man. Nayla (Sanaa Gamil) is a married woman in her forties from the old Egyptian aristocracy; a class Nasser hoped would eventually support the changes that the revolution was instigating in the country. Chahine himself appears in the film, playing the role of a member of the old upper class.

Nayla falls in love with Tariq, a young man studying at the university. He comes from a working-class background that allows him to help her see another Egypt, one a world apart from the Egypt Nayla knows. *Dawn* contrasts Tariq's down-to-earth attitude with Nayla's discontentment with the hypocrisy and shallowness associated with her own class; alluding to a crisis within a class which finds itself unable to deal with or absorb the new social, political, and cultural changes in Egypt.

The lives of Nayla and her family and friends, are uninspiring, tedious, and isolated from the changing realities that are taking place in the rest of society. In one scene, Nayla is at a party with a number of idle, upper-class Egyptians. The atmosphere is one of intoxication, with loud English music, and Latin American dancing. More importantly, the scene projects a sense of cultural alienation, alluding not only to the upper class's inability to see the realities of the lower classes' deprivation, but also to their lack of connection with their own cultural heritage. Fawal describes the scene: "In the heart of Cairo, the center of Arab culture, there is nothing Arabic, nothing Egyptian—except, perhaps, the opium or hashish. These people are alien to their country."[16]

As she meets Tariq and ventures with him into the world where most Egyptians live, struggle, and play, she discovers a new world with its own charm, dignity, and vivacity despite its poverty and limitations. But as she gets closer to Tariq and his world, Nayla is haunted by her past, and by her class inhibitions and reticence. After a heated argument with Tariq about her inability to come to terms with their age difference she decides to break up with him.

After weeks and months pass by, Nayla is reacquainted with a little boy in an orphanage she had met before her relationship with Tariq began. This time, however, she looks at him with a new eye; now she does not hold her earlier condescending—if charitable—attitude toward him. The boy becomes part of her life and Nayla starts to give him attention and take him to the places that Tariq introduced her to. One day, drawn to one of the couple's favorite spots, the Cairo Tower, Nayla meets Tariq again and he tells her that he is going overseas to finish his studies in Germany. In one particularly powerful scene, the camera moves with the characters as they go up the tower stairs and talk about what has been happening in their lives over the last few months. The higher they go the more we become conscious of their differing preoccupations and aspirations. Nayla tells him that now that she is divorced she wants to join him. But just before the couple are about to leave, she realizes that she cannot abandon the little boy she has befriended. Tariq is the past and the boy is the future. The film ends at this sad yet hopeful moment.

Accounts from the period testify to the extent to which the film was able to attract the attention of Egypt's critics and writers. Nonetheless, *Dawn* drew both critical praise as well as fierce criticism from local writers and media. While several round-table discussions and symposiums were organized to address the film's thematic and stylistic significance, several media critics felt that the film was not able to catch the hearts of post-revolution Egyptians, nor was it able to reflect the social and cultural experience of its presumed locale.

Dawn of a New Day was considered by some an unprecedented Arab cinematic event in its bold depiction of sexual relationships in conjunction with social criticism. One critic points out that the film "ventured a new route which parts with traditional themes and stylistic approaches," and that it "reflected the nation's determination to forge genuine revolutionary social and political change in the country."[17] But while critics had been anxiously awaiting its release, especially in light of Chahine's major success with *Saladin*, the film failed to attract audiences at the theaters, and reports by contemporary critics allude to the gloomy atmosphere which accompanied its screening in various Egyptian cities. Ahmad al-Houdari points out that he himself had a hard time understanding the film even after seeing it for the second time.[18] In another article, al-Houdari recounts that while critics expressed their admiration for the technical expertise manifested in the film, many in the external delegations that saw *Dawn* in an Alexandria film symposium, including French film scholar George Sadoul, expressed their unhappiness with the elitist attitude of the film in general.[19]

Egyptian filmmaker Tawfiq Saleh expressed a similar sentiment and wondered whether the film might have tried to ask too much from its audience. He argued that while he thought the film did reach its audience, it was not able to reach their hearts: "by demanding intellectual participation from his audience, Chahine made a significant stylistic and thematic leap but at a time when most people had not yet shaken their old film reception laziness."[20] Critic Hasan Fu'ad reiterates that while *Dawn* had some moments of brilliance that were deserving of study in film schools, Chahine had failed to reach the hearts of his audience:

> the film demonstrated Chahine's capacity in the art of filmmaking but he is still a student in his ability to relate to spectators. Furthermore, it seems that Chahine not only was not able to reach people, but also that he simply did not care about them . . . in fact Chahine himself was not even in attendance to see what kind of reaction the audience had when the film was first screened in Cairo.[21]

Several critics pointed specifically to the film's forced westernized approach, and its attempt to appeal to a non-Arab audience. While stressing the stylistic achievements of the film, Samir Farid argues that it was not in sync with Egyptian and Arab social reality: "a major flaw characterized the film, which can be summarized in its foreign accent which seems to dominate it on various levels." Farid even goes further, doubting Chahine's ability to look at Egypt from the inside: "In the end, most of Chahine's films feel like they take the point of view of a tourist looking at us."[22] Similar sentiments were expressed by other critics who even accused Chahine of essentially

Dawn of a New Day: Non-normative sexuality and revolutionary change.

62   Institutional Shifts and Political Divergences

rehashing other western cinematic themes in order to appeal to western critics and audiences. Ameed al-Imam saw a similarity between *Dawn*'s theme and storyline and that of Vittorio De Sica's *Indiscretion of an American Wife* (1953), which had been shown in Cairo ten years earlier.[23] Hilmi Halim argues that the film's script and dialogue seemed "written in a foreign language and then translated into Arabic, which eventually made Abd al-Rahman al-Sharqawi take his name out of the film credits."[24]

There is no doubt that the film was clearly fashioned with mainly international critical exposure in mind. In her defense of the film, producer Mary Kwaini argues that the film did attract a lot of local critical attention, and there had been many intellectual roundtables to discuss its significance. Responding to critiques of the film's editing style and what some saw as its lack of structural unity, she suggested that the film probably had fewer mistakes than any other Arab film and that the topic itself was quite accessible. Conversely, Kwaini does admit that she and Chahine had international exposure in mind.[25] Another contemporary critic alludes to how the producer and the filmmaker did not seem concerned with locally releasing the film:

> Although the film was finished last [1963] August, and a copy was sent to the previewing committee of the Venice Film Festival which began on the twenty-seventh of the same month, the film was not screened in Egyptian theaters until February, a full six months after it was finished.[26]

But not everyone agreed that the film's international appeal represented a curse for the film; one Lebanese critic even took a certain Arab pride in how *Dawn* echoed and even surpassed other western films. George Ibrahim al-Khoury wrote:

> The film which was officially shown at the Beirut International Film Festival was indeed a new dawn for Arab filmmaking, and Cairo was able to outstrip French and many Italian and British films. [Dawn of a New Day] represented a qualitative leap in the history of cinema in the Arab East, and I don't think I am exaggerating if I claim that it is probably the best film shown at the Beirut Festival.[27]

The differences of opinion on *Dawn of a New Day* were clearly substantial, but the fact remains that Chahine's new cinematic venture differed considerably from his earlier films. His attempt to present an in-depth look at different classes as they related to each other and to the changes affecting their society was a complex undertaking, one which had little or no chance of hitting a chord with mainstream Egyptian and Arab audiences. Given the technical complexity of the film, its dearth of movie stars (despite the fact that Sanaa Gamil was a well-known and highly respected theater actress), and its largely detached atmosphere with less emotional characters than were usually associated with Egyptian melodramas, the film seemed destined for a less than enthusiastic response from the average Egyptian filmgoer. However, considering the period, with its complex dichotomies that were affecting all of Egyptian society, the film offers a disturbing assessment of a critical moment in Arab history.

The film's emphasis on Nayla's struggles to affirm her identity as a woman even as she fights to transcend her class background to become part of the changes taking place in her society is indeed a complex position, but one that is at the heart of the contradictory political and social affiliations that characterized the Nasser period. To begin, the relationship that develops between Nayla and Tariq is structured with an eye for its irreconcilability, not simply due to the age difference, but based on the profound divergence between their class and cultural backgrounds. In one memorable scene, Nayla is in bed the morning after sleeping with Tariq. She looks at the mirror and smiles. She is happy and feels renewed and rejuvenated after the encounter with her lover. She then takes the mirror in her hand and lifts it up and sunlight is reflected across the room as she moves the mirror around. As the light hits her chaise-longue we notice her red gloves lying alongside an envelope which Tariq had given her earlier—leaving her money for the sandwich and drink that she had bought him during a previous outing. Nayla rises from her bed, picks up the envelope, and goes back to bed lovingly touching her face with it before calling her servant for breakfast. Chahine's masterful yet subtle visual storytelling approach summarizes the essence of difference between the two people, one which makes this relationship doomed.

Dawn of a New Day also offers a seamless plot structure that complements its main theme of post-revolutionary modernization in Egyptian society. As such, the film proposes a critique of the old upper class's reaction to the revolution's new social and national policies. Chahine himself saw the film as a reaction to how "the old Egypt attempted to derail the new experience and its new socialist orientation."[28] After the film's release, leading Egyptian Marxist Mahmoud Amin al-Alem reflected on the film's significance as a commentary on Egypt's former upper class. He argues that *Dawn of a New Day* made a significant contribution to understanding post-revolutionary social dynamics in the context of a dying social class and the rise of another:

Aside from some minor details, I think the film presented us with a very good story, a picture of a dying class on the eve of social revolution, and the brilliant and renewed Sanaa Gamil [the actress who plays Nayla] was fully powerful in her ability to depict the tragedy of this class ... because while this class is on its deathbed, its members are still seeking salvation and they can only find it through recreating themselves, through work, and through adopting the revolution.[29]

What al-Alem saw as the film's main weakness was its one-sided engagement with its intrusive portrait of the dying class. He argues that a more balanced perspective of the larger picture, which did not ignore the reality of the revolution, could have strengthened the impact of the film.[30] To the extent that the film depicts the life of a dying class in a post-revolutionary situation, *Dawn of a New Day* foreshadows Tomas Gutierrez Alea's *Memories of Underdevelopment* (1968) four years later. Coming out during a period where the issue of how various social classes sought to position themselves vis-à-vis revolutionary political change under 'third world' conditions, the two films acutely focused on and expressed the anxieties of the old bourgeois classes in Egypt and Cuba respectively.

Both *Dawn* and *Memories* present protagonists from the old pre-revolution dominating classes. Nayla and Sergio are both detached and wary, but around them is a whirlwind of life. The setting for the two films is in an immediate post-revolution period where emerging values and ideas clash with the old ones and becomes vehicles for the protagonist's own self reassessment. Both films place their main protagonists in relationships with much younger people. In the end, neither character is capable of pursuing any meaningful or lasting connection with their fellow citizens. Equally as important, both films follow the protagonist's attempts to rediscover their surroundings in a way that transcends the boundaries of their own bourgeois dwellings. In both films, the depiction of the visual and aural textures of the city's people and streets is achieved with available and natural lighting, in contrast with the dark and shadowy settings associated with the protagonist's private—and privileged—spaces.

But while in *Memories* Sergio begins his exploration by trying to rediscover Havana through the telescope on the terrace of his penthouse apartment and only later takes his problematic venture into the Havana streets, Nayla seems determined to embark as quickly as possible on her journey outside her social and cultural prison. In the end, both films draw effective portraits of individuals hesitantly and awkwardly seeking a place for themselves within new and unfamiliar spatial and historical contexts. Nevertheless, while *Dawn of a New Day* reflected upon a dying class, it also foreshadowed the re-emergence of the same class (as seen in Nayla's refashioned image of her self, perhaps as the compassionate mother of a new age), a re-emergence that will lead the revolution to the disaster Chahine would later contemplate in *The Sparrow*. While the film did not directly criticize the Nasser revolution, it nevertheless pointed out an important element that Chahine felt was hindering the implementation of revolutionary changes in the country.

Nasser had several Marxist-oriented members within his revolutionary council and government and these exerted a relatively important influence. Nevertheless, these individuals were not the only ones with political influence. By the mid-1960s leftist and Marxist groups who supported the government were cautioning against what they considered a naïve ideological view which hoped for a sort of unity with the bourgeois class in achieving the goals of the revolution. These groups were also warning against the increasing influence of a new military class that in many ways was beginning to replace—both in influence and in bureaucratic privilege—the old economically powerful upper class. The issue of class, and in particular the old upper class and the new class emerging from the ruling military bureaucracy, became important components of Chahine's cinematic characterization of the problems facing the Nasser revolution. Chahine's later films would continue to allude to the impact of these problems on the Arab national project as a whole.

Dawn of a New Day does not critique the emerging upper class, and instead it clearly points out classist nuances within the post-revolution social mosaic. In as much as it was cognizant of the impact of class on revolutionary politics, the film prefigures a progressively critical Chahine who was poised to echo the views of the more leftist elements of the revolution's supporters and their critical attitude toward the political and military bureaucracy.

Stylistically, the film presented an important divergence from Chahine's earlier films. It signaled an effort to incorporate new techniques of storytelling involving a more jittery editing style, which favored a rapid capturing of the image that did not allow the viewer the time to contemplate its details. The film particularly utilizes this technique during its depiction of characters from the upper class conversing with each other at their parties. While this film cutting technique would become a permanent feature in Chahine's later films, its extensive use in *Dawn of a New Day* represented an important departure from the more pensive editing practices associated with most of his earlier films (aside from the specific moments in *Saladin* noted above). Added to the shadowy *mise en scène* that distinguishes the shots inside Nayla's home, the nervous editing style enhances the film's impressionistic presentation of a class uncertain about its future or its place in post-revolutionary Egypt. A slower and more relaxed editing style and brightly lit settings set apart the scenes outside Nayla's home as she accompanies Tariq into the streets of Cairo.

Chahine's stylistic experimentation in the film clearly impacted the level on which the film was able to resonate with its audience. The tension between his daring stylistic approach and his well-known interest in being part of an effective movement for social and political change would go on to characterize Chahine's later cinema, and remains the most respected *and* disparaged feature of his work. In fact, this tension would become an important component in criticisms of Chahine's work, particularly in connection with his perceived elitist tendencies that seem more concerned with satisfying western critics and audiences.

The local criticisms raised against *Dawn of a New Day* hit a chord, particularly considering the attention that Chahine gave to showing the film in international film festivals. This fixation with an international audience was never denied by Chahine, neither did he believe that it decreased or demeaned his deep attachment to his people and their social and national concerns and preoccupations. Through an eclectic body of work utilizing varied stylistic and generic approaches to nurture links with his audiences, Chahine seemed determined to engage this audience in an open and uncluttered cinematic project. In this regard, institutional and stylistic innovation and renovation were never ends in themselves, but were rather a field of learning, discovery, and contemplation. Such an approach played a critical role in the evolution of Chahine's cinema and comprised a self-evident space for its intrusion into social and political discourse of the day. Given that Chahine's cinematic practice engaged itself in the arena of political struggle, it is important to acknowledge the extent to which the tension between form and content continued to preoccupy the work of this determinedly activist filmmaker.

THE PERSONAL AND THE COLLECTIVE IN *THE PEOPLE AND THE NILE*

The first Chahine encounter with international coproduction was with his 1968 film *The People and the Nile*, an Egyptian-Soviet production that was meant as a tribute to the cooperation between the two countries in the building of the Aswan High Dam. The first Egyptian–Soviet coproduction on a fiction film, it involved actors from both countries and was shot in seventy millimeter color Cinemascope. *The People and the Nile* cost over a quarter of a million Egyptian pounds—a huge amount of money by Egyptian film production standards at the time. Furthermore, the film faced a major financial

The People and the Nile: Middle class artists in the midst of revolution (photo: Gamal Fahmy).

hurdle when Chahine was forced to reshoot scenes with a new cast after complaints from both the Egyptian and Soviet governments.

The Aswan High Dam project initiated Egypt's entry into the industrial age, and symbolized Egypt's solidarity with other third world countries and the socialist bloc. The project's positive economic, social, and political implications for Egypt were massive, and signaled the beginning of a new era for the country.

Upon his return to Egypt from Lebanon where he had spent two years contemplating the failure of *Dawn of a New Day* and his disenchantment with the increased bureaucratic interference within the filmmaking industry, Chahine embarked on a new production. After spending time outside of Egypt like "a fish outside its sea," as he described his time in Lebanon, Chahine began a film that was to participate in Egypt's celebrations of its "euphoric victory in the building of the [Aswan High Dam]."[31]

Work on the film began just one year before the 1967 War, which represented a watershed in Egypt and Arab modern history. Upon his return to Cairo he discovered that a top government official was looking for him to propose making a film which paid tribute to the Aswan High Dam as a symbol of Egypt resiliency in the face of colonial antagonism. In addition to celebrating Egypt's achievement in completing the massive Aswan

68 Institutional Shifts and Political Divergences

enterprise, the film was to commemorate the country's successful stand against the United States and the west when they pressured the World Bank to refuse financial support for the project.[32] The film was also to observe the era of Egyptian cooperation with the Soviet Union and other socialist countries. Chahine himself saw the project as a reflection on the "long and hard struggle to build the dam, and the symbolic meaning it holds for the people of Egypt and for all third world countries."[33]

The events of the film take place over two days, the first in Aswan and the second in Alexandria. The film does not expand on any one of the individual stories of its characters, and instead depicts them in parallel to the stories of the other characters. As such the film avoids any elaborate character development, and focuses on creating a sense of the collective aspect of the group's experience. The plot is structured around flashbacks that give us further information about each of the characters and elaborates on their present-day stories. Among *Dawn*'s many characters are: Nadia, a fine arts student and her lover Amin, a doctor who insists, despite her objections, on going to Aswan to finish his research on the effects of the bilharzia disease on the local population; Alexei, a Soviet engineer working on the Dam and his homesick wife Zoya, who decides to go back to her work in Moscow because she refuses to spend her days just waiting for her husband to come home; Saad, an Egyptian engineer now in Aswan with his family; Nicolai, a Soviet worker and his Nubian Egyptian friend Barak; and an Egyptian writer—whose identity remains unknown—who is working on a story about his experience in Aswan in conjunction with the experiences of the workers on the project.

The film opens with Nadia's father, the chief engineer in the project, holding a press conference in which he alludes to the gigantic effort that has gone into the project. Soon the film cuts to documentary footage of astounding scenes of the divergence of the Nile path. Nadia leaves Aswan for Alexandria and on the train she meets Yehia, a young man who seems to be following her. On the trip Nadia also meets Zoya who is on her way back to Moscow. Back in Aswan, Dr. Amin decides to go to Alexandria to try to fix his relationship with Nadia. Barak is collecting names on a petition to keep his Soviet friend Nicolai in Aswan but the latter has made up his mind to leave. The farewell scene can only imply the love the men share as Barak says goodbye to his friend and gives him a basket of Egyptian dates. The film's ending takes place in Alexandria, where Amin and Nadia confront each other, and Zoya makes her decision to return to her husband. On the road to Cairo Nadia realizes the distance that separates her from Yehia, as Amin decides to quit his research in Aswan and return to Cairo.

Chahine's film eventually offered an epic portrayal and celebration of the massive human effort that made the titanic High Dam structure possible. The film was unprecedented in Egyptian cinema in how it engaged multiple and unconnected characters, with the monumental national project being the only element that bound them together. In the end, *The People and the Nile* offered a complex portrayal of the lives of workers and engineers—both Egyptian and Soviet—and of the people of the Nile Valley. The film was finally released late in 1968, less than a year after the 1967 War.

In its political context, *Dawn* represented a reaffirmation of unity among Egyptians and a confidence in their ability to overcome the consequences of their military defeat just one year earlier. Furthermore, inasmuch as it featured the Soviet Union's solidarity with Egypt and the Arab world in their efforts to modernize their economy and society, the film was seen as a tribute to Soviet solidarity in the rebuilding of Egyptian and Arab armies that was in full swing after the crushing defeat of 1967.

However, just before it was released, problems began to arise on all fronts. Both Egyptian and Soviet coproduction authorities were asking for their own changes. As a result, as one critic suggests, the film eventually "came out fragmented and hesitant." Chahine described the period as a very difficult number of months of "endless meetings and manoeuvres, and in the end a great disappointment and surrender."[34]

Chahine relates the story of the two versions of the film, one of which he considers to be really his, in the sense that he felt it presented his own original vision. According to Chahine, it all began in 1964 when the government's General Institute of Cinema asked him to do a major film on the High Dam project, offering him a big budget and major technical support.[35] But the film that was finished in 1968 and given the name *The People and the Nile* was rejected by the Institute after several objections by the Soviets. As a result, the film was not released right away, and another version was made and released in 1972. Many components of the two versions are similar, including the score by Soviet composer Khtachordian and the photography by Soviet Shlinikov Bertchenko, and while Chahine did film the second version, he nevertheless felt it did not truly represent him.[36] But he goes on to point out that President Nasser himself was very upset with how bureaucrats pushed the filmmaker to the edge, and personally asked him to come back to Egypt (from Lebanon, where he had been staying after the debacle of the first version), and assured him he would be given the respect he deserved.[37]

In response to the question of why he agreed to do the second version of the film, Chahine cites his concern over the symbolic significance of the first attempt to produce a Soviet–Egyptian film, an effort in which he felt personally and politically invested:

> At the time, we did not have a real market for Egyptian film and the Soviet market involved more than seventy thousand movie theaters. The Soviet bloc also represented an opportunity to connect with hundreds of millions of people within the socialist bloc as well as a solid grass root following among progressive people around the world.[38]

The original version appeared to have been lost until Chahine discovered a copy in the *Cinémathèque Française* and undertook the task of refurbishing it and crafting a new negative for it. Chahine renamed the film *al-Nil wa-l-hayah* (The Nile and Life) for its Paris debut, and according to him, the Paris version contains some of "the best scenes that I have created in my entire film career."[39] This restored version was also shown in 1998 at the New York Film Festival.

The film went well beyond its official goal of celebrating a major economic project and the work and skill that went into it, as well as expressing solidarity between the peoples of Egypt and the Soviet Union. Rather, the film focused on the personal dilemmas of those who were involved in the project: their loneliness, their suffering families and troubled love relationships, and their cultural displacement. And instead of merely exploring the impact of the project on the lives of ordinary Egyptians—particularly the dam's unprecedented capacity to deliver energy and water for the cultivation of vast new agricultural lands—it provided a vivid portrait of the lives of marginalized Egyptian workers. In this regard, the film alluded to continuing class differences, and, equally as important, it accounted for the demographic changes that impacted the lives of the local Nubian population, forcing them to abandon their ancestral homes and move to new barracks-like residential areas.

In any case, the official version of the film was mostly received negatively by local critics. Due to its seventy millimeter format that restricted it to the few theaters equipped for the format, the film received only a limited theatrical release, which further reduced its potential for reaching a wide audience. Some of the comments on the film were indeed hurtful, blaming Chahine for a product of which he himself was not proud. One critic directly connected the failure of the film to Chahine's "typical spoiled kid attitude," and stressed how he "kept abandoning the shooting and jeopardizing the filming by altogether leaving the country for two years and coming back to an undeserved fanfare."[40] Many criticized the whole effort as unworthy of the artistic talents of its contributors, claiming the only powerful images were from the documentary footage and the scenes illustrating the diversion of the Nile's pathway.[41] Others were disappointed with the failure of the film to measure up to the power of the event and its significance to modern Egypt:

> The film does not add anything new to his cinematic technique, this in addition to its explicit propagandistic features. The story and the plot both come across as fuzzy and dramatically unfocussed. The film was not even able to capture the tremendous power of the workers who, in their thousands, were involved in a giant venture. Some of the audiences were commenting in the theater: "Chahine must have shot these scenes during his holiday...." Also the film was shot in seventy millimeter, which is great, but also means that the producers did not consider showing it except in first-class cinemas, instead of thinking of mass audience.[42]

Another critic pointed out that in spite of all the resources made available to him, Chahine missed the chance to effectively engage one of the most controversial and politically significant world events of the 1960s:

> The film had every resource at its disposal, and the story was based on one of the world's largest projects, which was also the center of one of the most controversial international political debates of the decade. Yet the film was unsuccessful both in its artistic merits, and in how it was received by the public ... and in connection with the film's attempt to bring together documentary and fictionalized segments, Chahine's effort was not as effective as it could have been if the editing was more cohesive and its rhythm less anxious.[43]

Egyptian critic Mohammad Ouda was even more pointed in his criticism, describing what he saw as the film's rehashing of old colonial perceptions of Egypt and its people. Ouda criticizes the film's emphasis on the personal, and its downplaying of the political. He specifically expresses his indignation with how the film created a portrait of an Egyptian nation in need of a foreign hand in order for it to move forward in its technical, economic, and social modernization:

> The film presented Egyptians as a backward African tribe, where the white man once again comes to take its hand to help it modernize. This is an insult to both the Soviet and Egyptian peoples who embarked on the project as equals and as partners in one struggle against colonial domination and toward forging a new kind of world politics.[44]

The writer also criticizes the film's inability to focus on the role played by Egypt, from the struggle to nationalize the Suez Canal through to the tremendous human vigor that created such a huge physical structure:

> Building the dam was a watershed in Egyptian history and in its struggle against colonialism. The projects' significance was that Egypt has finally mastered and had at its disposal sources of energy and water that allowed it to become truly independent and free, and this is exactly what colonial powers resisted and desperately tried to jeopardize. Egypt was able to use its Suez revenue for its own national interest after a major war with the three colonial powers of Israel, Britain, and France. On the other hand, there was the other 'foreigner,' the Soviet Union who, in the spirit of genuine solidarity, came to our aid and changed the dynamics of how we perceived international relations.... Therefore, the story of the dam could not and should not have been presented as anything but political.[45]

Irrespective of the critics' harsh condemnation of the film, *The People and the Nile* reflected another turning point in Chahine's career, where his own personal vision of the events played a more prominent role in defining his cinematic interpretation of them.

The People and the Nile: Soviet solidarity and the modernization project (photo: Gamal Fahmy).

Personalizing the High Dam story in many ways echoed Chahine's heightened sense of his political and stylistic cinematic sensitivities. As with his earlier film, *Dawn of a New Day*, *The People and the Nile* saw Chahine forcefully engaging the personal as political and the political as personal. The private stories of Nadia, Amin, Yehia, Zoya, Alexei, Saad, and others were no less reflective of the actual reality of post-revolution Egypt than the stories of Nayla and her young lover Tariq in *Dawn*. Although each of the characters' stories reads like a self-contained essay, their resonance acquires its potential only through their relation with each other, and within the body of the whole film. As such, each of these stories is reconstructed via the collective frame of reference represented by the High Dam project.

Chahine's approach in *Dawn of a New Day* and *The People and the Nile* sought the broadening of the conceptual framework of what was at that point classified as political cinema in the Arab world, and the two films reflected Chahine's incorporation of his increasingly nuanced vision of the Arab national project. To the extent that *The People and the Nile* drew a heterogeneous picture of Egyptian society (and, for that matter, of Soviet workers) as it embarked on the momentous Dam enterprise, it also offered an alternative image of the nation that transcended the government's official version of national unity. It presented a vision of a nation rooted in unity as well as diversity. Such diversity does not discount what the nation entails in terms of class (manual workers and engineers), occupational status (builders and managers), ethnic backgrounds and specificities (Nubians, northern Egyptians, and Russians), and gender differences. Chahine's subtle and beautifully crafted depiction of the repressed love story between Russian worker Nicolai and his Egyptian friend Barak, for example, further contributes to the film's attentiveness to fine-shading the nation and its people's rich elemental mosaic as well as claiming possibilities for internationalist forms of personal and political connection between Egyptians and other peoples. In turn, the film's projection of a renewed imagining of the nation inadvertently acknowledges a new and nuanced understanding of its goals, political objectives, and how these impact the personal within it. In the end, the epic, operatic structure of the film is grounded in how its strategy is put to the service of an art that is at once subjective and communal, propounding the possibility of renegotiating the representational paradigm of nationhood.

CLASS AND NATIONAL LIBERATION IN *THE LAND*

With *The Land* (1969), Chahine went back to his earlier interest in the life of the peasant class in Egypt during the pre-revolutionary period. Based on

Marxist Egyptian author Abd al-Rahman al-Sharqawi's novel *The Egyptian Land*, the film chronicles life in a small peasant village in the 1930s, and the struggle of its inhabitants against the pasha, a local feudal landlord planning to build roads through the village that could eventually destroy the villagers' access to water as well as their entire livelihood. Al-Sharqawi's novel, a semi-autobiographical account of his youth growing up in a poor peasant village in Upper Egypt in the early part of the twentieth century, was first published in 1954 to wide critical and popular acclaim. It was the first major novel to appear after the 1952 revolution that depicted and critiqued the pre-revolutionary era and showed a politically engaged sympathy with the struggle against Egypt's traditional feudalist system.

The Land presents the powerful story of the stubborn resistance of one peasant who galvanizes the support of the entire village. The story draws connections between anticolonial and class struggles, and as such it emphasizes intersections between class emancipation and national liberation. By contextualizing the villagers' struggle within a period in which Egypt was undergoing a revolt against British colonialism, the film also links class and national resistance to the pre-revolutionary fight against the rule of al-Khidyawi royal family. The film also draws a complex picture of class resistance by pointing out that irrespective of good intentions and individual heroism, in the end it is the strength of collective resistance that determines the outcome of major social upheavals.

When the peasants meet to discuss the pasha's plan to divert the road, while some suggest the mayor should appeal his decision, they eventually decide to send the village teacher to Cairo to make their case to the government. But as the convoy arrives in Cairo he finds the city engulfed in anti-British demonstrations, and returns empty-handed to the village. As the situation worsens, the villagers forcefully redirect the water to their lands and embark on a revolt against the pasha. The government sends troops to quell the peasants, and throws their leaders into prison, but soon after they are released they renew their defiance. The film ends with a powerful freeze-frame of the bloodied hand of Abu Swailam, the leader of the revolt, as he grasps at the soil while mounted soldiers drag him across his land. In the best tradition of social realist filmmakers, Chahine brilliantly brackets the film with images of "the hands of the old peasant tending his delicate young cotton plants in the opening shot, balanced by the same hands clinging desperately to the mature plants as the man is dragged to his death in the very last image."[46]

The film breaks with the original story, which is written in the first person. Here the story is told from multiple points of view that allow the film to concentrate on the visual aspects of the events rather than conversational dialogue which is favored in al-Sharqawi's novel. A young boy, who in the written version is the storyteller, becomes just one of many characters in the film. Each character in *The Land* is portrayed as an extension of a social, class, and cultural dynamic, reflecting the complexity of the village's life. On one side, there is the Pasha and his protégé the village mayor, plotting to expropriate the peasants' lands by forcing them out after they shut down their access to water. On the other side, there is a group of villagers representing a range of positions and outlooks on the events. This group is led by Abu Swailam, who owns and works a small piece of land. He is introduced as a veteran of the First World War, an organizer in the Egyptian revolt against the British in 1919, and a chief guard in the village before he was ousted after voting against the pro-British Sidqi party in the 1930 election. Other characters include: Sheikh Hassouna, a local religious leader whose intentions are good, but who is incapable of standing up to the pasha's pressures, which leads him to his final betrayal of his fellow villagers; Sheikh Yusuf, a greedy village merchant who is bent on becoming rich as fast as possible, and has no problem selling food at higher prices to strangers than the regular prices he charges his fellow villagers; and Muhammad Effendi, the educated and respected village teacher who is sent on the village's behalf to lobby the government against the pasha's attempt to confiscate the villagers' land.

While women's roles in *The Land* remain marginal, there are two, Wasifa and Khadra, who add other dimensions to the events in the village. Wasifa is Abu Swailam's daughter, an innocent young girl that every young man in the village dreams of marrying. She also symbolizes the village's dreams and illusions about life in the big city. The opening sequence sees a young boy coming back from Cairo. Wasifa, who used to play with him when they were younger, is eagerly looking forward to meeting with him, but while she has clearly matured, the boy is still too young to fulfill her needs and dreams. His narrative and symbolic importance, however, stems from the fact that he is returning from the city, that magical faraway place that attracts the imagination of many people in the village.

Through Wasifa's dreams about the boy the entire village's relationship with the city is conceptualized. The big city is not simply the place where all the villagers' crops go, it is also the source of a universalized anticipation—the constant waiting for something to happen that might in some way help the villagers improve their lives and fulfill their dreams of a more just solution to their problems. Thus Muhammad's trip to Cairo to lobby for support on behalf of the peasants symbolizes this other aspect of the city's significance for the village.

The other woman with a significant role in the film is Khadra, a landless orphan who has a reputation as the village whore. Khadra is used, manipulated, mistreated, and eventually disposed of when she is killed by Sheikh Sha'ban; a religious fake who uses religion to make financial gains. As a landless woman, she symbolizes the fate that awaits those incapable of protecting their property from the pasha's expropriation.

Through its authentic capture of life in an Egyptian peasant village at a critical moment in the peasant's struggle for social change, *The Land* provided international audiences with an alternate conception of the realities of Arab history and daily life. The enthusiastic and warm reception at the 1969 Cannes Film Festival where it was nominated for the Golden Palm, testified to how authentic depiction of localized social and class realities effectively communicates universal stories about oppression and political struggle. After its success in Cannes, the film was later distributed across France, which marked the first major acknowledgment of Chahine's stature as an internationally renowned filmmaker.

The film clearly depicts class struggle as manifested in the peasants' resistance to feudal domination, and alludes to how lack of unity among the peasants contributes to their defeat. But the film also engages the colonial side of the story as it intersects with issues of class exploitation. In one scene teacher Muhammad Effendi arrives in Cairo and tries to arrange a meeting with government officials to grieve the pasha's practices. As he enters a small hostel to make a telephone call to the official's headquarters he is harassed by riot police in pursuit of demonstrators protesting the king's appointment of a new pro-British prime minister to replace the previous nationalist one. Here the film points to the multilateral intersections and interactions between the struggles against feudalism, British colonialism, and local governments that rely on this class-colonial hierarchical alliance. *The Land* alludes to how these struggles demand unity between the peasants and other marginalized classes and sections of society, in both rural and urban Egypt. Thus the scene that finds Muhammad Effendi inadvertently embroiled in an anti-British demonstration as he arrives in Cairo provides a telling allegory for the entangled roots and manifestations of the village's crisis and the political predicament of the entire country. But, nonetheless, the film specifically stresses unity as the critical element of empowerment for the villages' peasants.

One scene elaborates the notion of class solidarity when it draws attention to the characteristic strength of the villagers as they unite to save a cow that has fallen down a well, as opposed to the disastrous dissonance that divides them when their shared water supply is threatened. Ibrahim Fawal describes how the scene involving the saving of the cow not only denotes the importance of class unity, but, equally as important, it complements Chahine's wider preoccupation with the notion of Arab unity:

> A telling scene occurs early in the film. The farmers are fighting over the irrigation of their pieces of land. Each is trying to be first and to divert the water to his lot. A serious fight ensues and they trade blows without mercy. Then a woman wails; her cow has fallen in the well and she, the owner, is going to be financially ruined. Suddenly they forget all about their quarrel and work together to pull the cow out of the water. The contrast between these decent people and the ruthless regime is one of the hallmarks of the film. The metaphor of solidarity is in the novel, but Chahine makes it more powerful. And here we have a motif that is dear to his heart. Ever since Saladin, unity, cooperation, and collective effort have been a touchstone in his cinema. Unity is essential in this remote Egyptian village as it is on the pan-Arab scale.[47]

Some critics, however, argued that the film implicates the Nasser regime's problematic attempt to nationalize the land, and that the film's 1930s setting was retained to mask its real intentions in criticizing government bureaucracy.[48] Others saw the film as a commentary on political repression in Egypt and the Arab world as a whole, and that the story was a call for popular resistance against such repression.[49]

Chahine's problematic relationship with the government bureaucracy, as well as his increasingly critical attitude toward its undemocratic practices, might have been in the background. But if we look at the setting within which the film was shown, and at how Chahine places himself in relation to Nasser, we may reach a different conclusion from what these critics suggest. To begin, *The Land*, both in terms of its social and historical dimensions explicitly tackles a very specific economic challenge within an equally specific period in Egyptian history, and as such, it is hard to situate the film's presentation of social and political relationships under British colonialism as allegorical to the Nasser period.

There is no doubt that the political atmosphere within which the film was screened in 1968 was highly charged. But the main preoccupation of the time was with the 1967 defeat and the Nasser government's struggle to move forward in rebuilding the army, as well as on its pronounced efforts to combat bureaucratic abuse, corrupt government practices, and the repression of dissident views. While the government was indeed under public scrutiny, all signs were that the popularity of Nasser himself and his pan-Arab national project remained very strong. One clear indication of such support was in the huge demonstrations in the aftermath of the June 1967 military defeat, when millions of people poured into the streets to reject Nasser's resignation and to call upon him to continue leading through the next stage in rebuilding. Eventually, both critics and supporters of the Nasser regime agreed on the need to reorganize and revitalize Arab resources in the fight to regain Arab control of the territory occupied by Israel in 1967. As such, *The Land*'s call for resilience in defense of one's land and national dignity was more likely to be interpreted by local audiences as an affirmation of the call for buoyant resistance in the face of defeat, and for reorganizing the resources of the nation to battle corruption and bureaucracy. As film scholar Amina Hasan suggested recently:

> The land is the basis of the nation and its future survival, and attachment to the land is an attachment to life itself. The liberation of Egyptian land which was occupied by the Israeli army after the 1967 defeat, and reclaiming national sovreignty necessitates the reorganization of political and economic life and solidarity among national forces.[50]

The strong performance by veteran actor Mahmoud al-Miligi as protagonist Muhammad Abu Swailam enhanced the message of the film as a commentary on the determination to resist all kinds of subjugation. But there is no doubt that it spoke mainly to the contemporaneous national conflict with Israel in the aftermath of the 1967 defeat. In a scene in which he calls upon the villagers to defy the pasha's attempt to take over their land, Abu Swailam actually reiterates the postwar political discourse in the Arab world, and unequivocally calls for a change of attitude and the rejection of political defeatism and apathy. He then embarks on a long monologue in which he reminds fellow villagers of the old struggles in which he and others participated during the Syrian campaign against Ottoman hegemony over greater Syria and the Arabian Peninsula, and during the Egyptian revolt against the British in 1919:

> Back then we were men and we stood up like men! But where are we today? Everyone is for himself and has forgotten about the others . . . . We need to reawake, but where . . . and how? Those days of struggle seem so far away . . . . [Back then] we became symbols of our nation: its pride, dignity, and splendor. Today we sit back and talk, complain, and bewail like old women. Some say tomorrow will be better, others that patience is a virtue, and others only babble just to say something, while others still have nothing to say . . . .

> We go to sleep babbling and we wake up babbling.... We live in babbles and our lives have turned to nonsense!

Notwithstanding his continued respect and support for Nasser, Chahine was also showing signs of skepticism about the ability of Nasser to continue his ambitious Arab unity and modernizing project without first introducing major changes to rectify fundamental and systemic political, social, and cultural problems. This skepticism was seen in how Abu Swailam's determination to carry on the fight on his own, without the tangible support and unity of other peasants, results only in a heroic, but nevertheless tragic, defeat.

To the extent that the film succeeded in projecting a new look for Egyptian and Arab political cinema, it expressed a clear evolution of Chahine's potential of political cinematic engagement. This was manifested in the film's assured amalgamation of historical images with issues of social and political change, in conjunction with a cinematic discourse which envisaged a powerful convergence between social representation and political action. As such, *The Land* was able to take Arab social realist cinema to new heights.

Almost thirty years before *The Land*, Kamal Selim directed *The Will*, which was considered to be the first Egyptian or Arab film to take a social realist approach. This same approach was later strengthened by major contributions during the 1950s and 1960s from filmmakers such as Salah Abu Seif and Tawfiq Saleh. What *The Land* achieved, however, was the creation of a new sense of how film can allude to dynamic interrelationships between the personal and the social. Simultaneously, the film provided a new perspective on how social dynamics affect and are affected by individual and collective commitment and political struggle.

While the peasants' resistance to class repression—and, metaphorically, colonial repression—was localized in history and geography, the overarching concepts of community and national rebuilding were certainly symptomatic of the power of their resolve. Chahine's cinematic depiction of social and national injustice was thus offered in conjunction with a call for solidarity and political action. Through his story of a small village in the Egyptian countryside, the filmmaker focused attention on the rich dynamics that encompass the struggle for social and national emancipation.

THE CHOICE

In comparing his two films released consecutively in 1969 and 1970, Chahine comments, "*The Land* is a story about men who choose resistance over surrender. *The Choice*, on the other hand, is about a man who capitulates and accepts retreat. However, in the process, he also becomes a traitor to himself by surrendering his soul to schizophrenia."[51]

The Choice was the first of Chahine's so-called Trilogy of Defeat, which also includes *The Sparrow* (1972) and *'Awdat al-ibn al-dal* (The Return of the Prodigal Son, 1976). The trilogy addresses the state of loss and disillusionment that began to sink into the Arab collective psyche after the 1967 defeat, and again later following the death of Nasser. The series also marks important stylistic shifts in Chahine's cinematic language in which he showed "increased interest in impressionistic visual representation, and increased disregard of classical linear storytelling techniques."[52]

The screenplay of *The Choice* was written by Egyptian novelist Naguib Mahfouz and, according to Yves Thoraval, reflected the novelist's state of mind after the 1967 defeat. During this period Mahfouz "shut himself away in a silence broken only by a few symbolic stories," and the story of *The Choice* was typical of this reclusive period.[53] The film tells the story of Sayyid, an aloof but thriving writer who appears to have killed his identical twin brother Mahmoud, a down-to-earth working class man who cherishes life and enjoys a genuine connection with ordinary people. After the murder Sayyid takes on his brother's identity, along with his own, in a puzzling plot that foreshadows the stylized psychological twists of the thrillers of the 1990s and beyond.

When Mahmoud, a worker on Alexandria's waterfront is found murdered, his twin brother Sayyid—a well-respected and well-connected writer—becomes the prime suspect. As the investigators begin to work on the case they come to suspect an intimate relationship between Mahmoud and Sharifa, his brother's wife. They also begin to discover a troubling correlation between the stories told in Sayyid's novels and Mahmoud's uninhibited lifestyle. But when Mahmoud turns up alive, a schizophrenic union between the two brothers seems likely.

In an interview Chahine reflects upon his anxiety during this period as symptomatic of pan-Arab despair as they entered into a long phase of political confusion, self-destruction, and anguish. He stresses that war and government corruption following the 1967 defeat and Nasser's death in 1970 caused a state of national confusion. In this context, people began to suffer the consequences of losing a clear sense of their national identity. *The Choice* sought to tackle these emerging anxieties. Chahine contends that during the late 1960s and early 1970s, "it was difficult to convey a clear and cohesive story . . . one begins to talk about schizophrenia because there is something that is not right." This is why the film's main questions are posed in connection with a confusion about identity, Chahine explains:

> [W]ho killed whom? Are Mahmoud and Sayyid two brothers and one killed the other, or are they two people who physically resemble each other? When the film was made it was necessary, both politically and socially, to tell the story in this manner.... We were exhausted and very confused and the film had to be similarly constructed.[54]

The Choice works well as a thriller because the plot is structured in a way that emphasizes the dichotomies and confusions that characterize the lives of the two presumed brothers. The film's structure departs from earlier Chahine films in that it further reduces its reliance on classical linear storytelling: it is built around the hallucinations of the main character. Instead of relying on the linear rules of cause and effect in communicating the story, the film juxtaposes contrasting moments and episodes in the lives of the dual personalities of Mahmoud and Sayyid and their ambiguous relationships with Sharifa.

The film stylistically augments a sense of loss and anxiety that will become an increasingly important feature in Chahine's future films. This is expressed through its reliance on fantasy and dream sequences, stream of consciousness outbursts, flashbacks of imaginary events, nervous editing and the recurring use of a foreboding red color. All this is presented in conjunction with a complex storyline which defies any clear sense of a beginning, middle, or end. The characters are at once emblematic of the social and political variety within Arab societies, but are also unrestricted in how they react to specific situations. Kamal Ramzi argues that Chahine's characters after *The Choice* became vividly realistic, but also as unpredictable as the chaotic changes that were occurring on the social and political levels, in the end making them natural parts of the filmmaker's freewheeling interpretation of history.[55]

There is no doubt that an important aspect of the film's uniqueness is the originality of its cinematic language and its limited reliance on dialogue. As one critic pointed out, the entire film almost looks like an impressionistic painting with powerful color patterns. The film utilizes effective camera movement and frame compositions and angles, but it did not appeal to a mainstream audience.[56] While *The Choice* enjoyed an enthusiastic reception from most Egyptian and Arab film critics, many of them clearly pointed out the failure of the film to connect with the audience. Viewers in screenings would rise around the middle of the film and start complaining that they didn't understand anything.[57] Another explanation for the hostility with which the film was publicly received might have to do with the way *The Choice* denied the audience any chance of identifying with the characters: "all characters and for all intents and purposes were despicable, and as such they failed to give any sense of hope."[58] Several critics shared the view that despite its best intentions the film lacked the edge to bring its intended message to people. According to Darwish Bargawi, "the contradictory use of realistic and surrealistic styles," obscured the film's important critique of the crisis of some of our intellectuals as reflected in their two-faced personalities. In the end, the film was reduced into "an intellectual exercise that lacked artistic and content coherence."[59]

Not all critics, however, saw the complexity of the film as an indication of Chahine's inability to communicate his message. Sami al-Salamuni, for example, argued that Chahine once again proved that he is the only Egyptian filmmaker who, in light of the "current state of intellectual stagnation and idleness," remains capable of making great art. For Salamuni, such a skill is needed to challenge "dominant trends that our [Arab] audience suffers from today [1971]."[60] Salamuni argues that Chahine's genuine sensitivity to Egyptian hopes and concerns compels him to warn against confusion by demonstrating its nihilistic consequences:

> More than anyone who is trained cinematically in Cairo, Chahine remains an Egyptian artist to the bone with great sensitivity to Egyptian issues and concerns. To be clear, being Egyptian is never about language and accent, but is in the serious commitment to Egypt, and to dealing with Egyptian people's fears and hopes. Therefore Chahine's uniqueness is not in his techniques, but rather in his consistent and desperate commitment to say something of substance about his society. This clearly varies between times when things are more or less clear, and other times when things are confused and uncertain.... Chahine gives a sense of these fluctuations in his films. In The Choice, Chahine has reached his intellectual and political maturity at a time when the state of affairs in Egypt in 1970 began to force it to make a choice between Sayyid, the opportunist intellectual, and Mahmoud, the free spirited honest sailor.... The two are the same person, which means that they could be any one of us. This is why 'the choice' is ours to make.[61]

Rafiq al-Sabban shares al-Salamuni's view, seeing the struggle between the two contending personalities, and the death of the bohemian Mahmoud—who seeks spontaneity and passion instead of luxury living—as a message about our time, a time when it is increasingly impossible to reconciliate between the two archetypes.[62] And while al-Sabban expresses apprehension about Chahine's incorporation of "unnecessary elements of a Hollywood style thriller," he nevertheless considers the film a major achievement, particularly on the level of Chahine's original mastery of cinematic technique.[63]

For her part, Amina Hasan mainly saw the film as a commentary on the problem of the "inability of Egyptian bourgeois intellectuals to represent the aspirations of the popular masses, and [this class's] opportunist perplexity in mixing between holding power and personal profit."[64] Similarly, Samir Farid saw *The Choice* more specifically as an indictment of Egypt's intellectuals who were incapable of absorbing the changing needs of their society and their country in the aftermath of the 1967 defeat. He argues that the unsympathetic depiction of Sayyid functions as a self-deprecating indulgence into which Chahine boldly—and uniquely—ventures. More importantly, however, Chahine's reflection on his own hopes, desires, fears, and anxieties presents a clear indication of the kind of dilemma that most Egyptian and Arab intellectuals had experienced prior to and after the 1967 War—the kind of dilemma that forces them to make choices. Sayyid, Farid suggests, represents a "typical bourgeois intellectual who seeks power and is ready to sell his soul for the luxury apartment, the car, the trip to Paris, and who is also ready to kill the best of what he has: his dignity and his honesty."[65]

While critiquing *The Choice* for its structural difficulty, Saad al-Din Tawfiq acknowledged that many audiences utterly enjoyed the originality of this cinematic venture. He also praised Chahine's novelty in conveying his political statement: "the film offered a warning, and an alert of an incoming danger." The end of the film exemplifies this message in a beautifully crafted manner when we are left with the flashing red lights of a medical emergency vehicle. "The flashing red lingers for a long time, and no 'End' credits appear . . . a clear mark of Chahine's resistance to such an 'ending'."[66]

By the time Chahine made *The Choice*, he had gained a reputation as being a politically conscious filmmaker whose work, one way or another, held some kind of a serious message. Chahine's achievements with *Jamila* and *Saladin* and the less successful, yet highly praised, *The Land*, sealed this reputation, and shaped the way in which his later films would be received and interpreted by both local film critics and audiences alike. So when *The Choice* was released, critical expectations and attention were focused on solving the film's plot twist in conjunction with solving the significance of its political puzzle.

On the surface, the story pointed out the dichotomy between intellectuals who isolate themselves from the real world—and even from their own intellectual history—and working-class people who remained true to their collective cultural roots. The symbolic dimension of the story, however, impacts a broader discourse. *The Choice* presented an insightful and complex reading of various aspects of the Arab psyche in the aftermath of the 1967 defeat and the gradual disintegration of Nasser's pivotal role in providing a sense of purpose and embodiment for the Arab national liberation project. In this regard, the film mirrored the era's increased uncertainty, skepticism, and disillusionment. Furthermore, as Chahine was working on *The Choice*, the Arab world was entering a phase of internal strife. Just before his death in September 1970 Nasser hosted a special summit for the Arab League to deal with the bloody clashes between the newly emerging Palestinian resistance and the Jordanian army. Nasser died soon after bidding farewell to one of the Arab heads of state at the airport after the end of the summit. After its expulsion from Jordan and its relocation in Lebanon, the Palestinian resistance would soon become an element of instability in a country that would eventually explode into civil war in 1975. Further instability in the area would follow in the form of internal strife as well as in increased divisions between Arab countries.

Chahine's film stresses the contempt the writer Sayyid has for his adventurous brother as well as for the limitations and formalities associated with his bourgeois lifestyle. On one level, *The Choice* works as an allusion to the dilemma of Arab intellectuals regarding their role within the reality of social and political turmoil that engulfs their country and nation. In this regard,

The Choice: the dilemmas of post-revolutionary intellectuals (photo: Gamal Fahmy).

Chahine ponders his own role as an organic intellectual who has become skeptical about the direction that he is about to take during a complex period in his nation's history. Ibrahim Fawal describes how Chahine projects his own anxiety and confusion on Sayyid's character by directly referring to Sayyid as the writer of *Cairo Station*:

> In his indictment of the Egyptian intellectual, Chahine does not spare himself. A scene at the [culture] ministry is quite revealing. When Sayyid goes to the ministry to inquire about his invitation to attend a literary conference abroad, an official is so impressed by his writing that he queries him about the sources of all the rich characters in his dramas. 'And Qinawi ... and that delicious Hannouma,' he asks, 'where did you meet such wonderful people?' Those familiar with Chahine's cinema know that Qinawi and Hannouma are the main characters in his film Cairo Station. In The Choice Sayyid is presented as the author of that screenplay; in reality Chahine is the film's auteur.[67]

But Chahine also juxtaposes Sayyid's dead-end existence against the free and down-to-earth lifestyle of Mahmoud. While on the surface, Mahmoud's character is simply that of an individual who chooses to distance himself from responsibilities and commitments, the context within which he is presented makes his attitude an expression of authenticity, honesty, and substance in fundamental contrast to his brother's façade. And inasmuch as he becomes a model for those resisting the temptations of petit bourgeois opportunism, the role of Mahmoud offers hope for the revalidation of human authenticity over capitalist consumerism.

In a scene at the circus we watch a boy cry after he loses his grasp of the balloon that Mahmoud had given him. As the balloon flies away, Mahmoud gently wipes away the child's tears and allows his own balloon to slip away from his hand and float up to the sky. Two nearby women then free their balloons, and soon the rest of the children do the same and the sky is filled with the colorful beauty of dozens of balloons. Mahmoud's ability to sustain the child within allows him to more easily relate to children and see beauty in the simple things in life, even as it protects him from obsessing over shallow luxuries, as seen in the football sequence. Mahmoud is playing football with some children near the waterfront; as the ball is thrown his way, he catches it and robustly shoots it back in the kids' direction. The following shot finds Sayyid surrounded by a group of high-ranking officials at a meeting table; a ball slides across the table in his direction, and Mahmoud quietly seizes it and hands it over to his assistant who takes it and locks it in a closet.

On another level, Chahine develops a complex characterization of Sayyid and Mahmoud as archetypes of their respective bourgeois and working classes. But instead of simply pointing out dichotomies, the film expounds on the symbiotic love/hate relationship between the two brothers/classes. It is a relationship that mirrors the new form of manipulation tendered by a new class, the nouveau riche—a powerful group that knows how to draw on the sympathies of the working and marginalized classes of society because that is where they came from. For Sayyid, his brother's life experiences provide the inspiration for his stories—and thereby the financial resources that support his personal lifestyle and ambitions. Their interdependent relationship mirrors that shared by many who are now on the top, "having been able to climb the social ladder and now act and live with two faces and two masks."[68]

Mahmoud's interest in his sister-in-law Sharifa reflects his dream of becoming part of the upper class with all the privileges that such a status entails. Sharifa, the daughter of a high ranking bureaucrat in the Ministry of Culture who has a close relationship with Mahmoud, acts as a mediator between the two classes. But in the end Sharifa is incapable of defining or understanding where she belongs; like her husband she resists severing ties with her adopted class, but finds no comfort within the class from which she came. She remains alone in her own contradictions, a symbol of her inability to resolve the paradox of her ambiguous class identity. Other characters in the film reflect similar dialectics: the love/hate relationship between Farag, the veteran police officer, and his young assistant Ra'uf, functions as another parallel to the brothers' bond, as well as to the unresolved contradictions that mar Sharifa's attempts at self-realization.

The film looks at the issue of class and class anxiety as a pretext for understanding the contradictory dynamics of postcolonial politics. In this regard, *The Choice* poses the question of whether this entire political structural dynamic can recuperate a revolutionary role to move forward the goals of national and social liberation:

> The film does not talk about social struggles like in The Land, neither about government corruption like in The Sparrow, but rather talks about a whole social system with all new rationalizations, ways of thinking, values, and behavior. It is a system that sets up a different political and economic agenda from that of the old system, but is also incapable of actually departing from it.... Chahine indeed exposed and pointed out this dilemma for the first time in Arab cinema.[69]

Shmeit's emphasis on the film's political significance is of great importance. Equally as important, however, is to note that the film represented a watershed in how Chahine presented his films. On the one hand, Chahine was responding to the worldwide emergence of new approaches to popular culture that offered renewed hopes for creating production and reception models that provided alternatives to the commodity-oriented mass culture. On the other hand, the film also propounded a distinctive form of popular culture that, while originating in the classical generic traditions of the thriller, has transformed these generic conventions through plot ambiguity and through creating a basis for a more vigorous and challenging reception dynamic. Within these cinematic rudiments of a subverted genre, the film assumed an ideological significance as a statement on current-day politics. Within these parameters, Chahine engaged the question of popular culture in a challenging manner. Rather than endorsing popular cinematic traditions in an unproblematized approach, *The Choice* deconstructed and eventually reconstructed a new subversive power for such traditions. The film did not hesitate to use the state of confusion within the postwar Arab world as a point of departure for a different kind of popular culture that Chahine felt was in need of re-energizing.

The new phase through which the Arab national liberation movement was venturing differed radically from that of the 1950s and 1960s. The simplicity that characterized the way many looked at the struggle against colonialism and the notion of social change was itself coming to an end. Political discourse increasingly shifted its emphasis toward re-examination, reassessment, and self-criticism. Within such a paradigm, clear-cut linear models for popular culture's engagement with politically involved films no longer seemed sufficient.

5

THE PRODIGAL DIRECTOR

President Nasser's premature death at the age of fifty-two in September 1970 shocked Egypt in an unprecedented manner. Nasser died just after the closing of a summit of Arab leaders to discuss the clashes between the Jordanian army and the Palestinian resistance. His funeral the next day was considered the largest in history with more than five million Egyptians participating in it. Nasser's death sent shock waves across the Arab world, and signaled the beginning of a new era in contemporary Arab history. Much of the left–nationalist and socialist policies adopted by the Nasser revolution were gradually but firmly abandoned by President Anwar Sadat's new government. These political transformations would eventually reverberate across the Arab region and would result in a steady decline in the influence and strength of the pan-Arab nationalist left and the Marxist-oriented political groups in the region.

Newly re-established political relationships between Egypt and the United States would contribute to changes in Arab governmental positions on the Palestinian dilemma and pave the way for official discourse that would advocate *al-tatbi'*—the normalization of relationships between Egypt and Israel. Despite the Egyptian and Syrian armies' relative success in the October 1973 War against Israel, events in the aftermath of the war would bring about major divisions between Arab countries, particularly over Sadat's signing of the Camp David Accords with Israel.

The 1967 defeat and Nasser's death in 1970 eventually brought about major political changes in the Arab world. Policy changes on the national and international levels resulted in major shifts on the economic, social, and political levels. In Egypt, international alliances with the Soviet Union and the central emphasis on the role of the Non-Allied Movement (comprised mainly of third world countries just emerging from colonial rule), were progressively supplanted by the creation of a new alliance with the United States. Internally, earlier policies that had favored socialist and government-oriented intervention in the social and economic spheres were replaced with the Egyptian government's free enterprise-oriented policy of openness.

As these shifts began to take shape within Egypt—the largest and most influential Arab country—a general confusion and lack of orientation began to take hold in other Arab countries. The most vulnerable country in the region was Lebanon, which, due to its sensitive religious and political balance, along with the presence of large numbers of Palestinian refugees, and ongoing political squabbles between regional powers, began to slide into a new and dangerous state of affairs. With new political uncertainties, various internal forces were vying to claim new grounds, and by 1975 Lebanon was engulfed in a major civil war that continued through the 1982 Israeli invasion that saw parts of the country occupied until the year 2000.

The immediate post-Nasser period also represented a new stage for Egyptian cultural industries, as well as for Egyptian and Arab intellectuals. After the October War, the Sadat government began to implement policies that aimed at gradually abolishing publicly supported economic and social enterprises, and to encourage private enterprise in general. This policy resulted in the reprivatization of many components of the public sector.

Despite Egyptian cinema's many successes and the intellectual, artistic, and political engagement of many of its filmmakers, the industry was not able to sustain a commercially viable base for its development. The Egyptian film industry was already experiencing difficulties as a result of the growing influence of television, which was introduced in Egypt in the early 1960s. The number of movie theaters in Egypt "began a steady decline, from 350 in 1955 to less than 250 twenty years later [in 1975]."[1] Roy Armes suggests that despite continued taxes on foreign movies,

> the flood of foreign film imports in conjunction with remained taxes on cinema receipts were kept at high level, and as a result, losses by the state organization amounting to some five million Egyptian pounds had led to a virtual cessation of state production by the early 1970s, even before the effects of Anwar Sadat's new and very different policies were felt.[2]

But while the privatization of the economy was fast-tracked in most sectors, much of the cultural sector, including media and film production, remained largely under the institutional and political control of the government.

As a new generation of skilled television and film workers failed to make any significant international mark, and the older generation of filmmakers increasingly turned to foreign coproductions, Egyptian cinema's dominance began to wane:

> The situation was aggravated by the difficulties the older filmmakers experienced while working in Egypt during Sadat's rule: the three films Chahine made in the late 1970s were all produced with the Algerian state production company, ONCIC; Tawfiq Saleh, after making The Betrayed (1972) in Syria from Ghassan Kanafani's celebrated Palestinian story, Men in the Sun, went to Iraq to become head of the film institute in Baghdad; and Abou Seif's only feature film since 1978 was al-Qadissia, made in Iraq in 1980.[3]

On the political level, the new government was bent on moving the country away from the nationalist and left-oriented politics associated with the Nasser period; the Nasser government's bureaucratic corruption and repressive political excesses were used to attack the entire socialist and pan-Arab nationalist ideological viewpoint.

In cinema, the outcome of this ideological turnaround was the appearance of new kinds of films, among which were those that took aim at Nasser's socialist policies and what would become commonly known as their "'centers of power' *(marakiz al-quwwa)*, a term associated at the time with the previous government's internal security service."[4] Furthermore, the new regime was also seeking new allies in its struggle against the Egyptian left. A marriage of convenience with Muslim fundamentalism began to materialize in attacks on left-oriented intellectualism:

> In 1972 Sadat's government imposed severe restrictions on what could be seen or heard on stage or screen. It lumped all foreign and Egyptian films together, permitting only those that were fit for audiences of all ages: children and adults were treated as if they had the same mentality and taste. Ironically, on that same day, 14 June 1972, the Egyptian film critics announced the establishment of their own society, which pledged to defend freedom of expression.[5]

Since the mid-1970s Chahine's work had been becoming more daring in both its themes and its stylistic experimentation. After the major critical success of his 1972 ONCIC Algerian coproduction, *The Sparrow,* which dealt with the crushing effects of the 1967 *Naksa* (the defeat in the war with Israel), Chahine made his dark and politically charged musical *The Return of the Prodigal Son* (1976), which portrayed the inter-Arab strife and wars in the post-Nasser period. This film was also coproduced with the Algerian government's production institute, and signaled Chahine's increased reliance on foreign coproduction, and his move toward creating his own independent film production and distribution company.

Immediately following the production of *The Sparrow* Chahine created Misr al-'Alamiya (Misr International) with his nephew Gabriel Khoury, and since then the company had produced films of chahine and other independent filmmakers. The company's shrewd business practices provided Chahine with the alternative financing base he needed to survive following the collapse of the Egyptian public sector, and has gone on to provide career-launching support for emerging Egyptian filmmakers ever since. Later, the company would secure the financial support of the French Ministry of Culture and French television that allowed Chahine to make more expensive films, including *Adieu Bonaparte!* (1985), *Iskindiriya kaman wa kaman* (released internationally as Alexandria Again and Forever, also as Alexandria, Again and Again, 1990), and *al-Muhajir* (The Emigrant, 1994), along with several others.

CRISIS AND RESILIENCY IN *THE SPARROW*

The Sparrow is based on a real scandal, to which contemporary Egyptian newspapers referred as "the case of the big thieves and the little thieves." The situation occurred just before the war in 1967. From the outset *The Sparrow* lays out two parallel events. It begins with images of newspaper headlines from the days before the outbreak of the 1967 War. The headlines mainly focus on increased tensions with Israel, but a story in smaller print refers to Abu Khudr, a wanted man hiding in Upper Egypt. In the background we hear the voice of the leftist Egyptian singer-songwriter Sheikh Imam, singing a tune that we will hear repeatedly throughout the film, "We are all travel companions in a long and hard journey."

Based on a story by leftist writer Lotfi al-Khouli, who also cowrote the script with Chahine, *The Sparrow* is set in the few days before, during, and after the June 1967 War. Ra'uf, a young police officer, is sent to a village in Upper Egypt to investigate the actions of Abu Khudr, a crime lord who has been terrorizing the people of the area. As he arrives at the village, Ra'uf meets Yusuf, a young journalist, who is investigating the same case. The journalist, however, is reporting the issue in the context of a scandal involving Abu Khudr and the

The Sparrow: Sheikh Ahmad: rebellion from the midst of religion (photo: Gamal Fahmy).

high-ranking government officials and businessmen who are stealing and selling machinery originally destined for a major industrial plant in Upper Egypt. To cover their tracks, the officials send a large police contingent to the area, and Abu Khudr is killed in an ambush. But Ra'uf and Yusuf decide to continue the investigation in order to expose the real criminals behind the theft, setting up headquarters in the Cairo home of Bahiya, a mutual friend. As they embark on their investigative journey the young journalist begins to suspect that his own father, a high-ranking party official, former feudal pasha, and big businessman, might be involved in the cover-up of the scandal. As in his examination of the role of the intellectual within the revolution through the character of Sayyid in *The Choice*, here Chahine once again presents the image of a bewildered Arab intellectual—Yusuf—confronted by his own demons and failures in the midst of momentous social and political upheavals.

For his part, Ra'uf is inspired by the possibility that his birth father might not be the senior security chief who married his mother, but rather a musician who used to write songs about working-class Egyptians and sing love songs about his country. Just as the two men begin to connect the dots and recognize the extent of the officials' involvement, the war with Israel breaks out and Egyptian and other Arab armies suffer a humiliating defeat. President Nasser announces his resignation and millions of people spontaneously flock to the streets of Cairo to proclaim their refusal to surrender.

The Sparrow is structured around several stories, all of which connect with the principal storyline that begins with the investigation of the Abu Khudr case and ends with the postwar demonstrations in Cairo. The story of the investigation initiated by the film's two protagonists, the police officer and the journalist, branches out to become an exploration of the personal and the political in Egyptian society. The shocking final moments of the film culminate in unanticipated defeat and defiance.

A key character in the film is Sheikh Ahmad, who emulates in many ways the real life personality of Sheikh Imam, the singer of the opening song about Bahiya. Imam at the time was a well-known cult figure among young leftists in Egypt and around the Arab world, where his songs became anthems in demonstrations after the 1967 defeat. In the film, Sheikh Ahmad is a former student of religion at al-Azhar who now sells political and religious books. He loves women, drinking, and singing, and is a politically contradictory man: a left-wing religious person who was interested in attending an institution which is known for its conservative outlook on life and politics.

Sheikh Ahmad has not been allowed to open a small bookstore, and has also been refused entry to the army. He has become fixed on avenging a relative who was killed by Abu Khudr, and refuses to allow the government to deprive him of his right to kill the outlaw. But Ra'uf denies Ahmad his revenge when he ties him up as the police attack Abu Khudr and kill him. Ahmad eventually joins Ra'uf and Yusuf in their quest to expose the big thieves. Toward the end of the film, it is Sheikh Ahmad who sobs as he listens to Nasser tending his resignation on television, and speaks out the bitter reality—"we were defeated without even knowing it!" Sheikh Ahmad's words reflect the overwhelming sense of disenfranchisement felt by Arab peoples after the losses of the war.

While *The Sparrow*'s storyline develops through a chain of events instigated by Ra'uf and Yusuf as they embark on investigating the scandal, it is consistently sidelined by the stories of other characters. One such character is a smart and endearing boy from Upper Egypt who keeps popping up to insist Ra'uf and Yusuf allow him to hitch a ride with them to Cairo. The boy is hoping to go to al-Hussein where he plans to work and get some money to help out his poor family at home. The determined boy keeps appearing out of nowhere to remind the two of their earlier promise to take him to Cairo. In the end, we see him pass by on the road, squeezed into a crowded taxi, and throwing insults at them for reneging on their promise. The boy's resolve is symbolic of the new generation that Chahine hopes still has the innocence, determination, and focus to fulfill the dreams of the revolution and transcend the cynicism of its earlier generation.

Other characters include Bahiya's husband, an Egyptian nicknamed Johnny who is the neighborhood drunk who speaks lovingly of the good old days of colonialism; and Fatma, Bahiya's young daughter who is determined to be a responsible citizen during the war and to play a role in the investigation. She is also the object of Ra'uf's sexual fantasies, a dream that turns into a nightmare as he wakes up to the sounds of war on July 6, 1967.

The role of Bahiya, the strong working-class mother who determinedly supports her neighbors, functions as the symbol of Mother Egypt, and her story ultimately becomes the point of convergence that mediates all the others. It is Bahiya who later leads the flock of demonstrators through the streets Cairo shouting "No!" to Nasser's resignation. A high-ranking official in the Socialist Union (the ruling party) looking down at the crowd frantically asks one of his aids, "Who are these people? Are they ours?" And when the throng reaches a bridge, their sheer number creates a bottleneck that impedes the approaching caravan of trucks with their cargo of stolen industrial material. As Bahiya leads and then melts into the mass of demonstrators in the streets of Cairo, we hear Sheikh Imam's voice singing the film's theme song in the background:

Egypt is you, captivating Bahiya . . .
Age turns gray, yet you remain young and glowing
[Age] passes by, yet you are always thriving
Long nights are come and gone
But your endurance remains the same
And your smile remains the same

Just like *The Land*, *The Sparrow* was enthusiastically received at the Cannes Film Festival, and received two additional screenings "to accommodate the requests of film critics who wanted to see it after the first two screenings were sold out."[6] Chahine's film, along with another film dealing with the 1967 War by Ali Abd al-Khalek (*A Song on the Way*, 1972), was banned by the Egyptian government, and *The Sparrow* was released to the public only after the successful 1973 offensive against Israel—with thirty-eight scenes cut from it. As critic Osama Khalil noted, one can only wonder what could have possibly motivated its release at this juncture.[7]

The 1974 release accompanied the production and release of several films that strongly criticized the corruption and anti-democratic measures of the Nasser period. Hasan 'Abd al-Rasul draws a direct connection between the timing of the film's release and the Sadat government's campaign against *marakiz al-quwa*.⁸ Films such as *al-Karnak* (Ali Badrakhan, 1975) played a major role in pointing out the weaknesses and mistakes associated with the Nasser period, but they were also used by the Sadat government to enhance a campaign against the previous government as well as its political orientation. In this regard, the campaign channeled support for the new approach that was taking hold in Egyptian politics that by the mid-1970s would result in the severing of relations with the Soviet Union and the initiation of a new alliance with the United States; the signing of a peace treaty with Israel; and the reprivatization of most of the public sector.

However, even after numerous scenes were cut from it, the film was seen by few Egyptians. *The Sparrow*'s complex and deeply entrenched revolutionary sentiment resulted in a limited release to only a few Egyptian theaters for very brief runs. Today, the film remains banned from Egyptian television and is not available in video stores in the country.

The film received harsh criticism from right-wing circles. One critic even applauded the government's decision to not release it until after the offending scenes were cut. Hasan Imam Omar attacked Chahine's "opportunistic" cooperation with the Algerian government "which clearly had its own political agenda" to produce a film that appealed to western audiences and did not reflect "Egyptian taste and points of view."⁹ But while the film was not welcome in Egypt during—or after—Sadat's reign, it still assumed a cult status within the Arab world. It was warmly and enthusiastically received in most Arab capitals, and soon became a hallmark of new Arab leftist cultural criticism. One Algerian newspaper described *The Sparrow* as the first Arab film that sought to engage in assessing the objective conditions that led to the 1967 defeat.¹⁰ The warm reception of the film in Lebanon after it was shown at the Brummana Film Festival a couple of months before its release reflected the strong impact of the film on Arab audiences.

However, the film did receive strong criticism from some leftist critics. Osama Khalil, for example, accused Chahine and author Lotfi al-Khouli of reflecting "petit-bourgeois viewpoints," which were embodied in the film's adoption of the viewpoints of "a journalist, an officer, a simple Egyptian woman, a drunk, and an anglicized Egyptian girl." He argues that the film turns the critique of corruption into a moral, rather than a class, issue. discounting the petit bourgeois' responsibility in the failure of the public sector to play a positive role in forging a "genuine socialist and working-class-controlled economy."¹¹

While the film did not initially have access to an Egyptian audience, the opening of *The Sparrow* in Lebanon's Brummana Film Festival in September

1973 led to critical attention for it around the Arab world, as well as in Egypt itself. Critics welcomed the film as a major Arab cinematic and political event. Discussions about the film took place at the festival and critics signed a statement in which they called for lifting the Egyptian government's ban on the film, considering it among the most important films in the history of Arab cinema and that both artistically and politically it offers a self-critical milestone that Arabs and Egyptians in particular should welcome instead of suppressing.

Ali Abu Shadi saw in *The Sparrow* another new phase in the development of Chahine's cinematic language, particularly when it came to the filmmaker's use of unfamiliar camera angles, symbolic color patterns, and his multicharacter development strategy; citing the film's multicharacter survey, its effective use of music and dance elements, in addition to the symbolic employment of the characters. All this, the Egyptian critic stresses, might have threatened the film's ability to connect with mainstream audiences. Yet, such techniques still signaled an important step in the maturation of Arab political cinema.[12]

The Sparrow, along with the song by the Egyptian duo of poet Ahmad Fu'ad Nagm and singer Sheikh Imam, became emblematic within grassroots and popular left-wing movements around the Arab world in the mid- to late 1970s. The film, along with the entire Nagm/Imam repertoire of songs, eventually came to represent the movement that emerged in the aftermath of Nasser's death. Increasingly, this movement expressed indignation with Sadat's attacks on the revolution's achievements and anticolonial policies, but also acknowledged and strongly criticized the Nasser regime's inability to transcend its petit bourgeois roots.

Several writers and critics saw the film as the first serious Arab attempt to address the politics of defeat and social revolution in the aftermath of the 1967 War. One contemporary critic points out the film's unique contribution to Arab cinema and how it broke with the thematic and stylistic timidity of earlier politically conscious Arab films. Ra'uf Tawfiq gives a vivid account of the film's impact on the politics of filmmaking in Egypt and the Arab world:

> Finally, The Sparrow is being shown in Cairo. After numerous efforts to ban the film due to censors' objections and the nasty campaigns against it by critics, some of which even called for withdrawing Chahine's Egyptian citizenship and for burning the film and executing Chahine in Tahrir Square, the film can be finally seen by an Egyptian audience.... No film reflects the moment of resilience that erupted on the streets of Cairo and the rest of the Arab world after Nasser's resignation on June 9, 1967 more than the one Chahine captures toward the end of this brilliant film.... Through an

original and advanced cinematic structure, Chahine presents a first-rate political film which does not rely on slogans and instead subtly utilizes the power of cinematic storytelling.... For Bahiya, the strong Egyptian woman and symbol of Egypt who lives in al-Azhar district at the heart of Egypt, understanding the issues facing her society and country is instinctive, and her life has taught her not to be easily manipulated by anyone. When the entire country falls into the trap of defeatism and puzzlement in the aftermath of the horrendous events of June 1967, Bahiya is the first to shout her rejection and express determination to continue the struggle as mass resilience announces the new birth of Egypt.

The film represents the most important artistically ambitious event in Cairo today, and it signifies a new start for serious cinema in Egypt.... This can be easily seen in the reaction of the audience and how they cheer and clap during several sequences in the film.... This all proves that our audience has not been totally lost to the karate, sex, and cabaret films, and that our audience still recognizes good work when it sees it.[13]

Viola Shafik suggests, that *The Sparrow* is considered "one of the most widely circulated cinematic variations the raped nation allegory, namely that of the (female) nation under siege."[14] The film certainly presents a powerful allegorical depiction of Egypt's defeat during the disastrous 1967 events. More to the point, however, from its outset, the film establishes two parallel political dimensions for its thematic critique of the state of affairs in Egypt on the eve of the 1967 War. There is an external dimension which relates to the officer in the Egyptian army, and there is another that depicts his brother, the police officer. They are both leaving their family and home, the first to participate in the war, and the second to help hunt down a dangerous criminal in Upper Egypt. The film is therefore clearly conscious of the two dangers facing Egypt. Soon, however, the story of the army officer gives way to the second story and the focus of the film shifts to exploring issues of internal corruption and decaying social structure as critical elements behind the defeat on the front with Israel: no victory on the battlefront is possible without a strong and self-motivated people with a genuine stake in their revolution and their country.

Through its portrayal of a cross-section of characters within Egyptian society on the eve of milestone national events that will change virtually the entire political landscape of the area, the film offered testimony to the state within which the entire Arab national project was entering. No character in the film moves in a vacuum but rather through the specificity of the historical period of which they are part. This allows for some clarity as to the film's analytical perspective, and how it considers the political, military, social, and economic situation of Egypt at the time. But the film does not rely on any one star or elaborate on a single character's development by way of positioning itself vis-à-vis specific viewpoints on the issues involved. Rather, the film shuns conventional linearity within which a specific protagonist goes through a crisis and eventually reaches some point of resolution. Instead, the film utilizes a polyphonic observational outlook on a multiplicity of characters as they relate and interact with economic corruption, as it, in turn, interacts with the political events that are unfolding on the front with Israel. As such, *The Sparrow* allows its characters a space to more intensely interact with their political surroundings; providing an effective milieu for the discussion of the structural and political problems that contributed to weakening the Nasser regime and eventually aborted its pan-Arab and anticolonial ambitions, and its programs for social and political change.

Questions about the ability to conduct a war while people continue to be politically disenfranchised; the manipulation of socialist slogans by corrupt and profiteering bureaucrats; the Palestine question; the role of Nasser; and the concept of national self-determination, were all at the heart of the political discussions that preoccupied Egyptians and Arabs in the late 1960s and

The Sparrow: One destiny on a road trip to defeat (photo: Gamal Fahmy).

throughout the 1970s. *The Sparrow* brought all these questions to the fore. Chahine himself saw the film as his personal testimony to a watershed period in Egyptian and Arab history; one in which he still saw new possibilities for overcoming the dire situation following the 1967 defeat. The film opens with a prologue signed by Chahine himself that summarizes his motivation for making the film:

> On the streets of Cairo, Algiers, Tunis, and Baghdad and all Arab capitals young people stop me and ask, "tell us, Youssef, what really happened in June 1967? How did we end up with such a defeat, and why? We thought that we were ready to fight!" All these sincere and courageous people, these sparrows that I love, did not hesitate to flock into the streets in June 1967 to express their readiness to take on the new challenge.... To all these people, today we try, through The Sparrow, to illuminate few of the national and international elements which they, without their knowledge, became victims to.

While some western critics saw the film as an expression of his disillusionment with the Nasser revolution after 1967, Chahine himself was adamant in insisting that he saw himself as integral to the goals of the revolution and that his critique came from within this revolution rather from outside of it. In an interview, Chahine explicitly identified himself as a Nasserist and strongly condemned the events following Nasser's death and how they destroyed the hopes and dreams for economic and social change in Egypt:

> I am a one million percent Nasserist... even now. I can assure you that if Nasser was still alive today my views would not be different in this regard. One only matures gradually: one starts young and slowly learns politics and economics.... Today [2004] they have appointed us a 'disaster' [Egyptian prime minister Dr. Atef Ebeid] who, while supposed to be an economist, has no sense about 'ethics'.... He was in charge of privatization before he became prime minister... all they have been doing with this privatization is selling public property because they are broke. Three quarters of the money is going to Switzerland![15]

But the film's powerful message could not have reverberated without Chahine's technical mastery in projecting a feel for the tensions and anxieties associated with the progression of events. Chahine's use of the camera in particular seemed to dominate the affectivity of the cinematic text. The final scene, in which Bahiya embodies the allegoric sparrow of the film's title, exemplifies how Chahine's camera works to emphasize the film's main theme. Bahiya moves forward toward the camera with piercing eyes, as the chanting flock follows her, flailing their defiant hands toward the sky like the wings of birds finally released from their cages. The throng marches toward the camera, and then past it, symbolically breaking free of the limitations of the cinematic frame. The scene powerfully captures the film's message of resilience as well as its emphasis on the need for the Arab masses to take control of their own fate.

But the optimism of the film's politics transcends the issues of the 1967 defeat to illustrate Chahine's stance on the role of women in the struggle for national liberation. Bahiya's motherly image is constantly subverted by the film's references to her many contributions to the rebellion. She is presented as a working woman—a seamstress for a film company—whose hard work offers a reminder of the disparity between the illusory, constructed cinematic reality, and that of the material reality of film construction, taking place behind the scenes by hard-working men and women.

This reflexive reference by Chahine establishes Bahiya as a women whose symbolic role as Mother Egypt is transgressed through the materiality of its origin within the lives of working-class and peasant women in Egypt. And Chahine's Bahiya struggles with her repressed desires as a woman: even while she observers in her daughter the young woman she once was, Bahiya continues to admire and celebrate her own face and body as those of a desiring and desired woman. In one powerful scene after she first meets Ra'uf and realizes he might be the son of her lover who died twenty years ago, Bahiya tells him: "you have the same beautiful eyes as your father." Later that night we see her entering her bedroom, and staring at herself in the mirror for a long powerful moment, as if assessing the weight of the years that now separate her from the time of their affair. But the moment also acknowledges and celebrates the resiliency of her own desire, albeit repressed, as a woman who is still capable of discerning the beauty in the eyes of the young Ra'uf. The final scene draws attention to Bahiya's symbolic break with her repression; the free movement of her hands, her eyes glaring back at us through her direct gaze at the camera, and her challenging voice as she leads the masses on the streets of Cairo, all recontextualize the concept of Mother Egypt and redraw it in conjunction with all the materiality of its class, gender, political power, and contradictory dynamics.

The final ten minutes of the film are structured around rapidly edited shots that create a feeling of anxiety. With the voice on the radio in the background announcing the declaration of a ceasefire on the night of June 10, 1967, we watch Sheikh Ahmad walking aimlessly, his image alternating sporadically with flash-like shots of religious leaders preaching to congregations in the mosques. The scene shifts to a shot of the officer, Ali, walking out from behind street vendors like a living corpse, punctuated by fast-paced images of the wounds of Ra'uf's brother on the front. In contrast to the rest of the film where the streets of Cairo are crowded with people, the streets are now almost vacant, lifeless, and quiet. We are confronted with the image of an empty café, followed by one of a poor child accompanying a blind man, followed by a painfully serene image of the Nile river, and finally, through to the view of nearby high-rise apartments—their windows open and their balconies deserted. A long shot then takes us to a large hall where a group of young people are congregating around a television. This shot is followed by one inside Bahiya's home, where all are gathering in front of her television; President Nasser is announcing his resignation. There is a close-up of Bahiya's husband Johnny, as he slowly moves into the room, followed by the image of Sheikh Ahmad weeping, "We were defeated without even knowing it!" It is at this moment that Bahiya utters her refusal to accept defeat, and the camera follows the masses as they flow onto the streets of the city behind her, loudly voicing their rejection of Nasser's resignation and expressing their determination to overcome the disaster. The entire scene is built to emphasize the nature of the defeat as indicative of the long repression of the peoples' voice, which, in contrast to the earlier images of corrupt businessmen and political leaders conducting their business as usual, points to the direction of the future—not just for Egypt but for the entire Arab nation. There can no moving forward without listening to the voice of the people and without their presence at the helm of the decision-making process.

The Sparrow initiated a new phase in Chahine's cinema in the sense that it allowed the filmmaker to enter an era of institutional independence from the Egyptian government. This would become an integral element in Chahine's future work, which would eventually find him creating an independent production company to produce not only his own films but also those by first-time Egyptian filmmakers. Equally as important, on the political level the film engaged critically with the new and shifting realities of Egypt and the region. It probed into the root causes of the military defeat of 1967, ironically provided an essentially pro-Nasser critique of the Nasser period, and offered an outlook on the possibilities for overcoming defeatist attitudes in the wake of Nasser's death. In this regard the film stressed the importance of a leading role for marginalized segments of society, merging issues of underdevelopment in the Arab world with history, class struggle, and popular culture.

By de-sentimentalizing the 1967 defeat, the film explored the value of revisiting history, even a not-so-distant one, as a means of understanding the present. Through its dispassionate look at class corruption in conjunction with a national political disaster, the film invites a reflection informed by history and politics. In this regard, *The Sparrow* represents perhaps Chahine's clearest attempt to point out the contradiction between the goals of the revolution and the goals of those who took control of its direction. The film's illustration of a post-revolutionary ruling class evokes the military-based bureaucracy it suggests will eventually wrest political and economic control from the old upper classes. As such, the film takes a critical stand that dissects the complex dialectic of class and power, and offers, perhaps for the first time, a new self-critical view of Nasser's failed attempt to launch an Arab national liberation project.

IMPENDING CHAOS AND *THE RETURN OF THE PRODIGAL SON*

In 1975, in the wake of Nasser's death and the increased tensions in Lebanon that would lead to a fifteen-year civil war, Chahine's stance on Arab reality took an even darker turn than was manifested in *The Choice* and *The Sparrow*. The Lebanese civil war signaled a new era in Arab politics that would be marked by increased internal and inter-state strife and the radical retreat of the Arab national project on all fronts. This would translate into a major schism between Egypt and the rest of the Arab world over Egypt's signing of the Camp David Peace Accords with Israel in return for the Israeli withdrawal from the Sinai Peninsula and its restoration to Egyptian sovereignty. The accords were considered, in some Arab quarters, as yet another blow to the dreams of Arab unity, solidarity in the struggle to force Israeli withdrawal from other Arab lands occupied during the 1967 War, and the struggle to implement Palestinian rights.

The war in Lebanon would foreshadow the tensions and wars that would rock the Arab world through the 1970s, and into the new millennium. The civil war would also signal the era of inter-religious, ethnic, and inter-state tensions within the region. All this translated into a long list of wars and bouts of civil unrest in the area: a north–south civil war in Sudan; the rise of religious fundamentalism in Syria, Egypt, and Algeria, and the explosion of Islamist terrorism in these countries; the continuing war between Morocco and the rebels of the Western Sahara; the war between Iraq and Iran; a continuing civil war in Somalia; a war between North and South Yemen; the Iraqi invasion of Kuwait; the war in Darfur; and more recently, Shiite–Sunni tensions in Iraq and throughout the region, and Palestinian infighting between

Fatah and Hamas factions. Added to this is the continuing Palestine–Israel crisis, two Israeli invasions of Lebanon, the first Gulf War in 1991, and the invasion of Iraq in 2003, all the result of military interventions within the area. The Arab region clearly became a hub of tensions, wars, and instability. Within this atmosphere, the dream of unity, progress, and solidarity was replaced by the nightmarish reality of death, destruction, and adaptation to—what Chahine would suggest to be—neocolonial manipulations. Chahine's bleakest film to date, *The Return of the Prodigal Son* (1976), reflected the filmmaker's acute and despairing insight into how the Arab world had come to this new era of self-destruction.

The film, however, also reflected Chahine's anxiety over the direction the new Sadat government was taking, particularly in its reversal of the social and economic policies initiated during the Nasser revolution. Chahine began to work on *The Return of the Prodigal Son* in 1975, the same year the Suez Canal reopened after its Egyptian sovereignty was reaffirmed. But this was also when, for the first time in twenty years, the Egyptian press, largely reflective of the views of the government, began a campaign against Nasser's policies and the social and economic strategies associated with it. Some newspapers even began to praise the earlier regime of the monarchy. Peter Mansfield describes the intensity of the campaign and suggests that it eventually translated into a concrete reversal of earlier revolutionary social reform measures and as such resulted in the rise of a wealthy new class:

> There was talk of selling off the nationalized industries to the private sector, dismantling the Arab Socialist Union and restoring political parties. 'Could de-Nasserisation go further than this?' Indeed. One of the most tangible results of Sadat's policies was the emergence of a new high-spending millionaire class. Some were nouveaux riches; others were members of the old regime who had recovered some of their wealth as a result of the de-sequestration of property seized in Nasser's time. Their conspicuous consumption . . . was an insult to the poverty-stricken Egyptian urban masses.[16]

Clearly, for Chahine, the retreat from the ideals of the revolution was testimony to the interrelationship between Egypt's social, economic, and national roles within the Arab national project. *The Return of the Prodigal Son* reflected deep anxieties concerning the changes taking place inside Egypt and their impact on the social and political fabric of the entire region; the civil war in Lebanon having given the first credence to these fears. The film marked the second collaboration (after *The Sparrow*) between Chahine's Misr International and the Algerian government's Film Agency. Responding to questions about the reasons behind making such a dark film, Chahine told a major Egyptian paper:

> I was quite frightened, and it was this fear that pushed me to make this film. It was a kind of apprehension I felt I needed to share with my audience. I was fearful that things we had rid ourselves of in our society were now coming back. They [the government] understand 'openness' [Sadat's policy of reintroducing an open economic market system] the same way they wrongfully understood socialism before . . . . Today, 'openness' is equally designed for their own benefit, the same way socialism was manipulated earlier! This new [upper] class and those dealers only look after their own interests.[17]

The story is adapted from a novel by André Gide and depicts a family going through a fatal crisis. Ali Madbouli, a former social activist who went on to marry the daughter of a wealthy contractor with lucrative government construction deals, returns home to his family after ten years in prison. Ali had been imprisoned for his involvement in a cost-cutting scheme that had resulted in the collapse of one its buildings. But the Ali who returns is no longer the well-loved man they remember, which disappoints everyone, including his nephew, his former lover, and the workers in his father's factory, toward whom he assumes the role of yet another technocrat with no genuine regard for their demands and grievances. The Madbouli family is well-to-do, owning a large factory, a movie theater, and vast lands. His aging father Muhammad has chosen to run a farm and tries to stay away from the entire business. He is grandfatherly and sincere—a weak figure who had once hoped to become an artist but was eventually forced to take on the family business. Ali's mother is a manipulative figure who meddles in everyone's life and is called Frankenstein by the father.

Ali's cousin, Fatma, has been waiting for Ali's return in hope of marrying him. She has loaned the Madbouli family a great sum of money, which his older brother Tulba has reinvested in his factory and now refuses to repay. Tulba rationalizes this by reminding everyone that he has been taking care of Fatma, as she is his wife's sister. Ibrahim, Tulba's son, who has just graduated from high school, has dreams of traveling and becoming a space scientist. Tulba, however, has other plans for his son, wanting him to become a veterinarian to help in the farm's work. Even Tafida, Ibrahim's close friend, rejects his dreams, preferring he be more realistic and study at a local university. The only person who supports Ibrahim's plans is his grandfather Muhammad. Ibrahim looks to his uncle Ali to stand up to Tulba, whose only motivation is to make money and consolidate his power in the town. But Ali's youthful idealism has been thoroughly trampled by his years in prison and he is now incapable of dealing with anything beyond his own ghosts, disappointments, and fears.

The Return of the Prodigal Son contrasts Ali's troubled bourgeois household with Fatma's happier working-class family: her mother is a feisty and independent woman from Alexandria; her father, Hassouna, works in Tulba's factory; and her younger sister Tafida goes to school and loves Tulba's son Ibrahim. Tafida has her own dreams and hopes, but unlike those of Ibrahim, hers are realistic and perhaps more achievable.

As the family gathers to celebrate Ali's marriage to his cousin Fatma, its internal feuds come to a head and the ensuing gunplay results in a wave of bullets that leaves the entire family dead, except for the young Ibrahim. The film's few sympathetic characters—Ibrahim, Tafida, and her family—succeed in avoiding the massacre, escaping to exile in Alexandria, Chahine's favorite symbol of possibilities and dreams. The film ends with a song of hope for a new beginning out of the ashes of self-destruction:

> This is what happened, this is fate and this is destiny!
> We say goodbye to the past and its big dreams . . .
> We say goodbye to the good times and goodbye to the ghosts . . .
> What's gone is gone and now there are only a few steps left
> The only thing we can do, my friend, is when we part ways
> We can look forward to the sun of our dreams
> And enjoy looking at it steadfastly through the thick clouds

The song heralds the arrival of a new era that Chahine considered to be inevitable. But it also denotes hope for the young couple in their escape from the massacre. *The Return* directly targets the post-Nasser retreat from the principles of socialism that the new government chose to discard entirely. In an interview in 1977, Chahine pulled no punches in his political reading of the period, pointing out that the new regime was determined to introduce a new ideological perspective. Instead of studying the mistakes of the revolution and continuing to work to implement its ideals—most of which remained as mere slogans—the government, according to Chahine, chose to radically depart from them altogether, instead reintroducing an old fashioned Machiavellian interpretation of capitalism.[18] Such a reimposition of the old system, Chahine argued, could only result in violent chaos, upheavals, and massacres because it was not built on a rational understanding of the needs of Egyptian society and its economic reality.[19] In this context, he continued, *The Return of the Prodigal Son* presented an important element of Egyptian society in Ali, a bourgeois who had once enthusiastically engaged in the socialist project, even choosing to break with his own class to support it. But, in the end, Chahine reminds us that, irrespective of their good intentions, members of this class are fundamentally incapable of genuinely parting with the ideals of their class:

> Ali, a sample of the bourgeois class, abandons socialist ideals when they are not fashionable and quickly adapts to the new circumstances. He even begins to treat workers like the old capitalists did. He has no problem going back to capitalism especially as he has never really lived the real socialist experience. Now he has abandoned socialism altogether and chosen the easy way out by adapting himself to capitalism, yet in the end he is incapable of surviving this transformation.[20]

Commenting on the macabre scene that closes the film, Chahine clearly alludes to the Lebanese connection as well as to the direct impact of President Sadat's policies and how they were beginning to affect the entire region. He also directly refers to the impact of these changes on the notion of Arab unity:

> Politically, to begin, the scene reflected what was taking place in Lebanon. I felt that Arabs were now going to embark on killing each other particularly after Sadat began to unilaterally make decisions without involving other Arab countries in them. Perhaps we hadn't been able to achieve [Arab] unity so far, but up to that point we at least had some hope of realizing it. Now it looked like we [Egyptians] had no need to talk to other Arabs.... This was treason to all Arabs.[21]

Stylistically, the film departed radically from earlier Egyptian and Arab popular cinema traditions, combining generic conventions from the drama, thriller, and musical, such that dramatic scenes were punctuated by cheerful song and dance numbers performed by Lebanese singer Majida al-Roumi in her role as Tafida. *The Return of the Prodigal Son* often juxtaposes song and dance sequences with the darker plot elements, even during the explicitly violent conclusion, a combination previously unheard of in Egyptian and Arab cinema. However, these seemingly contradictory combinations prove essential in the dramatic development of the story; each of the four songs signals a specific stage in the film's plot.

The first musical number takes place at school where the two young dreamers Tafida and Ibrahim express their friendship and love for each other. The second song accompanies Ali's release from prison and introduces us to his character through flashbacks of his lost time in prison and his consequent disillusionment with his political dreams and hopes. The third follows the fight between Ibrahim and his father Tulba, as Ibrahim and Tafida join other youths in proclaiming "The streets are ours," reflecting the solidarity and determination of youth in the fight for social change and freedom. The final song is initially heard when Ibrahim is bit by a scorpion, and is heard once again as a mantra towards the end of the film as the bloody chaos explodes at the Madbouli household..

The Return of the Prodigal Son features an omniscient Greek chorus in the form of a clown who comments on the action, echoing Chahine's contempt for the world of the bourgeois family. Three times the blank-faced clown comments on events: the first time, he announces the name of the film that will be shown in the town's movie theater; the second time, he emerges at the end of a song and dance number to hail the energy of its youthful participants. The clown's final appearance comes following the Madbouli massacre. The ambivalence of the clown's facial features only enhances the film's resistance to closure and its ambivalence regarding the fates of its characters.

The film is constructed through expressionistic depictions of characters and events achieved through unnatural lighting, nervous montage, and abstract *mise en scène*. The extensive use of expressionistic lighting functions as a commentary on the Madbouli family's lack of direction, which can only end in its implosion. In one scene Ali seems to be walking into the reddish circle of the sun on what appears to be a journey without direction. The Madbouli's house is persistently dim and striped by shadows foreshadowing its eventual transformation into an arena of death. In the final scene, as the Madbouli family prepares to celebrate Ali's marriage, the colorful celebration bulbs illuminating the house's exterior and garden are filtered, casting the scene in a cold bluish light. In contrast, interiors of the Hassouna family home are bathed in natural light from its open windows, and its garden bright with sunlight.

For the critic Ali Abu Shadi the film represented Chahine's attempt to tackle the new realities of defeat, popular discontent with new economic policies, and the rapid procession of changes implemented by the Sadat government. This, Abu Shadi argues, explains the film's stylistic approach, "Chahine

The Return of the Prodigal Son: The elusive dreams of revolution (photo: Gamal Fahmy).

thought that a 'realistic' approach would not be able to reflect the chaotic picture of Arab world reality in the mid-1970s."[22] In this regard, Chahine sought an even darker representation of this reality than in any of his earlier films. Abu Shadi suggests that Chahine utilized impressionistic and surrealistic images, as well as aspects of the Brechtian alienation effect, to tell a story that begins with an endearing account of the Madbouli family and gradually and accumulatively leads us through the family's approaching implosion.[23]

Though mainly linear in plot structure, the story nevertheless oscillates between the past and the present, and between reality and imagination. The film's stylistic approach, however, is impossible to pin down within a specific genre, school, or even vis-à-vis classical Hollywood realism or other non-realist schools. This turn to generic confusion, initiated in *The Choice*, to bend the conventions of the thriller to incorporate an explicit political analysis, became with *The Return* a full-blown ménage of the conventions of the melodrama, the musical, the political thriller, and the teen movie. The film also incorporated various stylistic approaches including the Brechtian direct address and a self-reflexive allusion to cinema and the cinematic instrument (vs. classical realist/illusionist storytelling), and expressionistic camera work and frame composition (vs. the neorealist portrayal of marginalized social characters).

In an interview Chahine explicitly emphasized his interest in utilizing film practice as a communication (rather than expressive) medium, within which the conveyance of ideas, political or otherwise, is at its very heart:

> I'm not against 'realism' per se. Nevertheless, I do refuse all kinds of dogmatic categories. My intention is always to create a dialogue with my audience.... This is why I chose to have songs, along with other cinematic techniques.... Realism as some envision it is difficult to maintain. The issue here is that if I feel I need to present a song, I should be able to simply present it, as in the case of the song (The Street Is Ours) that I got the idea for when I was in Paris. The police were chasing students who were shouting 'the street is ours', streets which before the Paris demonstrations were always under the police control. As such, the sudden intrusion of the song allowed me to say what I wanted without forcing it.[24]

Some critics however did not agree that the film's stylistic approach helped facilitate its political message. Ahmad Saleh insisted that Chahine "lingers in symbolisms that push the viewer toward an uncertainty from which they cannot awake."[25] Saleh argues that a stylistic approach that interrupts the film's dramatic flow is not helpful if the filmmaker genuinely cares about reaching out to his audience. Samir Farid, on the other hand, suggests Chahine's approach brings about the political message of the film even more forcefully:

> Ali symbolically portrays a tragic Nasserite hero who looks toward the sky but loses the earth underneath his feet, who demolishes what was supposed to be demolished but was not able to build what needed to be built, and eventually stood alone crying on top of Egypt's ruins.[26]

Farid points to the brilliant Shakespearian ending, unique in Arab cinema, in which Chahine clearly alludes to the tragic end of the "Discreet Charm of the Arab Bourgeoisie" in the Lebanese civil war, a fate he counsels other Arab nations against.[27]

Clearly, the film resists categorization, and as such points toward an auteurist approach which can only be described as eclectic. My use of the term *eclectic* here is in reference to Chahine's stylistic attitude, to which some now refer as *postmodern*. As I will discuss in the last chapter, the filmmaker's use of multiple generic and cinematic textual techniques stems from his conscious preoccupation with finding more effective methods to communicate his political ideas, which in postmodern terms might be considered ideological *grand narratives*.

Most critics saw the film as a grave reflection on contemporary Arab history. For his part, Ibrahim Fawal emphasized Chahine's critique of how

Nasser's socialism was applied and then was eventually totally abandoned by the Sadat regime.:

> Under Nasser, Egypt became a socialist country.... The theory might have been correct, and the intentions might have been good, but in reality the experience was disastrous. A tiny segment of the population got richer and the rest became poorer. Colonels and retired generals could not run industries; what they were good at was neglecting the factories they had inherited and making appointments and granting concessions to those they favored. Nepotism ran rampant and the public suffered following Sadat's 'corrective revolution.'[28]

Chahine suggests that under Sadat, life became harder for ordinary Egyptians, "The replacement of socialism with capitalism continued to favor the rich and powerful at the expense of the poor.... Egypt witnessed the rise of a new class of multimillionaires.... Looking back at both periods [...] Socialism was for them, and capitalism was for them."[29]

The notion of class dichotomies has always been part of Chahine's cinema, but in *The Return of the Prodigal Son* Chahine pushes the issue even further, through his factory workers' consciousness vis-à-vis their class position, their rights, and their boss's capitalist status. In the end, the struggle to improve their condition is enhanced by their clear understanding of the workings of capitalism, and how profits are accrued by increasing the level of surplus value extracted from the laborers' work. The film therefore transcends Chahine's earlier vision of the good capitalist versus the bad capitalist as seen in his *Struggle on the Pier*. While workers in *The Return of the Prodigal Son* have their share of such illusions early in the narrative when they count on Ali to be a better boss than his older brother Tulba, their hopes are shattered when the defeated Ali returns from prison. Furthermore, Ali has now become keen on running an effective and profitable business, which, as he keeps telling Hassouna, does not change his "personal love and appreciation for workers."

On another level, *The Return*'s class-focused plotline also tempts critical observations on how these issues affect the politics of national liberation and the Arab national project as a whole. In a 1976 article, Egyptian critic Samir Farid noted the film's linkages between Chahine's specific Egyptian and pan-Arab preoccupations, bridging the gap between the period after Nasser's death and that which came before the October 1973 War. Farid notes that, through his portrayal of the Madboulis, Chahine was able to capture the contradictions faced by the Egyptian and Arab bourgeois classes that seemed destined to self-destruct, similar to those encountered by the bourgeois family in Louis Buñuel's *The Discreet Charm of the Bourgeoisie* (1972), who in the last scene of the film seem to be going nowhere.[30] Equally as important, Farid suggests that the film's powerful climax "not only pointed out the tragic ending of 'the discreet' charm of Lebanese bourgeoisie manifested in the Lebanese civil war," but was also symptomatic of "the fear from the slow reinscription of this 'charm' into the whole body of the Arab nation." As such, the film represented a "red light warning which Chahine flashed in front of the entire Arab world."[31]

Critic Kamal Ramzi is more specific in his reading of the film, ironically seeing the fate of the family as suggestive of the fate of "a patriarchal Sadat" who would later die in a blaze of bullets by a group of Muslim fundamentalists:

> The Madbouli family should be seen in the context of the period when the film was being made. During this period, the speeches by Anwar Sadat attempted to paint him as the 'patriarch of the Egyptian family' and stressed that all should live together under the homogeneity of this family. A few months after the release of the film on September 9, 1976, major strikes and demonstrations exploded across Egypt exposing the big lie of the 'one family'... In this respect, the film was not simply a portrayal of the current situation but also an omen of things to come.[32]

But while almost all critics emphasized the film's microcosmic portrayal of Arab society in the aftermath of the 1967 defeat, Nasser's death, and the reintroduction of pro-capitalist social and economic measures, they also noted the emergence of a new element in Chahine's reading of his society's political landscape: the traditional family structure.

While Chahine's emphasis in his earlier films was on class struggle as it was manifested in social relations, *The Return of the Prodigal Son* signaled Chahine's incorporation of class issues in an alternative Arab national project. *The Return*'s microcosm of Arab politics featured an explicit rejection of traditional bourgeois patriarchal family structures, and emphasized the connections between the dynamics of those structures and the environment of defeat in the Arab world and its state of underdevelopment. Chahine commented on the nature of family relationships and sexuality in the film by contrasting between two class-based social structures, pointing out that sex within the bourgeois family "is rotten and very sick, while within the working-class family it is simple, healthy and enjoyable," making the latter family much happier.[33] Chahine, however, goes beyond a simple comparison between the bourgeoisie and the working class, suggesting that the family itself is a bourgeois notion that is repressive by nature, and therefore must be ended:

> The family system itself is a bourgeois invention . . . yet healthy relationships do indeed exist within such a system. The bourgeois family system as such, however, with all its values and ways of thinking, has to be obliterated. The bourgeoisie represses and exploits others claiming, "I'm doing it for my children." This is the unscrupulous contention that the bourgeoisie resorts to in order to rationalize sustaining its power and control.[34]

But while his earlier films, particularly *Dawn of a New Day*, *The Choice*, and *The Sparrow*, addressed the issue of the bourgeois family structure by contrasting it with a working-class alternative, the bourgeois family in *The Return of the Prodigal Son* is shown to be hampering the evolution of Arab society on economic, social, and political levels. Thus, Chahine's quarrel with the bourgeoisie would now engage its hegemonizing ideological value system. Asserting that the family structure itself is a decaying and rotten system and that people need to understand that they do not, for example, own their children, Chahine stated that in *The Return* he wanted to show how the "bourgeois family tries to control its children through money."[35] Acknowledging his shifting understanding of the Arab national project now encompassed a more heterogeneous outlook on the social structure of the nation itself, Chahine argued that the family structure inhibits Arab social development, and is in fact responsible for allowing a parasite class to emerge, grow, and dominate. Positing a direct link between the bourgeois mantra of "keeping it in the family" and today's narrow, state-based Arab nationalisms, Chahine went on to appeal to Arab youth to cast off the family system as it exists today, and to break free from earlier, closed, notions of nationalism.[36] Only an alternative, collective system would allow Arabs to begin to utilize their resources for their own benefit, Chahine suggests:

> For example, there are some [families who rule some Arab states] who consider oil as solely their own property and that grains are theirs alone, etc. . . . As an Arab I believe that all Arab resources are my property. A real revolution cannot be achieved until all Arabs come together and think in a collective way rather than through their narrow familial or ultimately their state-nationalist predispositions.[37]

Traditionally, references to family structure in Arab cinema have been framed within a broad political perspective rooted in notions of homogeneity, safety, and harmony. *The Return of the Prodigal Son*, however, is characterized by a dramatic emphasis on the ideological contradictions and vulnerabilities of such structures. Equally, the film's metaphoric approach to the political context within which the story operates emphasizes the ideological limitations intrinsic to Arab hegemonic constructions. The inherently self-destructive nature of the traditional bourgeois family structure is exposed through a formally innovative approach that reifies the Arab national project, with all its decaying, stagnant, and unpredictable dynamics.

While modernism had long since been adopted in Egyptian and Arab cinema, few filmmakers had taken on the question of the Arab national project before Youssef Chahine. Through an examination of *The Choice* and *The Prodigal Son*, I sought to identify how Chahine's modernist strategies contributed to reimagining the place of the individual and the family within the dialectics of national liberation. Modernism's destabilizing strategies, as utilized by Chahine on the threshold of a difficult and complex era in contemporary Arab history, projected a fierce interrogation of prevailing modes of Egyptian and Arab cinematic spectatorship. As such, at this critical juncture of its development, Chahine's cinema sought to engage and expose the complex ideological underpinnings of Arab political culture and cultural politics. Whether Chahine succeeded in his modernist experiment—with its eclectic infusion of generic and stylistic approaches—to communicate the anxiety of the period to his audience, remains debatable. What is certain, however, is that Chahine did not hesitate to venture into new forms of expression to awaken his audience to the crisis that was about to transpire.

6

IDENTITY AND DIFFERENCE

The outbreak of the civil war in Lebanon, along with the signing of the peace treaty with Israel, the reversal of Nasser's pan-Arab solidarity policies, and the reintroduction of market-oriented social and economic policies all contributed to the rise of new social and political vulnerabilities in the Arab world. Bread riots erupted in Egypt in 1977 in conjunction with workers' strikes in Helwan and other major industrial centers. Peaceful demonstrations which took place on January 18 turned into riots and violence on the second day, and the governmemt declared a state of emergency and imposed a curfew, a measure which had not been enforced since the early days of the 1952 revolution. In the end, seventy-nine people were killed, more than 214 injured, and thousands were sent to jail. In the aftermath of these events, the Sadat government retaliated, launching a campaign against the remnants of the Egyptian nationalist and Marxist left within the trade unions and centers of power both inside and outside the government, specifically targeting journalists and intellectuals. The government began to encourage and rely on political Islamist groups to assist in the subduing of the left and its influence among workers and students. The leftist-led protest movement deteriorated, and Islamist-supported groups began to exert increasing influence among students and other marginalized members of Egyptian society. The leadership gap created in the popular protest movement through the weakening of the left was soon filled by government-supported religious fundamentalists. With the decline of the nationalist and Marxist left, and the growth of social and political tensions, the new Arab reality Chahine had warned of in 1976 in *The Return of the Prodigal Son* was coming to pass.

Economic, social, and political tensions and instabilities were now taking the form of religious tensions. As they had in Lebanon, tensions between Christians and Muslims in Egypt began to surface, and factional street fighting and riots erupted. In September 1981, Sadat exiled the head of the Coptic Church, Pope Shenouda III, and imprisoned hundreds of his supporters, citing their divisive involvement in politics. The new situation was taking its toll on the political and social culture of a region where religious and ethnic groups had historically lived in relative harmony.

Given their significance, it was paradoxical that only three Egyptian films out of nearly eight hundred made between 1977 and 1992 dealt in any way with the January 1977 events.[1] For its part, Chahine's cinema in the late 1970s would begin to tackle the issue of religious and ethnic difference within Arab societies, relying on personalized readings of Egyptian and Arab histories to point out the heterogeneity of Arab culture. This emphasis on the personal and historical in *Alexandria... Why?* (1978), would signal his perception of the Arab national project as a celebration of the integration of cultural and religious difference within class, national and anticolonial solidarity. In this context, Chahine's cinema of the late 1970s began to articulate a new political and esthetic approach to the issue of Arab national identity.

The film discussed in this chapter offers a new approach in dealing with the issue of religious variance within Arab societies. This represents an attempt to explore the dialectical relationship between cultural experiences of religious affiliation and national development and liberation, by drawing attention to the conflict between historical and contemporary patterns in Arab political discourse. As such, these films move away from ahistorical presumptions of identity and liberal celebrations of difference, articulating an alternative discourse vis-à-vis Arab national mythology and Arab national identity.

CHAHINE'S CINEMA AND THE NEW APPROPRIATION OF ARAB IDENTITY

Along with the new social and economic policies and ideological trends affecting Egyptian cinema in the mid-1970s came a new generation of filmmakers with various ideological and stylistic orientations. Key filmmakers emerging during the 1980s as the new realism generation (some of whom began their film careers in the late 1960s) included Mohammad Khan, Raafat al-Mihi, Khairy Bishara, Atef al-Tayyeb, and Daoud Abd al-Sayyid. This paved the way for yet another post-new realism generation in the 1990s, including Sharif Arafa, Yousry Nasrallah, Radwan al-Kashif, Said Hamid, Tariq al-Aryan, Asma al-Bakri, Muhammad Kamil al-Kalioubi, Khalid al-Haggar, Tariq al-Telmessani, Majdi Ahmad, and Osama Fawzi. According to Samir Farid, these filmmakers put Egyptian cinema "back on the international stage."[2] Stylistically, Egyptian new realism incorporated features from post-Second World War Italian neorealism and the local new realism of the 1980s, which was, in turn, built upon the social realist trends of Egyptian cinema of the 1950s and 1960s. As Farid suggests, the new realism generations "expressed contemporary conditions in a way that no other generation of Egyptian directors had done."[3]

While Egyptian cinema was witnessing an expansion of realist approaches, Chahine's cinema continued its incorporation of interactive models of modernist, realist, and generic approaches. Equally as important, Chahine's cinematic project was concerned with representations of the subjectivity within, and the subjective relay of personal and national histories. With the changing political culture in Egypt and the Arab world in the late 1970s, Chahine's cinema began to recognize and redress marginalized social elements within Arab national identity. While Chahine's cinema has consistently acknowledged class difference and its role within the process of revolutionary change and national liberation, it nevertheless tended to neglect the issue of religious and ethnic difference within Arab society and how it impacted the notion of Arab identity. With *Alexandria... Why?*, Chahine began to revisit and engage the cultural and historical elements of distinct groups he thought integral to the appreciation of a collective Arab identity.

Alexandria... Why? represented an autobiographical first in the history of Egyptian and Arab cinemas and marked a new phase in Chahine's stylistic appropriation of the personal as political and vice versa; it also presented an explicitly new outlook on Arab identity as heterogeneous. The film marked a new phase in Chahine's international, and specifically western, critical reputation:

> This film, the first in Chahine's trilogy about himself and his city, was a major cinematic breakthrough, for it focused on a Christian family in a predominantly Muslim society and showed an Egyptian Jew as a patriotic Egyptian, not as a traitor who left Egypt and emigrated to Israel and later fought against Egypt and occupied Egyptian land. But most important is the sophisticated cinematic style of the film. Chahine [was] the only Egyptian director to win an international award in a major international film festival (the Special Jury prize at the 1979 Berlin Film Festival).[4]

Farid argues that Chahine's Alexandria trilogy embodied a milestone in Arab filmmaking similar to Taha Hussein's autobiographical book *The Days* in Arab literature. As such, Farid argues *Alexandria... Why?* paved the way for other filmmakers such as Mohammad Malas *Ahlam al-madina* (Dreams of the City, Syria, 1985) and Nouri Bouzid (*Man of Ashes*, Tunisia, 1986) to venture into making their own autobiographical films. These efforts, however, were distinguished by a clear emphasis on the historical moment within which their personal memory is captured:

> All these films were testimonies about periods in Arab history. Alexandria... Why? talked about the generation which carried out the revolution against monarchy in Egypt in 1953, Dreams of the City gave a context for the union between Egypt and Syria, and Man of Ashes tackled the period of Tunisia before independence. They also represent loving testimonies about cities such as Alexandria, Damascus, and Sfaques.[5]

Chahine's Alexandria trilogy, which in addition to *Alexandria... Why?* included *Hadduta masriya* (An Egyptian Story, 1982) and *Alexandria Again and Forever* (1990), represented a critical addition not only to Chahine's repertoire, but also to Arab cinema's alternative film practice. Each of the three original films (a fourth, *Iskindiriya... New York* (Alexandria... New York), was released in 2004) addressed a moment of personal and national significance in Egyptian and Arab history. *Alexandria... Why?* depicted the period of dreaming about the revolution, while *An Egyptian Story* offered an intriguing memoir witnessing the crisis of the revolution in conjunction with Chahine's own health crisis. Finally, *Alexandria Again and Forever* offered a picture of the post-revolutionary struggle for democracy, affirming a more encompassing notion of national identity that did not exclude queer sexuality.

The filmmaker's daring reflection on his own life as a filmmaker and agent for social and political change also indulged a radically fresh approach to autobiographical cinematic narrative. Chahine's relentless leaps between fact and fiction, the individual and the collective, the personal and the public made these films unique in their challenge to thematic, generic, and stylistic norms in Egyptian and Arab cinemas. His other films of the 1980s and 1990s, including *Adieu Bonaparte!* (1985), *al-Yawm al-sadis* (The Sixth Day, 1986), *The Emigrant* (1994), and *al-Masir* (Destiny, 1997), all featured autobiographical undertones focused on interactions between the private and the public. Furthermore, these films marked the connections between historical, cultural and political events and present-day Arab dilemmas and struggles. Leading Lebanese film critic Ibrahim al-Aris provides a perspective on the continuity binding the Trilogy and Chahine's later films:

Adieu Bonaparte!, The Emigrant, and Destiny were in essence a continuation in his personal journey films that he launched through his autobiographical trilogy ... In the latter he contemplated his personal life and career experience, his desires and his outlook on cinema, politics and on the other, all in a style which stressed personal history, and the history of his feelings and desires. In the other films, and without leaving much room to expound on the personal, Chahine visited 'real' history (the Bonaparte Campaign, the Pharaohs and Akhnaton's propositions about the oneness of God, and finally the history of the Andalusian state and its intellectual renaissance, all by way of dealing with his own present-day personal and intellectual struggles. In both groups of films, the ever present Alexandria of Chahine's 1940s youth, with its rich and multicultural diversity never left Chahine's imagination and was always subtly or explicitly there to remember.[6]

To be clear, Chahine's bold and original intrusion into the world of autobiographical cinema in his Alexandria trilogy, and his reflexive readings of key moments in Egyptian and Arab history as exemplified in *Adieu Bonaparte!*, combined to rearticulate the Brechtian practice of nurturing a self-conscious audience. Within such parameters, Chahine's cinema engaged in a self-critical and self-conscious re-reading of Arab history. By positioning subjectivity—whether individual, class defined, religious, ethnic, or queer—at the center of the process of relaying personal and national histories, Chahine offered a clear challenge to popular cinematic traditions that allege an objective or universal conveyance of such histories. As such, Chahine offered a new perspective on Arab history that allowed for a critical examination of the present, a re-examination of Arab national identity in a way that was determinedly heterogeneous.

Addressing the notion of religious difference within the Arab world offers room for a new understanding of how cultural difference, identity, and otherness have been shaped within Arab history. Furthermore, and insomuch as religious difference in the Arab world was largely subsumed in the notion of *umma* (a term derived from the Muslim description of the community of Muslims, but used interchangeably by many Arab nationalists to refer to *al-umma al-'arabiya*, or the Arab nation), the need for revisiting Arab history to explore and elucidate its largely heterogeneous ethnic and religious dynamics became an important element in the recuperation of Arab identity, particularly in the contemporary context of increased religious tensions in Lebanon and elsewhere in the Arab world.

Religious difference gradually became an important aspect of the politics of representation in Chahine's cinema. While issues relating to race or ethnic portrayal were never included in Chahine's cinematic world, his explicit recognition of how the issue of religious diversity impacted Arab cultural discourse allowed him to articulate a fresh and much needed challenge to traditional narrow and homogenous conceptions of Arab identity.

ARAB IDENTITY AND CULTURAL HETEROGENEITY IN *ALEXANDRIA . . . WHY?*

Since its emergence in the mid-1800s al-Nahda movement had emphasized both social and cultural heterogeneity as integral to the goal of Arab self-determination and national independence. One key element in this regard involved the movement's advocacy of Arab unity. But while this movement saw itself as part of a process for religious, social, and cultural reform, it equally recognized colonialism as a major obstacle to the progress of this process. But later, in the twentieth century, the pan-Arab movement included groups and individuals from a wide cross-section of the region's rich ethnic and religious mosaic, contributing to the movement's advocacy of a largely secular form of government. Therefore, contrary to some claims, the notion of Arab unity has been perceived mainly as the materialization of a national project that reflects the heterogeneous nature of Arab societies.

Over the last fifteen years, as a direct reaction to the rise of religious fundamentalism, there has been renewed interest in discussion of the notion of Arab national identity. Similarly, new Arab cinemas have been increasingly, albeit subtly, tackling the issue of national self-determination with an eye to emphasizing the heterogeneity of Arab identity. More than ever before in the history of Arab cinema, films have been progressively showing interest in stories that deliberate on the notion of national unity as an embodiment of a culturally diverse society.

Drawing connections between fundamentalism and colonial politics remains a subtle practice in new Arab cinema; Arab films are more likely to make direct linkages between colonial politics and the politics of traditionalism and anti-modernization. One of the more pressing themes explores Arab national identity as a non-static and vibrant process which defies dogmatic exclusivity and conservative traditionalism.

Three decades ago, Merzak Allouache's film *Omar Gatalou* pioneered the practice of contemplating and redefining national identity. The Algerian film was released to overwhelming popular success in 1976 and amounted to a watershed in the history of Arab cinema. *Gatalou* explored the adventures of a sexist man from a working-class background, torn between his obsession with masculine behavior and his struggle to break with tradition and adopt what he conceived as modern western mannerisms. The film offers penetrating allegorical insights into its themes of national posturing, repression, and alienation. Today, these themes are more frequently and elaborately discussed by a much wider group of Arab filmmakers.

Lebanese filmmaker Randa Shahal's *The Kite* (winner of the 2003 Venice Film Festival's Silver Lion award for best film) reveals an emerging trend in the cinematic depiction of Arab identity. The film juxtaposes the dilemmas of an awakening national identity with those of a budding sexuality. An across-the-barbed-wire love story between Lamia, a young Arab girl, and an Arab Israeli soldier (both from the same Druze religion as her), *The Kite* is a commentary on the oppressive reality of occupation, which divides people and deprives them of their national dignity. Furthermore, the film vividly illustrates how military occupation wreaks havoc on the humanity of both the occupier and the occupied. Equally as important, however, the film renders Arab identity, materialized in Lamia's own personality, as an expression of the vibrant performative process of struggling against all forms of repression.

Earlier examples of this trend include Ferid Boughedir's *Asfour is-Stah* (Halfaouine: Boy of the Terraces, Tunisia, 1990), Khairy Beshara's *Ays krim fi-glim* (Ice Cream in Gleam, 1992), and Nabil al-Malih's *al-Compars* (The Extras, Syria, 1993), among others. All these films tackle the dilemma of searching for national identity through the foregrounding of marginalized lives in the streets and alleyways of large Arab cities. Instead of claiming national universalities, these films depict diverse social and cultural settings, characters, and materiality that offer complex renderings of a rapidly changing society struggling to reclaim its national identity.

On another level, several Arab films are showing renewed interest in the theme of religious heterogeneity. Recently a film by Mounir Radi (*An Indian Movie*, Egypt, 2003) created a major controversy due to its authentic depiction of the sensitive topic of a friendship between two young Egyptians, a Copt and a Muslim. But while this topic was considered problematic in light of the sectarianisms exacerbated by fundamentalist politics, an increasing number of filmmakers seem to be delving back into Arab collective memory to explore aspects of the multireligious history of Arab society. Less than a year after Radi's film, *Ana bahib al-sima* (I Love Cinema, Osama Fawzi, 2004) was released, this time presenting an even more explicit attack on fundamentalism as a multireligious phenomenon. A coming of age story about the adventures of a young Egyptian Christian boy sneaking into movie theaters to watch films against the will of his fanatically religious father (the father considers his son's love of cinema as a sinful act), the film emphasizes the moral and ethical bankruptcy of all forms of dogmatism. In its celebration of the Arab world's rich ethnic, religious, and cultural diversity, *I Love Cinema* affirmed the struggle against religious fundamentalism as a unifying element involving Arab Christians and Muslims alike. More recently, comedian Adel Imam and Egyptian actor Omar Sharif starred in *Hasan wa Murkus* (Hasan and Murkus, Ramy Imam, 2008), a big budget box-office hit concerning exchanged religious identities and religious intolerance in the context of recent acts of sectarian violence in Egypt.

Occasional references to Arab Christians as part of a multireligious Arab society have featured in many Arab films, but not necessarily as the main focus of the narrative.[7] Even attempts to tackle the rich history of Egyptian Jewish contribution to Egyptian cinema have been nonexistent, and when the topic was most recently approached in a study by an Egyptian scholar, it largely reflected an essentially cynical anti-Jewish 'conspiracy' attitude which only saw this contribution as a sign of how the Jews were trying to dominate and manipulate the rise of the Egyptian filmmaking industry since its early beginnings.[8] Allusions to Jews as part of the Arab cultural mosaic have been taboo in contemporary Arab cinema. Aside from Youssef Chahine, whose *Alexandria... Why?* offered a love story between a working-class communist man and a sympathizing Egyptian Jewish woman, Arab filmmakers generally avoided acknowledging the historically strong presence of an Arab Jewish community. In fact, other than *Alexandria... Why?*, the last film that dealt with the issue of Arab religious heterogeneity and included a Jewish character was Hilmi Rafla's *Fatma, Marika wa Rachel* (Fatma, Marika, and Rachel, Rafla, 1949). Ironically, the film was released one year after the creation of the state of Israel in 1948. In fact up until *Alexandria...Why?* was released in the late 1970s, the last film that dealt with the topic of Arab religious heterogeneity and included a key Jewish character was Hilmi Rafla's *Fatma, Marika, and Rachel*. Ironically, the film was released just one y ear after the creation of the state of Israel in 1948. Since the 1990s, however, the topic has been making a comeback among a new generation of Arab filmmakers.

For many western audiences, the presence of a Jewish central character in Ferid Boughedir's 1996 film *Un été à la Goulette* (A Summer in La Goulette, Ferid Boughedir, 1996) might be interpreted as an attempt to promote peaceful coexistence between Arabs and Jews. However the film's approach to this clearly sensitive topic belies deeper ideological preoccupations. With the story of three teenaged Tunisian girls — a Muslim, a Christian, and a Jew — the film examines a period of pivotal importance in Arab history; one sectarians and religious fanatics alike would prefer to forget. *La Goulette* revisits local history through an exploration of the religious and cultural wealth that has defined the social character of the Arab world for over fifteen hundred years. In this respect, the film rejects nostalgia and allows for a new reading of Arab history as a means of dealing with the present and understanding the dynamics of political and social change. It also indirectly testifies to the destructive demographic, political, and cultural consequences—especially for Arab Jews—associated with the creation of the state of Israel in 1948.

In the period during the creation of the state of Israel, Egyptian cinema's Jewish characters were depicted in the same unproblematic manner as its Muslim and Christian characters. Popular films focusing on Jewish characters included a comedy series featuring Shalom, a working-class hero who was widely known as the Charlie Chaplin of Egyptian cinema in the 1920s and 1930s. Other films with strong Jewish characters include *La'bit al-sitt* (The Lady's Puppet, Wali Eddine Sameh, 1946), *Fatma, Marika, and Rachel* (Hilmi Rafla, 1949), *Akhlaq li-l-bay'* (Morals for Sale, 1950), and *Hasan wa Murkus wa Cohen* (Hasan, Murkus, and Cohen, Fouad al-Jazirly, 1954), among others. Even after the creation of the state of Israel, well-known Jewish stars such as Leila Murad, Kamilia, and Nagma Ibrahim remained involved in making films—some of which praised the Nasser revolution and even voiced opposition to the creation of the Jewish state in Palestine.

Nevertheless, after the establishment of the state of Israel, allusions to Jews as part of the Arab cultural mosaic gradually became taboo in Egyptian and Arab cinematic texts. Robert Stam and Ella Shohat noted how *Alexandria . . . Why?* attested to Chahine's own perspective on the Arab national project itself, arguing that the film's

> subplots offer a multiperspectival study of Egyptian society, describing how different classes, ethnicities, and religions—working-class communists, aristocratic Muslim homosexuals, middle-class Egyptian Jews, petit-bourgeois Catholics—react to Egyptian-Arab nationalism. The subplots stress the diversity of Egyptian experience, but the unanimity of the reaction to European colonialism.[9]

Chahine's positive portrayal of Arab Jewish characters remained an anomaly throughout the 1970s and 1980s, but by the mid-1990s, a small number of Arab filmmakers, whether working at home or in exile, began to break with the taboo. These filmmakers began to tangentially recontextualize Jewishness as part of Arab identity; in the process relocating the three-thousand-year-old history of Jews in the Arab world. *Summer in La Goulette*, the Elia Suleiman segment in *Harb al-Khalij, madha ba'd?* (The Gulf War, What Next?, Suleiman, Palestine, 1991), and *Salut Cousin* (Merzak Allouache, Algeria, 1996) all celebrated the heterogeneity of Arab identity and the multifaith history of Arab culture. These films' stories and cinematic references challenged the simplistic conceptualizations of Arab versus Jew that had become standard in western as well as Arab political and cultural discourses. As such, these films tended to reconfigure the notion of Arab identity by offering a sense of a shared Arab collective that recognizes itself as part of an *imagined community*.

During the 2003 Ismailia International Film Festival for Documentary and Short Films in Egypt—the largest festival of its kind in the Arab world—the first prize was awarded to *Insa Baghdad: 'Arab wa yahud, al-mifsal al-'iraqi* (Forget Baghdad: Jews and Arabs—the Iraqi Connection, Samir, 2002). The film depicted the lives and struggles of four communist Iraqi Jews facing national alienation as Arabs living in Israel. It also explored the painful yet humorous stories of the next generation—the sons and daughters of these Iraqi exiles. These films may be at the forefront of a renewed and bold effort on the part of a new generation of Arab filmmakers to break away from the rhetoric of religious sectarianism, indicating a renewed momentum for progressive non-sectarian Arab politics and a more inclusive appreciation and celebration of the heterogeneous nature of Arab identity.

After the success of *Forget Baghdad*, the subject of Arab Jews and Arab Jewish history has been revisited by various Arab filmmakers. In 2004, Al Jazeera, the largest and most watched news television network in the Arab world, produced a series on Arab Jews in Israel. The series documented the experiences of Arab Jewish activists of the 1960s and 1970s who were members of various radical leftist Israeli organizations such as Matspen and the Black Panthers. Among the documentary and fiction feature films that have made the rounds of Arab and international film festivals over the last few years are: *Salata baladi* (Salad House, Nadia Kamel, Egypt, 2007), a journey of discovery of the director's own Jewish heritage; *Fayn mashi ya Moshé* (Where Are You Going, Moshé?, Hassan ben-Jalloun, Morocco, 2007), and *Maroc* (Maroc, Leila el-Marakshi, 2006), all of which deal with the Moroccan Jewish immigration to Israel; and *Qissa bahraniya* (A Bahraini Story, Bassam al-Thawadi, Bahrain, 2006), depicting the challenges of being Jewish in Bahrain after the 1967 War. *Alexandria . . . Why?* thus represented a critical first in contemporary Arab cinema of the 1970s.

AUTOBIOGRAPHICAL MEMORY AND RELIGIOUS HETEROGENEITY IN *ALEXANDRIA . . . WHY?*

From a historical perspective, Chahine's cinema of the late 1970s and beyond helped initiate a bold cinematic examination of Arab national identity with an eye for celebrating its social and cultural heterogeneity. As noted above, it was at least two decades after Chahine made his autobiographical portrayal of a religiously and culturally diverse Alexandria that other Arab filmmakers began to depict aspects of the multireligious, multiethnic, and multiracial diversity of the Arab world and expose the current attempts to erase the remnants of such diversity. To the extent that it celebrated and reintroduced Jewish identity as an integral component of Arab national identity, Chahine's *Alexandria . . . Why?* offered an Arab cinematic milestone in its heterogenic reexamination of Arab national identity.

The film was coproduced by Algerian television, and was presented at the 1979 Berlin Film Festival where it won the Silver Berlin Bear. As a result of festival exposure, the film was later screened commercially in several European countries. The release of *Alexandria . . . Why?* came on the heels of a succession of films preoccupied with present-day events and disillusionment. Clearly, after his heart attack while working on *The Sparrow* Chahine had become more contemplative about his own life, and the autobiographical *Alexandria . . . Why?* represented the culmination of this reflexive mode.

In its bold attempt to bare the artist's soul on the public screen, *Alexandria . . . Why?*, along with the rest of Chahine's Alexandria trilogy, represented a major landmark in Arab filmmaking and arts. According to cultural critic Ibrahim al-Aris, Chahine's autobiographical approach differed in a substantial way from earlier, coy attempts by contemporary writers and intellectuals to tackle their own histories.[10] By 1978 few films ventured into the autobiographical, most notable exceptions being Federico Fellini's *8 ½* (1962), *Roma* (1971), and *Amarcord* (1974). But Chahine's interest in baring his own history and soul in front of the camera did not simply begin with *Alexandria . . . Why?* and the Alexandria trilogy. As Ibrahim al-Aris argues, the film represented the culmination of an old Chahine cinematic practice that went back to his first film *Father Amin* (1950) and was seen in subsequent films such as *Cairo Station* (1958). The major difference, al-Aris suggests, is that the *I* here has assumed a higher and more intimate level of candor.[11]

Chahine's partly fictitious depiction of his struggle to fulfill his dream of studying film in America during his last year at Victoria College in Alexandria brings to the fore a complex interpretation of a moment in the history of a heterogeneous Arab society. From the outset Chahine positions the film within a specific time and place: Alexandria during the Second World War. The Nazis are on the offensive, and Hitler is readying an army of over two hundred thousand soldiers to attack Egypt's western front. Alexandrians are awaiting the triumphant arrival of Rommel's troops in the hope they will help them drive out British colonialists.

Some Egyptians, like Yehia (Chahine's character in the trilogy) and his friends, still have time to watch the Esther Williams musical comedy *Bathing Beauty* (1944). The teenagers—who come from various class backgrounds—spend their time watching movies or out on the Alexandria seafront road picking up prostitutes. The film offers a rich array of characters that includes Egyptian aristocratic and working-class patriots, bourgeois opportunists, English soldiers, and a generation of hopeful youths whose aspirations are hindered by the realities of class, war, Egypt's struggle for independence, and the emerging Palestine dilemma.

The film's representation of a critical period in contemporary Arab history alludes to the many political and social issues impacting on the struggle around Arab identity. It reflects upon the resistance against colonialism, colonialist designs in the region, and the major impact these issues had on framing the social, political, and demographic reality of the Arab world. Chahine presents a nuanced characterization of political struggles of the period through his depiction of a variety of unlikely relationships: the friendship between three Egyptian boys, a Christian, a Muslim, and a Jew; a love story between a Muslim communist man and a progressive Jewish woman; and the affair between Adel, an Egyptian aristocrat, and Tommy, an Australian soldier. Equally as important, the film's plot indulges a direct and bold rejection of Zionist ideological claims about a Jewish national identity. Chahine's depiction of the dilemma of an Egyptian Jewish family during the final phase before the Zionist creation of Israel as a Jewish homeland, exposes a central question that continues to impact the Arab struggle for self-determination. Released the same year that the Camp David Accords between Egypt and Israel was signed, *Alexandria . . . Why?* offered a reminder of the roots of the Palestine dilemma. Irrespective of how chauvinistic anti-Jewish Arab nationalists looked at the film as an attempt to vindicate the accord[12] simply because the film favorably depicted a Jewish Arab family, Chahine's film in fact presented a clearly anti-Zionist message at a time when the Sadat government was still struggling to rationalize its recognition of the state of Israel.

The film provided a complex picture of life in Alexandria during the Second World War as Egyptians, along with Arabs in other parts of the Arab world, saw their nation become a battleground for contesting colonialist powers. It depicted a turbulent period in Egyptian history where people struggling against Britain's colonial yoke were also faced with political divisions due to colonial attempts to manipulate and capitalize on the region's diversity.

The film also alluded to several tactics used by different social classes and political segments of the population as they confronted both colonialism and

Alexandria, Why?: Middle class dreams between the father and the son (photo: Gamal Fahmy).

the possibility of a German occupation. On the one hand, a group of leftist radicals implausibly plot to kidnap the British prime minister, Winston Churchill. They hope that by kidnapping Churchill they will help end the British occupation of their country. On the other hand, we have Adel, the young Egyptian aristocrat who cruises local nightclubs in search of British soldiers he can lure away and kill. During one such outing though, he meets and falls in love with Tommy, the Australian soldier. Adel's father is a big businessman who makes a living by keeping his options open regarding the colonial future of Egypt. The film also introduces us to Muslim Brotherhood leader who avoids getting involved in the struggle against the British through the pretext of concentrating on the moral and religious salvation of Egyptians.

Two stories unfold within the film: the first depicts a teenage Yehia who dreams about acting and making films. Yehia's middle-class Christian parents insist that he study at the elitist Victoria College despite their humble social and economic status. Yehia's close circle of friends includes Mohsen, a Muslim who is also Adel's little brother, and David, a Jew. David's sister Sarah, who is in her late teens, is in love with Ibrahim, a Muslim and a communist who is respected by Sarah's father, a patriarch of the well-known Egyptian Jewish family, Sorel. The depiction of the Jewish family and the relationship between the daughter and a leftist Muslim working-class man is intriguing. The father is portrayed as an old man who is deeply troubled by the events that surround him, particularly by what is being planned for the region. Sorel warns his friends that the Americans are showing interest in the huge oil reserves in the Arabian Peninsula, and they are increasingly keen about setting up a local policeman to guard their interests there. He sees Israel as the likely candidate to play that role.

The theme of oil and its centrality in colonial Middle East politics and its implications for Arab national liberation is reiterated in the film in a scene depicting a play directed and performed by Yehia along with a group of his school friends. In the play Allied and Axis powers are chasing each other across an Arabian desert speaking their respective languages as confused Egyptian and Arab characters powerlessly watch the events. While some Arab characters hold a sign claiming "No One Is Allowed to Pass through Here," European armies continue to chase each other in total indifference to the group.

After being jailed by the authorities for his anticolonial activities, Ibrahim is visited by Sarah, who tells him she is pregnant with his child, and they decide to keep the baby. As the fear of a German occupation of Alexandria increases, the Sorel family decides to leave Egypt for South Africa. The family arrives in Haifa just as the state of Israel is about to be declared. Sarah makes a trip to Egypt to visit Ibrahim in prison, this time with her son who she has named after his father. Meanwhile, Yahia's family has finally accumulated enough money for him to go to California to finish his theater education. The final scene mocks the middle-class Arab enthrallment with the notion of American freedom, particularly as it was being mythologized toward the end of the Second World War when the United States was forging its role as the alternative to the old colonial powers of Europe. As Yahia's boat reaches the New York harbor, the Statue of Liberty is transformed into a toothless, laughing woman over an image reminiscent of 1940s Hollywood back-projection. The technique emulates the flattened stock shots often used by Hollywood to show foreign locales, but is used here as an ironic comment on the illusionist fantasies of American consumer culture.

The film relies on episodic storytelling techniques in which the linear progression of events is replaced by a loose assortment that captures the stream of consciousness and selective memory of Chahine's alter ego, Yehia. Chahine's modernist cinematic language in *Alexandria... Why?* features a highly compromised chronology, interrupted and incomplete sentences by characters, and deliberately fumbled camera movements. As Yehia struggles to make the arrangements to travel to America to study theater, these formal aspects are punctuated by flashbacks and flashes forward in a selective reordering of events from Chahine's own childhood and teenage years. This rich mixture of events, periods, locations, and individual stories combine to produce an almost surreal sensation. The film is also marked by its rapid editing rhythm, which nervously jumps between scenes from Hollywood musicals and episodes from newsreel documentaries of the 1940s. Mirroring this intense and complex atmosphere, the film is loosely constructed through episodes of the various subplots, which although linear in their connection with the overall story, are impressionistically juxtaposed, conveying a sense of Chahine's own selective memory and his personal experience of events and history. The intercutting of Second World War footage into the film's action provides perplexing breaks in the movie's rhythm, but also injects events of an intimate, personal nature with a sense of historical resonance and context. The use of 1940s Hollywood footage (especially from Esther Williams and Gene Kelly films) situates Chahine's own personal memory within the framework of his preoccupation with, and love for, classical American cinema.

The film's free reinvention and repackaging of Chahine's childhood memories allows him to create a space from which the filmmaker excavates aspects of the past by way of relating to, and commenting on, the present. Of particular interest here is Chahine's emphasis on his own Christian background; his close friendships with a Muslim and a Jew; and the love story between two leftist activists, a Jewish woman and a Muslim man.

The film was widely acclaimed on the critical level, and seen as a new watershed in Chahine's cinema which, following his earlier Trilogy of Defeat (*The Choice*, *The Sparrow*, and *The Return of the Prodigal Son*), represented an attempt to explore the notion of merging the private and the public. Samir Farid suggests that in *Alexandria... Why?* Chahine seemed to overcome the anguish of the defeat which he and every Arab felt after 1967. This was achieved by reconstituting his anguish within a broader historical perspective that is never linear: "As a filmmaker who comes from a generation that was part of the revolution as well as its defeat, Chahine sought to re-explore his deeper roots." To achieve this, Farid suggests that "revisiting his personal history and the history of Alexandria was unavoidable."[13]

While the film was very warmly received in western circles and at European film festivals, *Alexandria... Why?* was not similarly appreciated among Arab critics. And while the film attracted a lot of attention in the local media, it was not able to attract wide audiences upon its release in Cairo. Equally as important, the film drew criticism from various nationalist circles that saw the film's sympathetic depiction of an Egyptian Jewish family's decision to leave Egypt and settle in Israel as an indication of the film's acceptance of the Egyptian government's attempt to normalize relations with Israel. And even Algeria, whose government was involved in financing the film, ultimately asked the producers to remove any reference to Algerian Radio and Television in the film's credits.

On another level, the stylistic approach in the film was also criticized from the view that, as with *The Choice* and *The Return of the Prodigal Son*, it prevented Chahine from communicating his message to Egyptian and Arab audiences. One critic wondered why Chahine, who is deeply rooted in Egyptian popular culture, would choose to ignore common Egyptians, electing instead to please only the elitist audiences of Egypt and the Carthage, Berlin, and Moscow festivals.[14] Sami al-Salamuni argues that if Chahine's goal was to find sources of funding and distribution, then he should have been more concerned about making films that are accessible to average people. After all, al-Salamuni contends, "it is this accessibility which should motivate the artist, and should become the highlight of the artistic process."[15] Al-Salamuni describes how the film's style hinders audience reception:

> For the first two thirds of the film it is very difficult to comprehend the dialogue, and it is impossible to figure out the relationships between the characters. Also, the direction and the montage transpose you from one episode to the other without any logical progression or continuity. Only toward the third part of the film, when the young Yehia struggles to go to America to study, that you feel attached to the events and find yourself witnessing a powerful artistic moment. In the end, if Chahine was capable of making such a powerful segment, then why was he determined to spoil the rest of the film with a confusing and pretentiously forced style that is enough to destroy any film and abort any message that he might have had?[16]

Other critics, however, refuted the criticisms against the film, both those regarding its style as well as those in relation to its political viewpoint on the Arab–Israeli conflict. These critics argued that Chahine's reference to religious diversity, which essentially reflected the social reality of Alexandria at the time, had nothing to do with praising the Camp David Accords with Israel.

Ibrahim al-Aris positions the film within the historical context of the late 1970s: over a decade after the defeat; years since the unexpected and tragic death of Nasser; the escalation of the Lebanese civil war; and the unexplainable peace forged with Israel by Sadat. Al-Aris suggests that within such rampant chaos, some self-criticism in conjunction with revisiting history was inevitable.[17] So now that Chahine needed to say more than could be said before, he needed to accept some responsibility when assessing his own history.

[He] needed to say something that was bolder and more razor-sharp.... Because if you have spent years of your life pointing your accusatory finger at others, criticizing and exposing them, then you are obliged at a certain moment to stop and look in the mirror and try to read your features by evaluating your own past and present. [At this point] you need to ask yourself, "Haven't you been integral to this game and [your nation's] history?" And consequently this actuality and this defeat?[18]

Samir Farid suggests that the film was meant to reflect upon the limitations of typically middle-class ambitions. Chahine's filmic treatment of Yehia, his own alter ego, portrays him as part of the generation that eventually forged the revolution. Through the film's emphasis on Yehia's family's struggle to find acceptance and a place for themselves and their son among the ruling-class elite symbolically alludes to how this ambitious class could become the victim of its own dreams and illusions.[19] Equally as important, Farid argues that at its essence, the film is about tolerance, emphasizing the possibility for human connections at a time of war and crisis. In this regard he suggests that the film reminds us that it is "the fascist military establishment in Israel" that is primarily and ideologically in opposition to the notion of coexistence between people of different faiths.[20]

Alexandria, Why?: A farewell to an unlikely lover (photo: Gamal Fahmy).

That part of Arab and Middle Eastern history is not depicted simply in terms of how it changed the demographics of an area that for centuries had remained richly multireligious, multicultural, and multiethnic but also how the creation of a religion-based state in the area was instigated, in part, by colonial interests and designs. What is of particular importance in *Alexandria... Why?* is how Chahine focuses on reaffirming the Arab identity of Egyptian Jews through the sympathetic portrayals of the friendship between David and Yehia, the love story between Sarah and Ibrahim, and, equally as important, through his depiction of Sorel, the middle-class Jewish father as a well-versed anti-Zionist. In one scene, as Sarah describes to Ibrahim her family's deep resentment about their move to Israel, there is a flashback of the war in Palestine before the declaration of the state of Israel. Sarah recounts how Zionism has turned Judaism into a nationality rooted in blood and violence. In the words of Ella Shohat and Robert Stam, Chahine's Jewish related plot fundamentally "undoes the simplistic equation of all Jews with Zionism, and with Europeanness," and as such undermines "the Eurocentric binarism of Arab versus Jew, evoking instead a complex history of nationalist [anticolonial] struggle which includes Egyptian Jews."[21] In an interview Chahine himself reaffirmed the anti-Zionist message of the film, noting that its notion of diversity

> is rooted in the city of Alexandria itself. Alexandrians are particularly diverse because historically they have lived among people from different nationalities and religions, such as Italians, Greeks and others. Jews were simply just another religious group, and only became an 'issue' as a result of the Palestine problem. But this only came later.... The problem was created by Zionism ... and this problem that it created, it will continue to pay for ... and of course we are forced to pay for it as well. [In the film] condemning Zionism comes from the Egyptian Jew when he says that Zionism is trampling the rights of the Palestinian people.... It is the Alexandrian Jew who realizes this dilemma.[22]

But while Chahine consistently referred to his condemnation of Zionism, he also condemned the trend among Arabs to adopt an anti-Jewish—as opposed to anti-Zionist—viewpoint:

> Today many do not make a distinction between a Jew and a Zionist anymore, and do not even fathom that many Jews support Arab causes ... and that there are even Israelis who support Palestinian rights.... It is a shame to lose the support of such people and push them away from expressing their solidarity with Arab rights.[23]

In the end, and in spite of the way *Alexandria... Why?* focused on the lost dreams of all its characters, Chahine's occasionally nostalgic look at a multi-religious city brought forward a particularly fresh and bold reassessment of Arab society and culture with important implications for Arab national identity. The film's depiction of Arab heterogeneity during a challenging moment in its history acknowledged this heterogeneity as an integral and critical tool in confronting contemporary tests of Arab unity and the historically persistent colonial attempts to divide the region. Coming at a time when Lebanon was struggling with religious-based prejudice that threatened to precipitate the creation of yet another scattered collection of faith-based states, the symbolic emphasis *Alexandria... Why?* placed on the dangers of nationalizing religion functioned as a warning against the deadly trap of religious and ethnic intolerance.

7

RESISTANCE, HETEROGENEITY, AND HISTORICAL MEMORY

Cinematic attempts to rethink historical memory employ visual and narrative strategies consistent with Foucault's theory of genealogy.[1] While traditional histories have been concerned with producing links that unite events into a coherent story, *writing genealogy* on the other hand, involves the recognition of disparity, of the dispersion of origins and links, of discontinuities and contradictions. As such, discourses (including filmic discourse) transmit and produce power and reinforce it, but they can also undermine and expose power, rendering it fragile and vulnerable. The cinematic juxtaposition of texture and history in *Adieu Bonaparte!* (1985) creates a trans-historical interplay between past and present that allows the audience to constantly contemplate traces of a forgotten and repressed history. In the process, viewers are challenged to re-remember a past where they appear different from themselves, or from what they thought they were, and thereby recover a sense of themselves as sites of difference, sites of possible transformation.

Chahine's first attempt to work with non-Arab coproducers after his difficult experience with the Soviets in *The People and the Nile* came in the form of an epic film depicting a critical period in Egypt's colonial history: the French invasion of Egypt in the late eighteenth century. *Adieu Bonaparte!* was partially financed by the French TF1 Films Production, and represented the beginning of a long association between Chahine's Misr International Production Company and French coproducers. While this involvement allowed Chahine the opportunity to further broaden his international appeal and audience, it also generated critical allegations that the foreign support was increasingly influencing Chahine to make films that appealed to western audiences and critics, hence promoting western viewpoints of the Arab world to Arabs.

While *Adieu Bonaparte!*'s story is based on events associated with the French occupation of Egypt and the revolt against it, its narrative thrust concentrates on individual reactions to a major event in Egyptian history. Through the depiction of a variety of relationships among Egyptians as well as between Egyptians and Europeans during a time of crisis, the film paints a complex picture of the Arab world's love/hate relationship with the west: a contradictory liaison reflecting the continuing Arab struggle for modernization—seen as a western-based concept—and the anxieties associated with this image in the context of colonial policies in the region.

AN EPIC ABOUT A COLONIAL CAMPAIGN

Adieu Bonaparte! followed Chahine's two autobiographical films *Alexandria . . . Why?* (1978) and *An Egyptian Story* (1982) and offered yet another way of contemplating anticolonial resistance. This time Chahine chose to challenge chauvinist forms of considering and dealing with the Other by focusing on the dialectics of anticolonial resistance as a modernist process of national transformation and liberation. Just as *Alexandria . . . Why?*, the film concentrates on connections and links that transcend religious and ethnic limitations, and features Yehia, Chahine's alter ego as the amiable but hesitant protagonist whose dreams are challenged by the realities of war and an invading colonial army.

The story is set in Egypt during the French occupation (1798–1803) and depicts colonialists unleashing their military force to oppress local resistance. Despite the film's title, the Bonaparte character is marginal to the plot; the central symbol of French occupation is General Caffarelli. Caffarelli is caught between his French aristocratic background and his fascination with Arab culture, as represented through his relationship with an Egyptian peasant he tries to help and learn from. The film tackles several themes but concentrates on anticolonialism, even while alluding to the conflict between tradition and modernization in the struggle for national liberation. Historical events, however, remain in the background of the more personal story of the encounter between three young Egyptians and General Caffarelli.

The story begins in July 1798 as Napoleon's army lands in Alexandria and conquers the Mamluk rulers. The military campaign, however, also involves scientists and civil servants who are pursuing their own projects in the country. As the French move to Cairo we are introduced to three brothers from a poor Egyptian family who loathe both the Mamluks (symbols of Ottoman domination) as well as the prospects of French colonization. The eldest brother, Bakr, supports armed rebellion and wants to help organize the resistance, and to that end has convinced the whole family to move with him to Cairo. Bakr's patriotism is matched by his religious devotion as a Muslim. His brother Yehia, on the other hand, is stoical and idealistic in his reaction to events. He speaks French, which he has learned from a Greek Alexandrian woman and from his work in a French Alexandrian's store. Ali, the youngest, is educated and loves poetry, and eventually develops a friendship with Caffarelli, one of Napoleon's top generals. The general is naively but genuinely interested in transforming Ali and Yehia into modern Frenchmen, helping them open a bakery and gradually becoming their close friend and tutor. A deep love and friendship develops between the two brothers and Caffarelli, with Ali spending many long hours discussing French poetry, literature, and theater with the general.

The Mamluks abandon the Egyptians and retreat to their castles, even firing at Egyptian demonstrators demanding arms to defend themselves. When Bonaparte arrives in Cairo he declares that he respects Islam and is in Egypt only to help modernize the country and help its people rid themselves of the parochial Mamluks. Egyptians, however, don't seem to buy Napoleon's rhetoric; resistance to the French grows as does the rift between Ali and his older brother Bakr, who accuses Ali of cooperating with the enemy because of his friendship with Caffarelli. Ali insists that to succeed in the fight against the French occupiers Egyptians need to learn to use their modern tactics and methods. To demonstrate his argument, Ali begins to work in a French-operated print shop where he secretly produces leaflets in support of the resistance. As the three brothers become embroiled in the resistance movement, Yehia is killed as he attempts to sneak out explosives from the French armory, and Bakr is arrested. Ali exploits his friendship with Caffarelli to gain his brother's release, but it comes at the expense of their relationship. Later, when Ali visits Caffarelli in Acre following the general's loss of his arm in the fight for the city, the general expresses his dismay over the violence of the campaign and its contradiction with proclaimed French ideals. The film closes with the image of Ali in the desert returning to Cairo after saying his final goodbye to his friend.

Adieu Bonaparte! specifically emphasizes aspects of unity among Egyptians from Jewish, Christian, and Muslim backgrounds. Despite the attempts by the French authorities to paint the resistance as a Muslim rebellion, we see how the struggle unites Bakr with Faltaous, a Copt, and David, a Jew. Chahine's depiction of a multifaith Egyptian resistance is further enhanced by an equally sympathetic portrayal of inter-ethnic relationships, which in turn transcend chauvinist hatred. Another character of interest is an Alexandrian girl of Greek background who speaks Arabic with a foreign accent. The girl's object of desire is an Egyptian boy who subtly shares her interest. The third character is a French merchant who has already made a home for himself in Alexandria but is excited about the opportunities for Egypt's progress with the coming of the French fleet. The merchant shares this excitement with an Egyptian boy who naively sees the French arrival as a possible alternative to the social and political repression of the Mamluk rulers. Chahine's depiction of Alexandria the morning before the French invasion paints it as a cosmopolitan setting about to fall apart as a direct result of colonial intervention.

A CONTROVERSY DESERVING OF AN EPIC

Adieu Bonaparte! was greeted with a polarized reception unequalled by any of Chahine's previous efforts. This time, however, the critical division of opinion transcended Egypt and the Arab world and carried over into Europe, with its opening in Paris garnering more attention than any previous screening of an Arab film in France. French media hailed the film in an unprecedented manner, with specialized film magazines and journals as well as local newspapers, radio, and television producing lengthy tributes to the film and its director. For several weeks before the film was screened at the Cannes Film Festival, Chahine became the subject of adulation to an extent that no other Arab filmmaker—and perhaps no other third world filmmaker—had ever received in France.[2] Ironically, however, French political reaction to the film was no kinder than Egypt's.

The film inspired impassioned debate, with French admirers of Bonaparte denouncing Chahine's depiction of events as unbecoming to the man's legacy.[3] Some French critics were dismayed by Chahine's emphasis on the Egyptian viewpoint of the story. In spite of the enthusiastic reception of the film at the Cannes festival and its consequent exhibition in French cinemas, Chahine was troubled by French media vilification of the film's anticolonial sentiment, its portrayal of the French campaign against Egypt as "tragic," and by the critics, artists, and historians who attacked the film as a contemptuous and scornful condemnation of Napoleon's image and legacy. One criticism that particularly stung Chahine was French historian Jean Tollard's comment that the film "concentrated too much on Egyptian peasantry instead of focusing on Bonaparte!"[4]

Conversely, Egyptian and Arab film critics accused Chahine of pandering to his French financial backers, seeing the film as a clear indication of Chahine's preoccupation with finding an international market for his films. Samir Farid considered *Adieu Bonaparte!*, as well as Chahine's next film, *The Sixth Day* (1986), as having been created with the goal of making a breakthrough in the international film market, and argues that—as with profit potential—such objectives should never be among a filmmaker's motivations. He contends that while Chahine's dream of entering the international market is shared by all artists, it should not be achieved at the expense of his art. And in any case, Farid insisted, "the international market will never be genuinely interested in screening films from countries such as Egypt, India, and similar nations unless their films are of good quality and display anauthentic reflection of their national culture."[5]

Chahine reacted angrily to both Arab and French attacks. When French critics derided Chahine for using French money to defame a French hero, he pointed out that the reported level of French support was, to begin, highly exaggerated. In one interview Chahine tried to de-mystify some of the controversy by putting the French production support in perspective:

> I did not take French money! I don't sell myself to anyone. The French's contribution did not exceed three million francs, an equivalent of 10 percent of the film's actual budget of 3 million dollars. People thought that the French support was 3 million dollars! Nonsense … this is not true! The fact is that the Egyptian Ministry of Culture contributed 3 million francs, and the French Ministry contributed another 3 million francs, and I had to put up the rest … my company, Misr Film International. The French contribution was also a loan which had to be paid from the film's screening income.[6]

Criticism against the film in the Arab press was vicious. Sami al-Salamuni, one of the leading Egyptian film critics at the time, described the Egyptian reaction in anticipation of the film's screening at the Cannes Film Festival:

> For a full month before the Cannes festival, there was unremitting blether about how Adieu Bonaparte! was so dangerous and harmful to Egypt, and how Youssef Chahine was rebuffing Egyptian people's resistance to the French Campaign. Even when Chahine acknowledges this resistance, he ends up attributing it to a Jewish boy who is depicted as the leader of the Egyptian struggle. There was also talk about how the film attempted to appease the French at our expense. The main source of all that campaign came from one 'genius' critic who claimed he had read the script and

discovered all these 'crimes.' He then went on to urge the 'festival committee' during its meetings not to allow, at any cost, the screening of the film in Cannes.[7]

Influential Egyptian critic Samir Farid wrote an extended analysis of the significance of the film's attempt to present a cinematic account of a critical period in Egyptian history. Farid's critique set the stage for much of the critical Arab reaction and as such represented the most cohesive negative reading of the film, arguing that Chahine failed to distinguish between the dynamics of writing one's own history and that of one's society.

Farid acknowledges that revisiting an historical moment does not equal an objective relating of events, that all histories are interpretive and subjective, and that artistic representations of history are grounded in the historical moment within which the artist is located and the artwork is produced. As such, no artist should feel obligated to prove the authenticity of her or his representation of events, rather, it is the representation of the artist's views on the *present*—through the work's inclusions and omissions—that is at stake.[8] Within this context, Farid argues that Chahine's depiction of the historical period rehashes a problematic outlook on the nature of the relationship between the west and the Arab world, one which underestimates the internal dynamics of the struggle for progress and reduces it to a one-sided passive reception and acceptance of what the west offers:

> The west for Youssef Chahine, and for some Arab intellectuals, represents progress and civilization, and from within this inferior perspective they feel that they need to follow the west in order to be able to move in the direction of civility and progress.... The French invasion of Egypt in 1798 (or the French Campaign as it is called in the west), signaled the official beginning of a complex relationship between the Arabs in Egypt and in the Arab world and the west.... Youssef Chahine is not alone in believing that the 'French Campaign' represented the beginning of the Egyptian modern era. But as Christopher Harold states at the end of his book Bonaparte in Egypt, the country in the late eighteenth century was already ripe for change, even if Bonaparte had never set foot at its shore... the same way Egypt's astonishing art in Luxor and Karnak was destined to be discovered even if Dizet never invaded Upper Egypt, and the hieroglyphics would have been deciphered even if the Rosetta Stone had been discovered a few years after the end of the campaign, and the Suez Canal would have been dug even if Napoleon had never ordered the first studies of the area.[9]

Farid then identifies the difference between the ideological resonance of autobiographical films such as *Alexandria... Why?* and *An Egyptian Story*—both of which manifest Chahine's own fascination with western culture—and *Adieu Bonaparte!*, which depicts the French invasion of Egypt and the Egyptian resistance to its occupation. Political depictions in the latter film cannot be isolated from how they impact the resistance to present-day western challenges to Arab political, economic, and cultural sovereignty: "Today we continue to face Bonaparte and Caffarelli together, embodied in the professional terrorism of Menachem Begin and in the archaeologist Moshe Dayan."[10]

Farid also critiqued what he saw as the film's misrepresentation of specific historical references, such as the idealized account of the relationships between Copts and Muslims at the time. Farid proposes that, contrary to what the film suggests, the French in fact succeeded in manipulating divisions between the two groups in consolidating their control of the country.[11] He also cites the film's allusion to the Egyptians' rejection of the Mamluks as equal in its intensity to their rejection of the French. This is historically erroneous, he charges, arguing that Chahine was indulging in the type of pharaonic Egyptian chauvinism that contends that Arabs themselves were also invaders, such that "the only real Egyptians are the descendants of the pharaohs." He suggests that such a perspective contradicts Chahine's own emphasis on diversity as the essence of Egyptian historical continuity.[12]

Even critics who tended to be sympathetic to Chahine's work seemed almost apologetic in their praise of the film. For his part Ibrahim Fawal suggests that the film was simply the outcome of circumstances that pushed Chahine to a particular way of depicting history. Fawal indicates that the coproduction followed the signing of a cultural treaty between Egypt and France in 1984. When the two governments decided to coproduce a film on Napoleon, each independently invited Chahine to direct the film. Under these circumstances, Fawal suggests, "it would have been impolite and counter-productive to flaunt the cruelties of Napoleon's invasion in the face of the French," and concludes that "Chahine shows enough of the military campaign, but stops short of embarrassing a new friend."[13] Viola Shafik, on the other hand, chooses to link Chahine's "de-historicization" of the events of the French campaign to the filmmaker's auteurist and deeply personal interpretation of history.[14]

For his part, Walid Shmeit recontextualizes the film and refutes criticisms against it, arguing that in making *Adieu Bonaparte!* Chahine was not as concerned with historical accuracy as with contemplating anti-imperialist

Adieu Bonaparte: The local versus the colonizing Other (photo: Gamal Fahmy).

struggle and the dynamics of its failures and successes. He poses the question, "Do we not as Arabs face today similar dilemmas as those faced by Egyptians over two centuries ago?" Shmeit links *Adieu Bonaparte!* to a familiar practice in Chahine's re-reading of history which tends to stress aspects of cultural and human resilience rather than military victories. He recounts how in *Saladin*, the focus was on the Muslim leader's respect for religious diversity and his reverence for human respectful associations even among enemies.[15] Shmeit also sees the film as an attempt to project a new understanding of the reasons behind today's current state of disarray—a condition that continues to affect the ability of Arabs to resist ongoing colonial designs and campaigns within the region. Therefore, the film is about the divisions, backwardness, and lack of organization that contributes to national defeat. In *Adieu Bonaparte!*, Shmeit suggests, the invading army achieves its military goals "because the conditions that are essential to face up to it never even existed." Egyptian resistance was scattered, unorganized, and unprepared and instead of uniting efforts to resist the invasion, there were intense disagreements regarding the best way to confront the colonial army. These divisions "resulted in creating further disorientation and weakness among Egyptians." But Shmeit also points to Ali's understanding of how to conquer the enemy by confronting it with humanity, clarity of perspective, and an ability to understand the contradictory dialectics in relationships with the Other, as exemplified in his friendship with Caffarelli.[16] As such, Chahine succeeds in portraying the struggle against colonialism as a long historical process involving complex connections between the economic, social, and cultural arenas that cannot be reduced to an easy dichotomy between 'us' and 'them':

> The French scientist General Caffarelli was able to understand the situation and as a result decided to part with [traditional colonial attitudes] because he began to learn the value and significance of forging a relationship based on mutual respect. But in the end Caffarelli is not Bonaparte, who leads his soldiers to Egypt to create his legacy of glory at the expense of others. For his part, Ali is the opposite of Bakr, who insists on monopolizing decisions and repressing other views, and ultimately calls on people to face Napoleon's guns with sticks. Ali, on the other hand, insists on learning from the other and on getting prepared for confronting the invaders instead of rushing into an adventure which will only result in inevitable defeat.[17]

To stress his point further Shmeit gives the contemporary example of the Lebanese resistance (the National Resistance Front) against the Israeli invasion of Lebanon in the 1980s, referring to its success in putting the Israeli army on the defensive.[18] This success, Shmeit argues, was due largely to the Lebanese resistance's ability to understand its own strengths and weaknesses, and eventually prepare, organize, and utilize this understanding to launch its effective campaign against the Israeli army.

RESISTANCE AND CONFRONTING THE OTHER

One certainly needs to problematize the clear tension between the anticolonial positions of Chahine and his self-identification as a Francophone and a Francophile. While it is critical to see how France and the French culture had an impact on Chahine's cinema, it is also seminal to contextualize the reception of Chahine in France as an emblematic 'Francophone' director. His influence on North African filmmakers, and the impact of coproduction with France on his international career, starting from *Adieu Bonaparte!*, offers an opportunity to open such a discussion, which has links to postcolonial love/hate relationships, theories of the Other, as well as to various Orientalist discourses.

Adieu Bonaparte! came out at time when Arab society was just entering a period of increased religious rhetoric and fanaticism. As the nationalist and Marxist left movements were losing political ground, and in the context of the problematic relationship between many Arab governments and political dissent, forms of political and ideological mobilization were gradually shifting and being taken up mainly by preachers in mosques. This contributed to the rise of popular rhetoric focused on chauvinist ways of looking at the colonial Other. Instead of engaging an historical and economic analysis of the west's colonial relationship with the Arab and Muslim worlds, fundamentalist rhetoric focused on religious difference, reducing the relationship between the Muslim world and the west to an ongoing religious crusade to defeat Islam. Such simplifications of history and politics can only result in the isolation that cultivates and exacerbates a fear of the Other. Meanwhile, the large Arab, North African, and Muslim populations in Europe—and France in particular—were being increasingly targeted for the racist rhetoric of local right wing groups. Anti-Arab and anti-Muslim racism, along with this heightened xenophobia, aggravated tensions between minority communities and the traditional European population.

Chahine's joint European-Arab cinematic enterprise seemed to echo two interrelated messages. On the one hand, the film addressed the Arab struggle against imperialism and colonialism, and the need to wrest the cause from the rhetorical fanaticism that had come to define it. *Adieu Bonaparte!* also insisted in recognizing that human commonalities that transcends boundaries, the modernization of society, and the utilization of new technologies and sciences, are all indispensable elements in the processes of emancipation and national self-determination. At the same time, through its espousal of a heterogeneous sense of Arab history and society, the film sought new contexts for belonging and difference that challenged traditional homogenizing perspectives on Arab identity and the struggle for self-determination.

Chahine's message to the west emphasized the need to forge a new kind of relationship with the Arab world, one based on the recognition of its colonial legacy and its ongoing social, economic, and political price. The message also emphasizes the need for a consistent effort to rectify divisions with the Arab world through building connections based on mutual respect and equality. As such, Chahine's reconstruction of Arab subjectivity and community in *Adieu Bonaparte!* complemented an increased and clearer emphasis on a more heterogeneous outlook on Arab identity and hence on the nature of the Arab national liberation project. While this approach represented a subtle footnote in most of his earlier work, it became an increasingly prominent feature in his films following 1978's *Alexandria . . . Why?*

On another level, one should also look at Chahine's increasingly self-reflexive work since the late 1970s as a reflection of tension between a more crystallized sense of identity in the filmmaker's cinematic approach, and his increasingly passionate insistence on seeing ideological and political

Adieu Bonaparte: Whose modernization is it anyway?! (photo: Gamal Fahmy).

intervention as an essential part of his work. This tension informed all his post-*Saladin* historical political epics beginning with *Adieu Bonaparte!* On the one hand, one should not overestimate the impact of Chahine's religious minority background on his artistic, political, and ideological evolution, and Chahine himself consistently rejected attempts by some western critics to look at his work with a skewed emphasis on his minority status. Chahine's rich personal history—rooted in his Egyptian, Arab Christian, Arab Muslim culture and society—in addition to his cosmopolitan academic background belie any reduction to the status of a minority or a marginalized artist. On the other hand, this same resonant complexity could not but have had an impact on his films and their marginalized characters who are determined to play an active role in the life of their society. Counter-hegemonic political cultural intervention, irrespective of the level of its engagement and intensity, is in itself a process which involves positioning one's self and ideas in oppositional proximity—if not on the periphery—of dominant ideological values and discourse. Such interventions require some degree of intellectual alienation in order to engage the creation of self-assertive cultural mechanisms. Within such parameters—the inevitable dialectic of daily challenges provoked by the political, economic, and social realities of the day—an activist and committed artist develops a sense of a human process, which, as Julio Cortazar suggests, "operates by synthesis, seeking to see things whole."[19]

In *Adieu Bonaparte!*, the character of Ali evokes a subtle alienation and somewhat shy indulgence in the struggle of resistance against the French occupiers. He also carries the baggage of his personal contradictory feelings about the Other, as represented in his ambiguous relationship with Caffarelli. Ali represents an embodiment of Chahine's own struggle to synthesize tensions between the personal and the public in his depiction of the dialectics of national liberation. As in *Alexandria . . . Why?*, the role of Chahine's alter ego is played by Mohsen Mohieddin, a role later repeated in *The Sixth Day* (1986) and explicitly remembered and lamented in *Alexandria Again and Forever* (1990). As such, Ali's elusive character is central to the film's reconstruction of Arab subjectivity and the collective process of national liberation struggles.

The character of Ali—most notably in his response to the French invasion—establishes a productive space in which to identify the impact of the personal on discursive formations. By responding to the disjunctured elements that led to his relationship with Caffarelli, Ali embarks on a journey of exchanges, encounters, and confrontations impossible under normal conditions. The ambivalent merging of personal identity, national identity, and otherness in Ali's relationship with Caffarelli becomes a site of struggle where identity is anchored in the contradictory dynamic of interaction and resistance; Ali's political agency is accordingly detached from angst and silence, and represents a defiant rejection of culpability and anxiety. Within this process of recognition and rejection, individual and collective subjectivity can finally be restructured.

Ali's seemingly contradictory sense of alienation and connection, inferiority and belonging, mirrors the Arab national project's genealogical recognition of discrepancy, of the diffusion of origins and links, of ruptures and of incongruity. Ali's subjectivity, however, is tangible and palpable. His dynamic communion with his brothers, family, community, and—crucially—with Caffarelli, is not a luxurious indulgence in intellectual learning, or an enhancement of self through the creation/naming of an Other; Ali's relationships reveal the complex negotiations individuals undertake to find their place within communal forms of political engagement. As such, Ali embodies the constant process of reassessment, a critical aspect of the unfinished nature of the Arab national liberation project itself . . . as Chahine envisions it.

8

QUEER TRANSGRESSION AND POSTCOLONIAL AMBIVALENCE

The question of how sexual norms are constituted within contemporary Arab cultural contexts remains a fascinating puzzle to which postcolonial scholarship has yet to offer more than an indifferent mention. Scanning contemporary Arab cinema through the lens of queer studies, however, reveals many films exploring issues of gender identity and sexual difference, and challenging patriarchal culture in the broader context of the struggle for national and social liberation.

Alexandria Again and Forever (1990), one of Chahine's most celebrated films, is a rich and complex example of Arab cinema that affirms non-normative personal identities by rethinking traditional notions of nation. This elaborately reflexive third installment of his biographical trilogy, though ostensibly dedicated to Egyptian artists and their struggle for democracy and freedom, materially exposed Chahine's perspective on his own art and personal relationships. As with his earlier autobiographical films, *Alexandria Again and Forever* plays like a docudrama, though this time with Chahine playing himself in the role of Yehia. Chahine's stylistic outlook on his personal experiences, despairs, and anxieties, as well as his hopes and aspirations are reconciled within loosely connected cinematic episodes of fantasy and reality. But the creative, political, and personal struggles of the filmmaker are laid out in a manner unprecedented in world cinema, let alone in Arab cinema.

There are similarities between Chahine's fantastical autobiographical vision and those of such filmmakers as Fellini or Bob Fosse (especially in *All that Jazz*, 1979), particularly in their choice of a modernist stylistic approach to depict their stories. However, Chahine's disclosure of the most intimate of his personal aspirations and anxieties (such as his bisexual fantasies and relations, and his apprehensions of aging) breaks major taboos in the history of self-reflexive cinema. What is unique about this film is Chahine's ability to convincingly link the private and public; an inherently postcolonial approach in that social and political issues are relentlessly superimposed over the private spheres of sexual liberation and individual hopes and anxieties, to the extent that distinguishing between them becomes virtually impossible.

Alexandria Again and Forever represented a critical juncture in launching a radically new outlook on non-normative and queer sexuality within Arab cinema. Chahine's approach in this film remains a unique Arab cinematic experience in its boldly complex integration of the body politic and the politics of liberation. In this chapter I provide a general context for scholarship on the approximation of queerness in Arab cinema. Such a brief survey is important in order to position my analysis within the broader framework of an area which remains an overwhelmingly untapped area of research. I then provide an assessment of the film that places it first within the complex framework of queer representation in Arab cinema, particularly over the last three decades, and then in the context of its public reception in an Arab world willfully blind to its queer significance. Finally, I discuss the film as a key example of the intersection of the politics of the personal and the public in postcolonial cinema.

A SURVEY OF SCHOLARLY RESEARCH ON QUEER DEPICTIONS WITHIN ARAB CINEMA

If scholarship on Arab cinema is limited then scholarship on queer representations in Arab films remains virtually nonexistent. Still, some present work on homosexuality in Arab culture and cinema is noteworthy. Brian Whitaker's 2006 book *Unspeakable Love: Gay and Lesbian Life in the Middle East* attracted attention in the west and in the Arab world itself. One chapter in the book focuses on gay images in Arab films. Frederic Lagrange's "Male Homosexuality and Modern Literature" (2002) makes important reference to homosexuality in Arab films. Garay Menicucci's 1988 article "Unlocking the Arab Celluloid Closet: Homosexuality in Egyptian Film," is an important attempt to explicitly discuss homosexuality in Arab films. Of interest are articles and interviews written and given by Youssef Chahine himself, some of which specifically deal with homosexual references in his films. Of particular interest is Chahine's 2004 interview with Ibrahim al-Aris. Other writers on gender and masculinity in Arab cinema include Martin Stollery and Rahiba Hadji-Moussa. Raz Yosef's 2004 book titled *Beyond Flesh: Queer Masculinities and Nationalism in Israeli Cinema* provides relevant insight to understanding possible intersections and divergences between cinematic queer representations in Israeli and Arab cinemas.

In a recent book titled *Desiring Arabs* (2007), Joseph Massad argues against a "missionary" campaign orchestrated by white western-based gay movements that seek to universalize their own colonial version of human rights and addresses the question of queer transgression in relation to postcolonial discourses. Massad criticizes and problematizes the notions of "homosexuality" and "gay culture" arguing (following Said's *Orientalism*) that they are western constructs. The book is of great importance for those interested in investigating further possibilities of a specifically postcolonial perspective on dealing with the notion of queerness within a specifically Arab context. An equally important book in the same regard is Robert Aldrich's *Colonialism and Homosexuality*. Walter Armbrust discusses issues of masculinity in contemporary Egyptian cinema in several writings, and Ghassobu and Sinclair-Webbs's book *Imagined Masculinities: Male Identity and Culture in the Modern Middle East* also includes various chapters on male sexuality in Arab culture. Of particular scholarly importance to discussions on gender in Arab society is Fatima Mernissi's book *The Veil: Male–Female Dynamics in a Modern Muslim Society* which gives critical insights into issues of male sexuality and culture in Arab and Muslim societies. There are several works dealing with homosexuality in Arab and Muslim culture and literature. Most important is the seminal book *Islamic Homosexualities: Culture, History, and Literature* by Stephen Murray and Will Roscoe as well as *Homoeroticism in Classical Arabic Literature*, edited by J. Wright and Everett Rowson, both published in 1997.

ALEXANDRIA AGAIN AND FOREVER IN THE CONTEXT OF QUEER ARAB CINEMATIC REPRESENTATION

Arab cinema has had a long tradition of homosexual themes or subthemes, but as in many other societies, latent homophobia had long since led to the creation of cinematic codes that masked—even while tending to imply— homosexual relations (*viz.* America's Hays Code). Over the last two decades, however, some Arab films have been dealing more openly with gay and bisexual relations within Arab society.

Since the early 1990s, Arab cinema, both in the Middle East and North Africa, has been undergoing major changes and transformations. Newer Arab films are increasingly informed by the far-reaching perspective of an Arab national project reshaping social, political, cultural and gendered experiences of history and memory. More recently a number of mainstream and experimental Arab films have been featuring gay and bisexual characters and issues that implicitly or explicitly critique heterosexism and patriarchal norms. In Egypt, Youssef Chahine has been instrumental in refashioning traditional modes and lending momentum to the emergence of a new Arab cinema, one informed by the political, social, and cultural turmoil that has plagued the area since the second half of the last century.

In the mid-1970s Chahine's cinema began to claim a public space for issues that were traditionally censored from the Arab public sphere. Beginning with *Alexandria ... Why?* (1978) his films were concerned with deconstructing the ideologies that sustain traditional stereotypical representations of homosexuality and bisexuality. With *Alexandria ... Why?* and *An Egyptian Story* (1982), the first two of his Alexandria trilogy films, Chahine embarked on the first autobiography in the history of Arab cinema.[1] *Alexandria ... Why*'s loving account of Adel's affair with the British soldier he had originally planned to kill was—and remains—a unique and daring moment in Arab cinema. As Rafiq al-Sabban suggests, the aristocratic Adel is portrayed as a man who carries the dreams of his personal social and sexual revolt like a cross:

> [Adel] 'buys' a British officer so he can kill him, but in reality is living an impossible dream of very special attributes, which are protected by magical butterflies, where the enemy can become a lover ... and in the end, the knife turns into a kiss.... This dream, however, is aborted by death and tragedy....The British officer dies in battle, and Adel visits him at the [Alamein] graveyard, a symbol with no meaning, his grief resonating with a mornful English folk song.[2]

But despite this film's sympathetic portrayal of a gay character, Chahine's sexual politics remained largely obscure. In *An Egyptian Story* (1982), Chahine introduced homoerotic tension through the knowing eye contact between Yehia (the character representing Chahine in his Alexandria trilogy films) and a London cab driver. And there were delicately woven insinuations of a queer relationship between Ali and Caffarelli in *Adieu Bonaparte!* (1985), and earlier, albeit on a much more modest scale, in the relationship between Nicolai and Barak in *The People and the Nile* (1968). Another non-normative expression of sexuality—in the form of an intergenerational relationship—is witnessed between Nayla and Tariq in *Dawn of a New Day* (1964), and later evoked in the relationship between Sadika and Okka in *The Sixth Day* (1986).

Depictions of non-normative sexuality had remained a marginal component of his oeuvre, but with *Alexandria Again and Forever* in 1990 Chahine produced a milestone in the cinematic representation of queerness in Arab cinema. Today Chahine's characterization of queer sexuality in *Alexandria Again and Forever* stands as a complex amalgam of his signature politics of change with the subtle politics of sexual liberation.

Syrian director Osama Muhammad was one of the earliest Arab filmmakers to connect—however obliquely—the repression of bisexuality and patriarchal oppression. His 1988 debut *Nujum al-naha* (Stars in Broad Daylight) explores the dissolution of a family during its preparation for a wedding. Set in a rural Syrian village, the divisive dynamics of patriarchal oppression, and the inherent links between familial and sociopolitical violence are exposed via a homosexual couple's relationship.

Similarly, Yousry Nasrallah's *Mercedes* (1993) approaches homosexuality in Arab society from a political perspective, depicting the relationship between a man who abandons his upper-class lifestyle with his gay partner in Europe, choosing instead a chaotic existence with his working-class lover in Cairo. The couple become part of a group of young marginalized Egyptians of indeterminate sexual preference. *Mercedes* exposes upper class Egyptians' hypocritical homophobia and links it to their self-loathing infatuation with western culture and its preoccupation with capturing a share of a globalized capitalist economy. As such, *Mercedes* deals with same-sex relationships by specifically accounting for the multilayered nature of postcolonial sexual repression.

More recently, Arab films have begun to deal with homosexuality as a matter-of-fact issue. While many of these films are produced by Arab exiles in Europe, they nevertheless point to a growing Arab cinematic practice that includes Daoud Aoulad-Syad's *Bye-bye souirty* (*Adieu Forain*, Morocco, 1998), which features a homosexual transvestite dancer in the lead role, and *Une minute de soleil en moins* (A Minute of Sun Less, Nabil Ayouch, 2002) where the principal character is a police inspector sharing a platonic friendship with a transvestite. Another film of interest is Khalid al-Haggar's *Room to Rent* (Haggar, 2000), about Ali, an Egyptian student who longs to remain in London after his visa expires. When he strikes up a friendship with Mark, a gay photographer, he must re-examine his attitudes and biases regarding sexuality and socially constructed gender roles. More recent examples include *'Imarat Ya'cubyan* (The Yacoubian Building, Marwan Hamed, Egypt, 2006), *Bosta* (Phillippe Aractingi, Lebanon, 2005), *Khalina nurqus* (Let's Dance, Inas Degheidi, Egypt, 2006), and *Caramel* (Nadine Labaki, France/Lebanon, 2007). Lebanese Akram Zaatari's *Kaifa uhibbuk* (How I Love You, 2002) and

Palestinian Tawfiq Abu Wael's *Yawmiyat shab 'ahir* (Diary of a Male Whore, Tawfiq, 2001) are among the more daring in their critiques of the sexual repression of gays and bisexuals, but due to their experimental character seem less likely to reach a wider audience.

THE IMAGE OF THE ARTIST AS A TROUBLED ACTIVIST

As with many artists who challenge societal norms of sexuality, Chahine attempted to make such issues integral to his examinations of social and national liberation, and thereby found a natural space to voice his personal anxieties within his autobiographical trilogy. Although issues directly impacting queer sexuality remained underrepresented in most of Chahine's work, their subtle incorporation into *Alexandria Again and Forever* represented an important challenge to the Arab and Egyptian cinemas that had almost entirely overlooked them. As such, *Alexandria Again and Forever* denoted a critical departure from traditional Arab cinematic interpretations of queer sexuality.

The central relationship portrayed in *Alexandria Again and Forever* is introduced in the context of an alliance between a struggling actor, Amr, and Yehia, the director who may be able to help him realize his dreams. Their disparate roles in the pact create a tension between the two that presages the relationship's inevitable disintegration. Commenting on the relationship between Yehia and Amr in the film, Chahine refers to its troubled essence as he sees it:

> [In the film] I have sought to understand the 'dictatorships' that govern my own relationships, and I saw how they kill everyone. I saw how the 'dictator' in my attitude finally caused a deformation in the relationship. This is what I did as I tried to force someone else to become who I wanted him to be, but this was never fair. I only recognized this later, but back then I always tried to rationalize my dictatorship and to defend it, just like our country's leader today rationalizes the creation of a new security force ... of course only for the service of the people.[3]

Yehia is happily married to an attractive and independent minded woman, yet longs for Amr, the young actor who now wants to leave him to try his luck in commercial television and embark on "a boring conventional life." Despondent, Yehia lapses into a state of deep creative idleness.

Yehia joins in an artists' strike to oppose government intervention in the affairs of their union. Taking a stand for democracy against the Egyptian government, he joins a hunger protest that has rallied Egyptian film artists of all persuasions. As the strikers increase their demands, Yehia is overcome by his desire for Amr, whose career he had launched with the (fictional) film *Alexandria... Why?* But this obsession is soon overtaken by his budding interest in Nadia, the self-confident activist/actress he casts in his next feature. Against the backdrop of a solidarity meeting of the Film Artists' Union, Yehia and Nadia, too, are united. Their accord brings about a new chapter in the filmmaker's life as he enters an equal, albeit unconventional, relationship with Nadia; one which reconciles him with the need for a stronger connection with his film audiences as well as with his own identity as a political and social activist artist.

As the film opens, Amr, a young actor who has just won recognition for his role in one of Yehia's films, is now refusing to play Hamlet in his next production. Rather than languish in Yehia's shadow and continue to endure the hurtful gossip about their relationship, Amr wants to get married, have children, and "live a normal life." So Yehia, who considers Amr his younger alter ego, shares with the actor his story of seeing John Gielgud's last performance in the role of Hamlet in Cairo in 1940.[4] Because Yehia never had the opportunity to play the role himself, he now wants Amr to be the Hamlet he could never be. Amr eventually agrees to play the part, but their unspoken love, along with Yehia's merciless perfectionism, conspire to make the process almost unbearable.

Just before they are to embark on a trip to the Berlin Film Festival, Yehia's wife Gigi is injured in a car accident and is unable to accompany him there. So when their entry wins in Berlin, Yehia and Amr, its star, break into a fantasy dance sequence set to the American classic, "Walking My Baby Back Home." But Amr's joy is short-lived when their next cinematic collaboration is not as successful, and his failure to garner an award leaves him devastated, as witnessed by the second fantasy dance in which Amr dances alone on the roof as Yehia can only watch. Amr is overwhelmed with grief as he dances to a sad rendition of a well-known Umm Kalthum song about the end of a love marred by heartbreak and suffering.

Later, when Yehia begins production on his Alexander and Cleopatra film, Amr joins him, but their passions have faded. By the time Yehia is ready to film a final shot of Alexander laying in a glass coffin, he replaces Amr with a dummy rather than have to interact with the man. Like Pygmalion before him, Yehia has tried to create a perfect image to adore, but now he finds he cannot give it life. When workers' drills send debris crashing down on the set, and Yehia fails to save the shattered coffin and body, he is forced to move on with his life. But by now his heart has moved on and he has become infatuated by the beautiful activist Nadia, who is playing Cleopatra.

Alexandria Again and Forever: Chahine performing his "popular culture" skills (photo: Gamal Fahmy).

At first Nadia tries to reconcile the men, but backs down once she realizes the depth of Amr's resentment. But after telling Nadia of his marriage and his new life, Amr admits that he still loves Yehia, and wonders if the filmmaker indeed loves him, or just the image he created. Eventually, Nadia mediates Yehia's return to political activism when she encourages him to join the actors' union strike. The two forge a curious relationship, where both probe for truth and art in their work and in their relationship.

With its allusions to Chahine's previous films, *Alexandria Again and Forever* presents yet another elaborately reflexive take on his filmmaking career. At times we are treated to scenes with Chahine, in the role of Yehia, watching and commenting on Chahine's films as if he were their director. The final scene of *Alexandria Again and Forever* crosses another diegetic line as it captures the real events of the 1978 cinema artists' strike. And in another scene, Yehia speaks for Chahine as he denounces new trends in television shows funded by businessmen from the Gulf states, arguing that these "intruders" have no interest except in making money. Yehia/Chahine goes on to make the case that through increasingly reactionary policies and practices, and the censorship of Egyptian and Arab cinema and television, the capitalists have effectively ruined the careers of many talented actors and artists.

Stylistically, the film plays like a docudrama. Chahine's depiction of his personal experiences, despairs, and anxieties as well as his hopes and aspirations are all reconciled within loosely connected cinematic episodes that fluidly fluctuate between fantasy and reality. *Alexandria Again and Forever* incorporates the generic conventions of drama, musical, comedy, and cartoon with a seemingly unsystematic swapping between locations and timeframes. In the words of Ibrahim Fawal, the film stages "baffling moments" that come across like a hybrid operetta "of straight-forward narrative, cinema verite, formalism, expressionism, and some animation." But while these different stylistic moments may cause some unease in the viewer, the final result is indeed "stimulating, its style fresh and original."[5]

QUEER SENSIBILITY AND TRANSGRESSION

My research into commentaries on *Alexandria Again and Forever* in Egyptian and Arab newspapers, art magazines, and journals reveals an indigenous reading of the film diametrically different from the way it was received by western critics and journalists. While western critics emphasized the personal in relation to the film's tacit reflection of Chahine's own homosexual desire, Arab writers and critics ignored or avoided any acknowledgement of the filmmaker's sexual orientation.[6]

Ahmad Youssef, for example, instead chose to focus on how the film was "the first and perhaps the only Arab film to date" to depict an agonizing and bitter experience with an honest moment of self-reflection by an artist who, for the most part of his life, "has been searching for and demanding freedom." Further, he writes that through this process Chahine realized he is seeking personal freedom: "this occurs as he poses the 'I' to interact with the collective." In the end, the film puts things in perspective: "the issue is not simply about the artist's freedom of expression, but is rather about the right of people to be free."[7]

For his part, Ibrahim al-Aris considers the film as an attempt by Chahine to reflect upon the three most important components of his personal universe: his 'I,' history, and cinema. This combination, however, is presented as being in a state of flux and rebellion where each component struggles to free itself from Chahine's strong grip. This is exemplified in various evocative images and situations in the film: "a yawning Alexander; a shattered underground museum; a group of cinema artists who collectively say no to 'postponing democracy'; Chahine being rejected by two personifications of his alter ego (Nadia and Amr); and finally in the form of an Egyptian cinema which seems increasingly submissive to the logic of the new market, the Gulf states, and the bitterness which is beginning to inflict the process of making the new film."[8]

Perhaps understandably, Arab critics are reticent to name things for what they are when it comes to defining the kind of personal freedom that is the subject of this film; dealing with the specificities of the personal is difficult when issues of sexuality are still largely taboo in the Arab world. This is somewhat contrasted by Chahine's own less than timid recognition of the personal significance of Amr's character in the film. In an interview with Arab journalist Kussai Saleh al-Darwish, Chahine spoke freely about his feelings on beauty, talent and love:

> It is one thing when I fall in love with people who are good looking, but if they are also talented, I'm in danger! Even with 'kids' [he uses the word awlad, which in colloquial Egyptian Arabic refers to younger men], when they were talented they would make a different impact [on me] than others who were less talented.... I always see beyond physical beauty.... Of course in the case of people like Amr you feel very attached to him because he is very attractive.[9]

My reading of *Alexandria Again and Forever* is in some way inspired by the general thrust of these local readings of the film, particularly in how they see it as a marker of the filmmaker's renewed interest in Egyptian and Arab politics. But I am also intrigued by these critics' subtlety in approaching the topic of sexual orientation. It is within this context that I was inspired to present this acutely *postcolonial* queer reading (rather than simply a queer or gay reading) of the film. Equally as important, this analysis is particularly interested in how the film creates a fluid inter-passage between the personal and the political through a nuanced depiction of struggles for personal liberation under postcolonial conditions. As such, my exploration of the film accounts for Chahine's new strategies in dealing with issues of sexuality and sexual liberation. Thus the rest of this chapter offers a new reading of *Alexandria Again and Forever*, one that concentrates on its queer discourse and how this discourse marks postcolonial challenges and tensions between the personal and collective, and the sexual and national. It also points out how the film's queering of gendered experiences informs and is informed by wider transformative Egyptian and Arab struggles for social and political liberation. Within this framework, I hope to do justice to Chahine's experience of the Alexandria film trilogy:

> We are managed by everything that is happening in the world—it's globalization. They say it's an open market, but who are they kidding?

Why were we not able to penetrate America? Because they've had all the monopolies, in films and other areas. You have to know what is happening in the world, because it influences your characters, your country—it even influences your sex life; what happens in bed depends on what is happening in politics.[10]

In my conversations with Arab scholars, film buffs, and movie fans over the years, I have often raised the issue of homoeroticism in this and other Chahine films. The discussions were always fascinating in that they were consistently diverted to issues of colonial and neocolonial heritage as they impact Arab national consciousness in terms of national liberation and democracy— leaving issues of sexuality and sexual liberation resolutely unspoken.

It was the French, and later, British colonials who first introduced anti-homosexual laws in Egypt and the Arab world. Bruce W. Dunne notes that "pre-modern and colonial Egypt had no law against homosexuality, in spite of the insistence of the British that there should be one."[11] For his part, Fredric Lagrange suggests that some of the values that are now considered to be *'adatna wa taqalidna* (our customs and traditions) within urbanized Arab societies are for the most part relatively new, having only emerged in the 1800s. More importantly, they are values "that are at odds with classical (or rather pre-modern) representations of virility, as exemplified in *adab* literature which allowed for a wider spectrum of male desire." Lagrange argues that modern Arab ideals of morality are at odds with traditional

> popular representations and male sexual practices—which see little harm in active homosexual intercourse—easily vilified as evidence of the residue of underdevelopment, ignorance and lack of education. The newly enforced values are a reformist construction resulting from the encounter between a theoretical Islamic ethics of normalized sexuality, the influence of colonial domination and the desire to adopt Victorian-style norms as a token of 'civilization.'[12]

This argument is important to the understanding of the dynamics of contemporary homophobia in the Arab world as an Othering practice. Depicting homosexuality (or any unconventional sexual relationships or practices, for that matter) as an element of foreign (read decadent/western) culture, essentially mirrors the way Europeans viewed Arab societies during the colonial period. Brian Whitaker pushes further, arguing that religious and national fanaticism regarding homosexuality in contemporary Arab societies is a "reversal" of an originally Orientalist western attitude:[13]

Western orientalism, as analyzed by Edward Said in his influential book, highlights the 'otherness' of oriental culture in order (Said argued) to control it more effectively. Reverse orientalism—a comparatively new development in the Arab world—taps into the same themes but also highlights the 'otherness' of the West in order to resist modernization and reform. Homosexuality is one aspect of Western 'otherness' that can be readily exploited to whip up popular sentiment.[14]

Irrespective of the plausibility of Whitaker and Lagrange's arguments (both tend to disregard or marginalize, for example, the consideration of the complex dynamics of more recent American and western neocolonialist attitudes in connection with the Arab world), they both nevertheless allude to what must be addressed in any serious study of queerness within contemporary Arab cultural practices: the intersection between colonial politics and national identity. In addition, Whitaker's argument reminds us that any effort to deal with queerness within Arab societies and culture has to go beyond the personal surface, a preoccupation that often accompanies identity politics-based studies and approaches.

Certainly the rendering of bisexual desire in *Alexandria Again and Forever* is more subtle and contained than those found in western cinemas in the late 1980s. Indeed, Chahine's representations are nowhere near as explicit as those celebrated in classical Arabic literature and poetry (*viz* the work of seventh-century Arab poet Abu Nuwas as referenced by Pasolini in his 1974 *A Thousand and One Nights*).[15] Nevertheless, Yehia/Chahine's desire transgresses and subverts the boundaries of gender and age as poetically as any of the classic scribes.

Alice Kuzniar suggests that the notion of queerness works with a double definition, "at times in consonance with 'gay' and 'lesbian,' and at times in contradiction." Furthermore, she argues, queerness

> can collapse distinctions between gay, lesbian, bisexual, and transgender, yet it does not deny their common allegiance to non-heterosexual pleasures. It partakes in the activism of gay and lesbian communities and furthers their concerns, yet also questions their identity politics.[16]

Through Yehia, Chahine consistently "collapses" any definitions that presuppose his sexual preference. Instead, Yehia projects a collage of interchangeable desires, and in the end Chahine's own subjectivity "shines as a play of scintillating mirrors."[17] An example of this play can be seen in a scopophilic sequence that indulges in foot fetish titillation. When Yehia asks Nadia why she is walking barefoot, and she answers "it's good for the arch," a surreal fantasy sequence ensues: Yehia is directing *Anthony and Cleopatra* with Yehia and Nadia starring in the leading roles. When Anthony/Yehia protests that his official statue in Alexandria makes him appear flatfooted, the sculptor suggests he audition forty male models to choose the most beautiful feet to replicate for the statue. But when Nadia surreptitiously enters her foot into the blind competition Anthony chooses hers as the most beautiful arch. In the final shot of this imaginary episode we see Anthony swimming through fog toward another male swimmer. On reaching the boy he staggers him with an embrace and a kiss on the mouth, calling him "Cleopatra." With his typical economy of scale, Chahine has effectively transformed the legendary couple's love story into an utterly whimsical game of desire, with Anthony recast as the capricious bisexual Yehia. The parallel is reinforced later in the film when, as he helps Amr dress for the awards event that will signal the end of their relationship and the initiation of Yehia's fascination with Nadia, the camera slowly tilts down to focus on Yehia's hand gently touching Amr's foot.

Another sequence illustrating Yehia/Chahine's sexual ambivalence regarding gender and ageing opens with Amr's confession to Nadia that although he still loves Yehia, he has had enough of the difficulties associated with their relationship. His last words allude to Yehia's love for giving flowers. In the subsequent shots Yehia is seen holding a bouquet of flowers as Nadia tells him that Amr is not coming back and that he should move on with his life and career. Yehia shoots back, "Do you think I'm at a picnic here, just running around looking for attractive boys who look like girls in their *galabiya*s [an Arab common dress] . . . and for girls in jeans acting like Rambo?!" The viewer is left to wonder who the flowers were meant for: are they for Amr who Yehia is hoping will come back? And now that he realizes that Amr is never coming back, will he give the flowers to Nadia? But Yehia keeps the flowers. Later when Nadia's mother tells Yehia which of his films is her favorite (with a television set in the background playing Chahine's *Cairo Station*), it is she who receives the bouquet . . . in yet another illustration of Chahine's play with ambivalence and transgression of sexual desire.

All the above scenes denote playful allegories to Yehia's multiple objects of desire, from male to female and vice versa. The Anthony and Cleopatra sequence in particular has the ambiance of a celebration of the filmmaker's capacity to shift fluidly between sexual fantasies, occasionally using foot fetishism as a mischievous mediator between unpredictable desires. As such,

Alexandria Again and Forever: Elusive tranquility in a changing Alexandria (photo: Gamal Fahmy).

the filmmaker's queer subjectivity operates in an evolving non-generic articulation of the eroticism of transgression. In addition to their queer allusions, these scenes also advance Chahine's struggle to locate his own ego within the shifting embodiments of his desire.

As actors and artists, Amr and Nadia function as aspects of Chahine's alter ego—his Pygmalions—as, on another level, does the character of Yehia. In addition to indulging the filmmaker's queer subjectivity, this triad of alter egos allows Chahine the freedom to choose—or blend—feminine and masculine sensibilities, youth and age, the performative and the disciplined, all within the paradigmatic sphere that shepherds Chahine's playful transgressions. This anti-normative sense of the erotic guides the filmmaker's novel approach to expressions of sexuality in a film where sexual identities and desires resist containment. Thus Yehia's sexuality does not reflect some natural essence, but rather is rendered as an excessive and erratic construction and deconstruction of itself.

As it questions static identity affiliations, the film redefines the sexual *I* as the site of virtual desire, forever hybrid and in a state of metamorphic flux. Within this context, any possible consolidation within the film's game of desires is sidelined for the sake of transformative elements that allow Yehia's identity to move across sexual boundaries more freely and fluidly. From a counter-political stance, the film offers a persuasive model for the remaking (as opposed to the confirmation) of identities and desires. It is this unpredictability that allows the film to counter paradigmatic models of sexual and gender conduct, irrespective of their origins.

POSTCOLONIAL AMBIVALENCE

From a postcolonial perspective, however, Chahine's cinematic transgressions can also be seen as manifestations of the ambivalence that functions at sites of colonial dominance—where cultural processes are always most productive when they are most ambivalent. Hybrid subjectivities within these sites tend to produce their own slippages, excesses, and difference, but as a consequence, they are able to establish themselves as sites for the relentless struggle imbedded in the various planes of personal, social, and political resistance. In *Alexandria Again and Forever* Chahine uses Yehia's personal drama to reflect upon the tensions between—and intersections of—the personal, the collective and the political as they interact and collide within a postcolonial setting.

When Yehia/Chahine first dances with Amr in a fantasy of overwhelming joy after receiving the Silver Bear at the Berlin Film Festival for his film *Alexandria... Why?*, the sequence reflects the dynamics of their relationship as one made manifest through emptiness and ensnared by the tensions between unity and competition, love and control. Isolated on a nearly barren snow-covered sound stage, they break into a dance routine à la Gene Kelly and Ginger Rogers; the camera constantly following, capturing and recentering the couple within the frame.

The camera movement works with the minimalist staging and cold bluish lighting to focus of our cinematic gaze on the couple, their contradictory relationship and Yehia/Chahine's continued struggle with his alter ego. The dance choreography itself keeps Yehia and Amr at the center of the frame, but it also intermittently pulls them apart into two performative solitudes— foreshadowing their imminent parting. Furthermore, and despite his youthful vigor, Amr's dancing allows him just enough freedom to remain within the filmmaker's orbit as he emulates a male bird flapping his wings to impress his female object of desire.

The scene reiterates Yehia's performing artist ego's struggle between controlling and loving Amr. It also contemplates a period in Chahine's career when he was criticized for becoming overly self-indulgent and elitist, and for losing his focus on Egypt's social and political problems. But on another level the sequence also functions allegorically as a sly expression of postcolonial resistance.

The dance takes place in a snowy European country, and the dance assumes its shape to the tune of an American song. Toward the end of the routine,

Yehia tells Amr of his lifelong obsession with playing Hamlet as inspired by the final performance of the role by Sir John Gielgud in 1940s colonial Cairo. Gielgud's performance of Hamlet is now considered among the earliest queer interpretations of the role, and the scene juxtaposes photographic images of Gielgud's Hamlet with a photo of a teenaged Chahine playing the same role. These images are interrupted with a filmic insert of Amr playing the role of Chahine in a theater audience watching himself playing a Gielgud interpretation of Hamlet. In this complex and confusing play of images, the postcolonial present is consistently destabilized by its contiguous relationship to the colonial past, as the present moment is suspended by memory. Chahine here masterfully manipulates the shocking effect of photography with the fluid flow of cinema to transmit the past into the present and vice versa.

As with other postcolonial texts, the subjectivity of the body in *Alexandria Again and Forever* stands metonymically for all visible signs of difference, and their varied forms of cultural and social inscription: the American musical, the American song, the British actor, the queer actor, the old filmmaker, the young actor, the alter ego, the staged Berlin setting and the Egyptian dancing couple, the colonized and the colonizer, the past and the present. The drive here is to provide a liminal space within which cultural differences articulate and actually produce once-imagined constructions of cultural and national identity. In this multiple deconstruction and reconstruction of subjectivities, Chahine's own image carries the heavy legacy of colonial power as instigator of hybridization, rather than the noisy command of colonialist authority or the silent repression of Egyptian and Arab traditions. The sequence achieves this by taking up basic characteristics of the colonial canonical text and unveiling them, thereby subverting the text of the dominant discourse and exposing its underlying assumptions. What at first glance appears to be colonial servility (mimicry), on closer inspection is revealed as a sly form of resistance.

It is easy to frame Chahine's performative approach in the film as postmodern. Commenting on the film, a key Arab film critic suggested that it had signaled Chahine's embrace of postmodernism, which at the time was a relatively new trend within international cinemas.[18] Nevertheless, Chahine's approach in the dancing sequence and in the film in general, functions as a retelling of Chahine's own drama, which transcends creating a plane for a troubled intellectual or his tormented conscience. Performative practice here rearticulates a site of struggle for producing and representing individual as well as cultural and national identities. This site of struggle provides a basis for a rigorous rethinking of nationalism, representation, and resistance that above all stresses the ambivalent and the hybrid in postcolonial cultural practices. But what consistently fascinates is the way it subsequently interrogates, and then moves beyond the limitations of the postcolonial text itself.

BEYOND SUBVERSION AND INTO THE POLITICAL

Yet another dance illustrates Chahine's contestation of the postcolonial ambivalence of his national identity while questioning his own indulgence in the personal, which had marked the Berlin sequence. In the new sequence Yehia and Nadia are in a crowded bazaar where a carnival is in progress. Nadia wants him to dance. He complies. But before he leaves the dance floor, Yehia's skill and physical strength are tested against those of an attractive and virile-looking young man. The exchange of glances between Yehia and the young dancer as they perform with their phallic sticks shines in its homoerotic significance. But the close-up shots of their sticks locked together, and the eventual draw between the two dancers, also mark a balance prompted by great tension, ecstasy, struggle, love, and, equally as important, a conscious acknowledgement of both the *I* and the Other. Where the Berlin sequence featured two dancers dressed in fashionable western tuxedoes, performing alone for themselves and for each other to the tune of a colonial past (and a postcolonial present), this one takes place within a crowd of working-class Egyptians celebrating a religious festival to the tune of traditional local folk music.

The scene is structured by its oblique and extreme low camera angles briskly cut with dramatic close-ups. The camera tracks around the dancers in a dynamic fashion as it follows the action. In conjunction with the scene's low key lighting, these visual cinematic manipulations add a sense of sinister anxiety and enhance Yehia's vulnerability as a dancer; an allegory for the vulnerability of Chahine the artist, and his relationship with his audience.

In contrast to the earlier dance where the choreography remains at the center, Yehia here is presented as a competing equal, struggling to find a space for himself among the indigenous crowd that is challenging him to prove that he really belongs among them. Here Yehia's dancing signifies more than a cinematic mediation of Chahine's personal dreams and dilemmas, which themselves are being challenged by the loud crowd enticing him to show more than his typical "cinematic tricks and gimmicks." "Movies are all tricks," the crowd shouts, "there is always someone else who does the hard work." At a moment when Yehia, the filmmaker, is rearticulating himself as a public performer and as a political activist, Chahine is heartened to acknowledge the dialectic between the private and the public, including the one between the artist and his audience. Of course, there is nothing new about the way Chahine's story is presented through allegories of the embattled private and its public destiny, but his hybrid subjectivity in this film goes beyond merely accepting itself as a crafty form of subversion or resistance.

In themselves, hybrid subjectivities and texts enable a form of subversion, founded on an unpredictability that turns the discursive conditions of dominance into grounds that are open for negotiation and intervention. In *Alexandria Again and Forever*, social and political struggles and the more private spheres of sexual liberation and individual desire incessantly overlap, to the extent that demarcating between them is virtually impossible.

In the Tahtib dancing sequence, Chahine seems more preoccupied with the fear of losing his political role as an artist than with the dubious consolation of the role of a resistant hybrid, thereby countering the example of other postcolonialists, who, in Robert Stam's tongue-in-cheek characterization, tell oppressed people, "Certainly you've lost your land, your religion, and they torture you, but look on the bright side—you're hybrid."[19] Toward the end of the scene, Chahine's pointed editing of the exchange of glances between Yehia, the young male dancer, the crowd, and Nadia, ultimately signals Yehia's vindication in Nadia's eyes—but only after he has vindicated himself in the eyes of the young dancer, and, equally as important, in the eyes of the observing crowd of ordinary Egyptians.

Even implied sites of tension between the private and the political are dramatically developed into vehicles advocating concrete social and political action. When Yehia realizes Amr is never coming back to him, he blames the breakup on the petrodollar that has seduced Amr into working for a Gulf state-sponsored TV soap opera, a direct reference to a situation impacting many artists and intellectuals in Egypt and around the Arab world since the early 1990s.[20] Through yet another redrawing of the artist's subjectivity, queer sensibility and transgression are reconstituted with an even wider underlying tension between the private and the public, and the private, and the political.

Chahine, clearly, opts to suggest a resolution to these tensions. The reconciliation of the private and the public is explicitly marked in the final scene of the film. As Yehia/Chahine aims his camera to record a meeting of the Union of Egyptian Film Artists, it is Nadia that is captured as Yehia's new object of desire; her hopeful face emerging from a crowd of militant artists singing the national anthem following their unanimously vote against the government's attempts to break their union. As the final credits roll, we learn Chahine has dedicated the film "to the struggle of Egyptian artists for democracy." Referencing the *Hamlet* motif, Ahmad Youssef has observed that, "the question in *Alexandria Again and Forever* shifts from 'to be or not be,' to 'to become part of the collective by way of completing one's identity' or 'to remain isolated, and thus risk being lost forever.'" Within such parameters, "one's freedom begins with journeying toward and linking with another person's freedom, and ultimately making links with the struggle for collective and human emancipation."[21]

As with his earlier explorations of class, Chahine's cinema since the mid-1980s has taken up an interrogation of national repressions and limitations, scrutinizing contemporary Arab national discourse via its myriad manifestations in religion, diasporas, gender, and sexual identities. While many of the early Chahine films, particularly those from the 1950s to the mid-1970s, tended to limit their gaze to the public spheres of popular anticolonial struggles, his later films monitored the private realm of the personal and the domestic, which are seen as integral though repressed aspects of national history and identity. So while a film like *Alexandria Again and Forever* appears on the surface to be concerned less with the public sphere of national liberation and anticolonial struggles than with the private sphere of the artist and his libidinal plays, the film does not abandon the notion that national emancipation is worth fighting for. Rather than fleeing from contradictions, the film installs doubt and crisis at its very core. Rather than the grand anticolonial metanarrative, it favors proliferations of difference within polygeneric narratives, seen not as embodiments of a single truth but rather as energized political and esthetic forms of a collective project for revamping Egyptian and Arab identity.

In this chapter, I have chosen to deal with one key film that rejects social realism in favor of largely modernist strategies to evaluate the impact of conventional modes of address on sexuality and on the political construction of sexual identity. In a cinema that has sought to contest or invert assumptions about existing social relations and to seek new ways of seeing and speaking about Arab national identity, Chahine's appropriation of his own sexual identity in *Alexandria Again and Forever* carries the potential of subtly displacing, questioning, and transforming the discourses that have excluded queer representation from Arab cinemas and limited the appreciation of sexual emancipation as integral to the process of social and national liberation.

Less than a year after the release of *Alexandria Again and Forever*, Chahine directed the short documentary *Cairo as Seen by Chahine* (1991), which signaled yet another shift in the filmmaker's political discourse. With the escalating Gulf crisis and war, political tensions in the area were once again on the rise, and increasing religious fundamentalism in reaction to aggressive American policies dominated the political agenda of the day. The film depicted Chahine teaching a film class in which he poses a question about what the west would expect from a documentary about Egypt. The students respond with answers such as belly dancing, the pyramids and the desert, while exoticized images of the stereotypical tourists' Egypt are intercut with images reflecting the filmmaker's perception of his land. Chahine's Cairo is a place where demonstrators against the U.S. and Allied forces' intervention in the Gulf clash with the police. It also includes disillusioned youths who, despairing of any possible improvement in their lives, are taking up Islamist extremism as an ideological and political alternative to their desperation. And while the film's Arabic title indicates that Cairo continues to shine *(Minawwara)* through the resiliency of its people, the documentary's final shot is indicative of Chahine's increasing anxiety vis-à-vis religious fundamentalist politics. The scene depicts the congregation of a group of young people in a meeting held by a religious leader. As the meeting is about to start, it is interrupted by Chahine's call to cut the shooting, leaving the viewer shaken to discover that contrary to the conventions of traditional documentary, both set and scene have been constructed. The reflexive nature of the scene foreshadows what will become Chahine's next pressing filmmaking topic: religious fundamentalism and its effects on Egyptian and Arab societies. Coming after *Alexandria Again and Forever*, a film at first glance indulgently devoted to his own subjectivity, *Cairo as Seen by Chahine* heralds the filmmaker's shift of focus toward an area of contemplation more in sync with the political moment in which Arab societies found themselves throughout the 1990s.

9

RELIGIOUS FUNDAMENTALISM AND THE POWER OF HISTORY

While the rise of religious fundamentalism in the Muslim and Arab worlds was gradually gaining hold following the anti-Shah revolution and the proclamation of the Islamic Republic of Iran in April 1979, the changes taking place in Russia, Eastern Europe, and consequently in Central Asia in the late 1980s and early 1990s inadvertently laid the foundation for the further weakening of already tired Arab nationalist regimes supported by the Soviet bloc. More importantly, independent left and left–nationalist movements in the Arab world suffered from the political and ideological confusions associated with the proclamations of the death of socialism, the triumph of capitalism and the end of history. This, while oil rich Gulf states were financing religious enterprises throughout the region and among immigrant Muslim and Arab communities in the west.

By the time the anti-communist Afghanistan war came to an end with the rise to power of the western supported fundamentalist Mujahidin, billions of dollars in weapons, logistical support, and financial aid had been spent in the region—much of which benefited the activities of an array of Islamic fundamentalist groups. The influence of these groups was gaining momentum on official as well as grass-roots levels. With the retreat of leftist and left–nationalist politics in the Arab and Muslim worlds, social and political rhetoric generated by fundamentalists began to hegemonically monopolize popular opposition discourse.

In response, the issue of fundamentalist dogma began to rise as a key theme in the work of liberal and leftist Arab filmmakers. These artists began to make films condemning fundamentalist practices and ideologies as a hindrance to the modernization of Arab societies. They also began to focus on reaffirming the diversity and heterogeneity of Arab national identity as a key ideological base in the struggle against religious fundamentalism.

Chahine's 1997 film *Destiny*, followed by *al-Akhar* (The Other) in 1999, boldly challenged the increasingly trendy ideological religious fanaticism which was affecting the way Muslims and Arabs looked at politics, their own personal lives, their social relations, their history, and their cultural practices. Chahine's contribution marked a watershed in intellectual and filmmaking circles in their refusal of the fundamentalist revisionism that was hegemonizing Arab culture and politics. Youssef Chahine's films during this period offered a popular cultural thrust to tackle the complexity of the phenomenon. To this end, Chahine's films offered a complex re-examination of Arab society, both past and present, by way of challenging fundamentalists' attempts to impose their own version of Arab history and culture. These two films presented a powerful response to the stagnation of the left and the Arab liberation movement's withdrawal from the arena of ideological struggle, and as such, they opened the door for other Arab filmmakers to share their views on the issue.

In this chapter I present a detailed analysis of Chahine's *Destiny* as a modernist thematic and stylistic attempt to counter religious extremism. The chapter offers an extended survey of the political circumstances that led to the making of the film, and the effect it had on the production of a group of films that pointedly tackled the rise of fundamentalism in the Arab world.

THE RISE OF RELIGIOUS DOGMATISM AND THE ARAB NATIONAL LIBERATION MOVEMENT

Many Arab intellectuals claim that today's rise in religious and ethnic sectarianism, and by extension religious fundamentalism, has deep roots in colonial policies of divide and rule dating back to the early nineteenth century. In response, today's struggle to affirm the role of civil society and to advocate modernization and secularism is variously perceived as integral to the struggle against fundamentalism and ultimately for national self-determination.[1]

An important component of the nineteenth-century al-Nahda's outlook on social and cultural renewal was largely associated with a new stance on religion and philosophy. Prominent religious intellectuals of the period, such as al-Afghani, Muhammad Abdu and Abd al-Rahman al-Kawakibi stressed the need to overcome the divisive barriers between Islam and philosophy that had been popularized following the backlash against materialist philosopher Ibn Rushd in the twelfth century. Al-Nahda's intellectuals urged breaking with dogmatic interpretations of the Qur'an and advocated openness in its elucidation. They also sought to modernize the process of reading the religious text in a way that—as Ibn Rushd had proposed over seven centuries earlier—respected the primacy of reason, fought intellectual repression and religious mysticism, and by extension promoted philosophical rationalism, scientific modernization, and social progress.

The development of Islamic fundamentalism in the Arab world in the early and mid-twentieth century ran parallel to attempts to establish a modernist united secular state in the Arab world. The fundamentalist project itself was seen by many Arab nationalists as an offshoot of colonial and neocolonial forces to counterbalance the emergence of movements that promoted Arab unity and self-determination.[2]

By the early 1990s, the work of Egyptian intellectuals such as Nasr Abu Zeid (persecuted for his 'blasphemous' interpretation of the Qur'an), Nawal Saadawi (a feminist who targeted the issue of female circumcision), and Noble laureate Naguib Mahfouz was clearly incompatible with the fundamentalist agenda of promoting spiritual salvation as a substitute for economic and social justice. However, the witch-hunt against writers and artists was not confined to Egypt.

From the Maghreb to Jordan and from Yemen to the Gulf states, Arab intellectuals were assailed by religious zealots for disseminating blasphemy: Yemeni writer Abd al-Karim al-Razihi was forced to seek asylum in Holland; legal charges were laid against Kuwaiti writers Layla al-Uthman and Afaf Shu'aib and Jordanian poet Musa Hawamidah; in Algeria, Wasinin al-A'rag's novel, *The Hostess*, was banned for impiety, and several rai musicians were targeted and assassinated as advocates of sexual impropriety and godless communism. Back in the Arab east, popular Lebanese musician Marcel Khalifeh was being charged with blasphemy for a song he had adapted from a piece by Palestinian poet Mahmoud Darwish.

The wave of Islamic fundamentalism had a direct effect on intellectual and cultural life in the film production center of the Arab world—Egypt. Youssef Chahine himself was taken to court over his 1994 film *The Emigrant*. While the film ostensibly depicted the story of the prophet Joseph (he is given the name Ram in the film), it also presented another personal account of Chahine's views on life and politics (Joseph is the English language equivalent of Youssef—Chahine's given name). Ram is intent on leaving his family to travel in search of knowledge and enlightenment. His interest in agriculture leads to new innovations that enable the cultivation of produce in the arid desert. The film was criticized for what appeared to be an allegorical reference to the Zionist colonization of Palestine, which Israeli propaganda celebrated in terms of its success in "making the desert bloom." Considering Chahine's fierce anti-Zionist and pro-Palestinian politics the accusation was absurd. But still, the film created controversy with its depiction of a prophet, which according to Islam and to al-Azhar's religious rulings is forbidden. A lawyer charged that since the film presented the image of the prophet Joseph it should be pulled from Egyptian movie theaters and its distribution outside the country halted. The six-month court battle led to *The Emigrant* being banned from movie theaters, but not before it joined the ranks of the highest grossing Chahine films to date.

As fundamentalism gathered momentum, Arab intellectuals were voicing their opposition to the extremist religious agenda. For their part, many Arab filmmakers were becoming more conscious of the need to play a proactive role in the struggle against what they saw as the rising tide of repressive religious dogma. Gradually, politicized religion and religious politics became an important theme in Arab films. Filmmakers in Egypt, Tunisia, and Algeria in particular presented strong cinematic polemics against fundamentalist practices and ideology. Chahine's *Destiny* marked a major attempt to counter the rise of religious fundamentalism. The film presented an impressionistic outlook on the struggle against fundamentalism through the subject-consciousness of philosopher Ibn Rushd. The film's plot reclaims the philosopher's story via a self-reflexive rendering of historical dichotomies between conservative forces and ideas and proponents of intellectual and social progress. Venturing back into twelfth-century Andalusia, the film concomitantly makes a statement against dogmatic religious repression in contemporary Arab and Muslim societies.

Chahine's *Destiny*, and later *The Other* in 1999, once again set a new pattern in Arab cinema. The two films also strengthened and gave substance to earlier efforts by other Egyptian filmmakers and actors to counter the rising influence of local fundamentalist terrorism. Two key films featuring the popular comedian Adel Imam—*al-Irhab wa-l-kabab* (Terrorism and Kebab, 1993) and *al-Irhabi* (The Terrorist, 1994) directly tackled the phenomenon of religious fanaticism and its dangers. But Youssef Chahine's films challenged the complexity of the phenomenon by offering a popular yet intrusive assessment and rebuttal of the situation, a task many Arab liberals, leftists, and nationalist leftists seemed hesitant to undertake.

Chahine's films offered a complex re-examination of Arab society, both past and present, challenging fundamentalists' imposition of a skewed elucidation of its history and culture. As such, his films opened the way for a number of Arab filmmakers to share their views on the issue. One of the more popular films to come out of Egypt over the last decade is Atef Hatata's *al-Abwab al-mughlaqa* (The Closed Doors, 1999, produced by Chahine's Misr International), which tells the story of an adolescent boy living with his widowed mother in a contemporary Egypt where religious fundamentalists are gaining influence. The plot draws parallels between the struggle against fundamentalism and the boy's search for identity in a social milieu where sexuality is not a subject that can be dealt with openly.

Several Algerian and Tunisian films explicitly tackled the issue of fundamentalist terrorism and offered moving accounts of its impact on youth culture. In Merzak Allouache's *Beb el-Oued* (1994), the protagonist Boualem steals the loudspeaker installed on his roof by religious fanatics who use it to increase their influence in the district while ensuring that the decadent rai music is not heard by the district's youth. What follows is a powerful rendering of the clashing realities facing Arab youth as they fight against religious dogmatism. And Yamina Bachir-Chouikh's 2002 *Rachida* looks at fundamentalist terrorism against women through the eyes of the schoolteacher Rachida, who refuses to abandon her profession to abide by the role prescribed for her by a group of religious fanatics.

While a few voices attacked Chahine's film *Destiny* based on longstanding hostility toward Chahine's work in general, and particularly its condemnation of religious fundamentalism, *Destiny* was enthusiastically received by most Arab film critics. The film was seen as a landmark in Chahine's enduring message in support of freedom of expression, and against religious dogmatism and repression. Ali Abu Shadi considered the film a timely and courageous attempt to warn against the consequences of allowing "ignorance to dominate over knowledge and enlightenment."[3] A similar sentiment was expressed by Ahmad Saleh who saw the film as a strong didactic response to terrorist attempts to intimidate artists.[4] For his part, Ra'uf Tawfiq suggested that the film supersedes a thousand symposia and lectures that try to deal with the ideas and practices of religious extremism. Chahine, Tawfiq argues, was able to push the envelope of public discourse using the most important Egyptian cultural event in recent years.[5]

Veteran Egyptian film scholar Rafiq al-Sabban, who considered Chahine's philosophical persistence on a par with Ibn Rushd's, focused his review on Chahine's rendering of the world and its history in a non-static manner. This, in his view, forces history to "tag along" with the filmmaker, instead of the opposite:

Since his Alexandria trilogy, in which Chahine's outlook began to move beyond his own little world toward the larger social and political spheres, and since he began to engage the sagas of history instead of losing himself in the endlessness of time, the filmmaker has been able to take hold of his topics and his cinematic deliverance of these topics.[6]

Among the most prominent critics of the film was Mustafa Darwish, who considered the film a "shameful exercise that essentially works against the cause of enlightenment." Darwish, who had read the film's script prior to its production, saw the dialogue as forced, artificial, and tasteless. As such, Darwish suggested, the script did not do justice to Ibn Rushd's persona, and ultimately deprived this great historical figure from effectively contributing to today's battle for enlightenment across the Arab world.[7]

A MODERNIST STORY ABOUT ARAB HISTORY

Tackling religious dogmatism and its rise in the Arab world since the mid-1980s, *Destiny* won Chahine the 1997 Cannes' Fiftieth Anniversary Palme d'Or and is now considered among his most popular films outside the Arab world. The film loosely interprets the events of twelfth-century Andalusia, and as such it functions as a piece of history in the sense that it presents a historical setting where a cosmopolitan Arab culture spanning across cities such as Baghdad, Fez, Damascus, and the Spanish cities of Cordoba and Grenada has made them centers of economic expansion, scientific progress, and philosophical and cultural innovation. The film is also a piece of history in that it speaks from a moment in history to comment on current Arab and Muslim political and ideological developments and issues. As it tackles contemporary anxieties associated with the rise of religious fundamentalism, *Destiny* provides a modernist strategy that presumes the agency of its subject and audience in and through whom the film becomes memory and history.

The film presents a story of struggle against religious fundamentalism through the subject-consciousness of Ibn Rushd (Averroes), the twelfth-century astronomer, medical scientist, and religious interpreter *(fakih)* whose philosophy informed atheist thinking during the Renaissance. As a materialist thinker, Ibn Rushd translated Aristotle and contributed to the emergence of an evolutionary interpretation of the notion of creation. In his treatise *Incoherence of the Incoherence*, a polemic against al-Ghazali's *Incoherence of the Philosophers*, Ibn Rushd professed the eternity of the world, implying the existence of uncreated matter, and affirmed the primacy of reason over faith. The philosopher was later exiled to the North African desert and his books were burned. His followers were condemned and persecuted in Europe during the Inquisition.[8] For an audience unfamiliar with Arab culture and history the film brings to light references long absented by Orientalist discourse on Arabs and the Arab world. As such Chahine's film counteracts perceptions that allege a long-standing historical clash between, on the one hand, a western civilization that is the beacon of secular and rational discourse and, on the other hand, an Arab/Muslim culture that is inherently irrational, fanatical, violent, and against progress.

According to the film, the fight against religious dogmatism in the Arab world is integral to the anticolonial struggle for liberation, national self-determination, and modernization. In this chapter, my utilization of the term *modernity* integrates an outlook toward lived experience that encompasses various political, ideological, and cultural paradigms. My use of the term *modernization*, on the other hand, refers more specifically to the processes of change that result from the introduction of certain technologies, such as the technology of cinema itself, into the various spheres of private and social life. My employment of both terms considers the specificity of their use in the context of Arab history, philosophy, and culture.

This section also discusses the broad historical and cultural subtexts imperative to the understanding of *Destiny*'s signifying codes and their ideological connotations for Arab audiences. While this methodological approach remains, in my view, critical to the reading of any film, I contend that it is even more necessary to the discussion of this particular cinematic experience. In light of the film's heavy reliance on references that, for the most part, are not readily accessible to non-Arab audiences, some elaboration on contextual, historical, and cultural issues becomes of paramount relevance to analysis.

Islamic fundamentalists were not able to assassinate Faraj Fawdah, a radical liberal intellectual and a lifelong campaigner against obscurantism and fanaticism, until 1992. Similarly, writer Naguib Mahfouz, who, for a period of over fifty years grappled with God and wrote passionately about prostitutes and homosexuals, celebrating working-class promiscuity while expressing disdain for middle- and upper-class hypocritical puritanism, was eighty-two before fundamentalist groups made an attempt on his life in 1994. Clearly, the government's discounting of the rising danger of such groups allowed them to proclaim themselves the Egyptian guardians of morality. Succumbing to pressure from religious groups, the Ministry of Culture granted al-Azhar, Egypt's central religious authority and censor, a free hand to deal with "blatantly sexual and offensive books and cultural products."[9] Condemning fundamentalist "intellectual terrorism," Mahfouz himself issued a furious statement, declaring, "The censor in Egypt is no longer just the state. It's the gun of the fundamentalists."[10]

The plot of *Destiny* ventures back into twelfth-century Andalusia to explore the story of Ibn Rushd, who has been appointed grand judge of Cordoba by the caliph. Caliph al-Mansur has two sons: al-Nasir, a follower of the philosopher, and Abdallah, a party animal who is lured into the camp of fundamentalists. Political schemes are rampant in the area. The caliph supports Ibn Rushd, but is opposed by an Islamic fundamentalist cult that hopes to overthrow him and to get rid of the heretical philosopher. Meanwhile, the elder son is concealing a forbidden love for the gypsy Manuella, and his trusted adviser is secretly working against his father. A clandestine project is set in motion when a group of Ibn Rushd's disciples decide to copy his books by hand and send them to a safer place, in case the originals are burned.

The film characterizes religious fundamentalism as generating intellectual regression, and benefiting powers that seek to curtail the struggle for emancipation and basic human freedoms. *Destiny* is constructed in a largely accessible fashion; its linear plot progression is a departure from the filmmaker's usual complex use of flashbacks and dreams. As the film opens, a follower of Ibn Rushd is being burned at the stake in France. Fed by the philosopher's books, the bonfire intensifies as the man calls out to his son Joseph to seek out Ibn Rushd. The scene sets in motion a story about the cross-cultural and cross-historical phenomenon known today as religious fundamentalism. The

Destiny: 'Organic Intellectuals' in the face of intellectual uniformity.

174 Religious Fundamentalism and the Power of History

trajectory between the first and the last scenes of the film, in which we witness the burning of Ibn Rushd's books in Andalusia, carries particular resonance for modern viewers. Together, the two scenes bracket and enhance the film's critique of religious dogmatism as a cross-cultural phenomenon.

Ibn Rushd himself is portrayed as part of an open and pleasant intellectual and artistic community living in a predominantly free-thinking atmosphere. The depiction of Ibn Rushd's character—his enlightened philosophical vision, his intellectual openness and his playful yet politically engaged lifestyle—is underscored by the film's plot, which pits the philosopher's determination to move across a range of religious, ethnic, gender, and cultural boundaries, against religious fundamentalism's self-inflicted imprisonment within controlled, secretive, and prohibitive structures and politics. Presenting an attentive portrayal of a multiethnic and multireligious twelfth-century Arab Andalusia, the film draws attention to the dangers facing today's heterogeneous Arab national society and identity.

Chahine's celebratory delineation of a carefree Andalusian lifestyle underlines his thesis of religious fundamentalism as an anathema to social progress, intellectual freedom, and the celebration of life's blissful pleasures. In many respects Chahine seems intent on depicting all the earthly delights fundamentalists loathe; much of the drama features exuberant dance, music, poetry, humor, sex, and romance and plays out over backdrops of colorful architecture and costumes.

Romantic subplots enhance the film's emphasis on social and intellectual heterogeneity and on combating dogmatic interpretation of religion. The relationships between Abdallah and Sarah (Manuella's younger sister), and between al-Nasir and Salma (Ibn Rushd's daughter) both work to enhance the film's main thematic preoccupations; while Abdallah and Sarah's relationship is interrupted by his involvement with the fundamentalists, the second affair leads to marriage.

The linearity of the plot, aided by the familiarity of its Arab audience with the history of the conflict between Ibn Rushd and the fundamentalists, infers a clear political statement in support of progressive change and against the rise of religious fundamentalism and sectarianism. As it traces the philosopher's story, *Destiny* reclaims aspects of Arab history by way of describing a continuous struggle between reactionary forces and proponents of intellectual enlightenment and social progress. The film posits history as an arena of exploration and recovery of collective identity; this history is offered as memory and informative for understanding and addressing present dilemmas.

THE FILM AS A STORY ABOUT ARAB UNITY AND MODERNIST TRANSFORMATION

Destiny makes reference to two critical components of Arab and Egyptian postcolonial politics, both of which allude to the role of colonial powers in combating the pan-Arab project for national self-determination through their encouragement of religious sectarianism. The first relates to the centrality of the notion of Arab identity, which the film depicts as a heterogeneous entity, and the second deals with the relationship between fundamentalist politics and colonial political manipulations.

Destiny's attentive celebration of a multiethnic, multireligious and politically pluralist Arab society in twelfth-century Spain is conducive to the pan-Arab political reclamation of heterogeneity as a defining character of Arab identity. In other words the film puts a great weight on depicting the struggle against religious fundamentalism as a struggle for a heterogeneous Arab identity and unity. It is within this breadth that the film also recognizes the polity of religious fundamentalism in the context of externally induced colonial politics in the region.

The plot of the film explicitly alludes to the role played by European leaders in fomenting support for fundamentalist sects in Arab-occupied Spain. In this context the stance of European monarchs is characterized as a medieval hostility toward what Andalusia's Muslim–Arab culture largely symbolized at the time—cultural and national heterogeneity, scientific progress, and intellectual freedom and openness. As such the film allegorically refers to the colonial[11] politics of divide and conquer as exemplified here in its collaboration with Islamic fundamentalism; the film exposes how Arab struggles against colonialism and neocolonialism have been consistently informed by the struggle for modernist renewal. Today, emphasizing this modernization/national liberation dynamic remains part of the way most prominent Arab modernist intellectuals challenge the rise of Islamic fundamentalism as a politically and ideologically regressive movement.[12]

Within its own specific historical and cultural parameters, the Arab intellectual articulation of modernity acknowledges a paradoxical disposition of a project not dissimilar to how modernity was articulated within, for example, a Latin American context, as "neither a break from the past nor a new way of describing and categorizing the present; [but] instead [as a rearticulation of] the process whereby historical and cultural formations mediate and condition contemporaneity" to quote Zuzana Pick.[13] Modernity, as a specifically Arab frame of reference, finds its origins within an intellectual and political paradigm that was part of an anticolonial project that sought progressive political, economic, and cultural renewal.

Al-Nahda movement epitomized the struggle to reaffirm Arab identity and Arab rights for national self-determination. Equally as important, Arab intellectuals in the 1900s aspired to a cross-fertilization and integration of Muslim and Arab heritages with the humanist traditions of the European Renaissance, the ideals of the French Revolution, and the nineteenth-century scientific and industrial Enlightenment. As such al-Nahda saw itself primarily as a modernist and modernizing movement.

Destiny reincorporates modernity and the struggle for modernist renewal in the Arab world into the larger struggle against religious fundamentalism. In this regard the film codifies a long-standing Arab approach to modernity. Chahine's selection of the story of Ibn Rushd as the subject of his film bears direct relevance to how modernity in Arab societies is conceived within a specific political, social, and philosophical/religious continuum. In the film the philosopher is quoted directly on the relationship between philosophy and religion:

> Wisdom guides the virtuous theologian in his study of what we call "syllogism." And divine law guides the philosopher in his study of what we call "reason." Reason is the study of wisdom. Everything that has been deduced from divine law is subject to interpretation. Reason is the sister of divine law. The supposed conflict between them is a malicious invention.[14]

As a postcolonial text, *Destiny* explores Arab modernist meanings not only through content, but equally through a reciprocal articulation of the textual mode itself. In such texts, as Russell McDougall suggests, the "interest is in the attitude of the image, the strategies of the narrative, the placing of the reader, and the cultural coding of those esthetic principles that inform the whole process of fiction."[15] The film's thematic accent on combating religious fundamentalism is juxtaposed with a modernist rearticulation of the cinematic text.

MODERNIST IMPULSES IN *DESTINY*'S STYLISTIC STRATEGIES

The film freely utilizes several generic and stylistic conventions to underscore its challenge of the sanctification of history and its embodiment within the artistic text. By employing a pattern intrinsic to Arab filmmaking practices since the late 1920s, *Destiny* works stylistically with and against an assortment of representational conventions. The dynamics of the struggle against fundamentalism in twelfth-century Andalusia assumes a multitemporal and cross-spatial political significance, one that acknowledges the retreat to fundamentalism of denominations worldwide.

Generically, *Destiny* assumes the appearance of a historical epic, but it is also largely constructed as a passionate melodrama that in turn incorporates all the conventions of a musical genre film. Classical stylistic techniques, avoiding, for the most part, the use of hand-held cameras, natural lighting or violating the rules of continuity editing, are countered by a complex of alternate representational systems in its articulation of conflict between political reaction and progress. The film also brings together music and dance tableaus that transcend the specificity of twelfth-century Andalusia and simultaneously incorporate contemporary, multiethnic and multireligious references. In the process, *Destiny* breaks down the artificial barriers—of form, geography, high and low art, performer and artist—that so often demarcate cinematic cultural practices in the west. This allows the film to effectively reach out to a wide audience with an urgent message of relevance to regional and world politics. Constructed within an elaborate system of multitemporal affectivity and through the cross-fertilization of generic conventions and cultural signifiers, *Destiny* is presented in a qualitatively different fashion from what is generally associated with postmodernist textual play.

In her article "Circling the Downspout of Empire," Linda Hutcheon points out the distinctiveness of the political agendas of the postmodern and the postcolonial. She notes that while the first concerns itself with deconstructing orthodoxies, the latter prioritizes social and political action. As such, postmodern strategies are ineffective in bridging this gap, and they rest within the sphere of deconstruction.[16] In contrast, Chahine's texts are offered as political commentary on the static reading of history and of the historical text, and on the need to mine history to understand and respond to today's struggles and dilemmas. To achieve this, the film relies heavily on music and dance tableaus to enhance narrative and thematic lucidity.

At times the narrative seems to unfold between dance and music sequences that appear almost superfluous to the development of the plot, but these sequences inhabit a conceptual space that points to the political preoccupations of the film. Music culture in Andalusia after the eighth century witnessed the creation of the world's first known music schools (the Zuriab school), to which students from across the Muslim world and Europe flocked to study music theory, history, and performance.[17] Here the film utilizes historical and cultural references to mediate and counter contemporary fundamentalist claims that music and dancing are incompatible with Islamic or Arab traditions and culture. As such the film also reaffirms the ongoing conflict between dogmatic traditionalism and dynamic modernism in human history.

Destiny: Singing and dancing in the face of dogma.

Destiny also draws on a coalescence of oral storytelling, poetry recital, and performative music and dance as long-standing traditions in Arab history. In postcolonial texts, such performative practices emerge "as a locus of struggle in producing and representing individual and cultural identity."[18] By depicting various aspects of cultural performance—those that have played key roles in the development and popularization of Arab cinema itself and in the shaping of its national identity[19]—*Destiny* reiterates its allusion to the modernist continuum in Arab history. As he combines Arab, Spanish, Gypsy, flamenco, old, and contemporary music and dance conventions in at least three sequences within the film, Chahine rearticulates for his contemporary audience a historically heterogeneous Arab culture. As such, physical performance becomes a cultural signifier, which in the tradition of the postcolonial text "stands metonymically for all the 'visible' signs of difference, and their varied forms of cultural and social inscription."[20]

By using multiethnic references, the film's embellished song and dance sequences render body performance as an act of defiance and resistance that transcends cultural boundaries. For example, the forceful and self-assured gestures associated with flamenco dancing echo the film's philosophy that bliss and pleasure are antithetical to fundamentalist repression. But clearly the reference here is not to the dominant Andalusian Arab dance form of the period (known as *al-Samah*), but is rather to one that was emerging at the time through the coalescence of Spanish, Arab, and Gypsy dance traditions. As such, the film's celebration of cultural heterogeneity is enhanced by the choices made in building the filmic text itself and its use as a means of commenting on the politics of contention between fundamentalism and modernism.

The film also employs iconographic patterns of costume, architecture, and landscapes to render its thematic dialectic. These patterns initiate a rather subjective, multilayered, and decentered rearticulation of history. By carefully choosing his visual and cultural references, Chahine challenges classical realist conventions that largely convey an illusion of a closed universe, which, as J. Paech would suggest, becomes a panopticon in which reality and fiction are rendered as one.[21]

Destiny's extravagant and colorful *mise en scène* and its highly coded imagery work against the dark plot, offering references that subvert static conceptions of Arab and Muslim societies and cultures. The film's representation of life in Andalusia selects landscapes, costumes, architectural exteriors, and interiors that, as signifiers, destabilize dominant western imaging (as well as fundamentalist ahistoric nostalgia for a misconstrued past) of an Arab Orient characterized by dusty deserts, clay architecture, and women covered in black from head to toe. Such images are contrasted with the film's green and mountainous Arab landscape (the film was shot mainly in Syria and Lebanon) nearly identical to the Andalusian setting. The interiors of the Andalusian houses, palaces, and alleyways are richly decorated and markedly nuanced with red, rose, pistachio, and apricot colors in addition to blues, purples, and ruby reds.

The film's excessive emphasis on the colorfulness of the set functions beyond the necessity of plot structuring and historical accuracy; it provides for a modernist challenge to classical realist cinematic traditions that rely on the dominance of the plot to subordinate all other stylistic elements—including *mise en scène*. On the one hand, this textual exposé bestows credibility on the film's historical setting and provides it with an ostensibly authentic feel. On the other hand, the careful construction of the *mise en scène* contrasts and belies the dark plot, drawing attention to itself as an embodiment of resistance against the dark intellectual uniformity of the film's fundamentalists.

On another level, the film emphasizes spatial and signifying patterns that claim our attention in their own right. Visual representations consistently re-envision images and episodes challenging spectators to reassess their perspectives. From the outset, the film's commentary on Islamic fundamentalism is subverted by an episode depicting the burning at the stake of a follower of Ibn Rushd in medieval France.

As we witness the execution, Chahine's camera directs our gaze with lingering close-ups that scrutinize the cathedral's architectural exterior, the deafening silence and heaviness of its gargantuan medieval stones, its statues and its crosses, and the army of Catholic clergy and their henchmen. Western viewers must quickly refocus to accommodate this unanticipated ideological dislocation, as we realize we are being set up to challenge and question our own preconceptions of religious fundamentalism, its history, its players, and its victims.

To the musical rendition of *al-dhikr* (ceremonial religious custom), a tentative and shaky camera (the only handheld shot in the film) follows Abdallah down a dark and narrow path beneath an old castle where the fundamentalist group is conducting one of their secret rituals. The camera's stumbling and menacing movement fuels a sense of anxiety and apprehension, one Chahine uses to reflect upon the world of religious fundamentalism.

In a sequence introducing the leader of the fundamentalist group, the compelling power of iconography is manipulated to secure the mass's submission. Al-Amir (the Prince) is a man who wraps himself in a halo of sanctity and power. He is dressed in a white robe astride a white horse, his head and face clean-shaven. His arrival is heralded by a full-scale celebration impeccably choreographed to reaffirm the myth of his super-human angelic stature and to stress his religious piety in the eyes of his followers. One of his supporters proclaims, "al-Amir commands knowledge of everything, and is able to see and interpret the past, the present, and the future," while another tells us the Amir's diet consists of only a single date per day. These cultural signifiers of purity and disdain for life's pleasures, symbolized by the Amir's white robe and horse and the references to his dietary abstention (fasting), demonstrate how iconographies of longstanding cultural and religious relevance enhance hegemonic consensus.

The film also reveals how notions of Arab modernity and modernization represent historical challenges to fundamentalist dogma. When Ibn Rushd and his assistant Marwan need to spy on the fundamentalists in their castle hideout, they employ one of the great Arab contributions to science: an early telescope that works by using the magnifying power of water. Seven centuries before the movie camera's emergence, the telescope had similarly assumed a symbolic modernizing significance in its mediation of the gaze. As the telescope allows Marwan—and us—a clearer view of the fundamentalists' activities, we are alerted allegorically to the need for vigilance in responding to sectarian and dogmatic politics of all sorts. The film symbolically accentuates the centrality of Arab modernity and modernization as part of the transformational endeavor for progressive social, political, and national unity and self-determination. It also self-reflexively emphasizes Chahine's interest in the processes through which the critical examination and analysis of phenomena can be enhanced—through the political utilization of modern and modernizing tools such as cinema.

Destiny deliberately juxtaposes images and sounds of young people singing, dancing, reciting poetry, drinking, and making love against images and sounds of fundamentalists expressing their detestation for "life's material pleasures." Through the religious practice of *al-dhikr* the sect recites verses deploring life's "joys as well as its sorrows," and members of the sect express their reliance on faith to help them "accept what has been already determined for them" and to remain content while they await their inevitable deaths. In contrast, Marwan's songs expressly call on people to celebrate life.

The primary phrase of Marwan's first song includes an appeal to "lovers of life" to reaffirm their defiance against attempts to silence their music and prevent them from indulging in what life offers. It also calls on people to "raise their voices as they sing" to express their resistance to all forms of repression and terror. It is important to note here that the imagery of the first attack on Marwan is constructed to recreate the one suffered by Nobel laureate Naguib Mahfouz at the hands of fundamentalists two years earlier. The song is repeated twice more in the film, first as part of a musical dance tableau and second in eulogy to Marwan following his assassination. In both cases, singing takes on symbolic significance as an expression of resistance to terror, violence, and fundamentalist interpretations of religion.

Similarly, Chahine's use of contemporary Egyptian vernacular in this historically inspired film represents a unique break in Arab film practice, which traditionally relies on a classical Arabic dialect in historical epics. The colloquial spoken word reflects Chahine's interest in an oral text accessible to his audience, while on the ideological level it also represents a break from the dogmatic presentation of history through the mediation of high and sanctified text. The free use of the popular Egyptian dialect for the film's dialogue and songs breaks with a traditional outlook on classical Arabic as the only means through which history can be transmitted and addressed. Here the film once again asserts its modernist approach, this time by emphasizing the role and function of language as a dynamic signifier of history. This is of particular importance considering that classical Arabic is customarily appreciated for its mythical qualities, which, as Viola Shafik suggests, reduces it to "a transmitter of divine revelation" based on its use in the Qur'an which itself "marks in every respect, politically as well as culturally, the beginning of Arab Muslim culture."[22]

Through their attempts to invoke a different use of the Arabic language, writers of al-Nahda "contributed to the separation of language from the context of religion and paved the way for its use as a basis of national, non-confessional identity."[23] These Arab modernists revolutionized the use of the Arabic language as a dynamic tool to address and analyze history for its lessons in future social and political struggles. Thus, in addition to allowing for a less pretentious and more reflexive articulation of history, Chahine's use of popular and popularized tools to address his subject denotes a continuity in the endeavor initiated by Arab modernists in the mid-1800s. Just as *Destiny* deliberately employs a free visual and cultural articulation of a twelfth-century Andalusian setting, it also juxtaposes contemporary colloquial Arabic against the official history of the period, and draws from this disparity an entirely new, synthesizing function for words, sketching from this dialectic a renovation so basic it would be alphabetic.

By rendering a rich and dialectically charged history and culture, with all their artifices and practices, Chahine forges an inter-textuality linking the past, the present, and the possibilities for future change: a sort of cultural memory, which in the words of Jesus Martin Barbero, has the capacity to exceed the "cumulative user-value function; [one which] is processual and productive, it filters, charges and empowers shaping a dialectic permanence and change, resistance and exchange."[24]

Chahine's film draws attention to itself as a cry against the sanctification of history and the historical text; it challenges preconceptions of the text as static, beyond interpretation, and with little or no relevance to the present. Rather than reducing it to nostalgia, *Destiny's* representation of a crucial moment in Arab history functions as an exploration of the dynamics of representations of collective memory. As such, resistance to religious fundamentalism is rendered synonymous with a postcolonial struggle for national unity, self-determination, and economic, social, and political progress.

The name and image of Ibn Rushd assume iconic stature in the transformation of a people and a space during a critical period in Arab collective memory. But Ibn Rushd also signals the childhood of Arab culture—its dynamism violently interrupted by the hegemony of colonialism and neocolonialism and its submission to its own political and religious regression and terrors.

10

NATIONAL LIBERATION IN THE AGE OF GLOBALIZATION

The solidification of capitalist globalization after the collapse of the Soviet bloc in the early 1990s signaled a tipping point in the balance of economic and political power. More specifically, free trade resulted in increasingly inequitable relationships between developing countries in Asia, Africa, and Latin America and advanced European and North American capitalist countries. The World Bank's policies essentially shifted economic and social infrastructures, further exacerbating the umbalanced state of social development in the southern hemisphere.

While capitalist globalization has now become an economic and political reality, it continues to pose a major challenge to local and national cultures. A key manifestation of cultural globalization has been the rise of the global cultural producer, and the marketing of this phenomenon through transcontinental corporations. Today there are fewer, more concentrated ownerships of the major media, program producers, and international film production companies. Bill Gates, Rupert Murdoch, Ted Turner, and infamously, Conrad Black have become household names, symbols of the amalgamation of culture and entertainment as globalized consumer products, over which international corporations exercise unprecedented power. Arab cultural critic Ali Omlile describes this phenomenon in his book *The Question of Culture*:

[Capitalist] globalization has transformed culture into a uniformed consumer product that targets consumers on a global scale, and this uniformity is designed for large scale and popular production. It is also introduced as an international culture with no national identity despite its western or westernized character. This, however, is resulting in a contradictory outcome: on the one hand, consumption of these products is taking place on a worldwide scale, but on the other hand, this consumption is creating a reactive resistance from local cultures that constitute an important challenge to cultural globalization. Such resistance, to be sure, is too weak to face the new reality, and therefore local cultures have one of two choices: to retract back into an isolated and traditional form of culture, or to indulge in a modernizing process that allows it to venture on its path toward modernity, which means to force a mutual form of interaction in the internationalized reality of cultural relations.[1]

Chahine's cinema since the mid-1990s encompassed a group of films focused on themes of cultural conflict, the adoption of ethically skewed versions of capitalism, cultural hybridity, and terrorism as a defensive cultural mechanism in the age of globalization. Once again, Chahine's seizing of a new sociopolitical reality affecting every aspect of Egyptian and Arab culture was unique but consistent with his tendency to thematically emphasize the need for a modernist transformation that remains cognizant of national cultural specificities.

This chapter begins with a survey of the general manifestations of the concentration of cultural production as they began to affect film production and reception within the Arab world. I will then concentrate on three Chahine films, *The Other* (1999), *Sukut ha-nswar* (Silence . . . We're Rolling, 2001), and *Alexandria . . . New York* (2004), discussing how they were received, and how they reflected the anxieties associated with the rise of cultural globalization within an Arab setting.

ARAB CINEMA SINCE THE 1990S

While the global concentration of cultural industries was reaching unprecedented levels, a parallel amalgamation of these industries within the Arab world was taking place in a way that directly impacted filmmaking practices. It should be stressed, though, that the shift to a concentrated form of Arab film production and distribution was characterized by the direct involvement of local capitalist cultural institutions—mainly those from the Gulf states, Lebanon, Syria, and Egypt. While these institutions were clearly profit-driven and as such were not necessarily concerned with maintaining national sovereignty over their enterprises, they nevertheless had to maintain some semblance of the hegemonic Arab character of their productions. In other words, while these rising industries were seeking a wider pan-Arab market, they were also cognizant of the historical, religious, political, and cultural factors that could not be ignored if they were to challenge international competition and still be profitable.

As a result of new local and international dynamics, major changes were beginning to affect Egyptian and Arab filmmaking in the 1990s. Some of these changes were linked to the amalgamation of various trends and traditions in the region's production practices. These changes were in turn influenced by the greater political openness and relative relaxation of official censorship within many Arab states. They were also enhanced by the work of a growing number of younger filmmakers, both at home and in émigré centers, with the latter receiving financial and logistical support from European producers and agencies. As a result new Arab cinema was becoming less Egypt-centered and more trans-Arab in terms of its production, themes, and audiences.

Along with these positive changes, however, new problems arose as a direct result of the increased role played by companies with little or no experience—or genuine interest for that matter—in the art of cinema. Huge corporations owned by Gulf billionaires (Rotana and ART are prime examples) began investing in film and television production, and distribution in Egypt and throughout the Arab region. There can be no simple evaluation of the role played by these companies. On the one hand, the Gulf companies produced and distributed countless vulgar comedies and bad imitations of western action films. As a result, many poorly trained filmmakers flooded Arab markets with low quality films, contributing to the deterioration of the Arab film culture of earlier periods in Egyptian cinema's history. As well, the conservative sensibility of many of these producers is clearly reflected in the self-censored nature of many of the films made in Egypt of late. Themes of social and political consciousness, and melodramas featuring physical intimacy were actively discouraged and even rejected from the outset, while projects that were creative in their storytelling or stylistic approaches were non-starters. On the other hand, some of these companies have supported important projects, such as the restoration of early films. Some have promoted the televising of older, high quality Egyptian and Arab films, stimulating the interest of new generations of film enthusiasts in their rich cinematic heritage. The involvement of these companies in the massive Arab music clip production industry has generated a new cohort of emerging Arab directors and technicians, most notably Nadine Labaki, whose film *Caramel* (2007) became an instant hit with both Arab and international audiences.

But the Egyptian and Arab film production landscapes have not been entirely dominated by Gulf state producers and distributors. The Egyptian producer Gamal Marwan, for example, recently surprised all with his decision to create a new production company. Marwan, who owns the Melody television group, created Melody Pictures, allocating $18 million dollars (a large sum by Egyptian filmmaking standards) to produce ten films, with additional investments earmarked for the purchase and reprinting of Egyptian and Arab films for broadcast on his specialty film channel. Along with the Good News Group, the Egyptian production company responsible for two of the most successful, most controversial, and most expensive Egyptian or Arab films— *The Yacoubian Building* (Marwan Hamed, 2006), and *Laylat al-babi dull* (The Night of the Baby Doll, Adel Adeeb, 2008)—Melody Pictures seems to be venturing in a direction indicative of a greater interest in alternative film production strategies than those dominating the industry since the mid-1990s.[2]

Though market regulations (that leave local Arab production and distribution industries unprotected against western films, while becoming more restrictive vis-à-vis films from other Arab countries) and religious and political censorship continue to take their toll on Arab cinema, it is fast becoming more inclusive and heterogeneous in its outlook and audience. Egyptian films, for example, are often produced by Lebanese and Gulf investors and feature stars from Lebanon, Syria, Morocco, and Tunisia. And filmmakers from Lebanon, Syria, Palestine, and North Africa are working on coproductions with European governments and private sector agencies such as Fondazione *Montecinemaverita* and La Sept-Arte.

On another level, a number of television dramas are being made for trans-Arab distribution, and Syria has become a huge production center for television drama and comedy, second only to Egypt. In 2004 more than seventy shows were produced in Syria, most of which were widely distributed and extremely popular around the Arab world—particularly in the Gulf states and North Africa. Greater relaxation of government restrictions on private industries, combined with the recent construction of film and television production facilities near Damascus, and the continued influx of business investments from Gulf countries, is creating the potential for a major trans-Arab film and television industry in Syria. And with the overwhelming majority of film theaters in the region still locally owned and operated, possibilities exist for increased diversity in film programming and more screen time for indigenous films.

Thematically, Arab cinema since the 1990s has been marked by anxieties associated with, on the one hand, the stagnation of the Arab national project, and on the other, the rise of religious fundamentalism. As a reactive impulse, many Arab films are informed by a modernist symbiosis, with a revamped national identity struggling to affirm its heterogeneity and find a new role in the fight for social and national liberation.

As I have argued, Islamic fundamentalism had a direct effect on intellectual and cultural life in Egypt, resulting in a flood of films dealing with the issue, including two of Chahine's—*The Emigrant* (1994) and *Destiny* (1997). Chahine's production company Misr International also produced the popular and critically acclaimed *al-Abwab al-mughlaqa* (The Closed Doors, produced by Misr International, Atef Hatata, 1999), which addressed fundamentalism from a more contemporary perspective. Algerian and Tunisian filmmakers have been tackling fundamentalist practices and explicitly depicting their impact on today's Arab youth and youth culture. As well, the highly charged political atmosphere in the region since the 1990s has resulted in the production of a number of films that comment on colonial and neocolonial practices and domination, including Osama Mohammad's *Sanduq al-dunya* (The Box of Life, 2002), a stylized depiction of life in a small Syrian village during the 1967 war with Israel, which links resistance to neocolonialism with the struggle to modernize social relations. In turn, Arab cinema tended to foreground social and cultural settings and characters that reflected a rapidly changing society struggling to reclaim its national identity against both internal and external neocolonial pressures. Lebanese filmmaker Randa Shahal's *Tayarat al-waraq* (The Kite, 2003), for example, turns an across-the-barbed wire love story of a young Arab girl and an Arab Israeli soldier (both followers of the Druze religion) into a stinging indictment of the oppressive reality of occupation.

Similarly, the Palestine dilemma remains among the more frequently visited themes in Arab cinema. Since the late 1980s, however, more emphasis has been put on approaching the issue through the eyes of its victims: refugees, peasants, fishermen, working class and unemployed Palestinians. The films of Michel Khleifi (*The Tale of the Three Jewels*, 1995), Elia Suleiman (*Divine Intervention*, 2002), and Hany Abou Assad (*Rana's Wedding*, 2002) are prime examples of this trend. But one of the more epical and highly stylized attempts to depict the history of Palestinian exile is Yousry Nasrallah's *Bab al-shams* (Door to the Sun, 2004), produced by Chahine's Misr International.

On another level, Arab filmmaking since the 1990s has directly reflected developments in communications technologies, such as the growth of Arab satellite television networks. Film festivals in the region are increasing, with annual events in Cairo, Beirut, Marrakesh, Damascus, and Carthage, as well as the new Dubai Film Festival created in 2004. The Ismailia International Documentary Film Festival in Egypt has become a major outlet for screening and discussing the latest trends in documentary and experimental Arab filmmaking. All this has been informing and informed by a renaissance in pan-Arab national cultural interactivity.

A national cultural revival is transcending divisions and borders between Arab states, regions, and peoples—divisions originally prescribed and designed by colonial powers in the first decade of the twentieth century. This revival is ushering in a qualitatively new period in the development of Arab cinema. On the one hand, political tensions in the Middle East—including the continuing ramifications of the Palestinian dilemma, and the implications of the Gulf (1992) and the Iraq (2003) wars (both understood locally as reflections of neocolonialist designs and interventions)—continue to inspire political and social consciousness of cultural settings and preoccupations. This complex backdrop has encouraged the emergence of new thematic trends and stylistic patterns in various areas of cultural production, allowing for the growth of filmmaking practices that have favored the breaking down of artificial barriers of form, geography, high and low art, and performer and artist that so often inform cinematic cultural practices in the west. Considered together, these developments can only signal a new beginning for a cinema that has never shied away from its responsibilities to its people.

Chahine's work since the late 1970s consistently foreshadowed this cinematic maturation that increasingly characterized new Arab cinemas. The fact that Chahine's Misr International has launched the careers of a countless number of young filmmakers, film technicians, as well as film actors in Egypt and the Arab world testifies to Chahine's role as a filmmaker and as an institution in the history of contemporary Arab cinema. More important, in my view, has been Chahine's vanguard role in depicting new themes and previously untackled topics, along with his experimentation with stylistic approaches formerly unheard of in mainstream Egyptian film practice. As we saw in earlier chapters, Chahine's cinema was consistent and unique in how it informed and was informed by the various changes and events affecting the Arab world over the past sixty years. Chahine's sensitive depiction of critical moments in contemporary Arab history inadvertently created a thematic and stylistic yardstick for Arab cinema.

Many of the thematic concerns and stylistic approaches associated with New Arab Cinemas can be linked one way or another to specific Chahine filmic ventures. From being among the first filmmakers to place and celebrate the presence of peasants and workers on the Arab film screen, to the steadfast support for anticolonial and pan-Arab struggles, to the inclusive and more heterogeneous outlook on Arab identity, to the anxious concern over the rise of religious fundamentalism, to the struggle for grass roots democratic change, Chahine's cinema has prefigured and inspired New Arab Cinema. Even the institutional readjustments that Chahine dared to take, particularly his coproduction film practices, foreshadowed what has become a near standard practice among independent Arab filmmakers.

Some Arab critics have focused on how later films, particularly *The Other*, *Silence... We're Rolling*, and *Alexandria... New York*, attempted to appeal to international, and particularly French audiences (due to the production connections with Canal+, France 2 Cinéma, and the Centre national de la cinématographie). These critics saw these films as part of a trend that began with *Adieu Bonaparte!* that gradually compromised Chahine's artistic integrity as well as his role as a political activist. Notwithstanding such criticism, Chahine's later work offered a sensitive, albeit perplexed reaction to a situation where the social and political mechanisms of resistance were themselves being compromised and marginalized. Within this atmosphere, Chahine's final films reflected his combative rejection of globalization, which he believed was destroying his society's ability to modernize and to move forward. But these films also revealed his pessimism regarding the possibilities of a collective resistance strong enough to meet the new challenges of a hegemonic culture of consumerism, fear, and inferiority.

APPROACHING THE DILEMMA OF *THE OTHER*

While themes of hegemony, domination, and control have been integral to Chahine's cinema, these preoccupations take on a new twist in *al-Akhar* (The Other). Here, they are approached in the context of the *new world order*, a term broadly describing the global political environment after the collapse of the Soviet Union and the socialist bloc. The 1999 film can also be understood as a commentary on the state of unipolar cultural globalization that followed the Cold War. Hegemony and globalization are not necessarily only politically or militarily rooted, but are also based on and enhanced by economic, intellectual, cultural, and media-based forms of control. *The Other* warns against the uncontrolled mushrooming of restrictive power structures that glorify consumerism, rationalize capitalist greed and the domination of multinationals, and pave the way for the emergence of fanatical and extremist forms of dissent and opposition within developing countries.

The Other works well as a simple story between Adam, the son of a wealthy Egyptian-American family, who is preparing for his doctorate on international terrorism at UCLA, and Hanan, a young woman who is just beginning her career as a reporter with a leftist opposition paper. As Adam returns home for a brief vacation he meets Hanan in the airport and this begins a strong love affair between them. Margaret, his mother, is not happy with the relationship and goes to desperate lengths to manipulate her son and destroy Hanan. The couple eventually get married, but troubles arise when Hanan's investigations of a religious peace project lead her to pursue a story about corrupt business deals involving Adam's family.

Adam's family is building a tourist compound sponsored by American companies in a Sinai desert resort that promotes interfaith understanding. (Historically, the project was indeed proposed by former president Sadat as an expression of his commitment to peace in the Middle East). But the reality, however, is that the project is a scheme designed to profit the family and allow American capital to further control Egypt's tourist industry. In contrast with the symbolism that associates Margaret and her family with American policies of domination and manipulation, the film presents a sympathetic portrait of Hanan's working-class Egyptian family (Hanan's mother is named Bahiya, which Chahine used in several films, including *The Sparrow*, to invoke the character of Mother Egypt). In her efforts to control her son, Margaret bribes her daughter-in-law's brother, a zealous thug who belongs to a religious fundamentalist terrorist cult, to lure Hanan into a deadly trap. The film ends with the tragic death of the young couple during a shootout between the police and a group of terrorists in the streets of Cairo.

Melodramatic, the film presents a passionate love story in the middle of intense political struggle, kitschy musical numbers featuring western upper-class grandeur spliced into vintage Hollywood production sketches with dancers spinning to a Strauss waltz. But the film also contemplates important political issues at the center of contemporary third world–western relations, such as Arab politics, Muslim fundamentalist terrorism, multiculturalism, globalization, political corruption, and technological development. The film also offers a grim portrait of Egypt's post-socialist upper class, presenting it as a clique of egotistical nouveau riche characters dazed by American power, money, and new technologies. One of the most intriguing scenes is when Margaret, in her effort to plot against Hanan, meets a co-conspirator from a fundamentalist terrorist group at the Eiffel Tower, but the meeting is a virtual one, existing only in cyberspace. Computers and satellite connections are seen as the means to maintain surveillance and control by those who are in power.

According to Chahine, the main question that he poses in this film is, "where do we stand as Arabs in relation to the western attempt to coordinate its hegemony, and, for that matter, how do we hope to deal with the consequences of possible inter-western rivalries in this regard?" He wonders about the reasons behind the stagnation and inability of Arabs to move in the direction of uniting and coordinating their efforts to deal with the consequences of globalization and the new world order.[3]

As with *Adieu Bonaparte!*, Chahine once again tackles the issue of national resistance to colonial hegemony, this time emphasizing the need to modernize this resistance and effectively utilize technological advancements irrespective of who has created them. The film's allusion to the opportunist cooperation—mediated by modern technology—between Adam's scheming mother and Hanan's fanatical terrorist brother, signals a call to Arab audiences to take a modernist path of resistance to hegemony that integrates an understanding of the complex dynamics of and between national and globalized cultures. From the outset *The Other* sets the tone for this theme, as in its first sequence we are presented with a conversation between the cultural theorist Edward Said and a group of students including the film's protagonist Adam. Said focuses on the need to approach cultural difference not from the view of creating artificial dichotomies based on chauvinist fanaticism, but rather through appreciating a more historical perspective of difference and how it informs and is informed by power:

> All those who believe only in the oppressive force of power are destined to attempt to exert their violence and hate against others. I wish we would stop asking 'what is your identity?'! [The west] has invented the computer, and we [Arabs] have created the alphabet! It is not important who gave what to whom and who has taken what from whom. The pharaonic culture, for example, is just like Beethoven's music, the property of all humanity.

The film received mixed reviews from Egyptian and Arab film critics. Despite this reaction, however, *The Other* attracted large audiences. As a result, Chahine was able to finally pay off the loan from a French government producer in support of his film *Adieu Bonaparte!*[4] Some suggested that the Romeo and Juliet love affair between the two popular young actors in the leading roles (Hanan al-Turk and Hani Salama) played an important part in attracting young audiences to the theaters. Once again, an important point of contention was what was considered by many a confusing stylistic approach.

Film critic Kamal Ramzi characterized the film as "muddled at all levels" and "agitated" in its depiction of events. He goes on to say that while the film does feature Chahine's traditional interest in characters who are anxious, rebellious, and confrontational in the pursuit of their goals and desires, it nevertheless "comes across as forced and artificiated."[5] For his part, critic Mustafa Darwish shares the view that the film is forced in how it presents its message—mainly as a result of trying to say too much.[6]

Several critics, however, looked at the film as an imaginative artistic portrayal of an issue close to the hearts of younger Egyptians over-infatuated by everything American. According to Ra'uf Tawfiq, *The Other* presents an original depiction of the linkages between the practices inherent to American policies and the logic of fundamentalist terrorism.[7] Tarek al-Shinnawi writes that the film carries the entire package of contradictions that characterize Chahine's films: typically mixing direct and subtle messages, and alternating the simplicity and complexity of his direction. The writer also notes that in concord with other Chahine films, *The Other* once again offers characters alien to their surroundings and their history. As such, the film's Other is not far from us... in fact, "that Other is inside of us and is symbolized within the film in the characters of the terrorist, the corrupt businessmen, and members of an upper class which seems to have sold itself to the Americans."[8] In another article, al-Shinnawi further emphasized that the film reflected the child in Youssef Chahine that remained overwhelmed by the conflicting influences of reality and imagination.[9]

Samir Farid characterized the film as a "Caricatured Fantasy" about the new world order. He considered it a third installment in a Chahine trilogy in which he called for a new perspective in dealing with the Other: *The Emigrant* explored ancient Egypt, *Destiny* depicted the period of the middle ages, with *The Other* presented a slice of contemporary life. The film, in Farid's view, condemns the phenomenon of Egyptian and Arab religion-based terrorism but clearly alludes to the American involvement in it. But Farid warns against dealing with the film as a realistic political story because such an approach would trivialize its message as well as its artistic integrity. He argues that film needs to be looked at as a caricature of musical fantasy within which characters turn into caricatures of themselves: "Margaret of the Americans, Bahiya of Egypt, and Adam and Hanan of Romeo and Juliet."[10] As such the film represented another phase in Chahine's cinema, because while it continued the tradition of the detailed and expansive *mise en scène* and thematic preoccupation with contemporary Arab social and political issues, *The Other*'s pastiche undertones made it less readily accessible, particularly when it came to communicating its political significance.[11] Nevertheless, the film was indeed very successful in attracting a different kind of audience—one which had probably never seen a Chahine work before. One Arab viewer reflected on how the film was received in this comment on the IMDb Web site:

> The Other succeeded in attracting more people had never been big fans of Chahine's previous movies. But, on the other hand, the majority of Chahine's fans didn't like the movie, or at least they said, "Maybe it is a good movie, but it's not Chahine's," and I am one of them. The characters in the movie are not described in a deep way and symbols used in each character are superficial most of the time. Fans of Chahine used to watch his movies to spend two hours of deep thinking and analysis, not only of the artistic way and the impressive mise en scène of Chahine—which were very good in l'Autre also—but also for the revolutionary ideas and the "Deep Diving" he used to make in his characters and the strong contradictions inside one character as well as between different characters. L'Autre was Me versus the Other, but this Me was not surely Me, and the other was too much the Other.[12]

If postmodernism represents a crisis of knowledge and legitimation which leads to a historically conditioned skepticism toward the meta-narratives of Enlightenment and related ideas about scientific progress and political liberation as Jean-François Lyotard once stressed,[13] then Chahine's *The Other* represents a powerful example of and commentary on the Arab state of angst in the age of globalization and the new world order. The outlandish approach that dominates Chahine's representation of the film's characters effectively captures the lineage between cynicism, apathy, and defeat. For those critics who were looking for the old Chahine, whose films *Jamila*, *Saladin*, and *The Land* spelled out the reality of a national collective in a state of resistance, *The Other* could not deliver the goods. For those who sought the hopeful and determined Bahiya of *The Sparrow* (who defies defeat and proclaims resistance as identity) or looked for the guilt ridden post-revolutionary Bahiya of *The Return of the Prodigal Son*, the film could only be a disappointment.

Some critics could not relate to the sensibility of the artist as he attempted to depict a nihilistic moment in Egyptian and Arab history with no room for a real sense of resistance, nor even a genuine sense of guilt and remorse for past mistakes. All that was left were the kitschy iconographies and hollow replicas that operate in crisis ridden meta-narratives. The dilemma here is one rooted in the contradictory nature of modernization (and of Fredric Jameson's *postmodernity*) in the age of late capitalism; as technology increasingly provides bases for interconnectivity that could potentially enhance collective and coordinated solutions to common problems, we become lonelier and more isolated. It is a contradiction to which Marx alluded as symptomatic of the capitalist contradictory dialectic between the unprecedented capacity of this system to develop and perfect the means of production and the consequent dilemma of materializing the full social potential of these developments beyond their profit driven bases. Meanwhile, manifestations of globalized capitalism and the divisive and destructive forces associated with this ironically *de*-linking process (one which Chahine identifies as an Othering process involving proponents on all sides of the political and cultural spectrum) continue to create havoc. In this regard, *The Other* draws connections between, on the one hand, local bullies who dominate the economy and politics in a postcolonial Arab world, and on the other, an array of powerful multinational financial interests that have the upper hand under globalization.

Chahine's imaging of capitalist globalization in *The Other* is more acutely concerned with its ability to disguise its teeth and claws with satin gloves and warm smiles. The Bahiya imported from *The Sparrow* carries all the shattered and worn-out symbols of a Mother Egypt reduced to a shallow facsimile of her former self. In turn, Hanan's idealized innocence in her investigation into capitalist corruption while attempting to maintain a relationship with the son of a key culprit in the scandal, becomes a metaphor for the post-Soviet Arab left and its inability to resituate itself within a new set of dynamics, to provide a self-critical assessment of its earlier practices, or to offer fresh answers to new Arab social, economic, and cultural realities.

Chahine's irony, however, is far from being blank or autotelic. Reading a Chahine film within an Arab context allows us to see both the failures and the successes of an organic activist intellectual. The dark postmodern sensibility of the film represented a major departure from his earlier films, which, despite their modernist reflexive attitude, remained inclined to optimism— even in *The Return of the Prodigal Son*, the final escape of the two young people from the Madbouli family massacre reflected a subtly hopeful stance. This darkness, however, is anchored in the self-destructive dynamics of hegemonizing capitalist globalization.

Margaret's seemingly uncaring attitude as she walks across the Brooklyn Bridge after the death of her son is a smack of reality in an otherwise detaching postmodernist exercise; it is a moment when Chahine's cinematic play pauses and his—and our—brief moment of reflection begins. A symbolic embodiment of the colonial and the local Arab power structures in the age of globalization, Margaret is indeed in control of events. But she also remains the ultimate loser, having lost both her son and her own identity as a mother, a woman, and a human being. Margaret's surreal demeanor of sophistication, power, and ultra-modernity mirrors the broken and false promises globalization offers developing countries.[14] It is within this reflective moment that Chahine points out to his viewers the need to take refuge from the loss of contact with nature or the real, as Baudrillard would characterize the postmodern era's social and cultural affectivity.

SILENCE... WE'RE ROLLING

After two years of work during which Chahine was admitted several times to hospital, *Silence... We're Rolling* was finally released amid wide publicity and anticipation. The film was coproduced by Chahine's Misr International, the Cité de production médiatique, the Centre national de la cinématographie (CNC), and several French television stations. However, Chahine's ill health during the filming meant his assistant Khaled Youssef had to finish several scenes. And later, during the final stages of editing and mixing, despite his illness, Chahine involved himself in the struggle of some thirty thousand peasant families on the Nile island of Dahab near Cairo. People were being forced off their lands to allow for the construction of tourist attractions, and Chahine's well publicized visit to Dahab created a nationwide solidarity campaign that saw all major newspapers debate the issue of big business' attempt to deprive people of their livelihood, comparing the

Silence, We're Rolling: Love in the age of globalized capital (photo: Maged Fawzi).

contemporary story to Chahine's 1968 film *The Land*. Though the production of *Silence... We're Rolling* did not run as smoothly as planned, it was screened at the Venice Film Festival to great fanfare accompanied by a special celebration of Chahine's work, and went on to garner popular success at the box office.

Silence... We're Rolling is structured as a film within a film where a filmmaker is working on a movie featuring his family and friends. The filmmaking process is itself punctuated by deliberations and discussions among the actors about their roles, the film's goal, plot, and development. The story involves a pre-1952 revolution bourgeois family consisting of a wealthy grandmother (played by Magda al-Khatib), her movie star daughter Malak (well-known Tunisian singer Latifa) and granddaughter Paula (Ruby). Malak is in a loveless marriage with a lawyer distracted by his work, making money, and having an affair with another woman. Set in a westernized cosmopolitan Alexandria—in contrast to the warmer Alexandria of earlier Chahine films—this film has a light tone and a happy ending in the comedy of errors tradition. When Malak's husband runs off with her best friend, she is pursued by the would-be star Lamei (Ahmed Wafik), a gold-digging con artist who is only interested in Malak for her connections and her family's money. From the outset, the politically and socially progressive grandmother warns her daughter to beware of falling for the schemes of the young opportunist.

Halfway into the film, Lamei shifts his attentions from the mother to the daughter when he is tricked into thinking that the grandmother's fortune will go to the young Paula. In a bid to expose the truth to Malak, Alphi (a screenwriter who himself has a crush on Malak) comes up with a plot to expose Lamei. Meanwhile, Paula is in love with Nasser, the son of the family's chauffeur, a university student who loves to talk about Gamal Abd al-Nasser and the dreams of the revolution. The young Nasser is interested in publishing a journal for young people to warn them against globalized capitalism and how it is destroying the country's social and economic fabric. Nasser's character seems to be the only one in the film with a clear political and intellectual awareness of himself and his role in society; in his view, the dream initiated and supported by Nasser remains alive, and he does not surrender his personal and ideological integrity to gain acceptance from the corrupt upper class. In many ways, Nasser's character embodies the hope for the future and the possibilities of resistance to the overwhelming wave of globalized capitalism. The wealthy and politically astute nationalist grandmother is a matchmaker hoping to bring the two young people together, though Nasser is reluctant due to his idealistic fears of selling his soul to the upper class.

With a range of song and dance numbers that showcase the talent of Latifa, Chahine lets reality and fiction slide together, so that the film-within-a-film becomes indistinguishable from the drama. The wisecracking grandmother, with her great desire to see everyone happily married off before she dies, is countered by Chahine's witty fantasy sequences in which reality gives way to daydreams. Behind this showbiz and comedy veneer the film presents a buoyant commentary, and a picture of what Chahine himself characterizes as "our economic, political, and social reality of today." It is a reality where "trendy opportunism in our Arab countries as well as around the world has now become a legitimate form of conducting business."[15]

While most of the local reviews of the film stressed its beautifully composed and colorful *mise en scène*, and its light and playful demeanor, many criticized its lack of seriousness in dealing with the theme of globalization. Yusuf al-Qa'id writes that although Chahine certainly departed here from his earlier direct critique of the phenomenon of globalization, he nevertheless failed in reconnecting with the reality of today's condition as it affects the actual lives of people, something that he had succeeded in achieving with his epic masterpiece *The Land*.[16] Tarek al-Shinnawi was much harsher in his criticism of the film, considering it to be naive both in structure and ideas, and attacking

> Chahine's tendency to 'hide behind the claim that critics are incapable of understanding his films because they lack the education and the sophistication,' at the time when his recent films have simply become oriented toward western audiences and critics and increasingly assumed chaotic and incomprehensible structures and topics.[17]

Al-Shinnawi is referring here to a comment made by Chahine during a press conference in which he described some film critics as "donkeys par-excellence."[18] Naturally, the comment was very controversial but was taken by most as a typical Chahine outburst in response to unwarranted attacks by some journalists. In an article supporting Chahine in the controversy, the prominent leftist journalist Raga al-Nakkash noted that those same critics customarily condemned his films in a hostile manner—often without having seeing them—while hiding behind religious and nationalist chauvinist rhetoric. Some of them, she continued, even publicly called and occasionally encouraged extremists to kill him for what they saw as his heresies.[19]

The film's playfully hybrid use of the cinematic traditions of the musical and the romantic comedy genres offered a light, popular, and unpretentious critique of the cynicism of a young generation that reduces politics, arts, and relationships to games of financial and personal self-promotion. It presented a reflexive account of a filmmaker's attempt to make a movie at a time when executives in the Egyptian and Arab film industries were changing the spirit of filmmaking. The film points to an industry increasingly dominated by money launderers and opportunists with no genuine interest in, or knowledge of, the art and science of cinema. As such, the film clearly reflected Chahine's anxiety and outspokenness on these issues during this period. In a 2001 interview he stated that as far as he was concerned, the danger facing Egyptian cinema in the first years of the new millennium had shifted from what it had been in the early 1990s:

> [Religious extremism] does not concern me today as much as the state of intellectual stagnation and even degradation among governmental agencies and individuals who are supposed to be a source of support for the artists ... even more important is the rise of monopolies which are beginning to put their hands on all kinds of film production and distribution channels, even through taking over movie theaters around the country.[20]

Chahine goes on to argue that the lack of any proactive action on the part of the government to protect artists, art groups, and industries in Egypt was creating opportunities for large financial firms to set up shop and start making "all sorts of trash," and could only lead to disaster.[21]

Chahine's anxiety over the changing face of the film industry is well reflected in *Silence... We're Rolling*, which playfully depicts the frustrated world of a filmmaker in action and how he contends with the local manifestations of solely profit-driven practices. Globalization materializes local cinema and causes young generations of Egyptian and Arab artists to begin to see and rationalize their role as moneymakers and agents for a globalized capitalist culture. Lamei's character symptomizes how such practices are being rationalized, and as a result, how artists and art products are also forced to become uniform global symbols designed only for large-scale consumption. His opportunist relationship with Malak, and his disregard for any meaningful connection with her beyond manipulating her financial success and star status, further exemplifies this globalization dynamic.

Coming on the heels of *The Other*, *Silence... We're Rolling* focused the discussion of capitalist globalization to more directly impact the topic dearest to Chahine, the world of cinema. As such, the film contemplated the emergence of new rationalizations affecting the filmmaking industry in Egypt since the early 1990s. For Chahine, the framework for the new situation is located in business conditions regulated only so far as to encourage opportunistic and monopolizing practices. This situation is negatively impacting cinema in Egypt and consequently in the entire Arab world. In 1996 the government created new film legislation that relieved film investment companies of all taxes, but this was conditional upon these companies retaining a minimum capital amount of 200 million Egyptian pounds. According to Chahine in a 2002 interview with Nader Adly, this was clearly designed to encourage and support big companies, and tighten the screws on smaller and independent producers:

> At the time I felt an urgent need to make a film about what everybody referred to as 'globalization' . . . a concept which most did not understand, but in essence it was all about encouraging, rationalizing, even celebrating sleaziness on all economic, social, and political levels. . . . People who were crooked, immoral, and ready to sell themselves for money (i.e., opportunists) were applauded and praised. These are the kinds of people that are treated as VIPs, and are often labeled as businessmen although they know nothing about business except its shady features and practices.[22]

Within the changing world of Egyptian and Arab filmmaking in the late 1990s, *Silence . . . We're Rolling* depicted globalization not as a linear progression predetermined by the uncontested power of capitalism. Rather, it was identified as an element of a complex paradigmatic dialectic that also paradoxically involved elements of resistance and contestation. While, on the one hand, capitalist-based production and consumption continues to affirm a hegemonic control over an increasingly globalized culture, it is, on the other hand, regenerating various forms of resistance and even counter-hegemonic movements providing the basis for alternative cultural practices. The young Nasser is certainly a nostalgic tribute to the dignified resistance that characterized an earlier period in Egyptian and Arab history, but he is also a symbol of the unswerving re-emergence of postcolonial forms of resistance that are conducive to the dynamic of capitalist globalization itself.

On another level, however, the film for some appeared to offer a conciliatory outlook on traditionally non-conciliatory opposites. Leading film scholar Samir Farid saw *Silence* as an attempt by Chahine to artistically and thematically reconcile conflicting dynamics manifested within the plot in "the black driver and the white grandmother, the rich and the poor, the left and right, the honest and the deceitful, and between three generations that live in a specific moment within history: the generation of the driver and the grandmother, the generation of Abbas, Malak, Ezz al-Din, and Oulifi, and finally the generation of Paula and Nasser."[23]

Silence... We're Rolling was still showing in theaters in Egypt and other parts of the Arab world on September 11, 2001. Both western and Arab reactions to the events in New York and Washington were largely shaped by the continuing and interconnected crises in the Middle East. Within these fast changing political circumstances, a new dynamic seemed to once again reshape Chahine's immediate political preoccupations and consequently his cinematic production agenda. More specifically, a bitter corollary was reshaping the relationship between the Arab world and the United States as a result of what some within the Arab world saw as another excuse to reaffirm American political and military hegemony over the region, and to lash out against Arab and Muslim values and cultures. Chahine's next two projects would revise what seemed like a reconciliation of opposites in *Silence*, and revisit his own unresolved love/hate relationship with America as instigated by the tragic events of 9/11 and their aftermath.

AMERICA AND I!

Just before he began to work on *Alexandria... New York* (2004) Chahine was asked to make a short film on the events of September 11. The 2002 anthology, titled *09'11"01* (also known as *Eleven Minutes, Nine Seconds, One Image: September 11*), was part of a project initiated by a French producer and involved eleven filmmakers from around the world. Each director was given a little over eleven minutes to present a cinematic outlook on what took place in New York and Washington in September 2001. Chahine's contribution was among the most controversial of the eleven shorts, and he was accused by several western critics of providing a rationalizing pretext for the terrorist attacks.

The short film features veteran Egyptian actor Nour el-Sherif playing the role of Chahine. It begins with the filmmaker in New York City preparing to shoot a film when he is stopped by the police because he does not have a permit. It then cuts to 'Chahine' in Beirut as he cancels a news conference about the upcoming film due to the events of September 11. The filmmaker is then seen sitting on a Lebanese beach, when the ghost of a young soldier killed in a 1980s attack on the American army barracks in Beirut suddenly appears to him. The two have a conversation about American policy in the region, which is intercut by flashbacks depicting the soldier's relationship with a Lebanese woman. The filmmaker then takes the soldier/ghost on a trip in which he witnesses the home and family of a Palestinian preparing to blow himself up in a suicide attack inside Israel. Chahine's character uses the trip to explain the background of American policies that have been bolstering anti-American sentiment in Palestine and around the world for several decades.

Little seen in the Arab world, *09'11"01* was viewed mainly by critics attending film festivals in Europe and North America. While most Arab reviewers critiqued what they saw as preachy proclamations lacking artistic subtlety, some western critics considered its linkage between American foreign policy and the September attacks as somewhat offensive. In an interview in *Cahiers du Cinéma*, Chahine shot back, accusing his critics of having an anti-Arab bias. He explained that when he was asked to make the film the idea was to answer the questions that had dominated American popular reaction: "Why did they attack us, and why do they hate us?" Chahine argued that all he tried to do was to give as sincere an answer as possible:

> I simply stressed that supporting [Israeli] occupation and the unjust American policies in the Middle East are creating the basis for violence and extremism.... Perhaps they wanted me to present a film to reaffirm their views... but I will never do that... I am an Arab, and this is my honest perspective," said Chahine. I oppose oppression and occupation, and occupation breeds violence.... Israel is killing women and children and the United States does not even criticize these acts. Once America feels the effect of supporting violence, it lashes out and demands that the entire world weep with it in unison![24]

He talked about his personal feelings about America in a 2002 newspaper interview:

> I used to love America... and it is there where I found my first love and where I first studied arts and film.... I always thought that American modernity would help humanity on the road to happiness... but what was happening made me stop and think again. You simply cannot help oppress people and deprive them of their dignity and then turn around and expect them to love you![25]

It was within this atmosphere, in the context of the September 11 events themselves and the consequent racist anti-Arab and anti-Muslim rhetoric dominating the west, that Chahine worked on his new film *Alexandria... New York*. As with most of his films since *Alexandria... Why*, the film was coproduced by Chahine's Misr International and a number of French producers including France 2 Cinéma, Canal +, and the Centre national de la cinématographie.

Proclaimed by most critics as the latest chapter in his now quartet film autobiography, *Alexandria... New York* reconsidered Chahine's ambiguous and contradictory relationship with the America he always professed to love. The film finds Chahine's traditional alter ego Yehia in New York for a film festival celebration of his cinema. There he runs into his presumed first love Ginger, whom he had met when they were nineteen year olds studying theater at the Pasadena Playhouse. Back then, American cinema symbolized American dreams and ideals for Chahine, but fifty years on these ideas have been replaced with bitterness and resentment. For this Arab filmmaker visiting the United States, any positive semblance of America's image has been long shattered as he cites the anti-Arab bias he claims now mars its foreign policies, and as he talks about its cinematic genius being replaced by formula filmmaking complemented by contempt for talent and creativity.

To his surprise, however, Yehia finds out that he has an American child, Alexander. Now a man, the son, swayed by the daily dose of anti-Arab and anti-Muslim stereotypes offered by politicians and the media, refuses to acknowledge his father because he is an Arab. This partly fictitious memoir of Chahine's life develops on various planes, the past and the present, older Yehia and younger Yehia, the father and the son, love for America and hate for America—and of course New York and Alexandria. Once again Chahine creates a generic fusion of melodrama, musical (including some intriguing hybrid song and dance scenes), some comedy, and political drama. The film also incorporates a brief interpretation of Bizet's *Carmen*, a recital of an excerpt from *Hamlet* (a play dear to Chahine), and a sequence extracted from Chahine's 1958 *Cairo Station*.

After the titles and the film's theme song, the film opens with the filmmaker Yehia and his life-long friend and revolutionary intellectual Adib in a discussion about the United States' refusal to finance the construction of the Aswan High Dam, in which Yehia compares that issue with the refusal of an American producer to finance the production of one of his films. We then recognize that the reference is to Chahine's film *Cairo Station* in conjunction with a converstion which Yehia had with Adel in a Cairo café in the mid-1950s. Another discussion between the two takes place as Yehia is supervising the editing of the film and is telling Adib that it was the United States that forced Israel, Britain, and France to cease fire and eventually withdraw from the Sinai Peninsula after it was occupied in 1956. Adib angrily responds, pointing out his friend's naiveté, "Are you going to remain so uninformed for the rest of your life? It was the Soviet warning which forced them to withdraw.... Don't you get it?" The scene reflexively depicts the early phase of Chahine's fascination with the ideas of the American Dream and his impressions about American politics at the time. The discussion is complemented by the dark editing room setting, as well as the editing process itself, which involves bringing together various pieces of the cinematic puzzle. Chahine's political formation is at its early stage and is being challenged by contesting feelings and ideas.

Flashbacks usher us through a range of phases in the filmmaker's life, including Yehia's preparation for his latest trip to New York to attend a festival in his honor where several of his films will be screened. When the September 11 attacks take place the filmmaker is hesitant to take the trip due to his mixed feelings about the situation, but he finally decides to go. As he arrives in New York, however, another set of challenges confronts him. We see him talking about how he always had warm relationships with several Jewish friends and acquaintances and how they respected him and his work. In a later flashback, he is seen at a press conference following a screening of *Cairo Station* accusing Zionist critics of unjustifiably attacking the film. In another scene Yehia is with a close Jewish friend who works in the film industry. They converse about the possibility of getting some American financing for his film *The People and the Nile* (1968), but his friend ridicules his naiveté: "You are crazy to think that the Americans are going to finance a film that praises Nasser.... These people will never really accept you, your friend Nasser, or for that matter any Arab." "But you are a non-Zionist Jew, and we have no problem supporting each other," responds Yehia. To his disappointment, his friend tells him, "You are my friend indeed, but if I'm given the choice between you and Israel I will not hesitate to choose Israel!"

The film's plot is structured to show different situations in which Yehia/Chahine is forced to express disillusionment with preconceptions he had held earlier in his life. The most important comes when he meets Ginger at the New York festival in his honor some sixty years after they had first met in America. In today's New York the two recall their relationship, and a flashback takes us to that period. Ginger tells Yehia about Alexander, the son he had fathered, and how he is now a renowned dancer in a famous ballet troupe. At this point, the film moves us through a critically sensitive journey.

In reality, Chahine does not have children, but the film relates deeply to his love for the idea of having a son, and perhaps of having a wife. (Chahine was indeed once married, but the terms and duration of the union remain enigmatic.) Yehia's wife Jean shares his longing for his son and shows no jealousy regarding his previous relationship with Ginger. The filmmaker's dream, however, is frustrated by his son's rejection, which is further exacerbated by Alexander's racism—an attitude Yehia sees as characteristic of most Americans' dealings with Arabs. Yehia eventually abandons his hopes for a relationship with Alexander and angrily tells him he is "fed up and disgusted with you and with America.... It is me now who is telling you, 'I reject you.'" The film ends with Yehia walking alone down a busy New York street, his eyes mirroring his anger and pain, and in the background we hear a song about a New York that "kills tenderness."

The film was warmly received by Arab audiences and critics. In light of the tensions following the September 11 attacks, the subsequent American invasion of Iraq, and the continued violence in Palestine, the film's symbolic resentment of American policies in the Middle East was favorably received for its well-developed plot and visual beauty. Kussai Saleh al-Darwish considered the film a creative articulation of Arab anger toward American policies in the Middle East, particularly in the aftermath of the 9/11 events. The film, al-Darwish suggests, was able to provide a sensitive yet rich reassessment of the contradictory love/hate relationship between America and the Arab world.[26] Ibrahim al-Aris wrote in *al-Hayat* newspaper, "the clear reference to the real Chahine through Yehia's character in the film smoothly allows him to reflect upon his disappointment with America. But the film does not deal with issues of Arab resentment toward America in a simplistic and vulgarized manner, and instead it tackles them through an exploration of a tender love story that is woven in superior artistry."[27] Film critic Fatma Nimr considered the film as probably the most important in his autobiographical Alexandria series,

> not only because it depicts a sixty year old journey of love and suffering between Alexandria and New York, but also because of its high level of courage, especially in how Chahine conveys his contradictory feelings that stimulate him and shape his relationship with others.[28]

The film, nevertheless, was critiqued for its lack of authenticity in relaying Chahine's personal history; his stories based on real life events had always drawn criticism locally. Walid Toughan summarized a related critical discussion that accompanied the release of *Alexandria...New York*. "It is important to acknowledge that any work of art is in the end a culmination of personal recollections, and is virtually an impressionistic outlook on events or on history," says Toughan.[29] Critics question whether Chahine's approach opens the door for further "reformulations of history and historical realities, a practice which, given today's present circumstances, could contribute to the collective national amnesia our society already suffers from."[30]

Throughout his work on the film Chahine consistently articulated his view of it as a statement on his contradictory relationship with America. While most local critics stressed the autobiographical aspect of the work and how it complemented his Alexandria trilogy, the film felt more in sync with Chahine's preoccupation with contemporary political anxieties. Even as he began to write the script about his "most important personal love story,"[31] the film's original title, *Anger*, reflected Chahine's distress over the increased tensions between the United States and the Arab world.

Such anxiety was not new to Chahine or his work, considering how many of his films tended to *tisaffi hisabat* (even the score) between him and those people and ideas he disagreed with, or when he wanted to relay specific views on particular present controversies.[32] Nearly two years before its release, Chahine explained his main motivation behind a film with such an unsavory title as *Anger*:

> The story of the film is about the contradiction with which I live in connection with the United States. I love Americans' modern and modernizing ideas ... and their respect for sciences, arts, democratic values, and the American people's love for life. At the same time, there has been a constantly repulsive foreign policy toward all [Arab] concerns.... This goes back to their refusal to finance the High Dam, and later their 'stupid' bias on the side of Israel, their policy on Iraq and vis-à-vis nearly all Arab states.... There is also an unexplained hostility toward my work and toward me personally. For over fifty years, the Americans never acknowledged me or my work and I never registered on their map despite all the awards and recognitions that I amassed.... Only two years ago they began to show some of my films at a New York festival. Over the years, my love for America has transformed into anger ... and as the French say, 'only the lover gets angry.'[33]

Chahine's position on an increasingly volatile Middle East in the new millennium—a volatility he anticipated in the violent ideological and political dynamics of *The Other* even before September 11, 2001—had always embodied manifestations of the age of globalization.

The term *globalization* itself is problematic in the sense that the phenomenon of an increasingly integrated world economy (and its consequent interactive social, political, and cultural manifestations) has been central to the capitalist growth process since the European colonial ventures of the Renaissance. This process has been accelerated since the collapse of the socialist bloc in the early 1990s, with the ramifications of capitalist globalization clearly impacting the Arab world on all levels.

The sudden structural shift from largely nationalized economic structures (associated with many Arab countries' earlier ties with the socialist bloc) to overwhelmingly capitalist configurations, led to substantial consequences within the social fabric of Arab societies. With most Arab countries more open than ever to foreign capital flow and exchange, the economic dynamics of local and cross-Arab economies were being radically reshaped, with the changes advantaging advanced capitalist countries and multinationals. The accelerated global capitalist expansion in the Arab region manifested itself in increased violence, which was only exacerbated by American military and political interventions in the aftermath of the 9/11 attacks.

Considering its rich oil deposits, one can argue that the phenomenon of capitalist globalization as embodied within the Arab region assumed from the outset a less subtle neocolonial face than it did in other less financially critical third world regions. More specifically, the post-9/11 Americans, through their invasion of Iraq and continued unqualified support of Israel, shaped the notion of globalization within Arab popular political discourse as a re-embodiment of old colonial practices under a new regime.

By the time he was preparing to release *Alexandria . . . New York*, Chahine was giving an unprecedented number of interviews in which he consistently stressed a pointed message of resentment toward American policies in the region, "I am more than angry at the United States," said Chahine,

> I cannot imagine why the States would sacrifice more than three hundred million Arabs for the sake of three million Israelis . . . and I also do not understand how the president of a great country like the United States essentially declares war on an entire religion such as Islam . . . . This is utter lunacy no matter how much he claims that he is only fighting Muslim extremists.[34]

Between 1999 and 2004 Chahine's work (three features, plus his *9'11"01* short) focused on how globalization—as expressed in religious extremism and violence; corrupt, unregulated, and mainly foreign-controlled local versions of capitalism; and American policies vis-à-vis Iraq and Israel—was continuing to affect the Arab world. While *Silence . . . We're Rolling* focused specifically on what he saw as a degradation of values governing social and economic interaction in a world that accepts financial and personal profit as its moral compass, the three other films were much more explicit in linking this condition to the geopolitical effects of a new world order under the unipolar hegemony of the United States. Chahine utilized the personal and social interactions of his own postcolonial post-socialist world as allegorical reflections of the political tensions and dynamics of the new Middle East. In a cinematic conflation of the geopolitical and the personal, *Silence... We're Rolling*, *9'11"01*, and *Alexandria... New York* placed the filmmaker at the center of the narrative, with the United States functioning as a symbol of upheaval and violence.

THE RETURN OF THE RESISTANT SON?

If Chahine's three previous depictions of the age of capitalist globalization and the assumed unipolar world of American hegemony described what seemed like an overwhelming reality affecting Arab society and politics, his last film represented a return to his earlier optimism for the possibilities of resistance.

Chaos (2007) involved little foreign support. While the 3B Production Company was a coproducer of the film, Misr International put up the lion's share of the production money. Toward the end of the shoot Chahine decided to give directorial co-credit to his collaborator Khaled Youssef, who had been working closely with him on all his films since the mid-1990s. The film was first screened in competition at the Sixty-fourth Venice International Film Festival in September 2007, to which Chahine had to be flown in on a private plane due to his deteriorating health.

While the film is set within the Cairo district of Shubra, it reflects circumstances across the Arab world, and perhaps throughout many third world countries. When the film was being made, the issue of police brutality was a

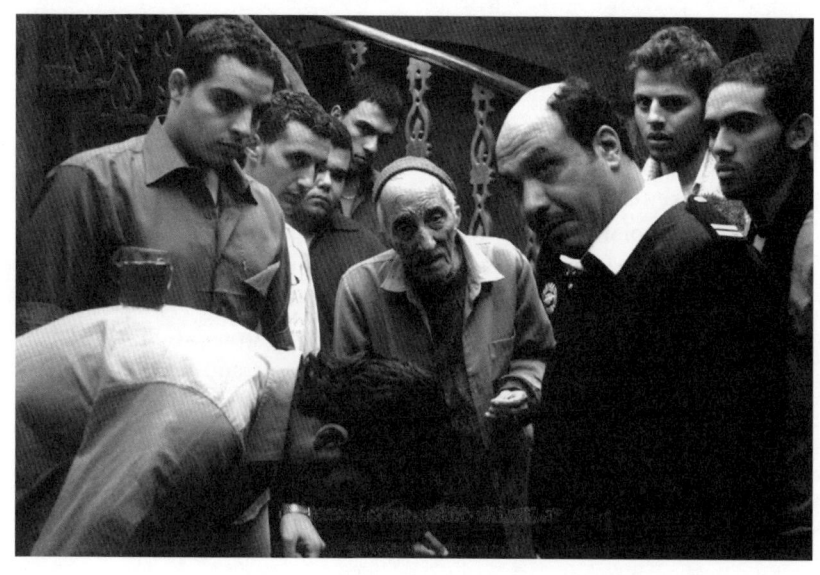

Chaos: Chahine's final 'popular cinema' rendezvous with politics.

major news topic in Egypt as outrage had broken out regarding cell-phone images of Egyptian security officers abusing and torturing prisoners. Equally as important, *Chaos* returned Chahine to the world of the marginalized, reminiscent of his films of the 1950s, as well as *The Land*. This time Chahine set his story within a working-class and lower-middle-class neighborhood. The message about corruption, police brutality, and government repression in a populist film clearly intended to attract the broadest audience possible, representing a return to his approach of three decades previous. But it was this accessible cinematic packaging of an urgent and subversive political message that made *Chaos* his most popular film in years.

The film opens with a violent scene of police brutality during a demonstration led by students in the Shubra district. Sherif, a young district attorney, has the case against the students dropped, but Hatem, a senior police officer, is seen throwing some of the demonstrators into a crumbling underground prison cell. Hatem, a ruthless, sadistic, and corrupt man is in love with his neighbor Nour, a young school teacher carrying an unreciprocated crush on the district attorney, Sherif. Hatem's mantra reinforces his character as an embodiment of the larger and more systemic problems of Egypt and the Arab world: "Whoever is ungrateful to Hatem is ungrateful to Egypt," he repeats to his neighbors on every occasion in order to reinforce his extortions and control. After all, he is not an isolated bad apple but a by-product of systemic corruption. Exacerbating the situation, both right and left wing opposition parties, as well as the Muslim Brotherhood, are concerned only with narrow, short-term political gains and are unwilling to become involved in any serious grass-roots action. The film is clearly marking what Chahine sees as the reduction of the role of the official opposition to mere window dressing. It also marks his views on how uninhibited political repression and the destruction of civil society have pacified and instilled apathy among Arabs.

Another key character in the film is Sherif's mother Wadad, the headmistress of the school where Nour teaches. Wadad is trying to encourage her son to take interest in the young teacher and to dissuade him against his unhappy love affair with his westernized, snobbish upper-class girlfriend Sylvia. The decoration in Wadad's home reflects her political orientation as a leftist activist with a great affinity for Nasser, Che Guevara, and the revolutionary traditions of past days.

Hatem's bullying and extortion, though profitable, reaps the resentment of the neighborhood, including Nour and her mother who happen to live in the same building as him. His unreciprocated love for Nour becomes a sick obsession. After some persuasion, Hatem eventually convinces her to go out, at which point he tries to explain himself and show her a different side from what the neighborhood sees. When Nour rejects his advances he abducts and rapes her.

The incident triggers a spontaneous rebellion by the people of the neighborhood, reflecting their long repressed outrage. The powerful final sequence is reminiscent in its sweeping impulsiveness of the final scene in *The Sparrow*, in which Bahiya leads the growing crowds of demonstrators as they express their rejection of defeat and of Nasser's resignation.

The film attracted audiences in Egyptian theaters for over four months and was widely acclaimed as a courageous and powerful attempt to deal with issues that had direct relevance to Egyptians. The film also attracted audiences across the Arab world where it was received with equal enthusiasm. For most local critics, the film represented a return to Chahine the realist, in reference to his earlier work that had marginalized and working-class Egyptians at its center. The Lebanese *al-Akhbar* newspaper lauded the film's story and setting as a microcosm representing the situation in all Arab countries today. It is a situation where "there can be no trust in the justice system, the police, religious figures, or anything that has to do with the state," the newspaper suggests. The paper also praises Chahine's "narratively strong and social realist perspective" in approaching events and social conditions with the mastery he demonstrated in his classic films *Cairo Station* and *The Land*. This, *al-Akhbar* says, contrasts with the "assertion of intellectual challenges" that characterized most of his later films.[35]

Othman Tazghart shares a similar appreciation of the "structural cohesiveness" of the film and the script, which allowed the filmmaker to develop his characters through a universal human dimension and significance in the same way he carved the characters of Qinawi in *Cairo Station*, Bahiya in *The Sparrow*, and Yehia in the Alexandria trilogy. In the same context, the writer sees the film as a departure from his more recent work including *Destiny*, *The Other*, and *Silence... We're Rolling*, which he sees as more internationally oriented and preoccupied. Chahine is at his best when he indulges the "specificity of localized Egyptian reality, and it is only then that this filmmaker's international appeal reaches its peak," says Tazghart.[36] Ahmad Farghaly agrees with this evaluation and points out that *Chaos* also signaled a "reconciliation" between Chahine and the public that had had so much difficulty in identifying with the stylistic density of his later films.[37] Farghaly also stresses the political importance of the film as a marker of Chahine's increased rage over the deteriorating social conditions and the Egyptian government's abuses of power. This situation, according to Farghaly, made Chahine feel the urgency of speaking out on every level, and led to his participation in public demonstrations.[38]

But in the end, as with all his films of the 1990s, *Chaos* presented a dark assessment of the social and political conditions in Egypt and the entire Arab region. And in a similar manner, Chahine and codirector Khaled Youssef saw the abuse of political power in interaction with the manipulation of economic (and consequently territorial) power as symptomatic of a worldwide phenomenon associated with capitalist globalization. In one interview Chahine commented on the universal relevance of *Chaos*' central character Hatem:

> The title of the film stems from the situation in which we live today where everyone who is in charge of an institution, corporation, district, and so on, considers it as his own fiefdom. These kinds of people are all over the place today and you keep hearing them declare, 'I am the Authority.' When we reach this point, you know that this is a condition which transcends individuals and symptomizes a general situation that has reached the point of danger.... This is not simply an Egyptian or Arab condition, it is occurring in every country all over the world, albeit in different forms and with different players.[39]

More to the point, Chahine once again pointed to the United States as the main perpetrator in the chronic abuse of state power to the predominant global norm, particularly in the third world,

> The notion of chaos is international, but the film more specifically focuses on despotism, which is mainly supported by the Americans... and let me reiterate that despotism is mostly the result of American support because the United States is the unipolar world power and particularly in the 'third world' where absolutism has reached [animalistic] heights. Third world leaders who are pampered by the American administration are turning their citizens into animals and treating them in this way. The film is therefore also about American repression of people around the world although it depicts a condition in a third world country.[40]

Unlike his other films of the period, however, *Chaos* transcended its own title to indicate that collective grass-roots resistance remains a viable, if not the only remaining alternative for confronting the deteriorating socioeconomic and political conditions of marginalized and working-class people in Egypt and the Arab world. Despite its very sensitive topic and its clear and strong criticism of government practices—the film was once described as among the "politically most daring films in contemporary Egyptian history"[41]—no scenes from the film were censored or changed. Most critics attributed the government's leniency to Chahine's international status and reputation, though it should be noted that in recent years several controversial films have been produced without major government intervention or censorship. This is exemplified in the relatively non-problematic release of films such as *Ana bahib al-sima* (I Love Cinema, Osama Fawzi, 2004), Inas al-Degheidy's *al-Bahithan 'an al-huriya* (In Search of Freedom, 2005), *'Imarat Ya'qubyan* (The Yacoubian Building, Marwan Hamed, 2006), and *Hina maysara* (Till Things are Better, Khaled Youssef, 2007). Though all infamous in their own right, none were as blunt in their direct condemnation of current government policies and practices as was Chahine's *Chaos*. The relevance of the film to contemporary Egyptian politics was manifested in the continuing reverberations of its political message. Two years after its release and almost one year after Chahine's death, codirector Khaled Youssef claimed that government attempts to censor his 2009 film *Dukkan Shehata* (Shehata's Store) were directly related to his participation in the making of *Chaos* two years earlier. Youssef says, "In spite of fact that my new film does not attack national institutions as such and does not tackle sexual or religious forbiddens, and considering that the film script acquired earlier the approval of the [censorship board] without any single complaint [. . .] the blunt truth about the government reaction now is that I am being persecuted because I codirected *Chaos*."[42]

The film echoes Chahine's *The Land* and *The Sparrow* in that popular solidarity and resistance is celebrated and given prominence particularly in the film's final scenes. And while the powerful ending of *Chaos* seemed like an unrealistic and nostalgic yearning for a long forgotten period in Egyptian and Arab memory, it only confirmed the state of tension and the impending popular resistance manifested in the strikes and demonstrations that rocked Egypt in the first months of 2008.

Chahine's films since the late 1990s seemed to become more political, and in spite of their largely unique address (at least from an Arab cinematic perspective) of issues of religious extremism, globalization, the relationship with the west and America, and finally state repression within Arab socities, still they rather magnified some stylistic shortcomings. In this regard, the artistic originality of Chahine's cinema of the earlier period (including in films such as *The Sparrow* or *The Return of the Prodigal Son*), remained more powerful in their intrusive building of characters and plot structure than his films from the latter period, most of which seemed content with eclectic recipes or social and political stereotypes. Yet playing with those stereotypes could have been one of Chahine's intentions during a period of retreat and volatility for the Arab national project.

11

CHAHINE AS AN AUTHOR AND AS AN ARAB ORGANIC INTELLECTUAL

It was during the period when *auteur* criticism assumed theoretical dominance within film studies circles in Europe in the 1950s and 1960s that Chahine's cinema first attracted international attention. Since then, most work on Chahine in the west has been characterized by an auteurist critical thrust which tends to stress thematic and stylistic elements of consistency, and as such has revealed the interactivity between his cinematic techniques and his artistic and personal preoccupations. Classically, auteur film criticism explores connections between the work and the persona of a filmmaker. Though post-millennial criticism tends to de-emphasize the role of the filmmaker in favor of a theoretical focus on representation, signification, reception, and history, I would like to conclude this book with a discussion on the place that authorial considerations hold within the cinema of Youssef Chahine and how they variously interact with his role as a political activist.

The emergence of Chahine's cinema overlapped with the most creative period of European and North American auteur criticism. The filmmaker's scholarly and pointedly self-conscious visual style that utilized his medium's affinity for communicating autobiographical and collective memory and history, along with his deep engagement with his films' scripts, clearly complemented the parameters of auteur criticism. Nevertheless, when Chahine's work began to attract the attention of critics in the west, it became increasingly evident that this approach was not going to be sufficient. Furthermore, the weight given by European and North American auteur criticism to the significance of art above other elements such as sociology, politics, history, and audience reception tended to drastically underestimate Chahine's use of cinema as an arena of ideological and political mediation.

AUTEURISM AND CULTURAL ACTIVISM

The political preoccupations of Chahine's cinema of the late 1960s tended to involve challenges to traditional mainstream Egyptian mechanisms of filmmaking. While his earlier films of the 1950s and early 1960s (and here I am thinking of his films that involved issues of social marginalization such as *Struggle in the Valley*, *Struggle on the Pier*, and *Cairo Station*, and themes of national liberation such as *Jamila* and *Saladin*) underscored the critical role of social and political commitment over creativity and individual expression, one could still recognize elements in these films (particularly in *Cairo Station*) that heralded his role as an Arab political activist with a genuinely creative vision capable of responding to the concerns of his society. While many filmmakers and critics, both western and Arab, probed the traditional ties between artist and society, Chahine moved toward a more defined political framework that necessitated the wresting of agency of meaning away from the restrictions of author and text.

Chahine's films, particularly since the mid-1960s, were largely characterized by stories presented in a compact manner resulting in complex narrative structures. As early as *Dawn of a New Day* and *People and the Nile*, Chahine's films became recognizable for their multiple stories involving a cross-section of characters in thematic interaction with each other. His films were also known for a stylistic approach that was recognizable for a liveliness manifested in long and complex scenes diligently composed and meticulously executed. These complex scenes involved elaborate camera movements that brought together his thematic dispositions and character variations resulting in a relentless process of locating and expunging. Ibrahim Fawal describes one of Chahine's most memorable scenes from *The Land*:

> The scene is shrouded with smoke. On the side of the frame is his cousin, Muhammad Effendi's mother. [He] emerges on top of the steps, enveloped with smoke as though he were emerging from a furnace. His descent down the staircase is a descent into hell. He stops by his cousin, speechless, and he leaves wrapped in disgrace.[1]

Within such scenes, Chahine exhibited a mastery of the art of *mise en scène* as well as his elaborate strategies for camera positioning and movement. The

Land exemplifies Chahine's use of social realism to describe the Egyptian countryside, its people, their lives, and their dreams. Each scene in the film creates dynamic interaction between the beauty of the landscape and the misery of the people of the village. The images from inside the homes of the peasants—and particularly the home of Abu Swailam—are characterized by detailed authenticity, capturing the genuine beauty of their homes. The *mise en scène* dramatically enhances Chahine's dialectical perspective on the clashing relationship between the means of production and the social forces of production under feudalism. The power of this approach is best exemplified in the contrast between the open and free landscape where peasants congregate and conduct their resistance against the feudal landlord, and the peasants' homes, where they retreat to their individual, private spheres, though this is ultimately the space of their defeat to the landlord.

But while Chahine was celebrated for his masterful and complex *mise en scène*—which naturally necessitated longer and more arduous shot construction involvement—he also became known for a nervous editing rhythm that kept the audience on edge, depriving them the opportunity to digest and contemplate a scene before delving into the next. While this montage style irritated many of Chahine's audiences, it nevertheless complemented the filmmaker's unabashed tendency to allow for mood shifts and contradictory sentiments in his characters, and even his proclivity for imposing himself on the screen. It also complemented his storytelling approach, which favored the incorporation of plot shifts and multiple voices, amalgamated finally in an ostentatious and dialectical whole. Similarly, by the early 1970s, Chahine's stories tended to revolve around moments of crisis, punctuated by brief and sometimes interrupted dialogues and flashbacks—often introduced without clear markers. These playful juxtapositions, often including moments of intermingled representations of the implausible and the real, expose the world according to Chahine, in which he avers "the fantastic is always [present], and fiction and reality are separated by a thread." In this mélange, Chahine suggests, "even the erotic arousal comes out of imagination, out of thought."[2]

But as Malkmus and Armes suggest, Chahine's complex stylistic layering of his stories, his ambiguous relationship with his characters, and the reflexive depiction of his own persona, all correspond with a deeply rooted artistic Arab tradition of decentering:

> In classical Arab poetry there is [a] dialectic of place and displacement; it exists in the 'traces in the sand' (atlal) motif.... The poem would begin as the poet returns to traces, to an abandoned camp site, and tries to name who

was there before him. Long misread as some kind of exercise in description, a search for a tribe, a manifestation of lack, of separation, of desire, as the classical poem develops, this feeling of incompleteness is assuaged as the poet leaves the desert and enters the state ruled by the perfect prince. All binary oppositions are then dissolved into the now perfect whole.[3]

These interrupted traces and reconnections as expressed in classical Arabic poetry can be observed in classical Arabic and Persian storytelling traditions as exemplified in *One Thousand and One Nights*, where stories emerge from one another and sometimes are revisited after a brief or elongated sojourn. This back and forth tug between the linear and the non-linear, the controlled and the spontaneous, easily traced throughout the narrative structure of Chahine's cinematic work, is therefore deeply entrenched within an authentic Arab artistic tradition. But while Arab classical poems, as Malkmus and Armes suggest, had the tendency to amalgamate or dissolve "into a new perfect whole," Chahine's films tend to move in the direction of overwhelmingly imperfect wholes and flawed characters, much like the never-satisfying endings of the sub-stories of the *Arabian Nights*, and never-fulfilled lives of their characters. Such are the stories and lives of Nayla and Tariq in *Dawn of a New Day*, Nadia and Amin and Nicolai and Barak in *The People and the Nile*, Abu Swailam in *The Land*, through to the tragic characters of *The Return of the Prodigal Son*, Hanan and Adam in *The Other*, to name just a few. Chahine's decentering of his characters and narratives is therefore characterized by its lingering dialectic that allows for further contemplation of possibilities that go beyond the immediacy of the filmic narratives. Furthermore, it is within a similar framework and dialectic that Chahine finds himself interacting with the politics of each of the historical periods depicted in his films. As a result, the body of Chahine's work assumes the same sense of uncertainty characterizing the unfinished social and national Arab project itself—the project that preoccupied his life and his cinema. Even Chahine's intense love affair with music and dancing, which saw itself translated at times into instances of utterly unpredictable perplexity and joy, reflected a dialectical appreciation of the cinematic experience as a political process.

Chahine's interest in the performative traditions of the musical genre was consistent throughout his film career. His interest in musical conventions was evident early in his career in films such as 1953's *Lady on the Train* featuring singer Leila Murad, and 1957's *You Are My Love* and *Farewell My Love* with the renowned Farid al-Atrash and Shadia, and later with the legendary Fayruz in *The Ring Seller* (1965). And since the 1970s Chahine's political use of musical and dance performances as commentary on the struggle for individual, social, and cultural emancipation has become a distinguishing feature of his oeuvre. While the conflation of politics with musical and dance performance reached its peak in *Destiny* with its explicit reference to music as a tool in the battle against intellectual and political repression, Chahine's interest in music as a political signifier also marked his work with Lebanese singer Majida al-Roumi in *The Return of the Prodigal Son*, and later in *Alexandria Again and Forever*, and with the Tunisian singer Latifa in *Silence... We're Rolling*.

Chahine's infatuation with song and dance is the embodiment of his love for the Hollywood musical. In *Alexandria... Why?* our first introduction to Chahine/Yehia sees him watching an Esther Williams film—not just any musical, a Hollywood musical. And after 1976, it seemed there was always a song and dance performer waiting in the wings for their cue. In *The Sixth Day* (1986), a film based on the novel by Andrée Chedid, Chahine explores a period in the British colonized Egypt of the mid-twentieth century. In a poor Cairo neighborhood, Sadika is taking care of her bedridden husband, and later, her cholera infected grandson. She shares a subtle love relationship with the young Okka, who makes his living performing song and dance numbers with a monkey. His performances are based for the most part on sketches from Hollywood films of the 1930s and 1940s. While Okka's joyful and life-affirming spirit is a welcome challenge to the atmosphere of death that overwhelms the impoverished neighborhood, it is also the vehicle through which Sadika finds resiliency, love, and social connection despite the isolation she suffers as her grandson's caregiver.

Equally as important, Chahine's interest in the elemental expressionism of the musical genre assumed a modernist political edge, seeking a Brechtian distancing of his audience through the enhancement of their appreciation of the ideological dialectic of the artistic process. In this regard, the interest in the decentered musical and dance performance in much of Chahine's cinema can be seen as complementary to his stylistic practices of decentering and multilayering the narrative structure and his interruptive and nervous editing approach. It is within the same thrust that one appreciates Chahine's fascination with generic traditions and his playful shifting between various generic conventions within the same filmic structure.

Chahine's rich body of work reflects this interest in generic play, especially within classical Hollywood genres. Over a period of more than fifty years, Chahine took on such varied genres as comedy *(Father Amin, Women Without Men, You Are My Love)*, musical comedy *(The Ring Seller, Goodbye to Love)*, social realism *(Cairo Station)*, social drama *(Son of the Nile)*, historical epic *(Saladin, Adieu Bonaparte!, The Emigrant, Destiny)*, classical political cinema *(The Sparrow, The Return of the Prodigal Son)*, melodrama *(Struggle in the Valley, Struggle on the Pier, Nida' al-'ushaq* (The Call of Lovers, 1961), *Man in My Life)*, avant-garde cinema *(Dawn of a New Day, The Choice)*, autobiography (the Alexandria trilogy), and so on. Chahine's relationship with all these genres and stylistic approaches, however, has always been ambiguous and interactive. As such, most of his films—and particularly those made since the 1970s—resisted rigid restrictions within these various conventions. Instead, Chahine's films tended to fluidly, at times abruptly, shift gear in their incorporation of generic and stylistic approaches. No Chahine film exemplifies more shockingly the filmmaker's tendency to subvert generic rules than *The Return of the Prodigal Son*. Years before inter-generic postmodernist play became fashionable, *Return* shocked audiences by concluding an upbeat musical comedy with a bloody massacre.

Chahine forged a cinematic discourse that subverts and reroutes his work away from "dominant determinations,"[4] and as such distinguishes his outlook on Arab identity and the Arab national project in a way that distances it from chauvinistic nationalism and static homogeneity. Within this framework, Chahine's cinematic lyricism never allowed ideological dogma to reduce social characters to stereotypes.

His political acuity, educational background, and central role in the development of contemporary world cinema allowed Chahine a greater appreciation of the role of human agency in all aspects of his life and work. His political agenda was sketched out through an interactive response to the ever-changing realities in the volatile Middle East. This was reflected in his cinema's consistent inclusion of themes pertaining to Egyptian and Arab events and struggles, and through his political pronouncements that complemented and often surpassed the bluntness of his cinematic messages. But while Chahine's political cinematic messages responded in an interactive fashion to conditions affecting the national Arab political discourse (an interactivity which remains unique in its longevity, consistency, and richness in Arab filmmaking history), his equally consistent utility of self-reflexive themes and characters provided an embodiment of an original approach to incorporating politically based messages into a cross-section of popular generic and narrative cinematic traditions.

Chahine's self-reflexive practice goes well beyond his autobiographical films and his embodiment in the character of Yehia in the Alexandria series. No other Arab filmmaker has publically exposed his feelings and sensitivities, his history and fantasies for all to see, as Chahine did in this series. But

Chahine's ultimate cinematic elation was always reserved for his delight in insinuating himself into his characters' lives and whims. The composure with which Chahine traverses genres and styles in his films is amply matched by his subtle transitioning of the imposition of his own persona across and among different characters within the same film—regardless of gender. In this regard the filmmaker, as Dave Kehr suggests, "makes the highest virtue of flexibility, of openness, of fluidity—of being as unfixable as water, his favourite element, and as various as Alexandria, his favorite city."[5]

Whether seen in the persecuted Yusuf in *The Emigrant*, the enlightened Ibn Rushd in *Destiny*, the determinedly Nasserist Nasser in *Silence... We're Rolling*; or in Nayla's loving admiration of the young and attractive Tariq in *Dawn of a New Day*, or Barak's of Nicolai in *People and the Nile*; or expressed in the camera's leering gaze over Yehia's naked body as he prepares to bathe in *Alexandria... New York*; Chahine's explicit or implicit presence is always palpable. This reflexivity is also manifested in the filmmaker's ambiguous relationship with his characters. In *The Choice* the assertion of the filmmaker's own paradoxical presence adds an alternative variation on self-reflexivity. Here, the director's presence is contradictory; it is manifested in the film's alternating empathy with the freewheeling, down-to-earth, and fun-loving working-class man, and his sophisticated writer/intellectual twin brother.

Chahine's reflexivity was also expressed in his long-standing interest in the theater. As his autobiographical Alexandria series—and particularly the film *Alexandria... Why?*— illustrates, Chahine's love for theater and theatrical performance was a primary component of his artistic development since his Victoria College school days. This later became an early training milieu for his filmmaking career when attended the Pasadena theater school in the 1940s. Unfortunately, his theatrical career was limited, though his 1993 directorial turn at Paris' Comédie-Française production of Camus' *Caligula* played to a great reception. The theater featured prominently in many of Chahine's films, whether as a theme, a stylistic muse, or as a point of reference. In addition to the explicit references in the Alexandria trilogy to his early performance in the role of Hamlet, and to his personal unfulfilled dream of making his own film version of the Shakespeare play—particularly as expressed in *Alexandria Again and Forever*—the theater motif popped up many times in Chahine's films. In *Alexandria... Why?* Chahine compels us to look at his Alexandria as a theatrical stage where the Second World War Egyptians are fighting the British and contemplating liberation at the hands of the Germans, even as Chahine/Yehia sees the world through the eyes of Hamlet. This is also clear, for example in *The Other* and *Silence... We're Rolling* where characters frequently seem to be performing on a theatrical stage, or as if facing a live audience rather than the conspicuous camera. Dialogues are often structured as monologues—intellectual extravaganzas exposing, analyzing, and commenting on the motives and actions of his characters.

Another key manifestation of the theatrical influence is in Chahine's discernible attention to *mise en scène* in each of his films. Set decoration in *The Choice*, for example, is analogous to that of a theatrical production, where the chill of the writer's flat is highlighted by its minimalist décor, bulky furniture, and its bluish-gray tones. In contrast, Bahiya's home, as part of the larger café compound, is a sensual space out of the *Arabian Nights* with its rainbow of striking colors and cramped eclectic furnishings that are further overcrowded by her many friends and visitors. To top it all, as Abd al-Fatah has noted, the film features the veteran Egyptian theater legend Youssef Wahbi playing himself and directly commenting on the essence of theatrical performance as "a play between the authentic and the constructed, between mirroring and masking."[6]

A critical aspect of Chahine's theatrical obsession was his lifelong fascination with Shakespeare's *Hamlet*, which was often reflected in his cinematic work. This preoccupation was part of Chahine's psyche since his early performance of the leading role in one of his English classes, as recreated in *Alexandria... Why?* Critic Issam Zakariya suggests that the shadow of the play began to emerge in Chahine's work as early as his first film *Father Amin*, where the ghost of a dead father haunts his family, expecting them, like Hamlet's ghost, to fulfill the obligations he was not able to in life. Later, in *Struggle in the Valley*, the protagonist, like Hamlet the son, hesitantly seeks to avenge his murdered father and recites monologues reminiscent of the Shakespearian character's. In *Cairo Station*, like Hamlet the father, Qinawi, as played by Chahine himself, is a character in love with a woman who loves another man. On another level, like Hamlet, Qinawi's sanity is questioned. But while Hamlet claims madness, Qinawi is indeed a mad obsessive. Zakariya also alludes to the essence of Hamlet's rejection of Claudius' right to rule as one that mirror's Chahine's defiance of oppressive and corrupt authority.[7]

This reflexive tendency in Chahine's work epitomizes what I would suggest to be his deeply personal investment in the thematic preoccupations of his films. As such his work embodied the possibilities for a politically activist cinema in the Arab world. Chahine's films manifested the vital connection between cultural politics and esthetic innovation that both neorealism and modernism had sought to activate. His consistent—if indulgent—engagement of his own image and history, equally provided the opportunities to indulge in larger social and political concerns. His eschewing of rigid generic conventions, along with his eclectic utility of discordant formal approaches, cultivated the unique artistic signature that was Chahine's for over fifty years. Loved by many and critiqued by some for his abandonment of social realist traditions, Chahine always refused to adhere to convention for its own sake, especially when it came to politics.

Clearly, Chahine favored a politics of authorship that allowed him to query the historical contradictions of Arab cinema, relocating its problematics in social and political relations rather than limiting authorship to expressive agency. Chahine insisted that film is most successful when it functions as an effective medium for communicating ideas and concerns that are relevant to collective social and national preoccupations. Within such a framework, no restrictive boundaries based on preconceived formal dogmas can be tolerated by filmmaker nor audience. What remains critical, as Chahine repeatedly stressed in numerous interviews, is the audience reaction, and in the end Chahine was more often than not successful in this regard, leaving behind a rich legacy encompassing a successful production company, the respect of his Arab audiences and fellow artists, and an international following of film buffs and critics alike.

Chahine's auteurism, therefore, cannot be divorced from the dynamics of cultural struggle and political commitment. Throughout his career, Chahine's socially and nationally oriented preoccupations and their cinematic expressions were developed in propinquity to modernist self-reflexive stylistic practices. As such, the filmmaker's work uniquely contributed to the evolution of the nationalist cultural thrust within Egyptian and Arab cinemas in general. As they developed and matured, certain key themes characterized his cinema: a socially and class conscious relationship with the lives, concerns, and struggles of working-class and peasant Egyptians (*Struggle in the Valley*, *Struggle on the Pier*, *The Land*); a reflexive re-reading of history grounded ironically in the filmmaker's preoccupation with the present (*Saladin*, *Destiny*); an assessment of the role of the intellectual in present-day political struggles (*The Choice*, *The Sparrow*, and the Alexandria trilogy); the theme of the Other and Othering as a pretext for dealing with issues of national struggle against colonialism and capitalist globalization (*Adieu Bonaparte!*, *The Other*, *Alexandria . . . New York*); and affirming national heterogeneity (again the Alexandria trilogy). All in all, Chahine's cinema, and particularly in the post-Nasser period, galvanized the collective state of anxiety affecting Arab society and the Arab political landscape. In response to this apprehension and uncertainty, Chahine's work took a critical look at the events that led to the 1967 defeat, as well as the dynamics of failure that thwarted the Egyptian revolution's attempt to move forward with social, economic, and political reform, and its goals of Arab national unity. And throughout the 1980s and 1990s Chahine's cinema created important touchstones for the long overdue discussion of the relationship between the Arab world and the Other, as well as its relationship with its own history and cultural reality.

As an advocate of social justice, Arab unity and Arab national self-determination, Chahine always recognized the importance of communicating his message to a broad audience. Therefore, accusations of elitism occasionally raised by local critics were taken very seriously by the filmmaker. Chahine often responded defensively to such claims, not only because he considered them unfair, but also because he felt that they represented a denunciation of what he considered to be central to his artistic project—his role as contributor to the politics of social justice and political change in Egypt and the Arab world. Chahine expressed a deep respect for his audiences, and always strove to connect with them. Furthermore, Chahine unswervingly rejected claims that the public is incapable of relating to complex artistic forms of expression. In an interview about *The Choice* Chahine did acknowledge that the density of the film might have resulted in its less than successful box office performance, but went on to defend the public's capacity to relate to stylistically and intellectually challenging films, citing the case of *Saladin*:

> Irrespective of how the audience reacted to the film [The Choice], I remain extremely respectful of their views. This audience almost never rejects a film I have made with genuine authenticity ... what we used to call the 'average audience' really understands better than anyone .... In the end, if there is no connection between the filmmaker and the audience, then it is the fault of the filmmaker and not the audience .... You cannot condemn the inability of the audience to relate to your films .... Instead you need to learn how to connect with them. In Saladin, for example, I introduced scenes that I could never imagine the audience relating to; I offered them battle scenes without one horse or one soldier ... shots with the color red splashed on a white robe ... yet they fully appreciated that and no one criticized me for it .... In other films, I presented scenes that people did not relate to ... so I sat and tried to analyze the reasons, and I found that I was to blame, and that is because I myself was not clear about what I was trying to do.[8]

Further, Chahine stressed that intellectuals should remain close to the pulse of the public, particularly when it comes to bread-and-butter issues. In the end, "if you do not offer the public something that is tangible, it will simply abandon you."[9]

On the surface, Chahine's work revealed a level of tension between his role as a public intellectual with a political agenda, and his distinct personal and artistic vision. As some critics would point out, Chahine's style occasionally affected his ability to communicate his pronounced social and political messages, and perhaps even played a role in the disconnect between specific films and mainstream audiences. Egyptian film critic Sami al-Salamuni describes how *The Return of the Prodigal Son*, despite its ingenious, unique, and technically superior style, failed to successfully communicate its political message. This stems, in al-Salamuni's view, from the filmmaker's overestimation of the Egyptian audience's cinematic experience and comprehension of modernist artistic traditions, in light of the predominant influence of commercial cinema on the tastes of Egyptian society.[10] But contrary to critical charges of elitism, Chahine never ignored the level to which his work was able to connect with wider audiences, and as such, he could not ignore the fact that some of his films, including *The Choice*, *The Prodigal Son*, *Adieu Bonaparte!*, *The Sixth Day*, and even the Alexandria trilogy were not as successful at the box office as he had hoped them to be. In fact, all these films were received much more enthusiastically internationally than they were among Arab critics and audiences. Thus his work in the 1990s appeared to be consciously struggling to rectify what he considered an imperative problematic, which, for him as a politically and ideologically engaged intellectual and activist, could not be simply ignored or underestimated. In a 1998 interview he candidly addressed the issue:

> [In my films today] I tend to favor simplicity. Before people would watch my films and come out saying, "I have no idea what he is trying to say." This is a problem for which both myself and my audience share responsibility. The audience is used to films that bring them joy, and are easy to follow. I used to make films that did not complement the level of [artistic and political] consciousness and expectations of the period's audience. Now I hope to make films that are simple, but that also carry a clear message and are presented in a decent cinematic language. This does not lessen the value of my work, and at the same time it allows the audience to genuinely enjoy my films. This is what I tried to do in The Emigrant and Destiny and what I will try to do in my upcoming film.[11]

The popularity of the two films cited by Chahine was indisputable, as was the popularity of the films that followed, as manifested in their box office success.

Whereas traditional critical appreciation of film authorship tended to validate individual and individually inspired artistry, Chahine's cinematic practice operated at the intersections between esthetic and political expressions, and personal creativity and collective responsibility. Chahine's rendezvous with politically committed cinema was among the earliest in Arab cinema. His sensitive approach to class and social issues in the 1950s gave way to the patriotic *Jamila*, and later, *Saladin*. As such, Chahine's work problematized the institutional framework of Egyptian and Arab cinema, pushing to the forefront the question of its social and national responsibility well before the 1970s when it became a general tendency in Egyptian and Arab cinema. But Chahine's film practice always reflected the presence of an author with a distinctive style and perspective on the politics of each period of his career.

With that in mind, I would like to argue that authorship in Chahine's cinema largely amounted to a critical map operating across a variety of fields. There is no doubt that creating a socially and politically involved cinema was an early and resolute concern. Initially, this preoccupation came to exemplify—and to respond to—the politically charged era initiated by the 1952 Nasser revolution. However, while alternative cinemas in many other third world countries in the 1960s and 1970s, particularly in Latin America, tended to stress ways of breaking radically with dominant Hollywood traditions, Chahine's work was becoming increasingly informed by the tension between his love for Hollywood movies and his engagement with the changes affecting his social and political milieu. As such, his work tended to defy prescriptive formulations, and eventually favored the creation of a cinema anchored in a joint engagement of subjective and social, experimental and popular cinematic perspectives. Thus, through Brechtian interventions ironically juxtaposed with nurturing interpellations, Chahine's cinema envisaged openness and resistance to reticence. While authorship was always integral to his cinema and eventually represented a self-evident hub for its intervention in social and political fields, Chahine's authorship was nevertheless implicitly marked by a pronounced attempt to extricate its image from the burdensome notions of elitism. As Roy Armes argues, the tensions created by this ongoing struggle were at the root of Chahine's signature formal methodologies:

> [T]he very diversity of the social and political development through which he has lived has fostered an eclectic approach, and his work offers a kaleidoscopic view of a shifting society in which the individual is constantly pulled in diverging directions. Chahine's openness to external events and to

his own moods and impulses means that his work is bound to be uneven. His work holds a great lesson, however: that it is possible for the Third World film maker to deal with social and political issues intelligently within the formal narrative structures of a cinema directed toward a mass audience and to combine this commercial concern with a totally personal style.[12]

In the end, Chahine's valued sense of 'organically intellectual authorship' defies the traditional tendency to draw a binary between the two, and by extension between activism and personal artistic originality. Moreover, claiming contradiction or demarcation between the western views of Chahine's cinema and the Arab nationalist and socialist understanding of his films, and confronting, for example, the mastery of *mise en scène* (authorial power) and the role of the activist as a spokesperson of his society (intellectual power), become an artificiated exercise which is counterproductive in an intrusive reading of Chahine's cinema.

Therefore, Chahine's cinema originates both intellectually and structurally from within the personal, and only as such does it indulge the collective; as his plots develop, a narrative commences its gyration around personal trepidation, expressing his dilemma—and thus his spectators'—within a society, a nation, and ultimately an entire world. Such dilemmas assume their shape as characters on the screen, and take on lives of their own that surpass predetermined or prescribed intellectual paradigms. The concern here becomes not as much to pander to the background of a character, whether it embodies Chahine himself or not, but to focus on and indulge characters within the world of social, political, and cultural incidences that inform them. As Egyptian Nobel laureate Naguib Mahfouz once commented on Chahine's work,

> Youssef Chahine does not seek the 'unique' (or the 'the unusual') for the sake of uniqueness itself. The close proximity of Chahine's cinema to Egyptian reality and authenticity makes this cinema of the socially committed kind which does not shy from taking clear positions on the problems facing Arab society.[13]

CHAHINE IN CONTEXT

Youssef Chahine's body of work evolved over a period of nearly sixty years, against the volatile backdrop of contemporary Arab history. Political events played a pivotal role in the retroactive formation of Chahine's oeuvre, and were indispensible to the discursive evolution of his work. These events shaped a cinematic practice that endured and grew, relying not on subjective esthetic and institutional paradigms, but on its incorporation of an ideological agenda that encompassed an interactive heterogeneous Arab national project.

Over the years Chahine's cinema became a landmark in Arab filmmaking and an important school for generations of Arab filmmakers. Among Chahine's apprentices were such major Egyptian filmmakers as Ali Badrakhan, Atef al-Tayyeb, Khairy Bishara, Yousry Nasrallah, Khaled Youssef, along with countless performers, cinematographers, editors, and film technicians. Within a broad historical context, the emergence of Chahine's cinema owes a great deal to the way that the circulation of ideas and films in the early 1950s was cultivated by a multiplicity of networks for their exchange and distribution. Therefore, Chahine's cinema cannot be pinned down to a singular foundational trace. Instead it needs to be looked at as a fluid amalgamation of Arab national political preoccupations and their articulation across a heterogeneous system of cultural and cinematic practices.

The bulk of Chahine's films dealt directly with specific contemporary political and social events in the Arab region, many continuing to impact current discussions of world events of the second half of the twentieth century. And through innumerable local and international interviews, Chahine always ensured his pronouncements were relevant and timely. Throughout his career he remained intellectually and artistically engaged in the struggles for political and cultural self-determination, liberation from colonial and neocolonial interference, freedom of expression, and social change. It is within this context that Chahine's cinema obtained its counter-hegemonic significance.

The evolvement of Chahine's cinema is marked by a richly varied intermingling of modes of production, consumption, and reception. Through his long career as a filmmaker, actor, producer, and activist, Chahine systematically sought to create the structures necessary to sustain his film work, its independence, and his role as an agent for social and political change. During the period between the early 1950s and the late 1960s Chahine's cinema owed a great deal to the way in which the left–nationalist Nasser government positively interacted with its ideas and helped create effective networks for its production, exchange, and distribution.

His interaction with the political and social realities of his environment allowed for the evolution of Chahine's cinematic strategies and played a major role in the discursive nature of Chahine's work. In many ways, Chahine's politicized contemplation of pivotal moments in contemporary Egyptian and Arab history influenced and consolidated his cinema beyond any temporary or official cinematographic and institutional paradigms. Despite death threats from his political opponents, Chahine enhanced his role as an organic intellectual in the protracted shaping and reshaping of the Arab national project through his films, his writings and his proactive participation in thousands of festivals, panels, interviews, political meetings, and street demonstrations. From his early rendezvous with nationalist themes in the 1950s and 1960s, Chahine's cinematic practice expressed a collective corollary to the persistent effects of colonialism within a postcolonial setting, bearing all the symptoms of underdevelopment, and a dynamic engagement with cultural and political militancy. Irrespective of its rich thematic and stylistic variants, a politically positioned cinematic practice remained integral to Chahine's work throughout his career.

Recognizing historical milestones in Chahine's cinema is constrained as much by the filmmaker's institutional undertakings as by the shifts that have been affecting the organizational structure of the Egyptian film industry since the 1950s. The instances of self-definition and social processes are mutually intersecting operations whereby patterns of cultural production are affected by ideology. The elements that have consistently constituted a level of cohesion in the work of Chahine within the broader Arab national project have had effects more far-reaching than box office records can adequately express.

By the time it entered the second half of its sixth decade, Chahine's cinema could no longer be assessed entirely on the filmmaker's political responses to social and political change. As such, Chahine's ability to transform and adapt to cultural and economic conditions and to successfully operate across the contradictory arenas of production and distribution should be understood as inherent to his resiliency both as an auteur filmmaker and as an activist. In fact, the dynamic adoption of alternative and mainstream stylistic and production strategies juxtaposed with a freewheeling mix of the two served to define the institutional and authorial framework of Chahine's cinema. Notwithstanding consistent positional shifts, amalgamations, and confluences, these strategies remained intrinsically grounded in a distinct form of cultural nationalism.

BY WAY OF CONCLUSION

No meaningful assessment of Chahine's cinema can be separated from the historical discourses on the Arab national project through which they were created and articulated. The unique profile of this cinema within Arab cultural practices was developed within interactive expressions of Egyptian, Arab, socialist, and third world anticolonial ideals, thus aligning its project with the Arab world as a historical entity facing a multiplicity of social, economic, political, cultural, and post- as well as neocolonial challenges.

The idea of an Arab national project and identity that emerged and matured since the 1950s, informed and shaped Chahine's body of work. Over the years, this cinema has probed the utopias of progress that displaced the colonial legacy since Nasser's 1952 revolution. Chahine's cinema always sought ways to illuminate and actively support the idea of a just society united by the legacy of a shared Arab identity, but following the death of Nasser, Chahine came to understand that the Arab national project could not be sustained without a conscious and explicit acknowledgement of the internal diversity that defines the Arab world. By accepting and embracing that diversity, Chahine's cinema presented an authentic attempt to refashion and redefine the ideals of Nasser's project, one for which Chahine had often expressed his admiration.

Since al-Nahda period Arab societies have been protractedly struggling to recuperate a sense of common history and destiny, and to envision an agenda toward an independent, socially just, modern, and united national community. This remained the essence of the romantic dream at the heart of the struggle against Ottoman hegemony, and later the struggle against the hegemony of European colonization. The carving out of nation states in the early twentieth century led to the creation of Arab national movements that struggled to overcome colonial divisions as a means to gain social, economic, and cultural entry into the modern era. Nasser's personal charisma inspired a project that made a major impact on the political history of the region for a short but critical period in the twentieth century. The failures of the Nasser experience, however, made an equally major, albeit negative, impact on the Arab project itself. But despite the official death of the movement, the lingering shadows of colonialism continued to necessitate the struggle for an authentically sovereign, economically interactive, modern, and just Arab society.

Chahine's cinema always interacted with the trials and tribulations of the Arab national project, seeking ways to adequately address its failures and actively redefine its parameters. As such, this cinema revisited the history of Egypt, and by extension the entire region, through the narrative negotiations of regional specificities of country, nation, class, religion, and—allegorically—gender and sexual orientation. In this way Chahine bestowed his cinema with a post-colonial perspective on Egyptian and Arab national identity that allowed it to move beyond the ineffectual chauvinisms of country, nation, religion, and ethnicity. Through his protracted examination of the notion of the Other, particularly in his films since the late 1990s, Chahine increasingly emphasized the nation as part of a heterogeneous regional culture and an anticipated humanist international solidarity. By envisioning such an identity, Chahine's cinema gave a tangible sense of a shared community that contented itself within inter-ethnic, inter-faith and inter-cultural variations to offset paternalistically determined allegiances and differences.

Chahine's work was contemporaneous with, and often presaged, Edward Said's articulations of a discursive formation whereby the history and imagination of the currently divided and underdeveloped Arab societies can be reclaimed free of false, Other-imposed memories of what Edward Said refers to as "mythic utopias."[14] Such a discourse operates within and across the fleeting memories of the past and the concreteness of the present, serving to articulate national autonomy and self-determination and counter failures of earlier pan-Arab organizations. On the other hand, Chahine's discourse serves to redefine an Arab nationalism enhanced by the desire for an autonomous sense of cultural identity. Such an idea has as much to do with ideology as with the resilience of the concept of Arab culture and identity. As Edward Said suggests,

> Culture is used to designate not merely something to which one belongs but something that one possesses and, along with that proprietary process, culture also designates a boundary by which the concepts of what is extrinsic or intrinsic to the culture come into forceful play.[15]

Thus, Arab cultural historians do not discuss identity as an obvious or transparent position of self-recognition.

Deliberations about national identity have often orbited around values characterized as either genuine or derivative, a forced binary that eclipses the ambivalent nature and development of identity. National identity is at once already attained in the form of historical continuities and interruptions— and still in process—in the form of a modernist break with the past. Within such a decentered, yet historical, notion of identity, Chahine's cinema sought a reflective and self-reflexive discourse on the nation and the place of the individual within it. As such, his cinema entailed an understanding of a history determined by resistance and struggle, diversity and unity, dependence, and autonomy. His cinema depicted a society concurrently enthralled with the past and the present, and with modernist cultural narratives of injustice and protest. Such a modernist enterprise can be understood as both an attempt to renew the forms and contents of Arab national political and cultural life, and as a site invoking a sense of the future so overwhelming it becomes inevitable.

Emerging from the tradition of popular mainstream Egyptian cinema of the 1940s, Chahine's work progressively carved its own space within and built upon this uniquely successful national cinema. While no obvious rupture separated Chahine's early work from other popular film traditions of the period, a budding identity began to characterize his work as it became more responsive to the political developments taking place in the Arab world in the early 1950s. This was first exemplified in Chahine's socially and class conscious films of the period. Within this framework, Chahine's films became identified with a new type of Egyptian and Arab cinema distinguished by its interactive response to the political events and challenges of the day, from the anti-imperialist struggles of the 1950s and 1960s to the recent challenges of capitalist globalization and neocolonial policies within the Arab region. Within these parameters Chahine's cinema increasingly asserted open expressive spaces and fresh admixtures of popular generic traditions. By the late 1970s Chahine was forging independent forms of production including the creation of his own production company, which nurtured a large group of new filmmakers who continue to enrich alternative and mainstream Arab filmmaking. And in 2005 Chahine's Misr International added film distribution and screening to its credits with its acquisition of a suburban Cairo cineplex complex.

There is no doubt that the political and institutional development of Chahine's cinematic project challenged the hegemony of traditional mainstream Egyptian and western models of cinematographic production and consumption. As such, this project advocated and succeeded in building a genuinely activist third worldist cinema at the cultural center of the Arab world. As an organic intellectual and artist, Chahine was constantly impacting the politics of contemporary Egypt, as well as pushing the boundaries of filmmaking artistry within the region. The continuous contradictory mix of mass public interest, controversy, praise, and criticism of almost all of Chahine's films, reflected the status and relevance he and his films achieved and sustained.

Chahine's cinema addressed from the outset contextually precise and idiosyncratic issues. Since *Jamila* in 1958, the release of each of Chahine's films was greeted by politically interpretive and widely covered reviews and interviews, occasioning expansive public debate and discussion in Egypt as well as in other Arab countries. These discussions led movie critics, reviewers, and political commentators to afford due contemplation to the latest developments in Arab and Egyptian politics, the relationship between Chahine's films and the people he hoped to champion, and the nature and dynamics of popular culture. In this manner, Chahine advanced reflexive critical approaches to cultural politics that indulged collective and new modes of address, even while attempting to bolster connections with wider audiences.

On another level, by bringing together various traditions and innovations in filmmaking and storytelling, Chahine's cinema encouraged cross-generational and cross-cultural audience interaction. It also stimulated projects committed to an alternative modernism, affirming the existence and the self-respect of a marginalized nation struggling for self-determination and liberation. Although the anti-imperialist rhetoric of the 1960s concealed the term *modernity* under the guises of Marxist and left nationalist theories of dependency and cultural resistance, the issue of modernity was never extraneous to Chahine's cinema. Through his films and his public pronouncements, Chahine engaged a filmic discourse of decentering and immediacy that consistently reminded his audience of the nature of his cinematic project as a stylistically deconstructive exercise aimed at contemplating new social, political, and cultural possibilities.

Thus, the cultural nationalism of Chahine's cinema engaged—but did not acquiesce to—hegemonic discourses on modernity. This cinema reflected modernity as an ideological project for progress and national self-determination. The modernist dialectic was translated into a stylistic compulsion grounded in the search for autonomy, originality, and representativity. These formative impulses constituted precisely the basis upon which this cinema has periodically redefined its ideological and esthetic project.

Chahine indulged elements relevant to the changing cultural, social, and political conditions bridging Arab and world film history. In this regard he sought to experiment with cinematographic and artistic concepts from both western and third world traditions such as neorealism, surrealism, reflexivity, montage, social (or socialist) realism, radical third cinema documentary traditions, as well as classical Hollywood realism. Chahine's eclectic approach, however, tended to refashion and transform his application of these concepts in order to make them more relevant to Arab social and cultural realities. Thus a typical Chahine film after the early 1970s, *Alexandria... Why?*, brought together elements that mirrored these concepts in a manner that allowed them to interact, often flawlessly, occasionally paradoxically. The first sequence of the film, for example, is a hub of reflexive, third cinema documentary interjections, classic and expressionist editing, and inter-generic postmodern cinematic stylistic applications.

Assimilating the pervasive political, social and cultural contradictions of the Arab world, Chahine's cinema reaffirmed the role of cinema as a critically interactive space of communication. Insofar as Chahine began exploring the realities of Egypt and the wider Arab world, he discovered a subjectivity comprised of his own social and artistic experiences as well as those of the richly diverse Arab cultural amalgam that has been the result of historical intersection and confluence of several major civilizations. He observed the sustained signs of underdevelopment, compounded by the twin challenges of modernization and postcolonial social justice, and the perpetual Arab struggle for national self-determination under globalization, and sought to remap the intricate dialectics of history, class struggle, national liberation, memory, and representation.

Consistently preoccupied with political agency and social process, and critical of the modernization tendencies of postcolonial Arab and third world nation-states, Chahine denounced a modernity based on self-confident promises of progress. With *The Sparrow*, Chahine began the long journey through which he began to see revolutionary experiences not as idealized elements along a linear trajectory—from colonization, injustice, and underdevelopment to emancipation, social justice, and progress—but rather as a protracted process problematized by regional, social, religious, political, racial, and sexual differences, and privileged by subjective and collective identities. This explains the major difference between Chahine's cinema before and after the death of Nasser, a difference implicated in his later cinematic emphasis on Egyptian and Arab national identity as a construct. Chahine's post-Nasser cinema served as embattled space for the evolving, rather than the foundational, essence of Arab national identity. By the 1980s, as he began to address issues of religious and ethnic difference, political intolerance, and non-normative sexuality, he simultaneously questioned historical presumptions and romantic celebrations of the notion of difference—insisting on treating it first and foremost as a political dilemma par excellence. At the basis of this evolving political engagement was a critical impulse that continually reinvented itself in and through the heterogeneous elements and contradictory discourses of a nation at once unitary and diverse.

As part of this evolution, Chahine's short and limited rendezvous with the government-supported institutional production paradigm to the independent and diversified film production model enabled his cinema to persist as a valid political endeavor. Institutional rearrangements and economic growth within the Egyptian film industry since the 1980s promoted commercial trends that affected national cinematic practices in the Arab world in a profound way. Simultaneously articulating new Arab and traditional western production techniques through the creation of his own film production company, Chahine ultimately found in independent institutional arrangements the possibility of energizing rather than weakening his cinema.

As a rich, varied, and at times seemingly uneven body of work (at least on the level of how some critics addressed the artistic originality of each of his works), Chahine's cinema still served to reinterpret and redefine the place of Egyptian and Arab film as a cultural and political practice within the complex social and political reality and history of the region. In a sense, this cinema originated from an insight and recognition of belonging, produced at a moment of volatility in contemporary Arab history. In the crucible of that volatility was formed the heart of Chahine's cinematic perception of Arab identity—and the Arab national project itself—as an ideologically and politically unfinished project.

NOTES

Notes to Introduction
1   Edward Said, "Orientalism," *The Post-Colonial Studies Reader*, 88.

Notes to Chapter 1
1   Contemporary pan-Arabism first began to take shape in the mid-nineteenth century in the Arab East (mainly Syria and Lebanon) and later in Egypt, and gradually assumed the stature of a heterogeneous movement with one of its main political goals the struggle against Ottoman hegemony over the Arab world. This struggle stressed the rejection of the medieval despotic and conservative rule during the final decades of the Ottoman Empire. Following the collapse of the Ottoman Empire at the end of First World War, the struggle for Arab unity and independence focused on the resistance to the isolating English, French, and Italian colonial projects. This mobilization generated the renewed sense of collective national identity that later inspired twentieth-century Arabs to continue to thwart and defy foreign designations of national boundaries in the region.
2   Irrespective of their varied approaches and political agendas, almost all major influential pan-Arab nationalist parties in the second part of the twentieth century advocated a secular approach to government. Most of the founders of these movements were from religious and ethnic minorities, including Christians Michel 'Aflaq (the Baath Party), George Habash (The Movement of Arab Nationalists), Antoun Saadi (the Syrian Social National Party), and the theoretical father of modern day Arab nationalism, Constantine Zureik. Marxists of pan-Arab orientation included Lebanese Christian Farajallah al-Hilou and the legendary Kurdish Syrian communist leader Khaled Bakdash.
3   Conference on *Renewing Nationalist Thought and the Arab Future*, which took place on April 15–19, 2008 in Damascus. For further details see *Champress* (April 20, 2008) at http: //champress.net/print_details.php?page=show_det&id=25580 (accessed April 22, 2008).

4   al-Madini, "Inhiyar al-dawla al-shumuliya," 9.
5   Said, "Orientalism," *The Post-Colonial Studies Reader*, 88.
6   From a cultural perspective, the pan-Arab project may be seen by some as somewhat problematic because it brings together diverse populations with various cultural and historical specificities (of which the problematic exclusion by some Arab nationalists of African, Kurdish, and Berber minority populations, for example, cannot be overlooked). However, the fact remains that the movement's intellectual and political leaders came from a cross-section of the region's diverse religious and ethnic minorities, including many from Christian, Jewish, and Kurdish backgrounds.
7   Pick, "The Politics of Modernity in Latin America," 43.
8   For an excellent account on the dynamics of the rise of the Arab Renaissance Movement see Hourani, *A History of the Arab Peoples*, 280–372.
9   By the early 1900s even critical interpretations of classical literary Arabic texts, including those of the pre-Islamic period *(al-Jahiliya)* came under fierce scrutiny. This paved the way for a spirited discussion on the interpretive value of language and text in addressing history, philosophy, and religion. A major development in this regard was the publication of Egyptian Taha Hussein's groundbreaking book *On the Jahili Literature*.
10 For example, most leading Arab literary and arts journals from the 1920s to the 1960s were initiated by and included contributions from intellectuals allied to various progressive and socialist-oriented movements and groups. Journals such as *al-Hilal, al-Thaqafa, al-Risala, al-Katib al-masri, al-Makshuf, al-'Arfan, al-Thaqafa al-jadida, al-Tariq*, and so on, were the first to publish material by the writers playing a major role in the rejuvenation of modernist Arab literature. Leading writers such as Salama Musa, Jirgi Zaydan, Taha Hussein, and later Naguib Mahfouz, Omar Fakhoury, Maroun Abboud, Tawfiq Youssef Awad, were among those who saw their first writings published in the above-mentioned journals. On its sixtieth anniversary, in its January–February 2002 issue, the Arabic cultural journal *al-Tariq* published a special issue mapping out the history of these journals and their significance to Arab cultural history.
11 On a recent research trip to Cairo I was pleasantly surprised to discover that, in any given week, Egyptian-made films constituted 70 to 80 percent of the films playing in movie theaters across the city. This, in a country where the state, in the interest of maintaining good relations with the World Bank and the government of the United States, has essentially abandoned all remnants of support for the production and distribution of its national cinema.
12 Shafik, *Arab Cinema*, 126.
13 Salah Abu Seif's 1953 film *Rayya wa Skina* is an early example of the effective integration of social realism, Soviet montage techniques, and German expressionist traditions in one film.
14 Khan, *An Introduction to Egyptian Cinema*, 34.
15 Ibid., 34–35.
16 Farid, "Periodization of Egyptian Cinema," 8.
17 Khan, *An Introduction to Egyptian Cinema*, 35.
18 Yusuf, *The Palestine Issue in Arab Cinema*, 13–14.

19 These regulations were amended in 1976 by the Minister of Culture under the Sadat government to include new restrictive interpretations.
20 Abu Shadi, *Cinema and Politics*, 53.
21 Farid, "Periodization of Egyptian Cinema," 9.
22 Armes, *Third World Film Making and the West*, 202.
23 Farid, "Periodization of Egyptian Cinema," 9–10.
24 Ibid.
25 Khan, *An Introduction to Egyptian Cinema*, 56–57.
26 Khan, *An Introduction to Egyptian Cinema*, 38 and Abu Shadi, *Cinema and Politics*, 53–59.
27 See Gordon, *Revolutionary Melodrama*.
28 Khan, *An Introduction to Egyptian Cinema*, 50.
29 Ibid., 56–57.
30 Farid, "Periodization of Egyptian Cinema," 11.
31 Ibid.

Notes to Chapter 2

1 Farid, "Periodization of Egyptian Cinema," 11.
2 al-Sawi, *Youssef Chahine: risala iydulujiya*, 100–104.
3 Nasri, "Chahine, sha'ir al-jamahir, 74.
4 al-Disuqi, *Sira' fi-l-wadi*, 63.
5 Abu Shadi, *Sira' fi-l-wadi*, 29.
6 Ibid.
7 Farid, *Madkhal ila tarikh al-sinima al-'arabiya*, 122.
8 Unlike western societies, in traditional Arab culture (i.e., among Muslims as well as Christians and Jews) marriage between first and second cousins remains a common, even preferable practice. As a reflection of this tradition, most Arabs still call their in-laws *'ammi* and *mirat 'ammi* ('my uncle' and 'my uncle's wife'), even if they are not actually married to their cousins.
9 Shawqi, *Sinimat Youssef Chahine*, 47.
10 al-Tayar, *al-Madina fi-l-sinima al-'arabiya*, 48–49.
11 Higazi, "Youssef Chahine al-muwatin, wa Chaplin al-gharib," 18.
12 Qasim Amin's 1899 book on the *Emancipation of Women* is a prime example of how al-Nahda writers saw the success of the task of Arab modernization as contingent on changing social and cultural habits of the common classes.
13 In Egypt, the folk dance group Firqat Rida would become an important feature of the art scene in Egypt after the Nasser revolution. The group made extensive Arab and international tours and received critical praise around the world. In Lebanon, much of the success of the Rahbani Brothers and the legendary singer Fayruz would be linked to the incorporation of Lebanese mountain peasant folk singing and dancing traditions into the operettas they began to present in Lebanon in the late 1950s.
14 Examples of this complex dialectic can be found in religious contexts (such as traditional Sufi oral and body performance traditions, Shiite theatrical ritual practices, and so on), and secular story-telling and theatrical traditions

(e.g., *al-hakawati*) and poetry, all of which continue to be part of the variant representational and technical forms of contemporary Arab popular culture.

Notes to Chapter 3

1. Shmeit, *Youssef Chahine*, 29.
2. Ibid.
3. Ibid., 37–38.
4. Nasri, "Chahine, sha'ir al-jamahir," 73.
5. Shukri, "Youssef Chahine yatahaddath 'an dawr al-sinima," 32.
6. Labib, "Youssef Chahine yaqul: banayt al-najah, 10–11.
7. Fawal, *Youssef Chahine*, 82.
8. Nadim, "*Jamila al-jaza'iriya*," 7.
9. Fawal, *Youssef Chahine*, 88.
10. Ibid.
11. Khan, *An Introduction to Egyptian Cinema*, 52.
12. 'Abd al-Malik, "*Jamila al-jaza'iriya*," 26.
13. Ibid.
14. Nadim, "*Jamila al-jaza'iriya*," 6.
15. Shmeit, *Youssef Chahine*, 193.
16. Nasser's well known interest in cinema is manifested in his support for filmmakers and for the development of the role of Egyptian cinema toward interacting with the social, national, and political priorities of Egypt is well elaborated and documented in a study by Jum'a Kaja and Bashar Ibrahim titled *Abd al-Nasser and the Cinema: A Study of the Problematic of Perspective*.
17. Shafik, *Popular Egyptian Cinema*, 43.
18. The word *faranga* is the term historically used by most Arab and Muslim historians and scholars to refer to what the west termed Crusaders. The term itself now connotes foreigners of any origin, though Arabs had originally used it to refer to people who came from the *faranc* region (modern day France). Some Arab historians argue that Muslims traditionally refrained from using the term 'Crusaders' out of respect for the Christian faith, which they did not want to associate with the European campaign. It should be noted, too, that Eastern Christian Arabs—most of whom fought on the side of the Muslims against the Crusaders' campaigns—represented an important component of the Arab population.
19. Shafik, *Popular Egyptian Cinema*, 45.
20. Shmeit, *Youssef Chahine*, 20.
21. Ibid., 193.
22. Fawal, *Youssef Chahine*, 160–61.
23. Farid, *Adwa' 'ala sinimat Youssef Chahine*, 126.
24. Ibid.
25. Shawqi, *Sinimat Youssef Chahine*, 73.
26. Khan, *An Introduction to Egyptian Cinema*, 52.
27. Fawal, *Youssef Chahine*, 159–60.
28. 'Abd al-Aziz, "Kullama tushadid hadha al-film taktashif shay'an jadidan," 66.
29. Ibrahim, "'Indama iltaqa Salah al-Din ma' Richard Qalb al-Asad," 9.

30 al-Khamisi, "Min film *al-Nasir Salah al-Din*," 41.
31 al-Hakki, "Fi-l-fann wa-l-adab wa-l-naqd," 17.
32 Rushdi, "Film *al-Nasir Salah al-Din*," 38.
33 Massad, "Art and Politics," 81.
34 Khan, *An Introduction to Egyptian Cinema*, 52.

Notes to Chapter 4

1 Farid, "Periodization of Egyptian Cinema," 12.
2 Ibid.
3 Ibid.
4 Ibid., 13.
5 Fayed, *The Revolution in Egyptian Cinema*, 47–48.
6 Darwish, *Dream Makers on the Nile*, 13.
7 Farid, *Adwa' ala sinimat Youssef Chahine*, 14.
8 Abu Shadi, *al-Sinima wa-l-siyasa*, 55–56.
9 Ibid.
10 Ibid., 56.
11 al-Salamuni, "*al-Ard* . . . Dhikrayat min al-ayyam al-jamila," 28.
12 Armes, *Third World Film Making and the West*, 201–202.
13 Ibid., 202.
14 Farid, *Adwa' ala sinimat Youssef Chahine*, 14.
15 Farid in *Adwa' ala sinimat Youssef Chahine*. The quotation is based on an interview with the filmmaker in 1976, 30.
16 Fawal, *Youssef Chahine*, 70–71.
17 Othman, *Round Table*, 21.
18 al-Houdari, Naqd film *Fajr yawm jadid*, 96.
19 Ibid.
20 Othman, "*Fajr yawm jadid* fi-l-mizan," 23–25
21 Fu'ad, "*Fajr yawm jadid*," 48–49.
22 Farid, *Adwa' ala sinimat Youssef Chahine*, 16.
23 al-Imam, "Mulahazat sari'a 'ala film jayyid!," 13.
24 Halim, *Fajr yawm jadid*, 25.
25 Othman, "*Fajr yawm jadid* fi-l-mizan," 24.
26 al-Houdari, Naqd film *Fajr yawm jadid*, 91.
27 al-Khoury, "Fajr yawm jadid li-l-sinima al-'arabiya," 38.
28 Farid, *Adwa' ala sinimat Youssef Chahine* (based on an interview in 1976), 127.
29 Othman, "*Fajr yawm jadid* fi-l-mizan," 25
30 Ibid.
31 Shmeit, *Youssef Chahine*, 47.
32 Ibid.
33 Farid, *Adwa' ala sinimat Youssef Chahine*, 18.
34 Nasri, "Chahine sha'ir al-jamahir," 76.
35 Diyab, "Youssef Chahine," B1.
36 Ibid.
37 Ibid.

38 Ibid.
39 Nasri, "Chahine sha'ir al-jamahir," 76. While it is important to note the presence of an original version of the film that deserves an assessment of its own, this book will concentrate on the publicly screened version. Given this book's emphasis on the contextual resonance of Chahine's cinema, the receptional element of the official version is indeed critical in addressing the film as a cultural product, which informed public discourse at the time in Egypt and the Arab world.
40 'Abd al-Gawad, "Jarima fanniya khatira," 10.
41 Gabr, "Film Youssef Chahine al-jadid," 38.
42 Subhi, "al-Bahth 'an al-nas," 45.
43 al-Fishawi, "al-Fulus wa-l-Nil," 35.
44 Ouda, *al-Nas wa-l-Nil*, 13.
45 Ibid.
46 Armes, *Third World Film Making and the West*, 248.
47 Fawal, *Youssef Chahine*, 76.
48 Armes, *Third World Film Making and the West*, 248.
49 al-Misnawi, "Youssef Chahine Finds His Own Voice," 48.
50 Hasan, *al-Ta'bir 'an al-najah*, 57–58.
51 Nasri, "Chahine sha'ir al-jamahir," 76.
52 Abu Shadi, "Qira'a fi thulathiyat al-hazima," 53.
53 Armes, *Third World Film Making and the West*, 249.
54 Shawqi, *Sinimat Youssef Chahine*, 114.
55 Ramzi, "'Umq al-judhur," 58.
56 Nathmi, 'Indama numathil shakhsiya ghayr shakhsiyitna," 10.
57 Tawfiq, "Man huwa al-ladhi ya'tabir," 19.
58 Ibid., 19.
59 Bargawi, "*al-Ikhtiyar*," 15.
60 al-Salamuni, "*al-Ikhtiyar*."
61 Ibid.
62 al-Sabban, "Thalathat haqa'iq hawl *al-Ikhtiyar*."
63 Ibid.
64 Amina, *al-Ta'bir 'an al-najah*, 61.
65 Farid, "*al-Ikhtiyar*."
66 Tawfiq, "Man huwa al-ladhi ya'tabir," 12.
67 Fawal, *Youssef Chahine*, 93.
68 Shmeit, *Youssef Chahine*, 60.
69 Ibid.

Notes to Chapter 5

1 Armes, *Third World Film Making and the West*, 202.
2 Ibid., 203.
3 Ibid.
4 Farid, "Periodization of Egyptian Cinema," 14–15.
5 Fawal, *Youssef Chahine*, 96.
6 Farid, "Cannes min Samir Farid," 12.

7   Khalil, "Ru'ya siyasiya," 167.
8   Hasan, "al-'Asfur 'ala shashat al-sinima," 30.
9   Omar, "'Asfur Youssef Chahine," 10.
10 Armes, *Third World Film Making and the West*, 249.
11 See Khalil, "Ru'ya siyasiya," 167.
12 Abu Shadi, "Qira'a fi thulathiyat al-hazima," 52.
13 See Tawfiq, "Aham hadath fanni fi-l-Qahira," 53.
14 Shafik, *Popular Egyptian Cinema*, 97.
15 al-Darwish, "Idha qult inanni la akrah Amrika," 15.
16 Armes, *Third World Film Making and the West*, 249.
17 Farid, "Urid al-takallum 'an haqiqati," *al-Gumhuriya*, October 14, 1976, 11.
18 Shmeit, *Youssef Chahine*, 150.
19 Ibid.
20 Ibid., 150–51.
21 Ibid., 129.
22 Abu Shadi, "Qira'a fi thulathiyat al-hazima," 52.
23 Ibid.
24 Farid, *Adwa' 'ala sinimat Youssef Chahine* (interview in 1976), 140.
25 Saleh, "Hal ya'ud al-ibn al-dal," 22.
26 Farid, "Al al-'asfur," 11.
27 Ibid.
28 Fawal, *Youssef Chahine*, 108.
29 Ibid.
30 Farid, *Adwa' ala sinimat Youssef Chahine*, 29.
31 Ibid., 32.
32 Ramzi, "'Umq al-judhur," 60.
33 Shmeit, *Youssef Chahine*, 145.
34 Ibid.
35 Ibid., 153.
36 Ibid.
37 Ibid.

Notes to Chapter 6

1   Ali Abu Shadi (*al-Sinima wa-l-siyasa*) specifies three films that coyly attempted to tackle these events including Mohammad Khan's *Zawjat rajul muhim* (The Wife of an Important Person, 1987), Tarek al-Arian's *The Emperor* (1990), and Muhammad al-Naggar's *al-Haggama* (1990), 164–65.
2   Farid, *Madkhal ila tarikh al-sinima al-'arabiya*, 16.
3   Ibid., 15–16.
4   Ibid., 15.
5   Farid, *Adwa' ala sinimat Youssef Chahine*, 92–93.
6   al-Aris, "Hawl al-shakhsi," 45.
7   The only exception is Hasan al-Imam's powerful portrayal of an early twentieth-century Christian dancer in *Shafiqa al-qibtiya* (Shafiqa the Copt, 1963).

8 See the study by Ahmad Raafat Bahgat titled *Jews and Cinema in Egypt* (2005). The book mainly chronicles the presence of Jews in the Egyptian film industry including its film stars and actors, directors, producers, movie theater owners, and film technicians. In the introduction to the book (p. 3), Bahgat suggests that there was an "actually significant role played by Jews in the development of Egyptian cinema up until after 1948," and that such role affirms that "Egypt, whether consciously or unconsciously, had become, in the period between 1917 and 1948, one of the most dangerous Zionist centers, if not the most dangerous, after the one created in Palestine."
9 Shohat and Stam, *Unthinking Eurocentricism*, 282–83.
10 According to al-Aris, "Generally speaking, Arab/Islamic culture from *al-Munqidh min al-dhalal* (The Savior from Deviation) by al-Ghazali, to *al-Ayyam* (The Days) by Taha Hussein, has known writings that were very close to autobiographies. Ibn Khaldun in his *Rihla ila al-sharq wa-l-gharb* (A Trip to the East and West), the personal autobiography Ibn Sina dictated to his pupil al-Jourjani, and *Hayati* (My Life) by Ahmad Amin among others, all mark the long journey undertaken by several Arab writers and intellectuals to articulate what can be described as 'confessions.' This journey also includes some convincing personal autobiographies (such as al-Mazini's *Ibrahim al-Katib* as an example). All these attempts, however, remained far from the personal autobiography in the real sense of the word. Most of what has been written in Arabic in this area tends to take the shape of 'moral explorations' which talk about the writer's personal struggles for 'repentance' (al-Ghazali), or relaying the story of an education which has led the writer into a specific intellectual path (like with Salama Musa, Ziki Naguib Mahmoud, and even Ibn Khaldun). All this remained, at least until the second half of the twentieth century, far from the original goal of the autobiography, which is in essence closer to the practice of 'exposition' rather than a rationalization of one's life approach and defending and celebrating its history." (From "Hawl al-shakhsi," 34.)
11 al-Aris, "Hawl al-shakhsi," 36.
12 Armes, "Youssef Chahine and Egyptian Cinema," 251–52.
13 Farid, *Adwa' ala sinimat Youssef Chahine*, 41.
14 al-Salamuni, "Fi'lan *Iskindiriya . . . lih?*," 203–204.
15 Ibid.
16 Ibid., 207.
17 al-Aris, "Hawl al-shakhsi," 34.
18 Ibid.
19 Farid, *Adwa' ala sinimat Youssef Chahine*, 41.
20 Ibid., 46–47.
21 Shohat and Stam, *Unthinking Eurocentricism*, 283.
22 Shmeit, *Youssef Chahine*, 172.
23 Shafiq, "Ana qaliq 'ala nas," 15.

Notes to Chapter 7
1 Foucault, "Nietzsche, Genealogy, History," 139–64.
2 Shmeit, *Youssef Chahine*, 179.

3   Ibid., 180.
4   Ibid., 179–80.
5   Farid, *Adwa' ala sinimat Youssef Chahine*, 84.
6   Shmeit, *Youssef Chahine*, 181.
7   al-Salamuni, "*Wada'an Bonaparte!*" 223.
8   Farid, *Adwa' ala sinimat Youssef Chahine*, 57–60.
9   Ibid., 72–74.
10 Ibid., 74.
11 Ibid., 65–71.
12 Ibid., 67.
13 Fawal, *Youssef Chahine*, 163.
14 Shafik, *Popular Egyptian Cinema*, 167.
15 Shmeit, *Youssef Chahine*, 44.
16 Ibid., 44–45.
17 Ibid., 84–86.
18 Shmeit, *Youssef Chahine*, 193. In this 1985 article, Shmeit is referring to an earlier stage in the resistance to the Israeli occupation of South Lebanon in which forces composed mainly of leftist and communist fighters initiated the fight against the Israeli army under the umbrella of the National Resistance Front. Later, the leadership of the resistance gradually shifted to Hezbollah (the Islamic Resistance Movement), which eventually succeeded in forcing the withdrawal of Israeli troops from South Lebanon in 2000.
19 Cortazar in Meyer, ed., "Letter to Roberto Fernandez Retamar," *Lives on the Line*, 75.

Notes to Chapter 8

1   Chahine's autobiographical series was completed with *Alexandria... New York* (2004), a fictional representation of the filmmaker's life and experience in the United States and their impact on his personal and political views vis-à-vis the west.
2   Rafiq al-Sabban, "*Iskindiriya... lih?*" 33.
3   al-Rubi, *al-Kuwayt*, October 2002, 109.
4   The *Hamlet* motif was featured in the two earlier films of the biographical trilogy. In *Alexandria... Why?* (1978) the young Yehia (Chahine) plays the part passionately for his Victoria College classmates, much to the appreciation of his English teacher. Later in *An Egyptian Story* (1982), *Hamlet* is quoted several times in conversations.
5   Fawal, *Youssef Chahine*, 144–45.
6   Two critical Arab readings of the film of note are Ibrahim al-Aris's "Hawla al-shakhsi wa lughat al-shakhsi fi thulathiyat Youssef Chahine" and Ahmad Youssef's "*Iskindiriya kaman wa kaman* li Chahine wa-l-sinima al-bahitha 'an al-hurriya." Examples of western readings of the film include: Dave Kehr's "The Waters of Alexandria: The Films of Youssef Chahine," and Bonice Reynand's "Everywhere Desire." See bibliography for sources.
7   Youssef, "*Iskindiriya kaman wa kaman*," 27.
8   al-Aris, "Hawl al-shakhsi," 44.
9   al-Darwish, "Idha qult inanni la akrah Amrika," 17.

10 Massad, "Art and Politics," 88.
11 Dunne, *Sexuality and the "Civilizing Process" in Modern Egypt*, 191.
12 Lagrange, "Male Homosexuality and Modern Arabic Literature," 90.
13 Whitaker, *Unspeakable Love*, 66.
14 Ibid., 69
15 Abu Nuwas (750–810) is widely regarded as one the greatest classical Arab poets. Challenging conventional song writing forms, his work celebrated life's physical pleasures such as drinking *(khamriyyat)*, and featured witty and erotic lyrics illustrating his sexual escapades with both males and females *(mudhakkarat* and *mujuniyyat).* Many poems explicitly described his lust for a beautiful boy, often embodied in the figure of the *saqi,* the wine boy at the tavern. The theme was often revisited by poets of the classical Arab era, including Omar al-Khayyam, Hafiz, Dik al-Jinn, and others.
16 Kuzniar, *The Queer German Cinema*, 257.
17 Reynand, "Everywhere Desire," 20–23.
18 al-Aris, "Hawl al-shakhsi," 40.
19 Stam, *Film Theory*, 294.
20 During this period, money from Saudi Arabis and other Gulf investors was funneled into buying TV and satellite networks, music production companies, newspapers, and other Arab media. This disconcerted many Arab liberal and left-oriented artists and journalists because of the political impact this was having on the mainstream media's positions on pan-Arab national political issues such as the relationships with the United States and Israel. There was also some concern about producers trying to please the ultra-conservative tastes of their financial backers.
21 Youssef, *Iskindiriya kaman wa kaman*, 32–33.

Notes to Chapter 9

1 For an excellent account of non-sectarianism in the Arab nationalist movement as exemplified by the struggle against early Zionist colonialism in Palestine, see Emile Touma's *The Roots of the Palestine Question.*
2 An important study of the rise of modern Islamic fundamentalism is found in Stephen Schwartz's *The Two Faces of Islam: The House of Sa'ud from Tradition to Terror.* The book provides an overview of the rise of the Wahabi movement in the late nineteenth century as the predecessor to more recent forms of Islamic fundamentalism. It also highlights the manipulation of these groups by the Ottoman Empire, and later by western colonials and neocolonialists in their efforts to counter the rise of Arab nationalism.

Another important study in this area is John Cooley's *Unholy Wars: Afghanistan, America and International Terrorism*, which specifically addresses the connections between the rise of Islamic fundamentalist groups, the Cold War, and anti-communist politics. The former ABC News reporter suggests that as far back as the 1950s, former U.S. Secretary of State John Foster Dulles pointed out the need to enhance a "common bond" with "the religions of the East" in fighting communism. Cooley argues that western analysts in think tanks and intelligence services in Washington, London, Paris, Rome, and elsewhere asked themselves, "who or what is the principal enemy of their enemy, communism? . . . The tacit consensus was that the Muslim religion, if translated into politics, could be harnessed as a mighty force to oppose Moscow in the Cold War" (50–160).

Eventually, the growth of Islamic fundamentalist groups in the Middle East and North Africa directly enhanced a simultaneous decline in the influence of the left-oriented secular nationalist movements. The death of Nasser in 1971, compounded by the Arab defeat in the 1967 war with Israel (which largely discredited the nationalist left in the Arab world), left the door open for a political alternative. A major shift in the political paradigm in the area began with the Lebanese civil war of the mid-1970s, which underlined the weakening support for leftist and Marxist groups in the Arab world. Islamic groups in the area subsequently began to assert themselves as the radical alternative to "Godless Communism."

3 Abu Shadi, "*al-Masir*: wathiqa tanwiriya," 74–75.
4 Saleh, "al-Afkar laha ajniha!" 14.
5 Tawfiq, "al-Kalima al-munasiba," 3.
6 al-Sabban, "Chahine wa-l-tarikh," 40.
7 Darwish, "*al-Masir*: fashal," 24.
8 For more on philosophical inquiry in Andalusia in general, and in relation to Ibn Rushd's contributions in particular, consult S. Jayyusi, *Legacy of Muslim Spain*, especially Miguel Cruz Hernandez's "Islamic Thought in the Iberian Peninsula" (777–803) and Jamal al-Din al-'Alawi, "The Philosophy of Ibn Rushd" (804–29).
9 For a detailed account of the role of the Egyptian government in strengthening the ideological grip of Islamic fundamentalists on culture in the 1980s and early 1990s and its effect on Egyptian cinema, see Ziyad Fayed's *Revolution in Egyptian Cinema*, 85–102.
10 Mahfouz, quoted in Shmeit, *Youssef Chahine*, 201.
11 There is no consensus when it comes to characterizing the nature of the Arab presence in Spain for over 400 years (i.e., whether this presence can be conceived as colonial or as liberatory). What is important here is to stress the dynamics by which Arab audiences perceive this presence, and consequently how Chahine himself utilized this perception to present a narrative about the colonial role in fomenting divisions among Arabs.
12 Adonis, "Ila Muhammad Jabir al-Ansari," 15.
13 Pick, "Politics of Modernity," 43.
14 Ibn Rushd, quoted in the film.
15 McDougall, "The Body as Cultural Signifier," 336.
16 Hutcheon, "Circling the Downspout of Empire," 130.
17 Among the few studies to be published in English on Arab music and its impact on world music history is Henry George Farmer's *Historical Facts for the Arabian Musical Influence*.
18 Gilbert, "Dance, Movement and Resistance Politics," 345.
19 Shafik, *Popular Egyptian Cinema*, 101–20.
20 Ashcroft, Griffith, and Tiffin, ed. "Introduction," in *The Post-Colonial Studies Reader*, 321.
21 Paech, *Literatur und Film*, 79.

22 Shafik, *Popular Egyptian Cinema*, 82.
23 Ibid.
24 Martin-Barbero, *Communication, Culture and Hegemony*, 148.

Notes to Chapter 10

1   Omlile, "al-Thaqafa fi itar al-'awlama," 13.
2   Khair, "Hulywud al-'Arab," http://www.al-akhbar.com/ar/node/67401.
3   Shmeit, *Youssef Chahine*, 246.
4   Farid, "*al-Akhar* yughdib al-jumhur," 10.
5   Ramzi, "*al-Akhar* yushabih film li-Chahine," 20–22.
6   Darwish, "*al-Akhar* fi-li-mizan," 20–21.
7   Tawfiq, "Hanan wa Adam fi muwajahat," 12.
8   al-Shinnawi, "*al-Akhar*: kul tanaqudat Chahine fi film wahid," 82–83.
9   al-Shinnawi, "Akhar Youssef Chahine," 11.
10 Farid, "al-Akhar: fantaziya caricaturiya," 12.
11 Ibid.
12 IMDb, Autre, L' (1999), User Comments, Author: Moheb, (mramses) from Egypt, March 8, 2000, "Chahine attracts more spectators, but . . . ."[sic], http: //www.imdb.com/title/tt0196355/#comment.
13 Stam, *Film Theory*, 302.
14 Fawal, *Youssef Chahine*, 397.
15 Ahmad, "Youssef Chahine: al-film huwa risala," 74.
16 al-Qa'id, "Youssef Chahine lam yarj' ila *Ard* al-waqi'," 15.
17 al-Shinnawi, "al-Mukhrij al-muhadhab jiddan," 13.
18 Ibid.
19 al-Nakkash, "Ittihamat wa rudud," 16.
20 Mazlum, "Suqut . . . Chahine yatkallam," 26.
21 Ibid.
22 Adly, "Ana ghadib 'ala Amrika," 14
23 Farid, *al-Mawja al-jadida*, 227.
24 "Chahine et Septembre 11." *Cahiers du cinéma* 573, 13.
25 Musa, "September 11 li Youssef Chahine," 9.
26 al-Darwish, "*Iskindiriya . . . New York*," 100–101.
27 al-Aris, "Youssef Chahine yuhaki khaybat amaluh," 14.
28 Nimr, "Tamarrud didd al-hilm al-amriki," 19.
29 Toughan, "Ra'yayn mutanaqidayn hawla film Youssef Chahine," 15.
30 Ibid.
31 Ibid.
32 al-Darwish, "*Iskindiriya . . . New York*," 100.
33 Gabr, "Film Youssef Chahine al-jadid," 14.
34 Noureddine, "Chahine yaftah al-nar," 51.
35 abi-Saab, "Awdat Chahine," 23.
36 Tazghart, "Youssef Chahine," 23.
37 Farghaly, "*Fawda* fi khidam al-tawaqu'at," 15.
38 Farghaly, "Nujum *Fawda*," 14.

39 Rashid, "Shabb fi-l-wahid wa-l-thamanin," 15.
40 Ibid.
41 Farghaly, "*Fawda* fi khidam al-tawaqu'at," 15.
42 Khaled Youssef quoted in the Egyptian newspaper *Al-Masry Al-Youm*, May 8, 2009, 1.

Notes to Chapter 11

1   Fawal, *Youssef Chahine*, 77–78.
2   Massad, "Art and Politics," 91.
3   Malkmus and Armes, *Arab and African Film Making*, 156.
4   Ibid., 156–57.
5   Kehr, "The Waters of Alexandria," 27.
6   'Abd al-Fattah, "Wujuh wa aqni'a," 69.
7   Zakariya, "Youssef Chahine," 43.
8   al-Salamuni, "*al-Ikhtiyar*," 118.
9   Ibid., 119.
10 al-Salamuni, *al-Ibn al-dal 'ad* falan yafhamu ahad," 48.
11 Khairallah, "*al-Muhajir* huwa al-sabab," 16.
12 Armes, "Youssed Chahine," 254.
13 Khallousi, "*Le Monde* fi hadith ma' Naguib Mahfouz," 31–32.
14 Said, *The World, the Text, and the Critic*, 8–9.
15 Ibid.

BIBLIOGRAPHY

'Abd al-Aziz, Hisham 'Id. "Kullama tushahid hadha al-film taktashif shay'an jadidan." *al-Fann al-sabi'*, September 1999, 66.

'Abd al-Fattah, Wael. "Wujuh wa aqni'a 'ala marah al-ladha al-fiqriya." *Sinima* (special issue) 24: *Youssef Chahine: 'Asfur al-mushakasa . . . wa-l-ghadab*, April–May 2004, 68–71.

'Abd al-Gawad. "Jarima fanniya khatira inkashafat hadha al-usbu'." *Thaqafa wa funun*, September 2, 1968, 10.

'Abd al-Malik, Anwar. "*Jamila al-jaza'iriya.*" *al-Iza'a*, December 20, 1958, 26.

'Abd al-Rasul, Hasan. "al-'Asfur 'ala shashat al-sinima al-masriya'." *Akhbar al-nujum*, August 3, 1974, 30.

Abdel-Malek, Kamal. *The Rhetoric of Violence: Arab–Jewish Encounters in Contemporary Palestinian Literature and Film*. New York: VHPS Palgrave, 2005.

abi-Saab, Rimon. "Awdat Chahine." *al-Akhbar*, December 12, 2007, 23.

Abu Shadi, Ali. *Khamsun filman min klasikiyat al-sinima al-misriya*. Damascus: The Publications of the Ministry of Culture—the General Institute of Cinema in the Syrian Arab Republic, 2004.

———. "*al-Masir*: Wathiqa Tanwiriya 'ala al-shasha." *Ruz al-Yusuf*, May 5, 1997, 74–75.

———. "Qira'a fi thulathiyat al-hazima." *Sinima* (special issue) 24: *Youssef Chahine: 'Asfur al-mushakasa . . . wa-l-ghadab*, April–May 2004, 50–53.

———. *al-Sinima wa-l-siyasa*. Damascus: al-Mada Publishing Company, 2002.

———. "*Sira' fi-l-wadi*: khutwa sahiha . . . wa nihaya kasiha." *Fann*, February 17, 1992, 29–31.

Adly, Nader. "Ana ghadib 'ala Amrika . . . wa filmi al-jadid yatanawal hadha." *al-Ahram*, February 24, 2002, 14.

Adonis. "Ila Muhammad Jabir al Ansari: da'wa li-i'lam bayan tarikhi fikri," *al-Hayat*, July 24, 2003, 15.

Ahmad, Soufian. "Youssef Chahine: al-film huwa risala li-l-intihaziyin . . . wa-l-lusus" *al-Sada*, October 7, 2001, 74–75.

Aldrich, Robert. *Colonialism and Homosexuality*. London and New York: Routledge, 2003.

Alexander, Livia. "Is There a Palestinian Cinema? The National and Transnational in Palestinian Film Production." In *Palestine, Israel, and the Politics of Popular Culture*, edited by Rebecca L. Stein and Ted Swedenburg. Durham and London: Duke University Press, 2005, 281–301.

Amghai, Mohammed. "Le cinéma arabe : Il s'impose enfin." *El-Moudjahid* 3, no. 102 (1973): 8–10.

Arab Cinema and Culture: Round Table Conference, 3 vols. Beirut: Arab Film and Television Centre, 1965.

Arasoughly, Alia, ed. *Screens of Life: Critical Film Writing*. Quebec: World Heritage Press, 1996.

al-Aris, Ibrahim. "Hawl al-shakhsi wa lughat al-shakhsi fi thulathiyat Youssef Chahine: bi ay hal, hal tahadath 'an ay shay' akhar fi sinima?" *Sinima* (special issue) 24: *Youssef Chahine: 'Asfur al-mushakasa . . . wa-l-ghadab*, April–May 2004, 34–45.

———. *Youssef Chahine: nathrat al-tifl wa qabdat al-mutamarrid*. Cairo: Dar al-Shuruq, 2009.

———. "Youssef Chahine yuhaki khaybat amaluh al-amriki wa yantaqil ila nahwa Hamlet." *al-Hayat*, May 22, 2004, 14.

Armbrust, Walter. "Bourgeois Leisure and Egyptian Media Fantasies." In *New Media and the Muslim World: The Emerging Public Sphere*, edited by Dale Eickelman and Jon Anderson, 102–128. Bloomington: Indiana University Press, 1999.

———. "Colonizing Popular Culture or Creating Modernity? Architectural Metaphors and Egyptian Media." In *Middle Eastern Cities, 1900–1950*, edited by Hans Chr. Korsholm Nielsen and Jakob Skovgaard-Petersen, 20–43. Aarhus, Denmark: Aarhus University Press, 2001.

———. "Egyptian Cinema." *Society for Visual Anthropology Section of the American Anthropological Association* (December 1997), 132–53.

———. "Egyptian Cinema On Stage and Off." In *Off Stage/On Display: Intimacy and Ethnography in the Age of Public Culture*, edited by Andrew Shryock, 42–68. Palo Alto: Stanford University Press, 2004.

———. "Farid Shauqi. 'Tough Guy, Family Man, Cinema Star.'" In *Imagined Masculinities: Male Identity and Culture in the Modern Middle East*, edited by Mai Ghassoub and Emma Sinclair-Webb, 199–226. London: Saqi Books, 2000.

———. "The Golden Age before the Golden Age: Commercial Egyptian Cinema before the 1960s." In *Mass Mediations: New Approaches to Popular Culture in the Middle East and Beyond*, edited by Walter Armbrust, 292–327. Berkeley: University of California Press, 2000.

———. "The Impact of the Media on Egyptian Music." In *Garland Encyclopedia of World Music: The Middle East*, vol. 6, edited by Virginia Danielson, Dwight Reynolds, and Scott Marcus, 233–42. New York: Routledge, 2002.

———. "Islamists in Egyptian Cinema." *American Anthropologist* 104, no. 3 (2002): 922–30.

———. "Manly Men on the National Stage (and the Women Who Make Them Stars)." In *Histories of the Modern Middle East: New Directions*, edited by Ursula Wokoeck, Hakan Erdem, and Israel Gershoni, 247–78. Boulder: Lynne Rienner Publishers, 2002.

———. *Mass Culture and Modernism in Egypt*. Cambridge: Cambridge University Press, 1996.

———, ed. *Mass Mediations: New Approaches to Popular Culture in the Middle East and Beyond*. Berkeley: University of California Press, 2000.

———. "New Cinema, Commercial Cinema, and the Modernist Tradition in Egypt." *Alif: Journal of Comparative Poetics* 15 (1995): 81–129.

———. "Popular Culture and the Decline of the Egyptian Middle Class." *The Journal of the International Institute* 3, no. 3 (Spring–Summer 1996): 8–9.

———. "The Rise and Fall of Nationalism in the Egyptian Cinema." In *Social Constructions of Nationalism in the Middle East*, edited by Fatma Müge Göçek, 217–50. New York: SUNY Press, 2002.

———. "Terrorism and Kabab: A Capra-esque View of Modern Egypt." In *Images of Enchantment: Performance, Art, and Image of the Middle East*, edited by Sherifa Zuhur, 35–59. Cairo: The American University in Cairo Press, 1998.

———. "Transgressing Patriarchy: Sex and Marriage in Egyptian Film," *Middle East Report* 206 (Spring 1998): 29–31.

———. "Veiled Cinema." *Visual Anthropology* 10, nos. 2 and 4 (1998).

———. "When the Lights Go Down in Cairo: Cinema as Secular Ritual," *Visual Anthropology* 10 (1998): 2–4.

Armes, Roy. *African Fimmaking: North and South of the Sahara*. Edinburgh: Edinburgh University Press, 2006.

———. *Dictionary of North African Filmmakers/Dictionnaire des cinéastes du Maghreb*. Paris: Editions ATM, 1996.

———. *Postcolonial Images: Studies in North African Film*. Bloomington and Indianapolis: Indiana University Press, 2005.

———. *Third World Film Making and the West*. Berkeley: University of California Press, 1987.

———. "Youssef Chahine and Egyptian Cinema." *Framework* 14 (1981): 12–15.

———, ed. "Youssef Chahine." In *Third World Film Making and the West*, 243–54. Berkeley: University of California Press, 1987.

Arts Academy. *Qadaya i'adat al-nazar fi tarikh al-sinima al-'arabiya*. Cairo: Arts Academy, 1994.

Asfour, Nana. "The Politics of Arab Cinema: Middle Eastern Filmmakers Face up to Their Reality." *Cineaste* 1 (2000): 46–48.

Ashcroft, B., G. Griffith, and H. Tiffin, eds. "Introduction," in *The Post Colonial Reader*, 321. London and New York: Routledge, 2006.

Assadi, Ginger. "Upholding the Palestinian Image in Israeli Cinema: an Interview with Mohammad Bakri." *Cineaste* 4 (2004): 41–43.

'Atiya, Hasan. "Judhur al-ghadab wa-l-tamarrud fi sinimat Chahine." *Sinima* (special issue) 24: *Youssef Chahine: 'Asfur al-mushakasa . . . wa-l-ghadab*, April–May 2004, 90–97.

———. *al-Rumantiqiya: utopia al-sinima al-misriya*. Cairo: Cairo International Film Festival, 2000.

de Baeque, Antoine. "Alexandrie; encore et toujours." *Cahiers du cinéma* 434 (July–August 1990): 64–66.

———. "Chahine, destin croisé." *Cahiers du cinéma* 517 (October 1997): 28–29.

———. "Dans le regard de Cannes: la catastrophe." *Cahiers du cinéma* 433 (June 1990): 68–71.

———. "*Le destin*," *Cahiers du cinéma* 514 (June 1997): 21.

Bahgat, Ahmad Raafat. *al-Yahud wa-l-sinima fi Misr*. Cairo: al-Qasr Company for Publication, Publicity, and Advertisement, 2005.

Baker, Raymond. "Combative Cultural Politics: Film, Art and Political Spaces." *Journal of Comparative Poetics* 15 (1995): 6–38.

Bakkar, Fatma. "Hazimat 1967 fi sinimat Youssef Chahine: thulathiyat min ajl al-isti'ab." *Sinima* (special issue) 24: *Chahine: 'Asfur al-mushakasa . . . wa-l-ghadab*, April–May 2004, 54–57.

Bargawi, Darwish. "*al-Ikhtiyar*." *al-Musawwar*, January 16, 1971, 14–15.

Benali, Abdelkader. *Le cinéma colonial au Maghreb: L'imaginaire en trompe-l'œil*. Paris: Editions du Cerf, 1998.

Berenice, Raymond. "Everyday Desire." *Sight and Sound* 8 (August 1997): 20.
Bergmann, Kristina. "Youssef Chahine," *Du* 7–8 (July–August 1994): 143–45.
Bernstein, Matthew, and Gaylyn Studlar. *Visions of the East: Orientalism in Film*. London and New York: I.B. Tauris, 1997.
Bhatty, Robin. "Islamic Fundamentalism at War against America: New Documentaries on Religion and Politics in the Islamic World." *Cineaste* 2 (2002): 20–26.
Bory, Jean-Louis. "Les géorgiques arabes." *Cahiers du cinéma* 506 (October 1996): 42.
Bosseno, Christian, ed. *Youssef Chahine L'Alexandrin*. Paris: CinemAction 33/ Cerf, 1985.
———. Khaled Osman, and Mona de Pracontal. "Youssef Chahine." *La revue du cinéma* 400 (December 1984): 103–18.
———. "Immigrant Cinema: National Cinema—The Case of Beur Film." In *Popular European Cinema*, edited by Richard Dyer and Ginette Vincendeau, 47–57. London and New York: Routledge, 1992.
Boughedir, Ferid. "Youssef, le fondateur," *Cahiers du cinéma* 506 (October 1996): 40–41.
Bouzid, Nouri. "New Realism in Arab Cinema: The Defeat Conscious Cinema." In "Arab Cinematics: Toward the New and the Alternative." *Alif: Journal of Comparative Poetics* 15 (1995): 242–50.
Bresheeth, Haim. "Telling the Stories of Heim and Heimat: Home and Exile in Recent Palestinian Films and Iconic Parable of the Invisible Palestine." *New Cinemas: Journal of Contemporary Film* 1 (2002): 24–39.
"Cannes," *Cahiers du cinéma* 514 (June 1997): 19–49.
Carter, Sandra. "Moroccan Cinema: What Moroccan Cinema?" Unpublished PhD thesis, University of Texas at Austin, 1999.
Centre for Arab Coordination in Cinema and Television (CACCT). *al-Sinima wa-l-thaqafa al-'arabiya*. Beirut: CACCT, 1964.
"Chahine et Septembre 11." *Cahiers du cinéma* 571 (September 2002): 13.
Chahine, Youssef. *Le Destin*. Paris: Cahiers du cinéma/L'Etoile, 1997.
Cinémathèque Québécoise/Musée du Cinéma. *A propos du cinéma égyptien*. Québec: Agence de coopération culturelle et technique, 1984.
Cluny, Claude-Michel. "Chahine Yussif." In *Dictionnaire des nouveaux cinémas arabes*, 161–72. Paris: Sindbad, 1978.
Cooley, John K. *Unholy Wars: Afghanistan, America and International Terrorism*. London: Pluto Press, 2000.
Cyr, Helen W. *The Third World in Film and Video*. Metuchen: Scarecrow Press, 1991.

Daney, Serge. "L'Alexandrie, encore et toujours." *Cahiers du cinéma* 431/432 (May 1990): 44–47.

Danielson, Virginia. *The Voice of Egypt: Umm Kulthum, Arabic Song, and Egyptian Society in the Twentieth Century*. Chicago: University of Chicago Press, 1997.

Darwish, Adel. "Youssef Chahine: An Intellectual for the Masses," *The Middle East* 157 (November 1987): 11–14.

Darwish, Mustafa. "*al-Akhar* fi-l-mizan." *al-Sinima wa-l-nas*, August 7, 1999, 20–21.

——. *Dream Makers on the Nile: A Portrait of Egyptian Cinema*. Cairo: The American University in Cairo Press, 1998.

——. "*al-Masir*: fashal wa 'alama mu'iba." *al-Sha'b*, September 30, 1997, 24.

al-Darwish, Qussai Saleh. "Youssef Chahine bi kul saraha: idha qult inni akrah Amrika akun kadhiban." *Sinima* (special issue) 24: *Youssef Chahine: 'Asfur al-mushakasa . . . wa-l-ghadab*, April–May 2004, 6–25.

——. "*al-Masir*: Youssef Chahine bayn al-haqiqa al-tarikhiya wa haqiqat al-yawm." *Sinima* (special issue) 24: *Youssef Chahine: 'Asfur al-mushakasa . . . wa-l-ghadab*, April–May 2004, 86–89.

——. "*Iskindiriya . . . New York*." *Sinima* (special issue) 24: *Youssef Chahine: 'Asfur al-mushakasa . . . wa-l-ghadab*, April–May 2004, 100–103.

Dikeleman, Dale F. and Jon W. Anderson, eds. *New Media in the Muslim World: The Emerging Public Sphere*. Bloomington: Indiana University Press, 1999.

Diyab, Mohamed. "Youssef Chahine: hadhihi al-hikaya al-haqiqiya li-filmi al-muzdawaj al-ladhi kana mukhtafiyan." *al-Hayat*, July 16, 1999, B1.

al-Disuqi, Ibrahim. "*Sira' fi-l-wadi*." *Shashati*, June 5, 2003, 63.

Donmez-Colin, Gonul. *Women, Islam and Cinema*. London: Reaktion Books, 2004.

Dougherty, Roberta L. "Badi'a Masabni, Artiste and Modernist: The Egyptian Print Media's Carnival of National Identity." In *Mass Mediations: New Approaches to Popular Culture in the Middle East and Beyond*, edited by Walter Armbrust, 243–68. Berkeley: University of California Press, 2000.

Downing, John D.H., ed. *Film & Politics in the Third World*. Brooklyn: Autonomedia, 1987.

Downs, Susannah. "Egyptian Earth between the Pen and the Camera: Youssef Chahine's adaptation of Abd al-Rahman al-Sharqawi's *al-Ard*." *Journal of Comparative Poetics* 15 (1995): 153–77.

Dunne, Bruce W. "Sexuality and the 'Civilizing Process in Modern Egypt," Unpublished PhD thesis. Washington, D.C.: Georgetown University, July 1996.

Dwyer, Kevin. *Beyond Casablanca: M.A. Tazi and the Adventure of Moroccan Cinema*. Indianapolis: Indiana University Press, 1994.

Eke, Maureen N., K. Harrow, and E. Yewah, eds. *African Images: Recent Studies and Text in Cinema*. Eritrea and New Jersey: Africa World Press, 2000.

"Entretien avec Youssef Chahine." *Cahiers du cinéma* 310 (1980): 21–25.

Farag, Alfred. *Shari' 'Imad al-Din . . . hikayat al-fann wa-l-nujum*. Cairo: Dar al-Hilal, 2005.

Fargeon, Michael. "Yousef Chahine." *UNESCO Courier* 9 (September 1997): 47–53.

Farghaly, Ahmad Radwan. "*Fawda* fi khidam al-tawaqu'at . . . Youssef Chahine yatasalah ma' jumhuruhu." *al-Hayat*, December 7, 2007, 15.

———. "Nujum *Fawda*: ikhtiyar al-film fi-l-musabaqa takrim lahu." *al-Hayat*, September 21, 2007, 14.

Farid, Samir. *Adwa' 'ala sinimat Youssef Chahine*. Cairo: Egyptian General Book Institute, 1997.

———. "*al-Akhar*: fantaziya karikaturiya . . . 'an al-nizam al-'alami al-jadid." *al-Gumhuriya*, May 12, 1999, 12.

———. "*al-Akhar* yughdib al-jumhur . . . wa yadfa' al-dayn." *al-Gumhuriya*, September 1, 1999, 10.

———. "al-Ard." *al-Sinima*, January 5, 1970, 11–12.

———. "Al al-'asfur: 'al-shari' lana'." *al-Gumhuriya*, 1976, 11.

———. "Cannes min Samir Farid." *al-Gumhuriya*, June 12, 1972, 12.

———. "*Fajr yawm jidid* min wijhat nazar sayih." *al-Gumhuriya*, January 12, 1964, 11.

———. "*al-Ikhtiyar* wa-l-bahth 'an ashkal jadida." *al Sinima*, March 25, 1971, 36.

———. *Madkhal ila tarikh al-sinima al-'arabiya*. Cairo: Egyptian General Book Institute, 2001.

———. *al-Mawja al-jadida fi-l-sinima al-masriya*. Damscus: The Ministry of Culture, 2005.

———. "Periodization of Egyptian Cinema." In *Screens of Life: Critical Film Writing*, edited by Alia Arasoughly, 1–18. Quebec: World Heritage Press, Quebec, 1996.

———. "al-Rihla al-tawila li-*l-Ard*." *al-Gumhuriya*, September 15, 1969, 12.

———. "Three Perspectives on Arab Cinema." *Journal of Middle Eastern Literatures* 2 (2000): 275–82.

———. "Urid al-takallum 'an haqiqati wa haqiqat hadiri." *al-Gumhuriya*, October 14, 1976, 11.

Farmer, Henry Gerge. *Historical Facts for the Arabian Musical Influence*. New York: Beaufort Books. 1988.

Fawal, Ibrahim. *Youssef Chahine*. London: British Film Institute, 2001.
Fawzi, Naji. "*al-'Asfur*: dars fi-l-haraka." *Exclusive Readings in Egyptian Cinema's Visuals*. Cairo: The High Council of Culture (2002): 213–42.
Fayed, Ziyad. *Thawra fi-l-sinima al-masriya*. Cairo: Egyptian General Book Board, 1999.
Feinstein, Howard. "Arab Films at Pisaro." *Cineaste* 2 (1993): 42–43.
al-Fishawi, Abd al-Fattah. "al-Fulus wa-l-Nil." *al-Kawakib*, January 25, 1972, 35.
Foucault, Michel. *Language, Counter Memory, Practice*. Ithaca, NY: Cornell University Press: 1980.
Frodon, Jean-Michel, ed. *Au Sud du Cinéma*. Paris: Cahiers du cinéma, 2005.
Fu'ad, Hasan. "*Fajr yawm jadid*." *al-Ahram*, February 3, 1964, 8.
Gabr, Khaled. "Film Youssef Chahine al-jadid: min al-hubb ila-l-ghadab." *al-Akhbar*, December 25, 2002, 14.
Gabr, Nahed. "*al-Nas wa-l-Nil*." *al-Kawakib*, February 2, 1971, 38.
Gertz, Nurith and George Khleifi. *Palestinian Cinema: Landscape, Trauma and Memory*. Edinburgh: Edinburgh University Press, 2008.
Ghali, Noureddine. "Reflets et mirages du cinéma égyptien." *Jeune cinéma* 83 (December 1984–January 1985):1–8.
Ghassoub, Mai, and Emma Sinclair-Webb, eds. *Imagined Masculinities: Male Identity and Culture in the Modern Middle East*. London: Saqi Books, 2000.
Giavarini, Laurence. "*Le Caire*," *Cahiers du cinéma* 448 (October 1991): 87.
Gilbert, Helen. "Dance, Movement and Resistance" in *The Post-Colonial Studies Reader* edited by Bill Ashcroft, Gareth Griffiths, and Helen Tiffin, 341–45. London and New York: Routledge: 2006.
Gordon, Joel. "Becoming the Image: Words of Gold, Talk Television, and Ramadan Nights on the Little Screen." *Visual Anthropology* 10 (1997): 247–63.
_____. "Class-crossed Lovers: Popular Film and Social Change in Nasser's New Egypt." *Quarterly Journal of Film and Video* 4 (2001): 385–96.
_____. "Days of Anxiety/*Days of Sadat*: Impersonating Egypt's Flawed Hero on the Egyptian Screen." *Journal of Film and Video* 54/2–3 (2002): 27–42.
_____. "Film, Fame, and Public Memory: Egyptian Biopics from Mustafa Kamil to *Nasser 56*." *International Journal of Middle East Studies* 31 (1999): 61–79.
_____. "Golden Boy turns Bete Noire: Crossing Boundaries of Unscripted Television in Egypt." *Journal of Middle Eastern and North African Intellectual and Cultural Studies* 1 (2001): 1–18.
_____. "Nasser 56/Cairo 96: Reimaging Egypt's Lost Community." In *Mass Mediations: New Approaches to Popular Culture in the Middle East and Beyond*, edited by Walter Armbrust, 161–81. Berkeley: University of California Press, 2000.

―――. "The Nightingale and the Ra'is: 'Abd al-Halim Hafiz and Nasserist Longings." In *Rethinking Nasserism: Revolution and Historical Memory in Modern Egypt,* edited by Elie Podeh and Onn Winckler, 307–23. Gainesville: University Press of Florida, 2004.

―――. *Revolutionary Melodrama: Popular Film and Civic Identity in Nasser's Egypt.* Chicago: The Center for Middle Eastern Studies and MEDOC, University of Chicago, 2002.

―――. "With God on Our Side: Scripting Nasser's Free Officer Mutiny." In *Rebellion, Repression, Reinvention: Mutiny in Comparative Perspective,* edited by Jane Hathaway, 253–72. New York: Praeger Publishers 2001.

Hadji-Moussa, Rahiba. "The Locus of Tension: Gender in Algerian Cinema," in "With Open Eyes: Women and African Cinema," edited by Kenneth W. Harrow, special issue of *Matatu: Journal for African Culture and Society* 19 (1997), 45–66.

Hafez, Kai, ed. *Mass Media, Politics, and Society in the Middle East.* Cresskill: Hampton Press, 2001.

Hajjaj, Nasreddine. "Youssef Chahine: The Experience of a Leading Filmmaker." *Index on Censorship* 10, no. 4 (1981): 39–40.

al-Hakki, Abd al-Mun'im. "Fi-l-fann wa-l-adab wa-l-naqd." *Alwan* (1963): 16–17.

Halim, Hilmi. *"Fajr yawm jidid."* *al-Musawwar,* January 13, 1964, 25.

Harrow, Kenneth, ed. *African Cinema: Postcolonial and Feminist Readings.* Eritrea and New Jersey: Africa World Press, 1999.

Hasan, Amina. *al-Ta'bir 'an al-najah al-ijtima'i fi-l-sinima al-misriya fi sanawat al-sab'inat.* Cairo: The General Directory of the National Book and Documents' Institute, 2007.

Hennebelle, Guy. "Arab Cinema." *Merip Reports* 52 (November 1976): 3–12.

―――. "Youssef Chahine, ou la quête d'un style nouveau." In "Les cinémas africains en 1972," edited by Guy Hennebelle. *L'Afrique littéraire et artistique,* no. 20.

Hesse, Reinhard. "Egyptian Intelligentsia Fights Back." *World Press Review* 2 (February 1995): 5–6.

Higazi, Ahmad Abd al-Mauti. "Youssef Chahine al-muwatin wa Chaplin al-gharib." *al-Ahram,* June 4, 1997, 18.

Hillauer, Rebecca. *Encyclopedia of Arab Women Filmmakers.* Cairo: The American University in Cairo Press, 2005.

al-Houdari, Ahmad. "Naqd film *Fajr yawm jadid.*"*Ruz al-Yusuf,* January 12, 1964, 91–96.

Hourani, Albert. *A History of the Arab Peoples.* Boston: Harvard University Press, 1991.

Hutcheon, Linda. "Circling the Downspout" in *The Post-Colonial Studies Reader*, edited by Bill Ashcroft, Gareth Griffiths, and Helen Tiffin, 130–35. London and New York: Routledge, 2006.

Ibrahim, Kamal. "'Indama iltaqa Salah al-Din ma' Richard Qalb al-Asad." *al-Kawakib*, March 11, 1963, 9.

al-Imam, Ameed. "Mulahzat sari'a 'ala film jayid!" *al-Gumhuriya*, January 14, 1964, 13.

Jayyusi, Salma Khadra, and Manuela Marin. *The Legacy of Muslim Spain (Handbook of Oriental Studies: The Near and Middle East)*, vol. 12, 1992.

Jonassaint, Jean, ed., "Chahine et le cinéma égyptien." *Derives* 43 (1984), 23–27.

Kabous, Abd al-Karim. "*Wada'an Bonaparte*/Marhaban bi-Youssef Chahine wa marhaban bi-i'adat qira'at al-tarikh." *al-Hayat al-sinima'iya* 29, March 1986, 2–10.

Kaja, Jum'a, and Bashar Ibrahim. *Abd al-Nasser wa-l-sinima: bahth fi ishkaliyyat al-ru'ya*. Beirut: Dar al-Tariq li-l-Dirasat al-Thaqafiya wa-l-Nashr, 2004.

Kamel, Saad. "*Fajr yawm jidid.*" *Akhbar al-yawm*, August 22, 1964, 9.

Kassem, Mahmoud. "Sirat al-fannan al-dhatiya fi-l-sinima al-'arabiya." *Alif: Journal of Comparative Poetics* 15 (1995): 22–37.

Kehr, Dave. "The Waters of Alexandria: The Films of Youssef Chahine." *Film Comment* (November–December 1996): 23–27.

Khair, Muhammad. "Hulywud al-'Arab . . . kayf tuqawim al-ijtiyah al-khaliji?" *al-Akhbar*, March 17, 2008.

Khairallah, Magda. "*al-Muhajir* huwa al-sabab wara qanun al-hisba." *al-Anba' al-dawliya*, June 30, 1998, 16.

Khalil, Osama. "Ru'ya siyasiya li-*l-'Asfur.*" *al-Tali'a*, November, 1974, 176–77.

Khallousi, Siham. "*Le Monde* fi hadith ma' Naguib Mahfouz 'ala sinimat Youssef Chahine." *Fann*, November 11, 1996, 31–32.

al-Khamisi, 'Abd al-Rahman. "Min film *al-Nasir Salah al-Din.*" *al-Musawwar*, March 8, 1963, 41.

Khan, Mohammad. *An Introduction to Egyptian Cinema*. London: Informatics, 1969.

Khatib, Lina. *Filming the Modern Middle East: Politics in the Cinemas of Hollywood and the Arab World*. London: I.B. Tauris, 2006.

Khayati, Khemais. "Bonaparte et le Moineau." *Télérama* 1814 (20–26 October 1984): 30–33.

Khouri, Malek. "Anxieties of Fundamentalism and Postcolonial Modernist Resistance: Youssef Chahine's *Al Maseer* (The Destiny)." *CineAction* 69 (Spring 2006): 12–23.

———. "Arab Cinema: Landmarks and Emergences." In *Schirmer Encyclopedia of Film*, vol. 1, edited by Barry Keith Grant, 97–104. Farmington Hills: Thomson Gale, 2006.

———. "Origins and Patterns in the Discourse of New Arab Cinema." *Arab Studies Quarterly* 27, no. 1/2 (Winter–Spring 2005): 1–20.

Khoury, Gabriel. "Visite de la maison Chahine." *Cahiers du cinéma* 506 (October 1996): 22.

al-Khoury, George Ibrahim. "*Fajr yawm jadid* li-l-sinima al-'arabiya." *al-Sayad*, February 26, 1964, 38.

Kieffer, Anne. "Youssef Chahine: Un homme du dialogue" and "Adieu Bonaparte, ou le respect de l'autre." *Jeune cinéma*, no. 168 (July–August 1985): 1–5.

Kiernan, Maureen. "Cultural Hegemony and National Film Language: Youssef Chahine." *Alif: Journal of Comparative Poetics* 15 (1995): 130–52.

Klawans, J., B. Stwart, and K. Parnassus. "Nine Views in a Looking Glass: Film Trilogies by Chahine, Gitai and Kiarostami." *Poetry in Review* 112 (2001): 220–31.

Kuzniar, Alice. *The Queer German Cinema*. Palo Alto, CA: Stanford University Press, 2000.

Labib, Foumil. "Youssef Chahine yaqul: banayt al-najah." *al-Kawakib*, October 13, 1959, 10–11.

Lagrange, Frederic. "Male Homosexuality and Modern Arabic Literature." In *Imagined Masculinities: Male Identity and Culture in the Modern Middle East*, edited by Mai Ghassoub and Emma Sinclair-Webb, 168–98. London: Saqi Books, 2000.

Landau, Jacob M. *Studies in the Arab Theatre and Cinema*. Philadelphia: University of Pennsylvania Press, 1958.

Larcher, Jonne. "Un jour, le Nil." *Cahiers du cinéma* 536 (June 1999): 72–73.

Leaman, Oliver, ed. *Companion Encyclopedia of Middle Eastern and North African Film*. New York: Routledge, 2001.

Le Peron, Serge. "Le Syndrome Alexandrie." *Cahiers du cinéma* 310 (1980): 18–20.

Madanat, Adnan. *Sinima tabhath 'an dhataha*. Damascus: Minsitry of Culture, 2005.

Malkmus, Lizbeth. "A Desk Between Two Borders." *Framework* 29 (1985): 17–29.

Malkmus, Lizbeth and Roy Armes. *Arab and African Film Making*. London: Zed Books, 1991.

Mansour, Mohammad. "Youssef Chahine: malamih wa zilal." *al-Hayat al-sinima'iya*, Summer 1995, 176–85.

Mar'a (New York), three supplements to *Cineaste*, 1970–80.

Marks, Laura U. *The Skin of the Film: Intercultural Cinema, Embodiment, and the Senses*. Durham: Duke University Press, 1999.

———. *Touch: Sensuous Theory and Multisensory Media*. Minneapolis: University of Minnesota Press, 2002.

Martin-Barbero, Jesus. *Communication, Culture and Hegemony: From the Media to Mediations (Communication and Human Values)*. Newbury Park, CA: Sage Publications, 1993.

Massad, Joseph. "Art and Politics in the Cinema of Youssef Chahine." *Journal of Palestine Studies* 2 (Winter 1999): 77–93.

———. *Desiring Arabs*. Chicago: University of Chicago Press, 2007.

Mazlum, Lina. "Sukut . . . Chahine yatakalam: ru'yatuna l-il-'awlama taquduna ila karitha." *al-Qahira*, September 4, 2001, 26.

McDougall, Russell. "The Body as Cultural Signifier." In *The Post-Colonial Studies Reader*, edited by Bill Ashcroft, Gareth Griffiths, and Helen Tiffin, 360-340. London: Routledge: 2006.

Menicucci, Garay. "Unlocking the Arab Celluloid Closet: Homosexuality in Egyptian Film." *Middle East Report* 206. www.merip.org/mer/mer206/egyfilm.htm.

Meyer, Doris, ed. *Lives on the Line: The Testimony of Contemporary Latin American Authors*. Los Angeles: University of California Press: 1988.

al-Misnawi, Mustafa. "*al-Ard*: Youssef Chahine yajid sawtuh." *Sinima* (special issue) 24: *Youssef Chahine: 'Asfur al-mushakasa . . . wa-l-ghadab*, April–May 2004, 46–48.

Moustaki, Elisabeth. *Youssef Chahine: L'Alexandrin*. Cologny, Swisse: Amicale Alexandrie Hier et Aujourd'hui, 1998.

Mulvey, Laura. "Moving Bodies." *Sight and Sound* 3 (March 1995): 18–20.

Murray, Stephen O and Will Roscoe. *Islamic Homosexualities: Culture, History, and Literature*. New York: New York University Press, 1997.

Musa, Mahmoud. "September 11 li Youssef Chahine yashhan al-jadal fi Vinicia wa Paris." *al-Ahram* September 11, 2002, 9.

Naaman, Dorit. "Orientalism as Alterity in Israeli Cinema." *Cinema Journal* 4 (Summer 2001): 36–53.

Nadim, Saad. "*Jamila al-jaza'iriya*." *al-Masa,* November 24, 1958, 7.

———. "*Jamila al-jaza'iriya* nasr li-l-film al-'arabi." *al-Masa*, December 15, 1958, 6.

Naficy, Hamid. *An Accented Cinema: Exilic and Diasporic Filmmaking*. Princeton: Princeton University Press, 2001.

al-Nahas, Hashem. *al-Hawiya al-qawmiya fi-l-sinima al-'arabiya*. Cairo: The General Egyptian Book Organization, 1986.

al-Nakkash, Raga. "Ittihamat wa rudud . . . wa qubla!" *al-Kawakib*, October 9, 2001, 16–17.

Nasrallah, Yousry. "Chahine, encore et toujours." *Cahiers du cinéma* 506 (October 1996): 31–32.

Nasri, Samir. "Chahine, sha'ir al-jamahir: min *Baba Amin* ila *Iskindiriya . . . lih?*" *Sinima* (special issue) 24: *Youssef Chahine: 'Asfur al-mushakasa . . . wa-l-ghadab*, April–May 2004, 72–79.

Nathmi, Iris. "'Indama numathil shakhsiya ghayr shakhsiyitna." *al-Kawakib*, January 19, 1971, 27.

Nazarenko, Jean-Marie. "Alexandrie, Toujours." *Cahiers du cinéma* 427 (January 1990): 9.

Nieuwkerk, Karin van. *"A Trade Like Any Other": Female Singers and Dancers in Egypt*. Austin: University of Texas Press, 1995.

Nimr, Fatma. "Tamarrud didd al-hilm al-amriki." *al-'Arabi*, May 23, 2004, 19.

Noureddine, Magda. "Chahine yaftah al-nar: yaghsilun amwaluhum fi-l-sinima al-misriya." *Kalam al-nas*, January 10, 2003, 50–51.

Omar, Hasan Imam. "'Asfur Youssef Chahine." *al-Musawwar*, October 25, 1974, 10.

Omlile, Ali. "al-Thaqafa fi itar al-'awlama." *al-Hayat*, February 26, 2006, 13.

Othman, Hussein. "*Fajr yawm jadid* fi-l-mizan." *al-Kawakib*, March 2, 1964, 21–25.

Ouda, Mohamed. "*al-Nas wa-l-Nil*." *al-Ahram*, February 12, 1972, 13.

Paech, Joachim. *Litartur und Film*, Stuttgart: Metzlersche J.B. Verlagsb, 1997.

"Penser Ciné, Youssef Chahine." *Cahiers du cinéma* 448 (May 1991): 19.

Pick, Zuzanna. "The Politics of Modernity in Latin America." *CineAction* 43 (1994): 39–51.

"Produire Chahine; propos de Humbert Balsan, Cedric Anger. Thierry Jousse." *Cahiers du cinéma* 506 (October 1996): 34–35.

al-Qa'id, Yusuf. "Youssef Chahine lam yarji' ila *Ard* al-waqi' aw ila al-'awlama al-munfalita fi *al-Akhar*." *al-Hayat*, August 31, 2001, 15.

Radwan, Noha. "Youssef Shahin: A Free Man in the Dragon's Den." *Middle East Times*, September 1997, 47–53.

Ramzi, Kamal. "*al-Akhar* yushabih film li-Chahine." *Fann*, May 24, 1999, 20–22.

———. "Umq al-judhur . . . wa-l-nazra al munfatiha." *Sinima* (special issue) 24: *Chahine: 'Asfur al mushakasa . . . wa-l-ghadab*, April–May 2004, 58–67.

Rashid, Arfan. "Shabb fi-l-wahid wa-l-thamanin yuwasil sun' al-aflam wa balwarat hadafuh bi fahm hayatuh." *al-Hayat*, September 21, 2007, 15.

"Revue de presse égyptienne." *Cahiers du cinéma* 506 (1996): 43.

al-Rubi, Muhammad. "Muqabla ma' Chahine." *al-Kuwayt*, October 2002, 108–10

Reynand, Bonice. "Everywhere Desire." *Sight and Sound* 7 (August 1997): 20–23.

Robinson, David. "Tashlin and other Pleasures." *Sight and Sound* 4 (September 1994): 5.

al-Sabban, Rafiq. "Chahine wa-l-tarikh: wajhayn li-'umla wahida." *Akhbar al-nujum*, August 23, 1997, 40.

———. "*Iskandiriya . . . lih?*" *Akhbar al-nujum*, March 12, 1978, 38.

———. "Thalathat haqa'iq hawl *al-Ikhtiyar*." *al-Ahram*, March, 20, 1971, 12.

Sadiki, Larbi. *The Search for Arab Democracy: Discourses and Counter-Discourses*. New York: Columbia University Press, 2004.

Sadoul, George. *The Cinema in the Arab Countries*. Beirut: Arab Film and Television Centre/UNESCO, 1966.

Said, Edward W. "Orientalism," in *The Post-Colonial Reader*, edited by Bill Ashcroft, Gareth Griffiths, and Helen Tiffin, 87–91. London and New York: Routledge, 2003.

———. *The Question of Palestine*. London: Routledge and Kegan Paul, 1980.

———. *The World, the Text, and Critic*. Boston: Harvard University Press, 2006.

Said, Mohammad. "'Indama intalaqa al-'asfur!" *Fann*, December 12, 1998, 29.

Said, S.F. "Island of Silences." *Sight and Sound* 6 (1995): 22–24.

al-Salamuni, Sami. "*al-Ard.*" *Al-A'mal al-kamila li-Sami al-Salamuuni*, edited by Ya'cub Wahbi, vol. 1 (July 2001): 68-80. Cairo: The General Council of Culture Houses.

———. "*al-Ard . . . Dhikrayat min al-ayam al-jamila.*" *Al-A'mal al-kamila li-Sami al-Salamuuni*, edited by Ya'cub Wahbi, vol. 3 (November 2001): 27-37. Cairo: The General Council of Culture Houses.

———. "*al-'Asfour.*" *Al-A'mal al-kamila li-Sami al-Salamuuni*, edited by Ya'cub Wahbi, vol. 1 (July 2001): 292-96. Cairo: The General Council of Culture Houses.

———. "Fi'lan *Iskindiriya . . . lih?*" *Al-A'mal al-kamila li-Sami al-Salamuuni* edited by Ya'cub Wahbi, vol. 2 (September 2001): 203-207. Cairo: The General Council of Culture Houses.

———. "Hal yumkin tu'amin hadha al-'abqari?" *Al-A'mal al-kamila li-Sami al-Salamuuni* edited by Ya'cub Wahbi, vol. 3 (November 2001): 321-28. Cairo: The General Council of Culture Houses.

———. "Hiwar hawla *al-Ard*" *Al-A'mal al-kamila li-Sami al-Salamuuni* edited by Ya'cub Wahbi, vol. 1 (July 2001): 81–88. Cairo: The General Council of Culture Houses July 2001.

———. "*al-Ibn al-dal* 'ad falan yafhamahu ahad" *Al-A'mal al-kamila li-Sami al-Salamuuni* edited by Ya'cub Wahbi, vol. 2 (September 2001): 47–50. Cairo: The General Council of Culture Houses, September 2001: 47–50.

———. "*al-Ikhtiyar.*" *Al-A'mal al-kamila li-Sami al-Salamuuni* edited by Ya'cub Wahbi, vol. 1 (July 2001): 113-19. Cairo: The General Council of Culture Houses.

———. "*al-Ikhtiyar* . . . Ikhtiyaruna nahnu." *al-Ahram*, January 19, 1971, 12.

———. "*Iskindiriya . . . lih?* Mulahazat tafsiliya." *Al-A'mal al-kamila li-Sami al-Salamuuni* edited by Ya'cub Wahbi, vol. 2 (September 2001): 214-24. Cairo: The General Council of Culture Houses.

———. "*Wada'n Bonaparte!*" *Al-A'mal al-kamila li-Sami al-Salamuuni* edited by Ya'cub Wahbi, vol. 3 (November 2001): 223–28. Cairo: The General Council of Culture Houses.

Saleh, Ahmad. "al-Afkar laha ajniha!" *al-Akhbar*, August 25, 1997, 14.

———. "Hal ya'ud al-ibn al-dal Youssef Chahine." *Ruz al-Yusuf*, September 6, 1974, 22.

Saleh, Rushdi. "Film *al-Nasir Salah al-Din* . . . wathiqat sharaf li-sina'at al-sinima al-'arabiya." *Akhir sa'a*, March 2, 1961, 38–39.

Salmane, Hala, Simon Gartog, and David Wilson. *Algerian Cinema*. London: British Film Institute, 1976.

Salti, Rasha, ed. *Insights into Syrian Cinema: Essays and Conversations with Contemporary Filmmakers*. New York and Sao Paolo: Arteeast and Rattapallax Press, 2006.

Salvin, David Henry. *Colonial Cinema and Imperial France, 1919–1939*. Baltimore: Johns Hopkins University Press, 2001.

Samak, Qussai. "The West as Seen Through the Arab Cinema." *Mar'a* 1, no. 2 (supplement to *Cineaste* 9, no. 4, Fall 1979): 32–35.

al-Sawi, Muhammad. *Sinimat Youssef Chahine: rihla idyulujiya*. Alexandria: New Publication House, 1990.

Schwartz, Stephen, *The Two Facs of Islam: The House of Sa'ud from Tradition to Terror*. New York: Doubleday, 2002.

Semmerling, Tim Jon. *"Evil" Arabs in American Popular Film: Orientalist Fear*. Houston: University of Texas Press, 2006.

Shaheen, Jack. *Reel Bad Arabs: How Hollywood Vilifies People*. Ithaca: Olive Branch Press, 2001.

Shafiq, Sulayman. "Ana qaliq 'ala al-nas hatta idha lam yakun lahum 'unwan: ghadab Chahine . . . 'ala al-tariq." *al-Ahali*, November 11, 2002, 15.

Shafik, Viola. *Popular Egyptian Cinema: Gender, Class, and Nation*. Cairo and New York: The American University in Cairo Press, 2007.

———. *Arab Cinema: History and Cultural Identity*. Cairo: The American University in Cairo Press, 1998.
Sharaf al-Din, Durriya. *al-Siyasa wa-l-sinima al-misriya, 1961–1981*. Cairo: Dar al-Shuruq, 1992.
Shawqi, Suʻad. *Sinimat Youssef Chahine: tatawwur al-ruʼya wa-l-uslub*. Cairo: General Institute of Culture Palaces, 2004.
Shebl, Mohamed. "Youssef Chahine: The Prodigal Son." *Al-Ahram Weekly*, March 17–23, 1994, 16.
al-Shinnawi, Tarek. "*al-Akhar*: kul tanaqudat Chahine fi film wahid." *Ruz al-Yusuf*, May 13, 1999, 82–83.
———. "Akhar Youssef Chahine." *al-Ahram*, August 4, 1999, 11.
———. "al-Mukhrij al-muhadhab jiddan wa nuqaduh al-hamir jiddan." *al-Wafd*, September 30, 2001, 13.
Shmeit, Walid. *Youssef Chahine: hayah fi-l-sinima*. Beirut: Riad al-Rayyis Books, 2001.
Shohat, Ella and Robert Stam. *Unthinking Eurocentrism: Multiculturalism and the media*. London: Routledge, 1994.
Shohat, Ella, ed. *Talking Visions: Multicultural feminism in a transnational age*. Cambridge: MIT Press, 1998.
———. *Israeli Cinema: East/West and the Politics of Representation*. Austin: University of Texas Press, 1989.
Shohini, Chaudhuri. *Contemporary World Cinema: Europe, the Middle East, East Asia and South Asia*. Edinburgh: Edinburgh University Press, 2005.
Shukri, G. "Youssef Chahine yatahaddath ʻan dawr al-sinima fi nahdatina al-ijtimaʻiya." *Watani*, October 4, 1958, 32.
Stam, Robert. *Film Theory: An Introduction*. New York: Blackwell Publishing/ New York University, 2000.
Stein, Rebecca L., and Ted Swedenburg, eds. *Palestine, Israel, and the Politics of Popular Culture*. Durham and London: Duke University Press, 2005.
Stollery, Martin. "Masculinities, Generations, and Cultural Transformation in Contemporary Tunisian Cinema." *Screen* 42, no. 1 (2001): 49–63.
Subhi, Abd al-Munʻim. "al-Bahth ʻan al-nas wa-l-sadd fi film Youssef Chahine." *Akhir saʻa*, February 6, 1972, 45–46.
Tarr, Carrie. "Questions of Identity in Beur Cinema: from *Tea in the Harem* to *Cheb*." *Screen* 32, no. 4 (1993): 321–42.
Tawfiq, Raʼuf. "Aham hadath fanni fi-l-Qahira: al-ʻAsfur." *Akhir saʻa*, October 3, 1974, 52–55.
———. "Hanan wa Adam fi muwajahat al-ʻawlama wa-l-irhab." *al-Akhbar*, May 12, 1999, 12.

———. "al-Kalima al-munasiba fi-l-waqt al-munasib." *Sabah al-khayr*, August 21, 1997, 3.

Tawfiq, Sa'd al-Din. "Man huwa al-ladhi ya'tabir Mahmud mathalan a'la?" *al-Ahram*, May 6, 1971, 11.

al-Tayar, Rida. *al-Madina fi-l-sinima al-'arabiya*. Beirut: The Arab Institute for Studies and Publication, 1981.

Tazghart, 'Uthman. "Youssef Chahine: al-shaykh ya'ud ila sibah." *al-Akhbar*, November 12, 2007, 23.

———. "Impression de tournage." *Cahiers du cinéma* 390 (December 1986): 8–9.

Techiné, André. "Un baroque cinématographique." *Cahiers du cinéma* 506 (1996): 38–39.

Tesson, Charles. "*Le Destin*." *Cahiers du cinéma* 517 (October 1997): 30–34.

Thierry, Jousse. "Le monde de Chahine." *Cahiers du cinéma* 506 (October 1996): 4–7.

———. "Youssef Chahine face à l'Egypte." *Cahiers du cinéma* 489 (March 1995): 30–34.

———. "Youssef Chahine: 'Les Cahiers m'ont aidé face à mon gouvernment.'" *Cahiers du cinéma* 556 (April 2001): 18–19.

Thierry, Jousse and Jean-Marc Lelanne. "Le spectacle et la vie: entretien avec Youssef Chahine." *Cahiers du cinéma* 506 (October 1996): 8–30.

Thierry, Jousse, Cedric Anger, and Emmanuel Burdeau. "Filmographie." *Cahiers du cinéma* 506 (October 1996): 48–66.

Thoraval, Yves. "Youssef Chahine, ou le renouveau permanent." In *Regards sur le cinéma égyptien*, edited by Yves Thoraval 26–31. Beirut: Dar al-Mashriq, 1975.

Tlatli, Moufida. "Moving Bodies." *Sight and Sound* 5 (March 1995): 18–20.

———. "La Saison des hommes." *Sight and Sound* 7 (1993): 38–39.

Toubiana, Serge. "Balles Neuves." *Cahiers du cinéma* 514 (June 1997): 19.

———. "Chahine à la conquête de Bonaparte." *Cahiers du cinéma* 364 (October 1984): 60–66.

———. "Entretien avec Youssef Chahine." *Cahiers du cinéma* 431/432 (May 1990): 48–50.

———. "*Le sixième jour*." *Cahiers du cinéma* 390 (December 1986): 4–7.

Toughan, Walid. "Ra'yayn mutanaqidayn hawl film Youssef Chahine: al-ibda' bayn al-khida' al-ikhlas wa-l-khayal." *al-Quds al-'arabi*, September 22, 2004, 15.

Touma, Emile, Judhur al-qadiya al-filistiniya. Beirut: Center for Palestinian Studies. 1972

Tournes, Andrée. "Interview with Youssef Chahine." *Framework* 14 (1981): 11–12.

Vatrican, Vincent. "J'ai toujours pensé que le cinéma était un instrument de pensée" *Cahiers du cinéma* 490 (April 1995): 70–75.

———. "L'émigré." *Cahiers du cinéma* 489 (March 1995): 28–29.

Vitalis, Robert. "American Ambassador in Technicolor and Cinemascope: Hollywood and Revolution on the Nile." In *Mass Mediations: New Approaches to Popular Culture in the Middle East and Beyond*, edited by Walter Armbrust, 269–91. Berkeley: University of California Press, 2000.

Walid, Mohamed. "Youssef Chahine: le pari de l'intelligence." *Adhoua* 3 (January–March 1981): 9–15.

Wannous, Naser. "Surat Ibn Rushd fi *al-Masir.*" Summer 1998, 78–84.

Whitaker, Brian. *Unspeakable Love: Gay and Lesbian Life in the Middle East*. Los Angeles: University of California Press, 2006.

White, Jerry. "Children, Narrative and Third World Cinema in Iran and Syria." *Canadian Journal of Film Studies* 1 (Spring 2002): 78–97.

Woffenden, Richard. "Eyes Wide Open." *Cairo Times*, April 29, 2004, 16–19.

Wright, J., and Everett Rowson, eds. *Homoeroticism in Classical Arabic Literature*. New York: Columbia University Press, 1997.

Yosef, Raz. *Beyond Flesh: Queer Masculinities and Nationalism in Israeli Cinema*. Piscataway: Rutgers University Press, 2004.

Youssef, Ahmad. "*Iskindiriya kaman wa kaman* li-Youssef Chahine wa-l-sinima al-bahitha 'an al-hurriya." In *Egyptian Cinema and the Rights of People*, edited by Hashem Nahas, 27–33. Cairo: The Cairo Centre for Human Rights Studies, 2001.

Youssef Chahine: 'Asfur al-mushakasa . . . wa-l-ghadab. Sinima (special issue) 24, April–May 2004.

Youssef, Khaled. *Al-Masry Al-Youm*, May 8, 2009, 1.

Yusuf, Yusuf. *Qadiyyat Filistin fi-l-sinima al-'arabiya*. Beirut: The Arab Institute for Studies and Publication, 1980.

Zakariya, Issam. "al-Nisa' fi aflam Youssef Chahine: Qinawi yarqa' wa yuhatam timthal al-umm." *Sinima* (special issue 24: *Youssef Chahine: 'Asfur al-mushakasa . . . wa-l-ghadab*), April–May 2004, 82–85.

———. *Sani' al-maraya*. The Cultural Association Sweden–Egypt; Caravan; Euromed, 2008.

Zalaffi, Nicoletta. "Sous le signe de Shakespeare." *Images et son* 298 (September 1975): 15–16.

———. "Youssef Chahine: sani' al-suwar." *Sabah al-khayr*, May 1, 2001, 39–46.

Zuhur, Sherifa. *Images of Enchantment: Visual and Performing Arts of the Middle East*. Cairo: The American University in Cairo Press, 1998.

INDEX

A

Abd al-Rahman al-Kawakibi, 8
Abdu, Muhammad, 168
Abi fawq al-shajara (My Father on the Tree), 59
Abu Shadi, Ali, 13, 23, 56
al-Abwab al-mughlaqa (The Closed Doors), 171, 189
acclaim in international film circles, 37
activism and auteurism, 216–27
Adeeb, Adel, 188
Adieu Bonaparte!, 51, 92, 118, 119; anticolonial resistance, 136–38; Chahine's self-identification as a francophone, 143–46; historical memory, 135
Adieu Forain (Bye-bye souirty), 151
Adly, Nader, 201
al-Afghani, 8, 168
Agrama, Farouk, 16
Ahlam al-madina (Dreams of the City), 118
Ahmad, Majdi, 117

al-Akhar (The Other), 168, 186; globalization, 191–97
al-Akhbar, 211
Aldrich, Robert, 149
Alea, Tomas Gutierrez, 65
al-Alem, Mahmoud Amin, 64
Alexandria . . . New York (Iskindiriya . . . New York), 118, 186, 203–209
Alexandria Again and Forever (Iskindiriya kaman wa kaman), 92, 118, 146, 147; and queer context, 149–52;
Alexandria trilogy, 37, 117, 125
Alexandria . . . Why? (Iskindiriya . . . lih?), xvi, xxii, 116, 117; identity and cultural heterogeneity, 120–24
Algeria: crisis, xx; French occupation of, 37; revolution, 35
Algerian National Liberation Front (FLN), 37, 38
alienation, sense of, 146
Allouache, Merzak, 120, 123, 171

All that Jazz, 148
A Lover's Call (Nida' al-'ashiq), 18
America and globalization, 202–209
Ames, Roy, 57
al-'Amil (The Worker), 28
Amin, Qasim, 9
A Minute of Sun Less (Une minute de soleil en moins), 151
Ana bahib al-sima (I Love Cinema), 213
An Egyptian Story (Hadduta masriya), 118, 150
Anglo-Egyptian agreements, 11
Anthony and Cleopatra, 159
anticolonialism, 8; in *Jamila, the Algerian*, 37–42; resistance, *Adieu Bonaparte!*, 136–38
anti-imperialism: groups, 3; struggles, 141, 142
anti-Zionist messages, 132
Aoulad-Syad, Daoud, 151
apprenticeship, 36
apprentices of Chahine, 228
Arab cinema since the 1990s, 186–91
Arab dance traditions, 179
Arab nationalist movements, 3, 230
Arab National Liberation Movement, 168–72
Arab national project, xi, 1–16; as an unfinished project, 2–6; development of, 1-16; Egyptian cinema before the revolution, 11–12; modernity as an Arab cultural continuum, 6–8; overview of Arab cinema, 8–11; revolution and the emergence of film discourse, 12–16
Arab Renaissance movement *(al-Nahda)*, xv, 7
Arafa, Sharif, 44, 116

al-A'rag, Wainin, 169
al-Ard (The Land), 19, 22, 56, 58–60; class and national liberation in, 74–80
al-Aris, Ibrahim, xiii, 118, 149, 206
Armes, Roy, 90, 226
ART, 187
al-Aryan, Tariq, 116
al-'Asfur (The Sparrow), vii, 59, 66, 81, 92, 125; crisis and resiliency in, 92–103
Assad, Hany Abou, 189
Aswan High Dam, xxi, 35, 67,
A Thousand and One Nights, 158
al-Atrash, Farid, 218
auteurism and cultural activism, 216–27, 223
author, Chahine as, 215–35
authorial power. *See mise en scène*
autobiographical works, 143–46
avant-garde filmmaking techniques, 10
'Awdat al-ibn al-dal (The Return of the Prodigal Son), 81, 92, 130, 195; impending chaos and, 103–14
Awlad al-fuqara' (Children of the Poor), 20
al-'Azima (The Will), 19

B

Baba Amin (Father Amin), 18, 20, 27, 125
Bab al-Hadid (Cairo Station), 10, 20, 26, 28, 86, 125, 204
Bab al-shams (Door to the Sun), 189
Bachir-Chouikh, Yamina, 171
Badrakhan, Ali, 227; *see also al-Karnak*

al-Bahithan 'an al-huriya (In Search of Freedom), 213
al-Bakri, Asma, 116
Barbero, Jesus Martin, 182
Bargawi, Darwish, 83
Bathing Beauty, 126
Bayn idayk (In Your Hands), 18
Bayya' al-khawatim (The Ring Seller), 58, 218
Beb el-Oued, 171
Berlin Film Festival, 117, 125, 161
Bertchenko, Shlinikov, 70
Betrayed, The, 91
Beyond Flesh: Queer Masculinities and Nationalism in Israeli Cinema, 149
bisexuality, 148, 158
Bishara, Khairy, 116, 227
Black Market, The (al-Suq al-sawda'), 19
Bouhired, Jamila, 37
bourgeoisie, 113
Bouzid, Nouri, 118
Box of Life, The (Sanduq al-dunya), 189
Brummana Film Festival, Lebanon, 96
Buñuel, Louis, 112
Butler, David, 51
Bye-bye souirty (Adieu Forain), 151

C

Cahiers du Cinéma, 203
Cairo as Seen by Chahine, 165
Cairo Film Society, 15
Cairo Station (Bab al-Hadid), 10, 20, 26, 28, 86, 125, 204
Camp David Peace Accords, 1–3, 89
Cannes Film Festival, 20, 36, 77; *Adieu Bonaparte!*, 138; *The Sparrow*, 95
Caramel, 151, 188
Carmen, 204
Carthage Film Festival, 59
Centre national de la cinématographie (CNC), 197
Chahine, Youssef: as an author and intellectual, 215–35; artist as a troubled activist, 152–55; beyond subversion, political activism, 163–66; as a budding activist filmmaker, 34–42; in context, 227–29; early public sector experience, 58–60; epics, drive to produce, 46–49; political evolution of, 35; post-Nasser works, 234
Chaos (Heya Fawda), xii, 209–13
Chedid, Andrée, 219
Children of the Poor (Awlad al-fuqara'), 20
Choice, The (al-Ikhtiyar), 26, 58–60, 80–88, 109, 130
Christians, relationships with Muslims, 44
cinema, early cinema and social class, 17–18
Cinémathèque Française, 71
"Circling the Downspout of Empire," 178
class. *See also* social class: anxiety, 87; dynamics of, xiv; early cinema and, 17–18; *The Land*, 74–80; peasants, 74–80; post-revolution upper class, 60–67; *The Return of the Prodigal Son*, 111; rise of wealthy, 104
classical Hollywood genres, 219
Closed Doors, The (al-Abwab al-mughlaqa), 171, 189

Colonialism and Homosexuality, 149
colonial power structures, xiv
commercial viability of cinema, 90
Communism, 4
Coptic Church, 116
corporations, role of in cinema, 187
Cortazar, Julio, 145
crisis and resiliency in *al-'Asfur*, 92–103
criticism, *Adieu Bonaparte!*, 138–43; *Alexandria . . . New York*, 206; *Alexandria . . . Why?*, 130–31; *Dawn of a New Day*, 64–67; *Jamila, the Algerian*, 41, 42; *The Land*, 78; *The Other*, 194; *The People and the Nile*, 72, 73; *The Return of the Prodigal Son*, 108, 110; *Silence . . . We're Rolling*, 199; *The Sparrow*, 96
critics of nationalism in film, 57
cultural heterogeneity, xx; identity and, 120–24
curfews, 115

D

Dagher, Asia, 48
Darwish, Mustafa, 55, 172
al-Darwish, Kussai Saleh, 156, 206
Dawn of a New Day (Fajr yawm jadid), 58, 68; failure of, 58, 68; post-revolution upper class in, 60–67
Days, The, 117
al-Degheidy, Inas, 237
De Sica, Vittorio, 63
Desiring Arabs, 149
Destiny (al-Masir), xii, xxii, 51, 118, 168, 172–75; modernist impulses in, 177–83

Devil in the Desert (Shaytan al-sahara'), 18
al-dhikr (ceremonial religious custom), 181
Dhulfuqar, Ezzaddine, 48
Diary of a Male Whore (Yawmiyat shab 'ahir), 152
difference, identity and, 115–16
al-Din Tawfiq, Saad, 84
Discreet Charm of the Bourgeoisie, The, 112
disillusionment: with the Arab national project, 4; with the Nasser revolution, 100
distribution, government's involvement in, 54
distributors, 11
Divine Intervention, 189
dogmatism: rise of religious, 168–72; traditionalism, 178
Door to the Sun (Bab al-shams), 189
Dreams of the City (Ahlam al-madina), 118
Dukkan Shehata (Shehata's Store)
Dunne, Bruce W., 157

E

Ebeid, Atef, 100
Effendi, Muhammad, 77
Egyptian Catholic Center for Cinema, viii
Egyptian Land, The, 75
Eisenstein, Sergei, 10
Eleven Minutes, Nine Seconds, One Image: September 11, 202
Emigrant, The (al-Muhajir), 92, 118, 169, 194
experimentation, stylistic, 91

F

Faculty of Communication and Culture at the University of Calgary, viii
Fahmi, Ashraf, 55
Fajr yawm jadid (Dawn of a New Day), 58, 68; post-revolution upper class in, 60–67
Farag, Lafred, 31
Farewell My Love (Wadda'tu hubbak), 18, 218
Farid, Samir, 13, 15, 54, 61, 84, 110, 139, 140, 194, 201
Farouk, King, 4, 12, 17
al-Fatah, Abd, 222
Father Amin (Baba Amin), 18, 20, 27, 125
Fawal, Ibrahim, xiii, 38, 78, 86, 110, 141
Fawdah, Faraj, 173
Fawzi, Osama, 117, 213
Fayruz, 218
Fellini, Federico, 148
films: analysis of, xiii; the film with a purpose *('al-film al-hadif')*, 54; restrictions on, 91
financial resources, *Saladin*, 47, 48
First World War, 6, 9
foreign coproductions, reliance on, 92
Forever Yours (Hubb li-l-abad), 18
Forman Hasan, 27
Fosse, Bob, 148
France: Cannes Film Festival. *See* Cannes Film Festival; coproductions with, 135; French Ministry of Culture, 92; French New Wave, 10; French occupation (1798–1803), 136, 140; French Revolution, 2, 8, 177
francophone, Chahine's self-identification as, 143–46
free cinema, 55
freedom of expression, restraint of, 91
freeze-frames, 47
fundamentalism, religious, 167–83; modernist impulses in *Destiny*, 177–83; modernist story about Arab history, 172–75; modernist transformation, 176–77; rise of religious dogmatism, 168–72

G

Galal, Nader, 55
Gamil, Sanaa, 60, 65
gay lifestyles, 152–55. *See also* queer sexuality: queer transgression and postcolonial ambivalence, 147–66
genres, 12, 219
Gibran, Gibran Khalil, 9
Gide, André, 105
Gielgud, Sir John, 162
globalization: America and, 202–09; Arab cinema since the 1990s, 186–91; depiction of, 209–13; national liberation in the age of, 185–213; *The Other*, 191–97; and September 11, 2001, 207; *Silence . . . We're Rolling*, 197–202
golden age of cinema, 14, 15
Gordon, Joel, 14
Great Clown, The (al-Muharrij al-kabir), 18
Gypsy dance traditions, 179

H

hadatha (modernity), xv
Hadduta masriya (An Egyptian Story), 118
Hadji-Moussa, Rahiba, 149
Hafiz, Abd al-Halim, 44
al-Haggar, Khalid, 116, 151
Halim, 44
Hamama, Faten, 20
Hamed, Marwan, 151, 188, 213
Hamid, Said, 116
Hamlet, 162, 221
Hamlet, 204, 222
Harold, Christopher, 140
Hasan, Amina, 79, 84
Hatata, Atef, 171
Hawamidah, Musa, 169
al-Hayat, 206
Hays Code (United States), 13, 149
hegemony, xiv, 35, 191, 232; counter-hegemonic political cultural intervention, 145; resistance to, 193
Helwan, strikes in, 115
heterogeneity, 7, 135–36; identity and, 120–24
Heya Fawda (Chaos), xii, 209–13
Higazi, Ahmad, 28
High Cinema Institute, 15, 55
Higher Council for the Protection of the Arts and Literature, 14
Hina maysara (Till Things are Better), 213
history, xx; authenticity of historical events, 50; historical memory, 135–36; recognizing historical milestones, 229; power of, 167–83
Homoeroticism in Classical Arabic Literature, 149

homosexuality, 148–49. *See also* queer sexuality
Hostess, The, 169
How I Love You (Kaifa uhibbuk), 151
Hubb li-l-abad (Forever Yours), 18
Hussein, Taha, 9, 117
Hutcheon, Linda, 178

I

Ibn al-haddad (The Son of the Blacksmith), 20
Ibn al-Nil (The Son of the Nile), 18, 19, 27, 36
identity, 81. *See also The Choice*; Chahine's cinema and the new appropriation of, 116–20; and cultural heterogeneity, 120–24; and difference, 115–16; search for, 35
Idris, Yusuf, 31
al-Ikhtiyar (The Choice), 26, 58–60, 80–88, 109, 130
I Love Cinema (Ana bahib al-sima), 213
Imagined Masculinities: Male Identity and Culture in the Modern Middle East, 149
Imam, Adel, 170
Imam, Sheikh, 92
al-Imam, Ameed, 63
al-Imam, Hasan, 59
Imam regime, 58
'Imarat Ya'cubyan (The Yacoubian Building), 151
IMDb Web site, 195
Incoherence of the Incoherence, 172
Incoherence of the Philosophers, 172
Indiscretion of an American Wife, 63
In Search of Freedom (al-Bahithan 'an al-huriya), 213

Inta habibi (You are My Love), 18
intellectual: Chahine as, 215–235; isolationism, 84; stagnation *(jumud)*, xiv, 8
international coproductions, 67–74
international markets, 139
interpretation of religion, 175
inter-religious love stories, 129
interview in *Cahiers du Cinéma*, 203
In Your Hands (Bayn idayk), 18
al-Irhabi (The Terrorist), 170
al-Irhab wa-l-kabab (Terrorism and Kebab), 170
al-Irshad (Ministry of Public Information), 13
Iskindiriya...lih? (Alexandria... Why?), xvi, xxii, 116, 117: identity and cultural heterogeneity, 120–24
Iskindiriya... New York (Alexandria... New York), 118, 186, 203–09
Iskindiriya kaman wa kaman (Alexandria Again and Forever), 92, 146, 147; queer context, 149–52; queer sexuality, 147–66
Islam: rise of fundamentalism, xii; separation of Arabism and, 2
Islamic Homosexualities: Culture, History, and Literature, 149
Israel, 12; declaration of state, 132; 1967 War, 92–103

J

Jahin, Salah, 31, 57
Jameson, Fredric, 195
Jamila, the Algerian, 33, 34, 35, 36, 37–42, 195, 232; Afghanistan, response to, 39; China, response to, 39; Czechoslovakia, response to, 39; Germany, response to, 39; Hungary, response to, 39; India, response to, 39; Pakistan, response to, 39; political intervention, 36–42; Soviet Union response to, 39
jumud (intellectual stagnation), xiv, 8

K

Khan, Mohammad, 14
Kaifa uhibbuk (How I Love You), 151
al-Kalioubi, Kamil, 116
Kamal, Hussein, 16, 1969
Kanafani, Ghassan, 91
al-Karnak, 96; *see also* Ali Badrakhan
al-Kashif, Radwan, 116
al-Kawakibi, Abd al-Rahman, 168
Kazan, Elia, 25
Keep Your Eye on Zuzu (Khalli balak min Zuzu), 59
Kelly, Gene, 161
Khalifeh, Marcel, 169
al-Khaliq, Ali Abd, 55
Khalli balak min Zuzu (Keep Your Eye on Zuzu), 59
Khan, Mehboob, 41
Khan, Mohammad, 11, 15, 41, 116
Khleifi, Michel, 189
al-Khouli, Lotfi, 31, 57, 92
Khoury, Gabriel, 92
Khoury, John, 18
Khoury, Marianne, vii
al-Khoury, George Ibrahim, 63
Khtachordian, 70
Khudr, Abu, 92
King Richard and the Crusaders, 51

Kite, The (Tayarat al-waraq), 189
al-Kouddous, Abd, 57
Kuwait, Iraqi invasion of, 103
Kuzniar, Alice, 158
Kwaini, Mary, 63

L
Labaki, Nadine, 151, 188
Lady on the Train (Sayyidat al-qitar), 18, 218
Lagrange, Frederic, 148, 157
Land, The (al-Ard), 19, 22, 56, 58–60; class and national liberation in, 74–80
languages, recovery and preservation of, 7
large-scale cinematic productions, 35
La Sept-Arte, 188
Latin America, 226
Laylat al-babi dull (The Night of the Baby Doll), 188
Lebanon, 3, 143; Brummana Film Festival, 96; civil war, 90, 103, 112, 115
left-liberal groupings, 8
left-nationalist government, 35, 41. *See also* liberation
left national theories, 233
Levantine countries, 3
liberation, 4, 87, 88, 215; in the age of globalization, 185–213; America, 202–09; Arab cinema since the 1990s, 186–91; *Jamila, the Algerian*, 36–42; *The Land*, 74–80; *The Other*, 191–97; *Silence . . . We're Rolling*, 197–202; struggle for, 8, 33–24

literature, recovery and preservation of, 7
Lotus Film, 14
love stories, 129
Lyotard, Jean-François, 195

M
Madbouli, Ali, 105
Mahfouz, Naguib, 31, 57, 169; attack on, 182; *The Choice*, 80–88; commenting on Chahine's work, 227; contribution to *Jamila, the Algerian*, 38; religious fundamentalism, 173
Malas, Mohammad, 118
al-Malik, Anwar Abd, 41
Man in My Life (Rajul fi hayati), 18
Man of Ashes, 118
al-Mansur, Caliph, 174
Marxist theories, 233
Marzuk, Said, 55–56
masculinity in Arab cinema, 149
al-Masir (Destiny), xii, xxii, 51, 118, 168, 172–75; modernist impulses in, 177–83
Masr yamma ya Bahiya (Mother Egypt, You 'Beautiful' Bahiya), vii
Massad, Joseph, 51, 149
McDougall, Russell, 177
melodramas, 12, 18
Melody Pictures, 188
Memories of Underdevelopment, 65
memory, historical, 135–36
Menicucci, Garay, 148
Men in the Sun, 91
Mercedes, 151
Mernissi, Fatima, 149
al-Mihi, Raafat, 116

al-Miligi, Mahmoud, 79
Ministry of National Culture and
    Guidance, 4
Ministry of Public Information *(al-Irshad)*, 13
Ministry of Social Affairs, 11, 12
mise en scène, 40, 180, 199, 222, 227
Misr International Production
    Company, 135, 232
Misr Studio, 11
modernist transformation, 176–77
modernity, xv, 173, 233; as an Arab
    cultural continuum, 6–8
modernization, 1, 6, 173
Mohammad, Osama, 189
moments of crisis, stories built upon, 217
Monster, The (al-Wahsh), 18, 27
montages, 108
Morocco, 3, 103
Moscow International Film Festival, 37
al-Muhajir (The Emigrant), 92, 118, 169, 194
Muhammad, Osama, 151
Muhammad Abdu, 8
Muhammad Ali, 2
al-Muharrij al-kabir (The Great Clown), 18
Murad, Leila, 218
Murdoch, Rupert, 185
Murray, Stephen, 149
Mursi, Ahmad Kamel, 28
musicals, 12, 18. *See also The Return of the Prodigal Son*
Mustafa, Hussam-Eddine, 16
My Father on the Tree (Abi fawq al-shajara), 59

N

Nadi al-Sinima fi-l-Qahira
    cinematheque, 57
Nadim, Saad, 41
Nagm, Ahmad Fu'ad, 97
al-Nahda (Arab Renaissance
    movement), xv, 2, 7, 30
al-Nakkash, Raga, 199
Naksa, 92
Napoleon, 141, 143
al-Nasir Salah al-Din (Saladin), 14, 33, 35, 36, 42–52, 58, 142, 195, 224
Nasrallah, Yousry, 116, 151, 189, 227
Nasser 56, 44
al-Nasser, Gamal Abd, 10, 13;
    Chahine's support for, 80; death
    of, 42, 81, 89; image of in the
    Arab cinema, 42–52; reversal of
    pan-Arab solidarity policies, 115;
    revolution, 34; Suez War (1956),
    35; revolution, 58, 66, 226, 230;
    disillusionment with the, 100
al-Nas wa-l-Nil (The People and the Nile), 58–60; American financing
    for, 205; personal and the
    collective in, 67–74
national identity, xvii, 116. *See also*
    identity; and heterogeneity, 120–24
nationalism in films, 57
national liberation, 87, 88, 215; in
    the age of globalization, 185–213;
    America, 202–09; Arab cinema
    since the 1990s, 186–91; *The
    Land*, 74–80; *The Other*, 191–97;
    Silence . . . We're Rolling, 197–202
National Organization for the
    Consolidation of the Cinema, 14
National Resistance Front, 143
national self-determination, 8, 44

national unity: *Saladin*, 42–52; struggle for, 33–24
neorealism, 10
New Arab Cinemas, 190
new cinema, 55
New York Film Festival, 71
Nida' al-'ashiq (A Lover's Call), 18
Night of the Baby Doll, The (Laylat al-babi dull), 188
nihilism, 83
Nile and Life, The (al-Nil wa-l-hayah), 71
al-Nil wa-l-hayah (The Nile and Life), 71
Nimr, Fatma, 206
1967 War, 92–103
Nisa' bila rijal (Women without Men), 18
Non-Allied Movement, 89
normalization of relationships between Egypt and Israel *(al-tatbi')*, 89
North African filmmakers, influence on, 143
nouvelle vague, 55
Nujum al-naha (Stars in Broad Daylight), 151
Nuwas, Abu, 158

O

October 1973 War, 55, 90, 111
Omar, Hasan Imam, 96
Omlile, Ali, 185
On the Jahili Literature, 9
On the Waterfront, 25
Oslo Accords, xx
Other, The (al-Akhar), 168, 186; globalization and, 191–97
Ottoman Empire, 2, 7; collapse of, 9
Ouda, Mohammad, 72
Our Mother India, 41

P

Palestine: colonization of, 4; infighting between Fatah and Hamas, 104; refugees, 90
Pasadena Playhouse, 18, 204
People and the Nile, The (al-Nas wa-l-Nil), 58–60; American financing for, 205; costs of, 67; personal and the collective in, 67–74
petit-bourgeois viewpoints, 96
plots: *Adieu Bonaparte!*, 136–38; *Alexandria... New York*, 205; *Alexandria... Why?*, 126; *Chaos*, 210; *The Choice*, 81; *Dawn of a New Day*, 60, 61; *Destiny*, 173–75; *Jamila, the Algerian*, 39–41; *The Land*, 75; *The Other*, 192; *The People and the Nile*, 69; *The Return of the Prodigal Son*, 103, 104; *Saladin*, 45; *Silence... We're Rolling*, 198–99; *The Sparrow*, 92, 93; *Struggle in the Valley*, 21
political events, pivotal role of, 227
Pope Shenouda III, exile of, 116
popularity of films, 225
postcolonial: politics, 176; subjectivities, xiv
post-independent Arab states, 3
power of history, 167–83
pre-revolutionary periods, peasant class during, 74–80
privatization, 100; of the economy, 91
production, government's involvement in, 54
profit-oriented approach to filmmaking, 12
public sector production, rise of, 55

Q

al-Qa'id, Yusuf, 199
queer sexuality: in *Alexandria Again and Forever*, 147-66; artist as a troubled activist, 152-55; scholarly research on depiction within Arab cinema, 148-49; sensibility and transgression, 155-161; transgression and postcolonial ambivalence, 147-66
Question of Culture, The, 185

R

Rachida, 171
Radi, Mounir, 44
Rajul fi hayati (Man in My Life), 18
Ramzi, Kamal, 82, 112, 193. *See also* criticism
Rana's Wedding, 189
al-Rasul, Hasan 'Abd, 95
Rayya and Skina, 18, 27
relationships: with bureaucracy, 78; severing of with Soviet Union, 96
releases: of *The Choice*, 84; *The Sparrow*, 95
religion: religious fundamentalism, 167-83; modernist impulses in *Destiny*, 177-83; modernist story about Arab history, 172-75; modernist transformation, 176-77; Muslim fundamentalism, 91, 112; Muslim relationships with Christians, 44; religious differences, 119; religious sectarianism, 44; rise of religious dogmatism, 168-72; rise of religious fundamentalism, 167
Renaissance *(al-Nahda)*, 2
repression, class, 80
resistance, 135-36; *Adieu Bonaparte!*, 136-38; Chahine's self-identification as francophone, 143-46
restrictions of films, 91
Return of the Prodigal Son, The ('Awdat al-ibn al-dal), 81, 92, 130, 195; impending chaos and, 103-14
reviews. *See* criticism
revolution: Chahine as a budding activist filmmaker, 34-42; disillusionment with, 100; and the emergence of film discourse, 12-16;
al-Rihani, Amine, 9
Ring Seller, The (Bayya' al-khawatim), 58, 218
riots, 115
Room to Rent, 151
Roscoe, Will, 149
Rotana, 187
al-Roumi, Majida, 107, 219
Rowson, Everett, 149
Rushd, Ibn, 8, 172, 174

S

Saadawi, Nawal, 169
al-Sabban, Rafiq, 83, 150, 171
Sadat, Anwar, xx, 90; policies, 111
Sadoul, George, 61
Said, Ahmad, 39
Said, Edward, xiv, 7, 157, 231,
Saladin (al-Nasir Salah al-Din), 14, 34, 35, 36, 42-52, 58, 142, 195, 224
al-Salam, Shadi Abd, 16, 55
Salama, Hani, 193
al-Salamuni, Sami, 56, 83, 130, 139, 220

Saleh, Ahmad, 110
Saleh, Rushdi, 50
Saleh, Tawfiq, 16, 91
al-Samah, 179
Sanduq al-dunya (The Box of Life), 189
al-Sayyid, Daoud Abd, 116
Sayyidat al-qitar (Lady on the Train), 18
Second World War, 11, 15, 125, 129; Algeria, 38
sectarianism, religious, 44
secular forms of government, 2
Seif, Salah Abu, 16, 18, 27, 31, 36
self-determination, 144; in *Struggle in the Valley,* 22
Selim, Kamal, 80
September 11, 2001, xx, 202, 206; globalization and, 207
sexuality, xx, xxii; queer transgression and postcolonial ambivalence, 147–66
Shadi, Ali Abu, 97, 108. *See also* criticism
Shadia, 218
Shafik, Viola, 98, 141
Sharif, Omar, 20, 25
al-Sharqawi, Abd al-Rahman, 31, 48, 57, 63, 75
Shaytan al-sahara' (Devil in the Desert), 18
Shehata's Store (Dukkan Shehata), 213
Shiite, 103
al-Shinnawi, Tarek, 199
Shohat, Ella, 132
Shu'aib, Afaf, 169
Shubra, 209. *See also Chaos*
Shubra al-Khayma, 12
Shukry, Mamduh, 55
al-Siba'i, Yusuf, 31, 48

Silence . . . We're Rolling (Sukut hanswar), 186, 197–202
Silver Berlin Bear (Berlin Film Festival, 1979) 125
al-Sinima, 57
Sira' fi-l-mina (Struggle on the Pier), 20, 28; urban dimension of revolution, 25–31
Sira' fi-l-wadi (Struggle in the Valley), 19, 27; and the revolution in rural Egypt, 20–35
Sixth Day, The (al-Yawm al-sadis), 118, 139, 146, 219
social awareness, xv
social change, xx
social class, early cinema and, 17–18
socialism, 8, 111
social justice, xvii, 1; advocacy for, 224
Society for Cinema and Media Studies, xii
solidarity, xvii; reversal of Nasser's pan-Arab solidarity policies, 115
Somalia, 103
Son of the Blacksmith, The (Ibn al-haddad), 20
Son of the Nile, The (Ibn al-Nil), 18, 19, 27, 36
Soviet montage, 10
Soviet Union, 90; *The People and the Nile,* 67–74; response to *Jamila, the Algerian,* 39; severing of relationship with, 96
Spain, 176; dance traditions, 179
Sparrow, The (al-'Asfur), 59, 66, 81, 92, 125, vii; crisis and resiliency in, 92–103; motivation for *The Sparrow,* 100; resiliency in, 92–103

Special Jury prize (1979 Berlin Film Festival), 117
Stam, Robert, 132
Stars in Broad Daylight (Nujum al-naha), 151
state intervention, 54–57
Stollery, Martin, 149
Struggle in the Valley (Sira' fi-l-wadi), 19, 27; and the revolution in rural Egypt, 20–35
Struggle on the Pier (Sira' fi-l-mina), 20, 28; urban dimension of revolution, 25–31
Studio Misr, 15
studio systems, 10
stylistic authorship, xx
Suez Canal, 33; reopening of, 104
Suez crisis, xx
Suez War (1956), 35
Sukut ha-nswar (Silence... We're Rolling), 186, 197–202
Suleiman, Elia, 189
al-Suq al-sawda' (The Black Market), 19
Syria, 3, 103; failure to unify with, 58; secessionist military coup d'état in (1961), 42
Syrian–Egyptian unity, xx
Syrian National Social Party, 4

T

taboos, 148
tajdid (renewal), xv, 8
Tale of the Three Jewels, The, 189
al-tatbi', normalization of relationships between Egypt and Israel, 89
Tawfiq, Ra'uf, 194

Tayarat al-waraq (The Kite), 189
al-Tayyeb, Atef, 116, 227
al-Telemessani, Tariq, 117
Terrorism and Kebab (al-Irhab wa-l-kabab), 170
Terrorist, The (al-Irhabi), 170
TF1 Films Production, 135
3B Production Company, 209
thrillers, 82. *See also The Choice*
Thoraval, Yves, 81
Till Things are Better (Hina maysara, 2007), 213
tisaffi hisabat (even the score), 207
Tollard, Jean, 138
Tough, The, 27
Toughan, Walid, 206
Trilogy of Defeat, 81, 129. *See also The Choice; The Return of the Prodigal Son; The Sparrow*
al-Turk, Hanan, 193
Twentieth Century Fox, 18

U

umma, 119
Une minute de soleil en moins (A Minute of Sun Less), 151
Union of Egyptian Film Artists, 164
United Arab Republic (UAR), 42, 44
United States, Hays Code, 13
unity, xvii, 8, 80. *See also* national unity
Unspeakable Love: Gay and Lesbian Life in the Middle East, 148
Upper Egypt, 92, 98
al-Uthman, Layla, 169

V

Veil, The: Male–Female Dynamics in a Modern Muslim Society, 149
Venice International Film Festival, 209
Vertov, Dziga, 10
Visit of Mr. President, The (Ziyarat al-sayyid al-ra'is), 44
Voices of the Arab radio station, 38

W

Wadda'tu hubbak (Farewell My Love), 18
Wael, Tawfiq Abu, 152
al-Wahsh (The Monster), 18, 27
western modernity, assimilation of, 10
Whitaker, Brian, 148, 157
Will, The (al-'Azima), 19, 80
Williams, Esther, 126, 219
Women without Men (Nisa' bila rijal), 18
Worker, The (al-'Amil), 28
World Bank, 185
Wright, J., 149

Y

Yacoubian Building, The ('Imarat Ya'cubyan), 188, 151, 213
al-Yawm al-sadis (The Sixth Day), 118
Yawmiyat shab 'ahir (Diary of a Male Whore), 152
Yosef, Raz, 149
You are My Love (Inta habibi), 18, 218
Youssef, Ahmad, 164
Youssef, Khaled, 197, 227
Youssef Chahine, xiii
Youssef Chahine: The Child's Vision and the Rebel's Fist, xiii

Z

Zaatari, Akram, 151
Zakariya, Issam, 222
Zaydan, Jirgi, 9
Zeid, Nasr Abu, 169
Zionism, 132
Ziyarat al-sayyid al-ra'is (The Visit of Mr. President), 44
Zuriab school, 178